Anarchism, the Republic and Civil War in Spain: 1931–1939

This groundbreaking new study, translated for the first time into English, is the first synthesis to relate and interpret the main evolutionary milestones of anarchism in Spain, and is crucial to understanding the social conflict of 1930s Spain.

Casanova explores the concept of anarchism as both a political ideology and a social movement during the Second Republic and the Civil War (1931–1939). Dividing the work into two parts, the author first explores anarchism's strained relation with the republican regime. He then goes on to analyse the revolutionary process that broke out in the summer of 1936. This complete new study also examines possible reasons why anarcho-syndicalism did not resurface after the death of the Spanish dictator Franco, and offers a commentary on other writings on anarchism in contemporary Spain.

Casanova's work will interest historians across a range of disciplines as well as readers with a general interest in Spain.

Julián Casanova is currently Professor of Modern History at the University of Zaragoza, Spain.

Routledge/Cañada Blanch Studies on Contemporary Spain

Series editors Paul Preston and Sebastian Balfour, *Cañada Blanch Centre for Contemporary Spanish Studies, London*

Anarchism, the Republic and Civil War in Spain: 1931–1939

Julián Casanova

Translated from Spanish by Andrew Dowling and Graham Pollok,
fully revised by Paul Preston

Routledge
Taylor & Francis Group

LONDON AND NEW YORK

London and New York First published 2004 by Routledge
2 Park Square, Milton Park, Abingdon, Oxon OX14 4RN

Simultaneously published in the USA and Canada
by Taylor & Francis Inc
270 Madison Ave., New York, NY 10016

Routledge is an imprint of the Taylor & Francis Group

Transferred to Digital Printing 2005

Originally published in Spanish as *De La Calle Al Frente* by Critica,
Barcelona, 1997
© Julián Casanova 1997
Translation © 2005 Routledge

Typeset in Baskerville by Taylor & Francis Books

British Library Cataloguing in Publication Data
A catalogue record for this book is available from the British Library

Library of Congress Cataloging in Publication Data

ISBN 0–415–32095–X

Contents

Acknowledgements

The preparation and writing of this book took place over a long period of time and there are many people to whom I owe a debt of gratitude. Anna Monjo, Mary Nash, Susanna Tavera, Eulàlia Vega and Mercedes Vilanova were kind enough to send me some of their work which I had been unable to consult. Arantxa Sarría and Emilio Blasco sought out and photocopied documents from the Internationaal Institut voor Sociale Geschiedenis in Amsterdam. In that archive I was always able to count on the help and advice of Mieke Ijzermans. I also received professional help from Carlos Gil, who provided me with documentation concerning conflicts and uprisings in La Rioja; from Pilar Maluenda, who gave me data on the insurrection of December 1933 in Huesca; and from Julita Cifuentes, who has helped in the correction of the manuscript. In my time in Salamanca, I recall the hospitality and generosity of Manolo Redero and Gloria García, as well as the help given by María José Turrión García, librarian of the Archivo Histórico Nacional in that city. José Álvarez Junco read the first two chapters, and as has always been the case during our long friendship, his sincere comments and criticisms have improved the final version.

I have also benefited from the help of institutions, particularly the DGICYT., which has provided financial support for my projects in recent years and allowed me to enjoy a stay during the academic year 1991–2 in the Center for European Studies at Harvard University. During those twelve months, I met colleagues who honoured me with both their friendship and professional experience. I would also like to mention Robert Fishman, Abby Collins, Jürgen Wilzewski, Jos de Beus, Tom Koelble, Jeff Richter and Charles Maier. It was thanks to Charles Tilly that I was able to debate and discuss many of the questions that emerged in the seminar series which he organised in the Center for Studies of Social Change of the New School for Social Research in New York. To José Casanova, I owe many things, not only as a brother, but also the intellectual help that he always gave me when it came to using sociological approaches to historical analysis. For the confidence that they showed in my work, I would also like to thank Mari Paz Ortuño and Josep Fontana, of the publishing house Crítica, who made the publication of the original Spanish version of this book such an easy task. Finally, I would like to express my thanks to Professor Paul Preston, both a teacher and friend, with whom I have shared so many things in the past twenty

years and for the interest that he has consistently shown in bringing this book
before an English-speaking audience.

Julián Casanova
Zaragoza, 1996 and 2004

Note to the English edition

Eighty years. That is how long it took for anarchism to take root, bloom and die, from the arrival in November 1868 of Giuseppe Fanelli, sent to Spain by Bakunin, until the forced exile of thousands of activists in the spring of 1939. Eighty years characterised by a frenetic propagandistic, cultural and educational activity; by terrorism and violence; by strikes and insurrections; by aborted revolutions and egalitarian dreams.

This anarchist presence has not passed by unnoticed. Its followers cultivated for decades a reputation for honesty, sacrifice and combat. Its enemies, on the right and on the left, highlighted in contrast the anarchists' enthusiasm for bomb-throwing and their easy recourse to the revolver. These are, without doubt, exaggerated, black-and-white images which have influenced historians using them as sources.

From the arrival of Fanelli to the post-Civil War exile, anarchism's red and black flag was followed by varied and wide sections of the population. Hobsbawm and others have suggested that there was something rather abnormal, exceptional, atypical, in all of this because the 'normal' thing would have been socialism, the 'scientific doctrine' that the proletariat needed. It was abnormal precisely because anarchism had put down roots in Barcelona, the most industrial and modern city of Spain, where, in consequence, organised socialism had never advanced successfully.

In reality, there were many other peculiarities to be found in the contemporary history of Spain, such as republicanism, anti-clericalism, regional nationalisms, civil wars and numerous *coup d'états*. On the other hand, in other countries, socialism did not achieve striking success. In Western Europe, the comparative context in which Spain is placed, until the First World War, only a small proportion of the working class belonged to socialist political organisations or trade unions and, in electoral terms, it was only in Germany that an influential mass socialist party had been consolidated.

It would be then useful to recall something indicated by the most recent research: anarchism was not an 'exceptional' and 'extraordinary' phenomenon in the history of Spain, if by 'normal' and 'ordinary' we mean the experience of the other countries of Western Europe well into the twentieth century, until the point at which the transition from anarchism to anarcho-syndicalism took place, from forms of organisation based on ideological affinity groups to the emergence of more formal and disciplined union structures. Only with the creation and rapid consolidation of the Confederación Nacional del Trabajo (National Confederation of Labour) as a mass movement in the years 1917–21 and 1931–7 did Spanish atypicality begin, because only then did revolutionary syndicalism, being both anti-political and centred on direct action, disappear in the rest of the world – except, it must be said, in Argentina and Sweden.

Until the conversion of anarchism into anarcho-syndicalism, Spain experienced trends in worker association that were very similar to those in France and Italy: the adoption of Bakunist positions, the decline of the First International, the emergence of terrorism in the 1890s and the expansion in the doctrine of revolutionary syndicalism in the early years of the twentieth century. Not even the CNT, which was founded in 1910, was a persistent and stable phenomenon: it was only well established in very specific periods. Furthermore, except for Catalonia and in some other cities such as Seville and Zaragoza, it shared its presence with the socialist trade unionism of the Unión General de Trabajadores (General Workers' Union). Until the coming of the Second Republic in 1931, even this socialist trade unionism also embraced the anti-state and anti-political tradition inherited from the First International.

Thus, even though anarchism was less stable and robust than has been supposed, and was characterised by both chronological and geographical discontinuity, it nevertheless existed. It would disappear from view and would reappear with explosions of protest, with a social project for freedom, the collectivisation of the means of production, the abolition of the state, the organisation of a future society without coercion. The distinguishing characteristic of the movement was the determination to achieve these objectives through the rejection of parliamentary politics and elections.

The anarchism that triumphed in Spain in the twentieth century, closely linked as it was to revolutionary syndicalism, was 'communitarian', and expressed 'solidarity' with the popular classes whom it trusted to make the revolution. It expanded greatly during the Spanish Second Republic (1936–9) and had its Golden Age during the Spanish Civil War (1936–9). This book, then, is concerned with this story of the egalitarian dream and of a revolution which would end in frustration and cruel defeat.

Part I

Power in the street

1 History accelerates

If their power lies in the Ministry, ours lies in the moral force which inhabits
the streets.

(*Cultura y Acción*, 10 December 1931)

On 2 July 1930, Valeriano Orobón wrote to Eusebio Carbó from Berlin. Orobón
was a CNT (National Confederation of Labour) delegate to the AIT
(International Association of Workers) at the time, and was in search of an
'anarcho-syndicalist synthesis' which would avoid 'both syndicalist opportunism
and anarchist particularism'. This was an aim he had pursued at various moments
during his life. Carbó had been a teacher, a journalist, a 'wild anarchist,' a union
organiser and a propagandist. He had been expelled from several countries for his
ideas and imprisoned in his own, and had only just regained his precious freedom.
'The liberal constitutional breeze which is blowing through Spain at the moment',
Orobón told him, 'will not be sufficient. We will need a hurricane.'

It was indeed a hurricane, and no mere breeze, which stirred the spirit of the
Spaniards on 14 April 1931. The declaration of the Republic captured the imagi-
nation of the masses and was welcomed with overwhelming enthusiasm. 'A
euphoria of enthusiasm', as Orobón described it a few months later. 'Was it not
wonderful to see the people enjoying themselves like children, as if they had just
won the lottery?'[1]

'The people', that collective invoked by everyone, welcomed the Republic and
many anarchists, the 'wildest' included, joined in the celebrations. In effect, the
Republic represented an opportunity for revolutionary syndicalism, which had
been smashed a decade earlier, by the gunmen of the anarchists and the
employers, and silenced by the dictatorship of Primo de Rivera. Above all, it was
a chance to re-enter the public sphere with the sort of rites of mobilisation
which had been identified with republicans, socialists and anarchists since the
beginning of the century. There were demonstrations with flags and music and
revolutionary hymns. But, above all, there were the mass meetings. These great
reunions were a mixture of festival, propaganda and incitement to revolutionary
action. The public sphere was the ideal tribune from which to 'speak to the
people' and demonstrate, 'with the lash of critique, the futility of laws made to
subjugate mankind'. The declaration of the Republic was a political fact. It had

to be converted into 'a revolution, which would transform all political and economic values', and this was to be done using the CNT's own typical methods of direct action and popular struggle on the streets.[2]

While the people were overwhelmingly enthusiastic and placed such hope in the Republic, the CNT could do no more than wait, until the people awoke. And while this was happening, or perhaps because the majority of CNT affiliates were also recovering from their euphoric inebriation, the main anarcho-syndicalist leaders never tired of acknowledging the new Republican regime (even if they did so with their characteristic a-political reservation) in the press, at mass meetings and syndicalist meetings, and in articles addressed to the authorities. In this sense, on 15 April, and in the name of the CNT and the working class of Zaragoza, Victoriano Gracia asked the civil governor to 'set an example of generosity befitting this moment of intense national joy' and disarm the urban militia the Somatén, 'an institution which endangers public freedom'.

The Republic 'emanated from the people' and was preferable to a 'monarchy by the grace of god'. A considerable number of anarchists had contributed to its coming with their votes and much was demanded of it. Above all, it was expected to bring freedom. The CNT had no confidence that the government of the Republic might modify the class structure of society. However, it did expect a more liberal regime, and one that would grant it the freedom to augment its union organisation. In other words, it hoped for a regime that would allow it to defend, effectively, and with greater success than its rival the UGT, the interests of the working class. This was the position taken in the main journals of the CNT and of the Federación Anarquista Ibérica, the semi-clandestine organisation of hard-liners dedicated to maintaining anarchist purity, journals which had seen the light of day only thanks to the triumph of the republican candidates.

These declarations were always heavily qualified, accompanied by an energetic affirmation of the revolutionary and anti-parliamentary character of the CNT. However, the refusal, from the very beginning, to attack the Republican regime reflected the intense hope which pervaded the atmosphere at that moment. This was the moment in which the King of Spain had been forced to abandon the throne. Galo Díez saw this clearly and said so to his comrades in the Special Congress of the CNT, which was held in Madrid two months later. One had to speak to the people not only of revolutionary dreams, but also 'of their desires, their needs, their misery and their rights'. In comparison with the dictatorship, the Republic had much to offer, and it would be imprudent 'to risk that little which was certain for a lot more which still remained uncertain'. This particular leader believed that the majority of Spaniards were republicans. 'Like children with a new toy', they were delighted with the Republic. The most sensible approach was, therefore, to 'wait for the moral exhaustion of the Republic and then, along with the disillusioned republicans, begin the march towards a better ideal'. Given the circumstances, a cautious approach had to be adopted, and one which would 'not be confused with the reactionary cause'. When the people had tired of their new toy, 'and they would tire', the CNT would emerge as the source of authentic hope.[3]

The Republic 'emanated from the people'. It had been 'brought into existence by the people', and the people were an obligatory point of reference in all discourse concerning the death of the monarchy and the birth of the Republic. But who were 'the people'? For Manuel Azaña, whom events had placed in the highest of political positions, the people comprised almost everyone: bourgeois liberals and employers, the middle class and the proletariat. The people included everyone who had not belonged to one of the families or traditional oligarchies of the regime. This line of argument, which attempted to adapt the populism of Lerroux to the current situation, was fairly common amongst Spanish republicans. However, with Azaña, unlike Lerroux, there was no inter-class discourse. This was because his aim was not so much to 'found' one specific power base as to articulate various political forces around a common project. Even the socialists, who governed in coalition with the republicans, had dropped their working-class rhetoric in order to laud 'the people', both bourgeois and proletarian, as the subject of history.

It was as obvious as it was tautological that, for the people themselves, the subject of history was 'the people'. However, the Spanish people were 'rebels by nature', and anarchist in essence and, therefore, the CNT represented 'the spirit of the people'. Given this presupposition, 'the people' were in reality the proletariat or, as they were often referred to, the lower social classes organised by the CNT. The rest were merely bourgeois politicians, socialist traitors who would cheat and trick the people, and who 'appealed to popular sovereignty only when they needed votes'. The people were not to be reproached for their euphoria of faith in the new regime.

In accordance with this rhetoric, the Republic could not disappoint the leaders of revolutionary syndicalism. They knew that 'whilst capitalism subsisted there would be little or nothing achieved through a change of political regime'. However, it would be amongst the poorest classes, where most was expected of the regime, that the greatest disappointment would be caused. It would be from there that the challenge to the regime would emerge. The traitors and 'merchants of illusion', who were currently in power, would find themselves confronted by the militants of liberty who would 'sacrifice themselves stoically and offer up their lives in order to redeem the nation'.[4]

The importance of these different perceptions of what constituted 'the people' should not be underestimated. The ramifications were far reaching when the form of the new state came up for discussion. For Azaña and the republicans, the state would be liberal and democratic and constitute the instrument of social change. This state would bring about a transformation, sweeping away the power structure of the 'caciques' and the military and ecclesiastical institutions. A project of that magnitude, however, could not succeed if left at the level of mere discourse. It required concretisation in the form of government measures. 'In the space of two years, it will be necessary to transform the role of the church, the Armed Forces, labour relations, education, the ownership of agricultural property, the autonomous government of the regions.'[5]

It is difficult to imagine a government with more plans for social and political reform. Almost all of those who had participated in the historic encounter in San Sebastián, plus the representatives of the Spanish socialist party and the

UGT (General Workers' Union), were in the provisional government. Even before the first Parliament had been inaugurated, the provisional government had put into practice a law on the reform of the Armed Forces, which was the work of Manuel Azaña. There was also a series of decree laws which were the work of the Minister of Labour, Francisco Largo Caballero. These aimed radically to modify labour relations and included the decree on Municipal Boundaries (28 April), the creation of joint panels of arbitration for agrarian labour disputes (7 May), the collective leasing of rural estates (19 May), a loan for the National Institute of Social Provision to assist with unemployment (28 May), the right of intervention of government delegates in regional labour disputes (29 May) and the law on the eight-hour maximum working day (1 July). The Law of *Términos municipales*, or municipal boundaries, meant that employers had to offer jobs to people of the town concerned before making offers to outsiders. It removed the landowners' freedom to hire labour from outside in order to break local strikes. There were a number of important provisions relating to ecclesiastical institutions which still had to be dealt with and, above all, there was the projected law on agrarian reform. However, taken together, this reformist project embodied the faith in progress and modernisation, and the confidence in the triumph of reason over corrupt traditional practices, beliefs that were deeply rooted in Spanish republicanism.[6]

In contrast to the *laissez-faire* policies of previous governments, this state-in-construction attempted, as the record shows, to intervene in the regulation of labour relations, both in agriculture and industry. However, this veritable fever of legislation was insufficient on its own, and there was no powerful capitalist class behind the proposals which could reciprocate with the necessary concessions. The middle class and its republican representatives were seriously split over the ramifications of the reforms and the proposal to include representation of the CNT had also failed. As we shall see below, this organisation channelled the activities of the working class and the unemployed in a very different direction from that intended by Largo Caballero's Ministry. This was nothing new. The rivalry between these two different forms of trade-union practice had a long history. The difference lay in the fact that one was now in power, attempting to strengthen socialist positions within the apparatus of the state, whilst the other was on the street. And occupation of the street, that stage of the 'anti-political' battle and opposition to the state, always ended up with a problem of public order. There, on the street, the security forces were always willing to maintain order with a loaded mauser, the rifle most often associated with the Civil Guard.

The question of public order was not a minor issue, although it might appear so in comparison with the situation which the new government had inherited. The state was in crisis. It had a ridiculously small budget and the loyalty of the armed forces was in doubt. As a result, public order became an obsession for the political and military authorities. It was a justified obsession, but one which quickly undermined the prestige of the republican regime and created an obstacle, on all sides, to the consolidation of the reformist project.

Both Manuel Azaña and Miguel Maura, the first Minister of the Interior, have left abundant testimony to the reasons for this obsession. A state which is in construction and a government which is undertaking reform must posses the instruments of coercion and enforcement of the law. As Azaña pointed out in his speech to the Cortes on 21 January 1932, strikes and the disputes between workers and employers and the fulfilment or otherwise of the labour agreements are one thing. The occupation of factories and telephone exchanges and attacks on government buildings and the security force are something very different. 'The latter are never justified and are not carried out by citizens exercising their rights. Those who carry out these actions are not strikers. They are rebels and insurgents and will be treated by me as such.' Faced with a legal and peaceful strike, Azaña was willing to stand aside. Faced with outrage and the disturbance of public order, he would send in the armed forces. Already in July 1931, according to his notes, 'as a result of the strikes which the CNT was stirring up everywhere, we examined the situation and decided that drastic action was urgently required'. In that same government meeting, Maura outlined a decree which would be 'an instrument of judicial repression'. This was the future Law of the Defence of the Republic. Largo Caballero suggested 'going even further, because of the threat which the syndicalist movements posed to the Republic'. And the Minister of Justice was even charged with the writing of a decree 'to impede and correct the cowardice of judges who did not dare to proceed against the *Sindicato Unico*'.[7]

Maura wrote in his memoirs that, after the 'suicide' of the monarchy, he had 'taken part in the nascent revolution in order to defend the principles of conservative legitimacy within it', rather than leave a free hand to the left and the working-class organisations. He also made it clear that he had an understanding of authority 'which the masses and even some republican politicians would find difficult to accept and share'. Referring to the latter he asked 'what sort of understanding of authority and leadership they could have. 'From the minute they were born they have seen and heard of nothing other than revolts, conspiracies, coups, strikes, and riots and breathed the spirit of hatred against the forces of public security, the authorities and everything established.' Furthermore, the masses were manipulated by politicians and anarchist agitators who neither accepted the authorities nor the laws which regulated labour. As a result, they thought there should be no 'law of assembly nor association nor any other which supports them'. Such was his concern for public order that Azaña often wrote jokingly of the 'whirlwind' Maura. 'What Unamuno said of Primo de Rivera could be said about him – first he fires and then he takes aim.'[8]

One thing that Maura and Azaña agreed about was the unpopularity of the Civil Guard amongst the working classes, although Azaña pointed out that others loved them and saw them as 'the only upholders of social order'. Hatred of the Civil Guard was especially intense amongst the agricultural workers, who saw them as the embodiment of an inquisitorial regime and the purest representation of violence and repression. As Don Manuel noted, 'the Civil Guard has always been tough, and what is worse, irresponsible'. This situation did not improve with the beginning of the Republic, 'because many of the usual victims of the Civil Guard have been councillors and mayors who have not reconciled themselves with the new authorities'.

Given these declarations, and many more which the governors of the coalition would have to make until the massacre of Casas Viejas in January 1933, it is surprising that there was no reform of that part of the administration. In the words of Manuel Ballbé, 'the republican governments were incapable of bringing the administration of public order into line with the principles of democratic government'. The republican governors used the same mechanism of repression as the monarchy, and failed to break 'the direct relationship which existed between the militarisation of public order and the politicisation of the armed forces'. The armed forces maintained their presence in a considerable part of the civil administration of the state. Their influence could be felt in the headquarters of the security forces, the Civil Guard and *Guardia de Asalto* (Assault Guards). It was transmitted *en route* by a number of civil governors and ran all the way up to the *Dirección General de Seguridad*. The leaders of the *coup d'état* of 1936, Sanjurjo, Mola, Cabanellas, Muñoz Grandes, Quiepo de Llano and Franco himself, were all good examples of the connection which existed during the 1930s, just as Pavía and Martín Campos had been examples of it in 1873.

The subordination and surrender of public order to the armed forces began with the very declaration of the Republic. On 16 April, Cabanellas arrived in Seville in order to take command of the Captaincy General of the 2nd Military Region and declared a state of emergency. This was maintained for almost three months and served as the pretext for the closure of all of the CNT's labour centres. According to the proclamation of 22 May, these were 'run by a brazen minority of foolhardy persons without identity papers, many of them ex-gunmen, professional rebels and instigators who had been a model of meekness and reserve under the dictatorship'. A few days later, on 5 June, the Minister of the Interior sent a telegram to Cabanellas. The National Committee of the CNT had asked for the reopening of the centres which had been closed in Andalucia. This was in order to allow them to nominate delegates to the Special Congress which was going to be held in Madrid from the 11th of that month.

> Would your Excellency consider the possibility of acceding to this petition which I consider useful because the Madrid Assembly might possibly reach an agreement which is more in the public interest than the tension [which exists] between the Confederation and the Government.' If your Excellency finds it possible to accept this request, he is authorised to close once more those centres which are a threat to public order. I have also been asked if you can permit the normal sale of the journal *Solidaridad Obrera*. Please let me know if you are able to accept this request.[9]

According to the reply of 6 June, Cabanellas accepted the request. However, he was replaced three days later by General Ruiz Trillo and the state of emergency was then lifted thanks to the electoral campaign for the Constituent Assembly.

Needless to say, this surrender of the control of public order to the army fed the anti-military feeling of the labour movement. It also increased the antagonism between the labour movement and those military men who, steeped as they were in conspiracy theory, saw the labour movement as the work of 'gunmen, professional agitators and the enemies of law and order'. This threatening and disparaging attitude towards the socialists and anarco-syndicalists was typical of the military men in charge of the repression of social conflict. It was not coincidental, for example, that Sanjurjo should have adopted this tone with Manuel Azaña the day that, following the clashes between peasants and Civil Guards at Castilblanco and Arnedo, he was replaced as Director of the Guardia Civil. Nothing was said of what Sanjurjo thought of the atrocities committed by his subordinates in the Riojan village, but the General had no doubt who was to blame. 'The dregs of society' had taken control in many of the socialist councils. These people were 'undesirables' who 'threaten law and order, terrify land owners, damage property and inevitably come to blows with the Guardia Civil'. The socialists, he concluded, should not be in government, 'because their presence only encourages the trouble-makers'.[10]

This picture of disorder, painted by the man who would lead the first uprising against the republican regime a few months later, ignored the regime's constant recourse to exceptional measures. Shortly after coming into existence, the provisional government passed a legal statute authorising its own use of exceptional measures. This state of exception which was maintained until the Law of the Defence of the Republic was passed on 21 October 1931. Within these first months there was already abundant evidence of the way in which the Republic intended to deal with the problem of public order. Bloody incidents in the northern town of Pasajes in May were followed in July by even bloodier events in Seville. Different versions would be given of these events and police accounts of workers' conspiracies would be given credence and their dismissal of anarchist accusations accepted. However, there seems to be little doubt that a considerable number of these early incidents of bloodshed were the result of demonstrations and collective acts of protest to which there was always an armed response. Intimidation and the failure to guarantee the exercise of fundamental rights became the norm.

It could never be argued that the eventual recourse of the anarchists to insurrection, which will be analysed in depth below, was a logical response to the failure to guarantee the exercise of fundamental rights. Nevertheless, it was understandable that this barrage of exceptional measures, which limited rights essential to the functioning of their organisation, created a persecution complex amongst wide sectors of the CNT. Once the initial period of necessary co-existence had come to an end, the republican authorities demonstrated an incapacity to discern between social conflict and 'acts of aggression against the Republic'. Meanwhile, the CNT membership began to proclaim itself the victim of an 'Azaña–socialist dictatorship'.[11]

Even before these reports appeared on the front pages of their publications, CNT demonstrations had provided evidence of brutal conduct on the part of the security forces, equivalent to that of the monarchy. It was obvious that the

UGT was not responsible for the repression. However, as far as anarchist propaganda was concerned, they were governing in coalition with the republicans, had the benefit of associated privileges and were, as a result, co-participants in the errors committed by the authorities. The 'socialists persecutors' were now to be added to the traditional enemies of the working class, capitalism and the state. From the autumn of 1931 this argument was constantly repeated. The people demanded that their 'ruinous governors' make 'suitable amendment' and the condemnation always ended with a threat. 'You are in time, not to save the failed regime which you serve, as that is entirely impossible, but to save yourselves.'[12]

This verbal aggression fulfilled a purifying function. It showed that pacts were impossible with class enemies and constantly emphasised the potential for martyrdom of every activist. The blood of these martyrs was not just any blood, but the blood of the proletariat, and this fact served to highlight even more the socialist betrayal. At stake were the defence of human liberty and dignity against the structures of power and, 'above all', the defence of the poor and hungry against 'that order which guards the tranquillity of a legion of parasites, whilst thousands of human beings die through lack of the basic necessities of life'. If necessary, blood would be shed. This was where the distinction was to be found between 'bourgeois, in other words republican or monarchist morality' and revolutionary morality. At first this rhetorical exaltation of revolutionary morality was limited to a few isolated groups of anarchists. Though very influential in some of the media, their presence within the unions was minimal. However, as time passed these unions were unable to fulfil the demands made on the employers and the social and labour policy of the republicans and socialists was of little benefit to the poorest. When this happened, and it did so within a short space of time, rhetoric became the principal, and often the only, stimulus to mobilisation.[13]

While all of this was going on the anarchists were taking advantage of the first moments of freedom and expectation, in order to strengthen their organisation. Even though syndicalism had not yet fully emerged from the long night of dictatorship, the initial growth was noticeable. A considerable number of syndicalist unions had remained active during the dictatorship, above all in Catalonia, by infiltrating the Free Unions (*sindicatos libres*), scab unions financed by the employers. They had used their presence on the *comités paritarios* (arbitration committees) to maintain contact with the workforce. A number of their leaders had chosen to avail themselves of closer relations with the republicans and had become involved in conspiracies against the monarchy. This situation explained the welcome with which many veteran anarco-syndicalists greeted the Republic. It also explained the reticence of others, especially those who had remained clandestine or on the fringes of the unions, about dealings with politicians. Even Valeriano Orobón Fernández shared this concern. In his letter of 2 July 1930 to Eusebio Carbó, cited above, Orobón argued that in one of the future 'National Conferences' anarcho-syndicalism would have to resolve certain urgent problems: 'defend the CNT against the attacks of those who wished to subordinate it to the influence of a party' and 'perfect the basic structure of the CNT by making the existing structure (unions, local and regional federations) more flexible and by creating federations within industry.'[14]

Both of these issues came to the fore in discussion at the CNT's Special Congress, held in Madrid a year later. The creation of national federations within industry (which Eleuterio Quintanilla had proposed in vain at the National Congress held in Madrid's Teatro de la Comedia in December 1919) were now approved by 302,343 votes to 90,671 against, with 10,957 abstentions. In reality, as can be seen from the information existing on the assemblies held by the syndicates in the run-up to the Congress, the argument was clear and the situation was ripe. As a result, only a few anarchist activists, not all of whom were members of the FAI, were vehemently opposed to the agreement. The most prominent of these, Julio Roig, José Alberola and Juan García Oliver, represented a few hundred members. Almost 47,000 of the 90,671 negative votes came from the construction unions, the largest of which were Barcelona 24,000, Seville 9,509 and Zaragoza 5,000. Of course, the creation of national federations in industry was an idea supported by the main leaders, including both the purist anarchists of the FAI and the moderates who would go down in history shortly after as the 'treintistas'.[15] It should be noted that The *treintistas* were the followers of the thirty (*treinta*) leading anarchists who had signed a manifesto in August 1931 advocating cooperation with the Republic and opposing the FAI's aspirations to lead the CNT into revolutionary confrontation with the state. The FAI were able to have them temporarily expelled from their positions on committees and in the CNT press.

Opposition to the creation of national federations seemed to be linked to fairly abstract and outdated notions of social and union relations. The central arguments were based on José Alberola's defence of the free communes, and a critique of the supposedly 'Marxist reasoning' to be found in the proposal, which was supported by Julio Roig of the Santander Construction union with his individual vote. As usual, García Oliver went much further with his praise of the 'purely Spanish' character of the CNT organisation. 'The Federations of Industry are a German idea and look as if they have come out of a barrel of beer. The International Working Men's Association [to which the anarchists were affiliated, with its headquarters in Berlin, rather than the Marxist international] know nothing about Spain, and they show that they know nothing when they make the mistake of thinking that Spain is the place to try out this new fashion.' The most serious problem was that 'they carry the seed of disintegration within them and dissolve the mass movement we have kept ready in order to be able to smash the state'. True to his reputation as an 'anarcho-bolshevik', García Oliver concluded that the problem with the Confederation was 'the lack of revolutionary intelligence amongst the most prominent activists'.

The report on which these discussions were based had been prepared by Joan Peiró, who had already put forward his arguments in a series of articles which appeared in the Vigo-based journal *¡Despertad!* These arguments were well known and the central theme was that the working classes needed to adapt their methods of struggle to the ever-increasing intensification of capitalism. The national federations in industry would serve 'to unite the actions and initiatives of the proletariat ... in a national project of opposition to capitalism' and help to prepare 'the structure of the economic apparatus of the future'.

Although the process of setting up and developing the national federations in industry was slow, the arguments between those in favour and those against were resolved very quickly. It is not true, therefore, as is sometimes suggested, that the struggle over this issue was a reflection of the later split between syndicalists and members of the FAI. It is true that, during months following the Congress, some members of the FAI, such as José Alberola and Manuel Rivas, argued against the agreement. They did this in the columns of their journal *Tierra y Libertad*, with the well-known argument exalting the individual and the commune. However, they were no longer very powerful and the most influential anarchists had already opted for changes in the syndicalist organisation. Furthermore, this was not the time for indulgence in theoretical debates and many anarchist leaders chose to avoid the issue.[16]

Discussion of the report 'The position of the CNT on the Constituent Cortes' (the new Republican parliament) went to the heart of the anarcho-syndicalist conception of politics. The proposals which emerged from these discussions reconfirmed the Confederation's long-standing commitment to direct action and anti-parliamentary principles: 'Whatever happens, whether the Constituent Cortes legislates in reactionary or democratic fashion, the CNT has to follow its principles of direct action. In order to transform the political reality which has been produced in Spain into a revolution which will transform all political and economic values, the CNT must lead the people in the direction of libertarian communism.' These declarations were accompanied by what, given the exceptional nature of the moment, was considered a 'list of minimal requirements' which 'the people' were to demand of the government. These related to education and the economic crisis, individual liberties and freedom of the press, the right of assembly and the legalisation of strikes. They ended with the usual warning about what would happen 'if the people feel themselves betrayed'. The CNT, 'which is a part of this very people, will proceed, in the moment it finds most opportune, to put its weight behind the dissolution of the Constituent Cortes and proceed to the opening of a new revolutionary period'.

The ambivalence which arose from the ratification of a commitment to anti-political principles, whilst simultaneously making demands on the state, caused a certain amount of tension. Three of the speakers, Joaquín Ramos of the Sagunto steel and engineering union and the delegates of the Madrid construction union, Feliciano Benito and Cipriano Mera, refused to back the final motion on the basis that 'the mere act of formulating a petition ... to the Constituent Cortes implies recognition of its legitimacy and authority. The activists of the Confederation affirm, or should affirm, that this legislative body is a bourgeois mechanism whose purpose is the consolidation of the regime of constant exploitation.'

The personal votes of these three influential anarchists stimulated widespread reproaches against the moderates who were accused of collaboration with bourgeois institutions. As a result of this polemic, it has come to light that leaders such as Ángel Pestaña and Joan Peiró had undertaken, with the Catalan President Francesc Macià, not to take part in an anti-parliamentary campaign. Others, such as José Villaverde, had realised that the first concern of the CNT, given that it represented only a small part of the working class, was to achieve gains in basic liberties and union rights. The motion was finally agreed with some modifications. However, several delegates demanded that, in return for their acceptance of the motion, their protests should be noted in the minutes. Amongst them were Vicente Ballester, José España, José González, José Alberola, Germinal Esgleas, José Xena, Progreso Fernández, Joaquín Aznar, Miguel Mendiola and those delegates who had used their personal vote – in other words, the delegates of the main construction unions and almost all of the FAI members at the Congress.

However, this verbal radicalism failed to produce a split in the CNT and the Congress should not be interpreted as a triumph of the moderates or the defeat of the FAI. It had been twelve years since the CNT had been able to hold a meeting of this sort, and many anarcho-syndicalists were unwilling to throw away the historic opportunity for union expansion which legality entailed. Those who occupied the leading positions on the National Committee, on the Regional committee of Catalonia and in the Local Federation of Barcelona were not, as García Oliver suggests in his memoirs, 'tired working class activists' who had abandoned 'the active revolutionary position' and 'occupied' these posts 'through the persecution of dissenters'. This sort of argument ignored the fact that there were to be found amongst them anarchists of the FAI, such as Manuel Rivas, and moderate trade unionists, such as Ángel Pestaña, Progreso Alfarache, Francisco Arín, Ramón Artoneda or Joan Peiró from the editorial board of *Solidaridad Obrera*. These people had spent years searching for ways to get the syndicalist organisation out of the quagmire it had been dragged into by the 'excesses of the extremist minorities in 1922–23'. They were now reaping the fruit of a continuous struggle for legality which, for some time, had been showing its effectiveness in the factories, workshops and union meetings. They had accumulated a certain prestige, which derived from the many hours they had dedicated to propaganda work and union reorganisation.[17]

Four hundred and eighteen delegates attended the congress at Madrid, representing 511 unions and 535,566 members. This was considerably less than the CNT had mustered in December 1919 and very similar to the figures for the May 1936 Congress in Zaragoza. Between the congress of 1931, shortly after the declaration of the Republic, and the congress of 1936, two months before the military coup which began the Civil War, three phases can be distinguished in the membership of the CNT. The first phase, of exceptional growth, was especially obvious in Andalucia. This was followed by a noticeable decline, which began well into 1932, above all in Catalonia, Valencia and Andalucia, and continued for most of the next three years. There was then a slight recovery in the first months of 1936. The CNT reached its apogee in the autumn of 1936, with nearly 800,000 members and more than 300,000 in Catalonia and Andalucia.

These two regions, along with Valencia and Aragón, were the main centres of CNT influence, although it was only amongst the organised working class of Catalonia that it held an undisputed lead over the UGT. At the beginning of the Republic, the goal set by the revolutionary socialist leaders for this social movement, which was strong in the urban centres but, with the exception of Andalucia, much less so in the rural world, was the improvement of the material and cultural conditions of the working classes and the consolidation of a strong union organisation based on the principles of anti-politicism and direct action.[18]

A movement of this type cannot be fully explained only in terms of its internal institutional and ideological evolution. Ideologies can contribute to the radicalisation of protest, but they are not the only things that determine the level of consciousness amongst workers and unions. Nor is it enough to add an examination of the attitudes of other sectors of society, such as the bourgeoisie and the Spanish state, towards this sector of the working class. The limited capacity of the Spanish state for reform (in spite of the attempts made by the first Republican governments) and the knee-jerk repression and intolerance of any sign of rebellion or disobedience are important. These factors are especially relevant when comparisons are made with other more advanced societies. However, this still captures only one aspect of the problem. It is worth, therefore, evaluating three common interpretations of the movement. The first attributes the radicalisation of the CNT to 'take-over' by the FAI and those anarchists who were more intransigent and less syndicalist. The second interprets the violent and insurrectional attitudes of the CNT towards the Republican regime as a reaction to the repressive mechanisms and coercion of the state. Finally, there are those who interpret this development as the consequence of the very abnormality of the libertarian phenomenon, something seen as destructive, against everything and everyone, 'embarked upon the daily enterprise of revolution' and determined to face an 'inevitable clash with the state'.

However, neither all the forms of protest nor all the strikes which took place during the Republic can be attributed to the CNT. These perspectives are useful, therefore, only when placed within the context of other variables which affected collective protest, such as the political objectives of labour legislation introduced by Largo Caballero as Minister of Labour, the resources mobilised against unemployment and the success or failure of labour disputes, the lack of attention to and understanding of agrarian questions (in a society in which rural structures carried considerable weight), the expectations (millenarian or otherwise) stimulated by the coming of the Republic, to the concept of revolution (loaded with religious references impossible to fulfil yet shared by a substantial sector of anarchist activism), and the conditions in which this social movement had to operate, in a period and under a regime beset by adverse circumstances.

If the question of rivalry is left aside, it can be seen that, although the cultures and union practices of the CNT and the UGT were very distinct, there had also been elements of convergence, during the previous decades. However, the potential for convergence became a motive for intra-union hatred with the first breaths of republicanism. With the consolidation of a corporatist system of labour, a process which began under the dictatorship of Primo de Rivera, the integration of the UGT into the apparatus of the state gave it power which went beyond 'traditional union activity'. The blatant favouritism shown towards the socialist labour organisation amounted to the concession of control of labour, a coveted commodity in those times. In the words of Largo Caballero, this control required 'a reduction to the minimum of so-called direct action'. The CNT was aware that this situation blocked its own aspiration of achieving that same monopoly of labour negotiations which the UGT was achieving by other means. As a result, the CNT entered into open dispute. This initially limited itself to threats and warnings but then turned to coercion and violence. The behaviour of the security forces, who often acted on their own initiative, the persecution of peaceful demonstrations and the arrest of hundreds of CNT activists blocked the initiative of the more moderate leaders and played into the hands of the most intransigent. The prisoners' support committees, the real 'hinge' between this radicalism and the CNT, flourished everywhere and dominated the agenda at many union meetings. In the months following the Congress, the protests degenerated into an open struggle against the republican regime and its mechanisms of defence. After the first attempted insurrection in January 1932, the break with the regime was already irrevocable and the split within the anarchosyndicalist organisation was complete. The 'euphoria of enthusiasm' was not followed by a 'wakening of class consciousness' once the 'democratic illusion' had evaporated, but rather by a strategy of insurrection which ended up drowned in blood.[19]

On 6 April 1932, Valeriano Orobón Fernández spoke at the great republican debating club, the Ateneo of Madrid.

> For a few days the advent of the Republic brought the ineffable apotheosis of class confusion... Soon, however, the guns of the Civil Guard ... arrived to mark out implacably the boundaries of class and reminded everyone that the Republic was essentially a capitalist power ... As a result of their dogmatism and their limited sociological basis, the political parties are unable to bring about a comprehensive social revolution. The wide participation of the proletariat provides an indispensable basis for revolution and is a prerequisite for its victory.

The 'fraternisation' between 'sheep and wolves' had come to an end and history was accelerating. The economic crisis, the inadequacy of a state which was both incompetent and repressive of reformist projects, the rivalry between two projects of labour organisation which both tried to channel the mobilisation of the working class through opposing and incompatible procedures and the hostile reaction of thousands of agrarian landowners – fragmented at first but later organised by the authoritarian Catholic party, the CEDA (the Confederación Española de Derechas Autónomas) and the employers' associations – came together as important elements of instability in the scenario which had opened with the departure of the King. The working classes appeared in the streets and in the parliament and institutions, with their organisations, collective protests and demonstrations as powerful participants who could not be excluded from the political system. And once the echoes of the first democratic and republican change, 'which has brought nothing more than a harvest of poor rhetoric', had died down, they demanded their own second, social, change which would bring 'bread, freedom and social justice'. This book is about this story and its tragic outcome.[20]

2 The seeds of confrontation

The change of regime and political system that took place in April 1931 was charged with hope and expectation. It seemed to herald the 'regeneration' of a corrupt and decadent system, and, as a result, many expected transcendental change. They hoped for a state that would be a benefactor, willing to assist the most needy. They expected a government which would understand the problems of the working class and the struggle of agricultural workers for land, and take heed of those who, for so long, had complained of economic stagnation. These aspirations were expressed in petitions to the authorities, in public meetings and demonstrations, in electoral campaigns and in strikes and other acts of civil disobedience. Collective protests and mobilisations swept aside the barriers that had previously contained them. Some of these protests bore the unmistakable stamp of class struggle, in which groups confront each other on the basis of their relationship to the means of production. Others, a considerable number of them, were related to more traditional problems, such as the unresolved question of land use and exploitation. This was a recurring problem in rural Spain, which could lead to anything from robbery to the occupation of estates. Finally, there were the less visible and scarcely articulated manifestations of dissent, with protagonists and means which Rudé identified some time ago as pre-industrial forms of protest.

Until very recently, historians have concerned themselves predominantly with the analysis of class conflict. Charles Tilly has identified a series of fundamental processes (the concentration of capital, the proletarianisation of the workforce and the increasing power of the nation-state) to explain the decline of the eighteenth-century repertory of collective action and the rise of new forms in the nineteenth century. However, these processes are much more difficult to locate and identify in Spanish society, and undoubtedly developed much later. Furthermore, the advent of the Republic brought with it an important novelty. A radically different distribution of power, by parliamentary means, led to the development of forms of collective action which were either previously unknown or dangerous for those who practised them. Three basic factors, to which others would be added, can be indicated in order to explain the expanding field of mobilisation during this period.[1] These were: the presence of republicans and socialists in the government; the ability of UGT union leaders to make use of state power in the resolution of labour conflicts; and a deeply rooted anti-political anarco-syndicalism, which mounted staunch resistance to the corporatist framework.

The search for possible causes of the heterogeneity of forms of protest has led to explanations to suit all tastes but, in the main, historians have concentrated on the economic, political and ideological aspects of analysis. However, none of these approaches are satisfactory on their own. Furthermore, much depends on the conceptual and theoretical framework adopted and the type of protest on which the investigation focuses. There seems to be little doubt, for example, that the international economic crisis (which shook most advanced societies and Spain to a lesser extent) hindered the governing coalition of republicans and socialists in their plans for reform. This in turn contributed to the fragility, or instability, of the regime. However, the relationship between economic factors and protest is always extremely complex. There is, of course, no automatic causal process which leads from misery, oppression and injustice, on the one hand, to disturbances, strikes and rebellion on the other. Nevertheless, it is also clear that groups of people with the same problems, grievances and expectations in common can sometimes develop a collective consciousness. These groups might then go on to create social movements and organisations, with the aim of achieving their common objectives, and they may well act under the stimulus of specific ideologies. However, as a result of the abundant data which historical investigation has produced, this analytical framework requires qualification. Even if we accept E. P. Thompson's primacy of experience, which has done much to demystify the working class and debunk the dogma of 'objective' interests, the existence of elements and circumstances which are marginal to the discourse of class and the relations of production has to be acknowledged.[2]

Let us concentrate our attention, therefore, on those groups which, having been powerless until that moment, discovered opportunities, institutional or otherwise, for political influence. These opportunities appeared thanks to the change of regime and the weakening of the position of those who, until that moment, had exercised hegemony. The opportunities presented by a situation of crisis and change have to be placed in context. The social structures connecting actors to each other, and also to their antagonists, provide one context. The coercive capacity of the state to control, encourage, tolerate or eliminate collective action provides another. As various studies have shown for other countries, democratisation does not put an end to the efforts of the state, or the dominant groups, to limit protest and utilise repression and force against strikers, demonstrators and dissidents. The Republic was neither more nor less democratic because it used repression. Rather, what was decisive was the way in which its security forces dealt with what was often the simple exercise of fundamental rights, but which they saw as deliberate and illegal actions of enemies of the established social hierarchy. The mechanisms of state coercion can transform ordinary political struggles against the existing order into violent actions, in the same way that the intransigent positions of certain groups can encourage the heavy handed and brutal reaction of its repressive apparatus. We should, therefore, take seriously the actions and beliefs of protesters and of those who opposed them. The logic and the rationality of their behaviour should be examined within the context in which the protest took place, and not from the perspective of contemporary ideas and assumptions.[3]

Once the republicans and socialists were in government, messages of both hope and fear quickly began to be heard throughout the Spanish countryside. Pressure was felt, both from above and below, and this either aimed at blocking the revolution in progress or eliminating the remains of the monarchical past. The essence of the transformation can be grasped in relation to two inextricably interwoven dimensions of rural society. These were the structure of local power and the application of the relevant legal norms, such as the decrees on obligatory cultivation of the land, municipal boundaries (the prohibition of the employment of outside casual labour until all those workers resident within a given municipality had been taken on) and the '*bases de trabajo*' (the wages and working conditions agreed for each agricultural task).[4] This changed the social and labour relations anchored in the traditional domination of the landowners and, as can be seen from the existing documentation, this was the area in which the first confrontations and resistance emerged.

It seems inevitable that a change of the magnitude of April 1931 (which was more noticeable and more celebrated in the cities than in the villages) should generate tension between those local authorities which remained loyal to the monarchy and the new incumbents of local power. Whilst republicans and socialists complained about the continued existence of pro-monarchist authorities, the officials of the new regime faced obstruction from landowners and the supporters of 'order', who saw themselves displaced from the central mechanisms of decision-making and influence over the rural communities. The Association of Landowners of Trujillo, in Cáceres, protested in July 1931 against the '*alojamientos*' (the 'billeting' of unemployed labourers on estates) which the Mayors have begun to practise systematically and in periods in which there has never been a shortage of employment'. They went on to ask the government to prohibit this 'totally'. In this particular case, the owners eventually chose 'the immediate establishment of a surcharge of 10% on the contributions of all classes, in order to provide funds ... and avert a possible crisis'. However, many landowners accepted the paternalist and discriminatory system of 'billeting', as long as it did not get out of hand.[5]

The employers' resistance to republican legislation was precipitated by the loss of control of the town councils, the increase in socialist influence through the creation of joint panels of arbitration in agriculture and the Ministry of Labour's new legal framework of labour regulation. This hostility was particularly virulent in the areas of *latifundia* – the great estates in Extremadura and Andalucia – where there was a rural proletariat and social conflict was most intense. The employers' failure to comply with the regulatory norms of agrarian labour and, in general, with the social legislation of the Republic, was one of the most common causes of protest by agricultural workers, be they union affiliates or not, in the first two years of the Republic. What was demanded in these disputes was definitely not social revolution, the expropriation of the rich or the collectivisation of land, although these demands might well appear in the theoretical models elaborated in the most radical propaganda. Rather, what was demanded were wage rises, employment and free access to the use and exploitation of the land.[6]

'Untenable situation' – these were the words most often repeated in the telegrams which the mayors and civil governors regularly sent to the Ministry of the Interior, asking for funds for public works and unemployment assistance: '400 laid off, Council funds exhausted, starving beggars in the streets, untenable situation, send funds urgently.' This telegram (from the mayor of Casariche in Seville to the Ministry of the Interior) was already being repeated, in 1931, by many of the towns of Andalucia and Extremadura. There was always an attempt to suggest, between the lines, that if, as often happened, the funds were not forthcoming, then the result would be robberies, attacks on farmhouses and the occupation of estates. All of which amounted to 'a grave threat to the maintenance of public order'.

This situation forced the civil governors to maintain a difficult balance between the pressures of the mayors, the local citizens of the provinces and the authorities in Madrid. The idea that a solution would be forthcoming from above was widespread in the early days of the Republic, when optimism still persisted. This can be seen from the quantity of petitions, which arrived from all over, soliciting the intervention of the central authorities in the provision of social justice and the amelioration of problems as diverse as starvation and natural disasters. This was partly a hangover from a paternalistic era which had still not entirely disappeared, but it was also a reflection of the desperate state in which the unemployed and their families found themselves in a society in which there was no unemployment insurance. With the exception of the decree law of 28 May 1931, which allowed for the concession of loans to the National Institute of Social Provision, 'for the assistance of the unemployed', there was no advance made in this area during the government of the republican–socialist coalition. The potential solutions, which are easily identified in the history of Spain, appeared to be unviable at the time. There was no money to finance public works. Those who could provide employment refused to hire workers who were affiliated to the unions and workers were often forced to leave the unions as a condition of employment. Threatening messages might not meet with strong resistance. Even if they did, they had the double effect of identifying the 'politically conscious' workers, who could then be sacked and a lower daily rate paid. The civil governors had to content themselves with noting the cases of success, intervening in favour of a potentially 'peaceful' solution, imposing these where necessary and, where all else failed, maintaining order.[7]

'Deploy the Civil Guard' was, effectively, another of the most common requests which the local authorities, civil governors and landowners made of the Minister of the Interior. There was no mystery behind these requests. It required only for a strike to be called by one of the local sections of a union over 'disputes with the employers over wage rates'. As the unions 'exercised the right to employment coercively', the local mayor would request the intervention of the civil governor. The civil governor would, in turn, request the minister to authorise the 'deployment of the Civil Guard as he considered necessary' in order to avoid 'the disturbance of public order'. At other times a private landowner would address himself directly to the minister, during the harvest period, requesting armed intervention and offering to 'facilitate lodgings and cover the cost of extra expenses incurred'.[8]

That the employers and the councils should have to cover the costs, when reinforcements of the Civil Guard were requested, is highly indicative of the Spanish state's lack of funds, and of the structural problems of its police force. This lack of funds usually went hand in hand with ruinous financial administration. The forces of law and order were badly paid, poorly equipped and, as was the case with the administration in general, relatively inefficient. Furthermore, the Civil Guard was thinly spread out over the territory and when trouble broke out reinforcements had to be called in from another locality. They were often transferred from small provinces to the capital cities and, as their towns of origin were left 'abandoned', fear spread throughout the affected authorities regarding the threat from 'extremist elements' who might take advantage of the situation in order to demonstrate against 'order and property'. The prisons where these 'extremists' ended up were also the focus of conflict. Full of extremists, as they must have been towards 1932, the situation was 'alarming', and the 'social prisoners' caused altercations and complained of 'brutal beatings'. The civil governors voiced concerns over the possibility of escapes or attacks, given the lack of 'reinforcements of Civil Guard necessary for the level of vigilance appropriate to the critical situation in the countryside'. Manuel Azaña, prime minister on the day that the cabinet had 'finally managed to "execute" Victoria Kent', that is replace her as Director of Prisons, noted in his diary by way of justification that: 'The prison situation is alarming. There is no discipline. The prisoners escape whenever they like.'[9]

The hope of a radical change in the relations of domination in the countryside evaporated very quickly. Or at least this was the perception of numerous groups of agricultural workers in the north and south. Without ceasing to implore the government to protect them, they manifested their discontent in demonstrations charged with both myth and immediate reasonable demands. The dream of social revolution was always close on the horizon, but always out of reach. The legislation put in place by the government was probably the most appropriate and (with the exception of the agrarian reform which was always under discussion, but never seemed to arrive) many day labourers and tenant farmers benefited from the initial winds of change. Nevertheless, unemployment rose to an unacceptable level – 'starvation, misery, lack of basic necessities', repeated the telegrams, but the government did not have the means to improve the situation. Many landowners began to express their aggressive hostility towards the 'republican burden' openly, whilst the security forces could not preserve order without shooting people.

From September and October 1931 onwards there was an increasing number of occupations of estates and of incidents in which workers would go to the homes of the landowners and demand their wages. They would often be turned away at gunpoint or by the Civil Guard. There were also violent demonstrations in which unionised agricultural workers clashed with the employers' associations. This type of incident brought two different worlds of culture, loyalty and friendship into confrontation. An astonishing number of occupations and 'illegal cultivations' of properties took place in provinces such as Huesca and Teruel, which was all the more surprising since it was not Andalucia. In the northern parts of Aragon, some of these protests took place under the auspices of anarcho-syndicalism. Rejecting the official arbitration committees (*jurados mixtos*), they declared revolutionary strikes, which infringed the 'honourable rights of modest, working land owners' and could lead to the imprisonment of the 'strike committee'. However, in other cases, such as Puebla de Valverde in Teruel, it was local groups (two hundred in this particular case) who

> invaded a private estate in Puerta Escandón and proceeded to plough up the land, cut trees and collect wood, until the mayor of the town arrived. At that point the locals desisted in their activities, but only on condition that the authorities agree to obtain the title deeds from the proprietor, as the locals believed that the village had a rightful collective claim to the property.[10]

These were long-standing disputes over the rightful ownership of public property, in which accusations were constantly made that common lands had been enclosed in the nineteenth century and usurped by local landowners. Activists of the socialist land-workers' federation (*Federación Nacional de Trabajadores de la Tierra*) took a leading role in demands for measurements to be made so that public lands could be separated out and marked off. These demands had become so persistent, and were perceived as such a threat, that many of the landowners prepared for battle before the conflict had even begun. This is what happened at Olite, in Navarra, where the landowners complained directly to the Minister of the Interior that they had been 'expelled by locals and tenant farmers who had taken over the lands'. Maura, displaying his characteristic love of order, wrote to the Civil Governor on 29 May, urging him to 'take whatever urgent and energetic measures necessary to put an end to such abuse'. 'No action is required yet', came the reply from the provincial authorities the next day, because 'it is not true that the tenant farmers have expelled the cattle-breeders, or taken control of their property. They have merely made demands to the council for the return of enclosed lands.'[11]

The mayors and local authorities were sometimes blamed for the atmosphere of unease which reigned in many towns, as they were seen to be 'linked to the promoters of disorder'. It was not unusual, for example, in those regions of Aragon where revolutionary syndicalism had a strong hold for the republican authorities to join with anarchist activists in revolutionary proclamations. These proclamations were the expression of a common culture. 'Long live Anarchy!' shouted a republican councillor from the balcony of Beceite town hall (Teruel, July 1931), following which both he and the mayor had to resign. One month later, the leading authority in Albalate de Cinca in Huesca 'addressed the population from the balcony of the town's cultural centre, urging them not to pay land rents and attacking the clergy and the bourgeoisie'. As was to be expected following such a declaration, the head of the local Civil Guard asked the Civil Governor if he thought it was best to 'proceed directly to the dismissal of the mayor or punish him for this shameful abuse of authority'.[12]

Of course, not all disputes were organised by the labour organisations. The precarious situation of salaried workers, the hostile attitude of many landowners, who left their land uncultivated, and simple hunger and need all generated forms of delinquency and dissidence. The pattern was fairly consistent in the rural world of Spain, especially in the areas where large-scale property predominated, and examples abound in the republican period. The illegal appropriation of property, robberies with violence and thefts all fall into this category of dissent. They might be carried out by groups or individuals and the value of the property stolen was usually small. However, it was fairly common for these acts of delinquency to be repeated and this led to heavier sentences. The penalties imposed were also usually 'small, although when this was placed in relation to the individual's level of wealth, the effects might be considerable'. The problem did not end there because 'the need to feed their families ... drove them not only to steal, but also to insult the authorities'. Demands for employment were made forcefully, and might even be accompanied by death threats. If this failed they 'took directly what nature had to offer'. The fact that the majority of those involved in these crimes were day labourers is not without significance. They put up with the worst conditions and were the most wretched and uneducated sector of the community. As a result, the sentences imposed sank those condemned 'into a ruinous spiral of marginalisation.'[13]

Judging by the descriptions of the authorities, there was no shortage either of the type of protest thought to be characteristic of the 'pre-industrial masses' (although numerous studies have, of course, confirmed the persistence of these forms of protest in societies considered to be industrialised). Bread was the staple and its consumption was a good indicator of standards of living and social position. Hunger was accompanied by the search for bread and this generated conflict. However, if E. P. Thompson's views are accepted, this conflict was also due to popular belief in the immorality of the governors, who tolerated hoarding, price increases and speculation. Women were especially prominent in this type of collective protest, confronting the authorities and the security forces and occupying the front-line in demonstrations. This was exactly the sort of incident that took place at Peñaranda, in Salamanca, on 28 September 1931. Following a public meeting called by the socialists, 'rebellious crowds' attacked the bakery'. The Civil Guard repelled the 'aggression', leaving two 'strikers dead' and four wounded. At Almedina, in Ciudad Real, on 9 May 1932, the Civil Governor informed the Ministry of 'disorder resulting from the lack of bread and the rise in prices', which had been caused by the 'shortage of flour' in the whole province.[14]

These agrarian conflicts emerged against a background of faith in the good intentions of the Republic and an expectation that its legislation would prove efficacious. Bloodshed was minimal, up until the incidents spanning Thursday 31 December 1931 to Tuesday 5 January 1932, when there took place a sort of second 'Tragic Week' (anti-clerical rioting and the subsequent bloody repression in Barcelona in 1909). The republican regime was not under any particular pressure at that time, and nothing at the end of the year would have led one to imagine what would happen. The Constitution had been approved with an ample majority in parliament on 9 December. Niceto Alcalá Zamora was elected President of the Republic on the day after, and on 15 December Manuel Azaña formed a government.

As has been recounted a thousand and one times, it all began in Castilblanco, a town in the north-east of the province of Badajoz in the district of Herrera del Duque. The provincial Federación de Trabajadores de la Tierra had convened a strike for 30 and 31 December. This was a protest strike aimed at the civil governor and the colonel in charge of the Civil Guard, who were accused of supporting the landowners and 'caciques' in their failure to comply with the new social legislation. The strike was relatively peaceful, with only a few sporadic clashes between the Civil Guard and the labourers. However, on the 31st, whilst the demonstrators at Castilblanco were returning home, the mayor, or one of the landowners according to a different source, asked the Civil Guard to disperse them. There was a struggle and one person was shot dead by the Civil Guard. The labourers, in an attack of rage and hate (that hate of which Azaña spoke), threw themselves on four of the Civil Guards with sticks, stones and knives and massacred them.[15] Enraged and undisciplined, the Civil Guard took mortal revenge for several days, during which time the governing authorities stood passively by.

However, with the exception of Zalamea de la Serena, where three labourers were killed and three more wounded, the most outrageous incidents took place in areas where the unions and employers were in conflict over issues closely related to the shortage of work, far away from Castilblanco and the big estates. At Épila in the province of Zaragoza, the sugar workers demanded that employment be given preferentially to residents of the municipality. Employment was to be restricted to two persons per family, and those without local residency were to be laid off. On Saturday 2 January, there was a strike in the factory, the agricultural labourers did not report for work and some commercial establishments were closed. On the Sunday about five hundred people assembled in the town square. In anticipation of the strike, the Civil Guard had called in reinforcements from several towns in the province of Zaragoza. They attempted to clear the square and opened fire, leaving two day-labourers dead and several more wounded. The next day, at Jeresa in the Valencian district of Safor, a demonstration of agricultural workers, who were in dispute with their employers over new work contracts, showered the mounted Civil Guard with stones and insults. The guard responded with a sabre charge and this was followed by shooting which left four dead and three wounded, two of them women.[16]

Finally there were the incidents at Arnedo, a town in the province of La Rioja with five thousand inhabitants centred on the footwear industry. The events which took place in this locality raised a 'storm' of protest against the Civil Guard as a result of the rivers of blood spilt in the town's Republic Square. Six men and five women were killed and eleven women and eighteen men were wounded. Five of the wounded were permanently disabled and unable to return to work ever, whilst one Civil Guard suffered a minor gunshot wound. There were victims of all ages. A woman of seventy and a child of four were found amongst the dead, and amongst the wounded there were men and women of over seventy and a child of five who had to have a leg amputated. It is not surprising that in such a bloody aftermath the 'storm' was, as Azaña noted, 'thunderous'.

There is an abundance of varied and reliable documentation which leaves little room for doubt in the interpretation of these incidents. Almost a year before the incident in Arnedo, a dispute had begun in the Muro family's shoe factory. One of the owner's sons had sacked a worker who joined forces with a group of other sacked employees. The civil governor convoked meetings, initiated arbitration and even managed to achieve a 'verbal agreement, although without legal force', before an 'arbitration committee' attempted to resolve the conflict 'by legal means'. Meanwhile, the employers refused to comply with their commitments and continuously infringed the legislation on the length of the working day. The workers 'having gone along with all of the government's attempted solutions, showed an admirable spirit of solidarity and a long-suffering desire to find a peaceful solution'. However, as this was unsuccessful they decided to call a strike, which was announced within the period prescribed by the Law of the Defence of the Republic and began on 5 January 1932. The local branch of the UGT and the factory strike committee called on 'all conscientious citizens' to unite in solidarity with the 'suffering' workers 'to demand our daily bread, and that of our children, which these heartless employers want to steal from us ... by closing commercial and industrial establishments, abandoning work and so helping to resolve a situation which could bring great suffering to Arnedo'.

That same day the civil governor, Ildefonso Vidal, arrived to chair a meeting in the town hall which was attended by the mayor, a number of councillors, the lieutenant colonel and commanding officer of the local Civil Guard and a few employers who agreed to the presence of the employees sacked by Muro. Meanwhile, the strike was continuing peacefully as 'the sabotage and coercion common in these situations took place without violence or aggression and there was no disturbance of public order which required the intervention of the security forces'. The demonstrating strikers, with women and children leading the march, entered the square where the Civil Guard were already assembled with a sergeant, four corporals and twenty guards under the orders of lieutenant Juan Corcuera y Piedrahita. Without coming to attention or issuing any previous warning or firing shots in the air, 'they opened fire suddenly and unexpectedly' and did not stop 'until they were ordered to by the lieutenant colonel, who came down from the town hall'. There was no 'collective aggression nor any collective resistance' and the people fled in terror. According to the conclusions of the report drawn up on the orders of the Civil Governor of Vizcaya, 'the lieutenant in charge of the security forces should not have dispersed the demonstration … because his superiors, the civil governor and the lieutenant colonel, were in the town hall and had not issued him with instructions for the dispersal'. According to the military sentence given two years later, 'the officer had received the normal instructions from his lieutenant colonel, to exercise prudence but act forcefully and not to allow himself to be taken by surprise'.

In their summing up, both the military judge and another special judge found no indication of responsibility on the part of any of the locals. There were, however, divergent opinions on whether the bullet that injured the Civil Guard came from the pistol of one of the demonstrators or, as was stated by the doctor who attended to the wounded, from a standard Civil Guard-issue Mauser rifle. The military sentence, which was pronounced in Burgos in January 1934, absolved the lieutenant of 'homicide and wounding through reckless imprudence, due to the lack of evidence, and the same ruling was applied to the unit of Civil Guard under his orders'.[17]

The dead were buried, Sanjurjo was sacked or was 'transferred to another post' as Azaña put it. The events of Arnedo were forgotten, because many other incidents were still to take place (only a few days after there was an attempted insurrection in Figols) and with the tragedy of Casas Viejas, exactly a year later, the incident in that Riojan town seemed to pale into insignificance. In reality, the two incidents had little in common. In Arnedo, there was no uprising to be put down but the workers' will towards conciliation and the UGT's attempts to channel the conflict through the legal mechanisms were of little avail. According to the summing up, the memory of Castilblanco, the state of despondency of the Civil Guard (as a result of what were perceived as unfair and systematic attacks on the institution), confused orders and the lack of leadership and discipline all provided possible explanations of such a bloody and sudden response – the shooting lasted 'less than a minute'. This analysis fed the legend, which had a basis in reality, that the state could not control its mechanisms of coercion, even when the military and governmental authorities were present. It also betrayed an inability to enforce the new legislation. A few days after these 'tragic events', Andrés González, president of the provincial Socialist Federation and member of the county council, informed the Civil Governor that the agreements of the arbitration committee on the reinstatement of the sacked workers

> have still not been implemented. Your Excellency must be made aware of the enormous damage which the failure to comply with the law does to the maintenance of order. When the citizens fail to find the support, to which they have a right, discipline is broken. What is worse, when they see themselves cheated of their rights, desperation overpowers the exercise of reason and results in violence with terrifying consequences.

These reflections on the dramatic events would continue to be relevant for quite some time.[18]

In spite of these confrontations and the impunity with which the security forces would continue to act, it seems obvious that there was still a considerable difference between the type of conflict characterising the smallholding areas of northern Spain and that of the large estates where day labour was predominant. There was much more evidence of successful government mediation in the former, and resistance to the application of social legislation, on the part of the authorities and employers, was much more marked in the latter. This distinction became even more marked with the advent of agrarian reform.

For many reasons, including the cunning with which large landowners had managed to obscure the scale of their holdings, and because of various technical clauses relating to 'rotation' and 'systematic leasing', the law of agrarian reform seemed to threaten the expropriation of small proprietors more than of large-scale landowners. The confusion and fear generated by the law were skilfully exploited by militant Catholic organisations. Many of these 'very poor proprietors' who were so common in the north of Spain were 'propelled' into a generalised offensive against the Republic. Amongst the day labourers, who were probably the sector of Spanish society which held out most hope that the regime would eradicate the excesses of class privilege, the effects were not as negative. The initial support and wage increases which accompanied government legislation and policy augured a noticeable improvement in their standards of living. In comparison with previous epochs the fate of the rural proletariat seemed to have taken a favourable turn. However, this vision began to run aground as the slowness of agrarian reform became obvious. Unemployment continued to flood the horizon, resources were failing and some of the more radical expressions of agricultural protest ended with severe punishment meted out to the protesters.

The year 1932 was not uneventful, but it was in 1933 that the rivalry between employers and workers and between the two union organisations over the distribution of work and jobs reached its peak of intensity. The socialist FNTT had rapidly put down solid foundations in the countryside in the first months of the Republic. Given the incapacity or lack of will to implement reform on the part of the state, many FNTT sections now began to rely on the strike as a practical response to the offensive of the employers. The year opened with an insurrectional challenge, which had far-reaching consequences, in spite of it doing nothing to subvert the established order. By the end of the year, following another revolutionary skirmish, the socialists had left the government and many had already decided that the phase of reform from above was over. The importance of these events should not be underestimated and they will complete our vision of the social struggles in the rural world in a separate chapter. However, we shall now make our first incursion into the different expressions of conflict in the cities.[19]

There were many things happening in the cities, right from the first moments of the Republic. Although agrarian structures still carried too much weight in Spanish society, the effects of a slow industrial development, which had been particularly noticeable in the previous decades, were unmistakable. This had led to an 'urban explosion' in certain cities. Fifty-seven point three per cent of the population had been occupied in the primary sector in 1920. This had descended to 45.5 per cent in 1930. The percentage working in the secondary sector had increased from 21.9 per cent to 26.5 per cent and the population active in the service sector had risen from 21 per cent to 28 per cent. Agriculture still accounted for half of economic production in 1935. However, as recent studies have pointed out, the Spanish economy was advancing along the route of modernisation in those years. Furthermore, new ideas and new institutions were appearing on the scene. The classic form of worker organisation, the trade union, emerged in that period. The popular classes, who occupied a variety of urban spaces, also found their characteristic forms of organisation and mobilisation in certain parties. It was in these cities that the coalition of popular and new social classes was able to put an end to the electoral domination of the corrupt local bosses known as *caciques*, and ultimately of the supreme authority that presided over it – the King – and enthusiastically welcomed the Republic.[20]

The characteristics of conflicts in these urban centres, during the government of the republican and socialist coalition, were very different from those seen in the rural context. Proof of this has emerged from the analyses carried out through a large number of case studies. The struggle to control the distribution of employment was inextricably caught up with the distribution of union power. During crises of unemployment, the unions effectively became employment exchanges. As a result, confrontation around the corporative structures of labour constituted the underlying thread in the bitter confrontation between the two unions, both of which already had competing organisational traditions within the urban working classes.

Obviously there were other contributing factors, and one of these was the vision of the strike held by many anarchists, and not just those of the FAI. The strike was seen as an 'introduction' to the organisation, and the cultivation and abuse of it was to be used as a way of attracting the unorganised proletariat. García Oliver referred to it in his most extreme expressions as 'revolutionary gymnastics'. We will continue to observe the attitudes of the state, with its mechanisms of coercion and special legislation, and the desire of certain socialists in government to 'clip the wings' of the CNT. We will encounter other types of conflict, which were more strictly related to the development of industrial capital. These took place between employers and employees and concerned terms of employment, salaries, the length of the working day, holidays, and insurance against injuries and ill health. Finally, local differences will be noted, with Madrid and Barcelona providing the opposing poles of union practice. However, it was the increasing hegemony over labour, which the UGT was developing from within the government and the apparatus of the state through legislation, which determined the primordial rivalry. This was perceived as unfair interference, which enormously limited the CNT's legitimate field of action. The ensuing struggle provoked accusations and insults and placed the Republic in an antagonistic relationship towards a large section of the working class.

This type of analysis undermines the typical characterisation of the CNT as a form of unionism with a high level of revolutionary and working-class consciousness, radicalised by the pernicious influence of the FAI. The principal, although not the only, difference between these two types of unionism, during the first two years of the Republic, was that the socialists opted for the inclusion of labour relations within the legal framework agreed between the various competing forces and the state. They believed that this would lead, gradually and inevitably, to the emancipation of the working class and to socialism. The CNT adopted direct forms of action which eschewed government mediation as the street became the site of struggle and confrontation with the state. They began to announce the arrival of the revolution within a fixed term, and this was to be ushered in through rebellion and insurrection.

Participation in government was no bed of roses and the socialists found themselves attacked on all sides. However, the CNT did not escape persecution either. Its presence on the street and the insurrectional nature of its movement provoked numerous arrests and imprisonments and a generalised repression. There was little doubt about the consequences of being one side or the other. When the socialists left the government in 1933 (some of their leaders claimed that they had been 'expelled'), reformism and the struggle for a legal route to social change lost all meaning. The Republic was no longer of any use and social revolution had become the only viable option. As we shall see, the socialists now travelled paths already trodden by the anarchists: accusations of persecution and repression, general strikes and insurrectional ventures which were unrelated to the day-to-day concerns of the workforce. Ironically, many anarcho-syndicalists had grown tired of the continual strikes and insurrections and days of demonstration and protest. October 1934 would find them thinking about the futility of individual actions which lacked wider social support.[21]

The mobilisation of the CNT in response to the *jurados mixtos* (arbitration committees) soon made itself felt in those cities such as Barcelona, Seville and Zaragoza, where the CNT was strongest. In Zaragoza, a number of unions declared strikes in an attempt to negotiate recognition outside the context of the *jurados mixtos*. These strikes were now accompanied by coercion and threats against the rival UGT. As in Seville, the reaffirmation of direct action was not directed so much against government mediation, which was accepted and at times even requested, as towards 'the disabling of the corporatist organisation'. 'Unions attempting to oblige employers to negotiate directly, circumventing terms approved by the arbitration committees' – this was the message which the Civil Governor of Zaragoza telegraphed to the Ministry of the Interior on 17 September 1931, following the announcement of a strike by the CNT Transport Union. In this particular case, the terms of employment, which were supported by the UGT, were awaiting the outcome of an appeal lodged by the employers, 'which I believe it would be useful to resolve quickly'. Government intervention, intimidation on the part of the CNT, UGT members who did not support the strikes and the opposition of the employers to the arbitration committees were characteristic factors in these conflicts and they would be repeated time and again.[22]

Not surprisingly, Barcelona was the most contested forum in this struggle. The rapidly reorganised CNT was in expansion. The UGT had never had a favourable reception in Barcelona and they were willing to take advantage of the situation in order to try and make inroads. From the very beginning of the Republic, both the industrialists and the UGT had been complaining about the infringements, abuse and 'brutal coercion' carried out by the CNT. A census had been drawn up for the election of speakers on the arbitration committees, but the CNT union leaders did not register their affiliates. Manuel Azaña captured the importance of this 'civil war' between the two union practices, with his habitual precision, when on 26 September he describes them as

> perhaps the most vigorous political realities in Spain at this point in time. The CNT unions have been refusing to comply with social legislation in Catalonia. They do not recognise the arbitration committees nor accept the work inspections. This has caused considerable trouble in the Cabinet. Largo Caballero has fought hard not to give in to the desires of the Catalans and to bring the undisciplined unions under the control of the Ministry of Labour.

The socialist Minister of Labour, Francisco Largo Caballero, who 'represented the UGT in the government', was against the idea that 'the social legislation and its application should be left to the autonomous regions'. The matter arose again during the discussion of the Catalan autonomy Statute. On 7 May 1932, after a meeting with Largo Caballero and the socialist Minister of Justice, the prime minister Fernando de los Ríos put it even more clearly:

> The Socialists are determined to maintain control of social affairs in Catalonia or, in other words (because at the moment they do not have that control), to use their power in the ministries to ensure their own defence against their terrible enemies the anarcho-syndicalists of the CNT.[23]

Azaña never hid his 'lack respect if not downright aversion towards the leaders of the CNT'. Nevertheless, he made an effort to give the impression that he was not taking sides with

> any of the proletarian organisations, because I am above that. Their struggle in the economic field does not concern me, nor do I have any intention of hindering them, ... However, violence, which damages the Republic, will not be tolerated. Above all else, they must respect social peace. If they do not respect social peace, I will impose it.

This was a logical reaction from a man who, in the words of his brother in law, had 'little or no sympathy for the disorder of anarchist thought, let alone action'. He did not usually receive the anarchist leaders. When he did, he hardly let them speak, and paid even less attention to their complaints about repression, the closure of unions and the arrest of activists.[24]

The response of the CNT emerged very quickly, and in the same place that their activists had chosen as the battleground – the street. Between May and July

1931, the CNT declared a series of strikes, in which the communists sometimes participated. These led to a considerable number of deaths in the street, as in Pasajes and Seville, and put an untimely end to the aspirations of the more moderate socialists. The 'civil war' between the two union practices grew more intense in June, with the strike convoked by the Sindicato Unico de Mineros in Asturias (a union controlled jointly by anarchists and communists). It moved further towards the abyss with the nationwide national telephone strike, called by the anarcho-syndicalists for all of Spain at the beginning of July. This emerged 'within the framework of inter-union rivalry and against the background of promises made by the leaders of the republican–socialist coalition before the declaration of the Republic', to regain a sector of such primary importance as telecommunications, which had been sold to a North American company by the monarchy. The other three unions with members working at the company refused to support the strike and Maura opposed the idea of the strikers negotiating directly with the owners. There were clashes with the security forces which resulted in a number of deaths, numerous arrests and hundreds of sackings. Far from causing reflection on the hasty organisation and failure of the conflict, this outcome merely heightened mistrust in the regime which, 'having failed to respect the channels and procedures of equality and rights ... is condemned to a premature death'.[25]

For the purist sectors of anarchism, these deaths and the subsequent repression served as a way of mobilising support against both the Republic and those leading the CNT at that point in time. 'Crime as the method of government' began to appear in the anarchist media after the events of Pasajes and Seville. As these conflicts became increasingly violent, so protests increased against repression, against the Law of the Defence of the Republic and against the deportations following the first insurrectional attempt in January 1932. Many of the disputes were of a non-political nature and concerned issues such as medical insurance and sick pay, objections to obligatory maternity insurance, better wages and attempts to force employers to comply with the terms of employment. However, the rhetoric and the actions sustaining it evinced apocalyptic visions announcing 'the total collapse of the capitalist and authoritarian world'. Moderate positions did exist, and there were calls from Asturias at that time for 'a period of calm, without so many strikes and disputes ... so as to present a well-established confederal organisation'. However, it was the extremist view which won the day and insisted that Spain had been 'kidnapped by the Civil Guard', and turned into 'a workers' prison'. This all served as confirmation of their thesis 'that where social democracy governs, it is much more authoritarian and ferocious than any authoritarian and feudal monarchy'.[26]

From January 1932 onwards, the rhetoric of the spilling of 'the blood of the proletariat' became a permanent feature in the anarchist press. Following the massacres of Arnedo, the insurrection of Figols and the subsequent deportations of CNT members, it seemed impossible to bridge the distance between the 'repressive' Republic and 'a proletariat which is increasingly detached from any democratic illusions'. In reality, these illusions had not lasted long and some authorities were obsessive and severe in exercise of repression. There was no possible truce. On 14 January 1932, Casares Quiroga, who had replaced Maura as Minister of the Interior, asked the Civil Governors of eight provinces (Valencia, Zaragoza and six in Andalucia) to 'inform me of the most extremist and dangerous persons who are to be found in these provinces, with their names and the reasons for which they might cause breaches of public order, so that the Law of the Defence of the Republic can be applied, if necessary'.[27]

The situation was already very tense, but things were strained a good deal more by the Law of Professional, Employers' and Workers' Associations promulgated on 8 April 1932. This law made it obligatory to present the provincial delegate of the Ministry of Labour with a copy of the 'Statutes, Regulations or agreements on the basis of which the association would be organised'. As was to be expected, the law was quickly condemned by the National Committee of the CNT as 'an arbitrary imposition of governmental intervention in the conflict between labour and capital', the sole object of which is to 'deny the right to strike and removing the possibility of direct action from the hands of the proletariat'. This proletariat, 'organised by the CNT', would struggle 'from below, in the street' against a 'government dominated by the UGT and the Socialist Party'. The only thing that the government would achieve with this 'interminable series of laws aimed at controlling the activities of an essentially anarchical people' was the multiplication of protest and the 'overthrow of the current state of affairs, which is only .maintained by police batons and mausers'.[28]

Regardless of the extent to which the spilling of the 'generous and humble blood' of the proletariat became an emotional focus of propaganda, the 'batons and mausers' were not the principal cause of the breach which had opened between the two unions. The struggle for control of the distribution of employment lay behind many of the clashes between the UGT and the CNT during that period. The economic crisis and the reduction in public spending, with its consequent reduction in public works, and the impossibility of migrating to the cities caused a considerable increase in the number of unemployed. In June 1932, official figures already estimated the number of unemployed at 446,263, of which more than half were agricultural labourers. During the previous two decades there had been a high degree of structural change in industry which had led to the influx of a large new workforce. Many of these young workers, having benefited from the dictatorship's policy of growth, had joined the labour organisations at the beginning of the Republic. They had great expectations but no union experience. The majority of them had no specialist qualifications and when the crisis arrived, above all in the construction sector, they joined the ranks of the unemployed. As there was no unemployment insurance in Spain at the time, unlike other countries, this meant that the unemployed suffered greatly. The Republic found itself with a delicate problem, which it had not foreseen, and did little to counteract it, other than create a 'National Fund for Involuntary Unemployment'. In reality, the question of unemployment never took centre stage in the politics of the regime. Given this situation and the expectation which the arrival of the Republic had created, frustration soon turned into protest.[29]

A person's job determined their income, where they lived and their social position. In the cities, work occupied the greater part of a person's time and for many it was not only a way of earning a living. It also determined their way of life, who their friends were, their culture and their leisure time. Unemployment, on the other hand, signified not only difficulty and hunger but also feelings of inadequacy and the loss of identity. This would all be obvious to an observer from a society such as England in the 1930s, but in Spain things were not quite that clear. The perception of a permanent job as something normal and indispensable, which is a prerequisite to perceiving unemployment as a problem, was a recent phenomenon in Spain and one which was limited to a small sector of industry. Spain was a country with a high percentage of agricultural workers and high levels of militant union membership amongst the construction industry. Construction work was seasonal, largely unskilled and during several months of the year it was done by workers from the agricultural sector. The labour organisations demanded public works as a way of ameliorating the effects of unemployment. For the authorities the 'conflict of those without work and without bread' was 'a volcano in eruption'. These were different perceptions which, in times of crisis, afforded no solution.[30]

Faced with a problem of this magnitude, the CNT made ingenuous and unviable proposals, such as the adoption of the six-hour day. At the same time it reproduced the typical analyses of the 'moral, political and economic bankruptcy' of capitalism. Everything could be blamed on the 'excess of production which flooded the markets and the inadequate purchasing power of the people continued to decrease as unemployment increased'. Given that 'bourgeois society' had no solution to 'structural unemployment', what was required was 'social revolution' and the 'introduction of libertarian communism'. Until this felicitous moment arrived, as it soon would, half measures were a waste of time. The 'capitalist system' was to blame and it was 'the capitalist system itself' which had 'the duty to ensure the means of subsistence for the unemployed workers'. This analysis explains the diatribes against any form of subsidy from the state and the demand that work should be 'distributed amongst all wage earners'. The refusal to make use of the mechanisms of the state, even if this was to the benefit of the working classes, was a logical consequence of the belief in the need to destroy the existing order. In practice this meant rejecting outright any type of reform be it of labour relations or land ownership.[31]

The idea of strengthening the labour organisation through the state and using intervention as an instrument in the resolution of disputes was not, therefore, a project which the two labour movements shared. This was the principal source of anarchist resistance to the relations of institutional dependence which the UGT had developed. Anarcho-syndicalist practice made headway in proportion to the extent to which the economic crisis hindered the representation of workers' interests via the corporatist channels. This was because, while union affiliation might guarantee employment, when there was little employment to distribute, the advantage held by those in control of contracting disappeared. With no strikes to declare, discontent established itself in the assemblies of unemployed workers and from there was transmitted to public demonstrations and channelled against the government, amongst whom there were now to be found the well-connected 'socialist old boys' who were ultimately held responsible for the situation. Obviously this mass of unskilled labourers, who were inexperienced in union struggles, could contribute to the radicalisation of protest and cause disturbance. However, contrary to what has commonly been supposed, they could never construct a powerful labour movement which would be a threat to capitalism. In reality, in a state such as Spain, they would never be more than a problem of public order. The vicious circle of mobilisation-repression-confirmation of the fact that all authority was the same would be completed time and time again. It is highly significant that in the Spain of this period the principal strikes did not start in the factories or one sector of production and then spread to the rest of the workforce. 'Rather, they were convened by the union leadership in response to the negative responses of those in power to the demands of the workers.'[32]

The struggle of the CNT against the intervention of the state in disputes between workers and employers contributed to the failure of the mechanisms of 'reconciliation' which were essential to the functioning of the corporatist system. However, they gained very little as a result. That the Republic did not, or could not, fulfil the expectations of workers, will be seen from its inability to realise the majority of their aims. As a result, the more radical postures quickly began to elicit a positive response amongst wide sectors of the unemployed urban and rural proletariat. The internal struggle within the CNT led to a split in which thousands of activists left the union in the most industrialised areas and where affiliation was strongest. Amongst those who left were some of the most able leaders. Losing support amongst the industrial workers in order to gain it in the sector of unemployed and construction workers (a volatile workforce which could be mobilised with the same rapidity with which it deserted the ranks of the protest) was not a step forward. Two years after the declaration of the Republic with numerous disputes and several insurrections behind it, the CNT was much weaker and, with some important exceptions such as Madrid, had suffered a noticeable reduction in membership. Things had not gone much better for the UGT. The socialists had left the government, something which the employers and the republicans of the radical party had been crying out for during 1933. The inability of the party and its union to articulate the interests of the workers led to a fragmentation of the socialist movement, 'the basic problem and weakness of the left in general during the period of the Second Republic'.[33]

It would seem logical to conclude from the results of this analysis that the struggle between the two unions and the opposition of the CNT deprived the Republic of part of its social foundation. It would, however, be an over-simplification to attribute the weakening of the liberal democratic alternative to the radicalism of the anarcho-syndicalists. The middle classes were divided over the consequences of the republican reform package. This legislation did not facilitate the resolution of labour conflict, nor the organisation of those sectors of labour marginal to the control of the UGT. The state was lacking in economic resources and inefficient in administration whilst the security forces were wont to adopt measures of violent repression in the resolution of conflict. As a result, the consolidation of republican democracy had many obstacles in its path. The anarcho-syndicalists contributed in good measure to this culture of conflict. However, it is obvious that they were not responsible for the political fragmentation of the middle classes nor the inability to form lasting coalitions which they demonstrated. Those who had traditionally dominated Spain's political institutions, from which they had been evicted with the declaration of the Republic, returned after the elections of November 1933. For several months, and with the unconditional support of hundreds of thousands of small and medium rural landowners, these forces had begun an offensive against the republican regime which would not end until they had succeeded in bringing down the reform project and extirpating the revolutionary threat. We will not anticipate events any further here. It is time to examine in some detail the political and ideological components, and the internal world and most important expressions of the anarcho-syndicalist phenomenon.

3   The symbols of identity

A union movement without a party

Anarcho-syndicalism never had a party which represented and defended its interests via the mechanisms of parliamentary politics. The absence of strong, organised, working-class political parties was a phenomenon common to many European countries up until the First World War, and it was also characteristic of Spain during the entire Restoration period. There, an inefficient oligarchical state continued to preside over a corrupt pseudo-parliamentary political system. Given the persistence of this state of affairs, the Spanish trade-union movement, be it that of the UGT or the CNT, developed powerfully anti-political and anti-state characteristics. These came to the fore in its revolutionary practice which, in effect, constituted the essential difference between the Spanish working-class movement and that of the most advanced European countries. The participation of socialist and UGT representatives in government, during the first years of the Republic, modified this situation substantially. Having excluded themselves from political representation, the leaders of the CNT (and especially those who began to dominate the organisation from the beginning of 1932) were able to maintain the purity and strength of the anarchist message, against the background of this perverse social and political reality. This was the root of Spain's atypical nature. In Spain, there existed an anti-political mass-labour movement, which was able to defend its project without participation in the parliamentary and political institutions. In the rest of Europe, by the 1930s, a labour movement of this type had already become an object of merely historical interest.

The CNT was without political allies and alienated from the government, whose project of reform had important consequences for the movement. Their response was to mobilise their members in the occupation of the streets, a political space from which they would both reproach and combat the state. This occupation of the streets and the associated idea of 'less talk and more action', became the 'revolutionary act, par excellence'. The streets also provided the arena in which the differences existing within the revolutionary organisation itself would be resolved. This was what Durruti told Ricardo Fornells, one of the *treinta*, the signatories of the 'manifesto of the thirty' expelled from the Barcelona Food Union. Durruti would shake hands with the *'trientistas'* only 'in the street when they had shown themselves to be revolutionaries'.[1]

As a movement, the CNT was primarily concerned with union matters and remained independent of the political parties. However, in order to accede to control of the organisation, a minimum grasp of anarchist ideology was necessary. As a result, a distinction was established between the leaders, the grass-roots militants and the membership at large. The leaders were the most politically conscious sector. They had achieved a familiarity with the basic principles of the organisation and its doctrinal arguments, and had done this through the reading of books, pamphlets and the press. This qualification, of course, 'required by the acquisition, or prior possession, of an acceptable level of literacy'. These leaders were always surrounded by a large group of militants, who were well informed on political and social affairs and the organisation's position on these. This group would read the press, attend union meetings and frequent the local study and debating centres known as *ateneos* and libraries, in search of the information necessary for their activism. Finally there was the membership at large. With some variations this was always around several hundred thousand during this period. Their relationship to the organisation was generally quite loose. They paid their dues, but often they had to be badgered to do so. They would not normally attend meetings at the union centres or branch offices, and their participation in labour conflicts and protest demonstrations depended on the degree of success these could be seen to have. For the majority of this sector, the CNT defended the standard of living of the workers and fought to better them. For the leaders and the activists anarcho-syndicalism was a force destined to bring about revolutionary change in society.

The ideological preparation necessary for a leadership role had to be obtained somewhere other than union itself. Various sources existed, such as the libertarian *ateneos*, the rationalist schools, groups of fellow travellers and a variety of cultural organisations, and these became the real symbols of identity of the activist 'with ideas', above all in the urban centres. As this preparation could not be obtained within the structure of the union, the ideological debate within the organisation was dominated by the leaders and the most active sector. It did not extend to the whole organisation and, as a result, a barrier arose between this trained minority and the membership at large. The latter were excluded from any type of internal debate. As an almost inevitable result of the importance given to this preparation and familiarity with ideas, the level of militancy and cultural preparation went hand in hand. This was because 'the worker who was sufficiently concerned to participate actively in union life had to be aware of the situation in the CNT and have the ability to debate any issue that arises'. In a society with high levels of illiteracy, especially amongst labourers, day-field workers and women, these requirements conditioned, and impeded, the active participation of the majority of the membership in the internal debates. Those who imparted ideology went on 'propaganda excursions' to the towns and cities, participated as orators in the public meetings and might be members of the editorial board of the anarchist press. They constituted a minority of men, and sometimes women, whose faith in the power of culture and ideas was unbreakable.

It would be misleading, therefore, to suggest that the CNT was different, in this respect, from any of the other mass organisations. The myth of the active participation of all of the membership in decision-making falls down when it is set against the guiding principles and habitual practice of the organisation. This analysis also forces a distinction to be made between the workers, members and leaders, and between the working class and the anarcho-syndicalist movement. The distinction between active commitments and mere adhesion to the revolutionary syndicalist cause could be seen clearly in the rural unions, which were often run by teachers and activists from the urban world. This was a distinction, at the end of the day, 'between those who played cards in the bar and joined the union as a social necessity, and those who went to centres to study and participate in the planning of social action'.[2]

The grandiloquent declarations and the revolutionary rhetoric, which were used as prompts to mobilisation in disputes, were also accompanied, in the Spanish case, by the creation of an autonomous workers' culture. This pervaded the daily life of the working classes. It was a mixture of the 'essays on the programme of libertarian communism' (which abounded in the writings of authors such as Isaac Puente or Federico Urales), and visions of the society of the future. It was diffused through channels of information as diverse as conversations and conferences to the reading of the press and pamphlets in the union libraries and libertarian *ateneos*. This faith in the revolutionary power of culture explains the tremendous efforts which the anarchists made to save the people from ignorance. Ignorance was seen as a root cause of oppression and inequality. 'Good schools and good teachers will bring a definitive end to illiteracy and *caciquismo*, these two burdens which keep the people subject to the greatest of iniquities.'[3]

It is true that the press was the most extended form of revolutionary propaganda and that anarchist journalism was a well-recognised form of activism amongst the members of the organisation. Control of the editorial board of *Solidaridad Obrera*, for example, became the prize over which the factions fighting for hegemony of the CNT struggled. With a circulation of more than 31,000 copies at the beginning of the Republic, and a history which ran parallel with that of revolutionary syndicalism itself, the Barcelona paper was the most desired of prey, in the rivalry between the anarchist groups and the union leaders. Following its reappearance in the summer of 1930, it was edited (albeit with several interruptions) by Joan Peiró. The prototype of the 'journalist' worker and industrial activist, Peiró was also on very good terms with the left republicans in Catalonia. Coming under attack from the journals of the Urales family, from the FAI and from libertarian journalists, such as Felipe Alaiz, who remained aloof from labour militancy, Peiró resigned on 21 September 1931. Along with him went the editorial board of Sebastià Clara, who had run the paper for a few months at the beginning of that year, Ricardo Fornells, Agustí Gibanel and Ramón Magre. All of them, with the exception of Magre, had signed the 'manifesto of the thirty'. Their letter of resignation, 'an irrevocable decision', was a premonition of the cracks which would open in the organisation. They went from *Solidaridad Obrera* to *Cultura Libertaria* and from the CNT to the so-called *sindicatos de oposición* (the opposition unions of the *treintistas*). With the exception of a brief period of collaboration during the spring and summer of 1932, not until after the outbreak of the civil war would Peiró return to the paper in whose service he had developed as a leader.[4]

The fact that Felipe Alaiz replaced Peiró as editor is a good indication of the dark and turbulent times which awaited. Officially Felipe Alaiz was appointed as editor of *Solidaridad Obrera* at the October Regional General Meeting of the CNT Unions of Catalonia. However, the decision was, in reality, taken by the activists of Barcelona's Industrial Union of Fabric and Textile workers. This union was lead by Joan Montserrat and Dionisio Eroles and their meetings were often attended by Francisco Ascaso, Buenaventura Durruti and Juan García Oliver. Alaiz's problems with the unions began very quickly. He was arrested in 1932 and replaced first by Josep Robusté and then Liberto Callejas. Taking advantage of Aliaz's absence, the Regional Committee of Catalonia invited Joan Peiró to collaborate with the paper again. In Peiró's opinion, the Regional Committee wanted to 'get rid' of Felipe Alaiz because he was 'a serious threat ... to the existence of the Catalan Regional Committee's paper'. Alaiz had an acrimonious confrontation with Peiró. He complained about the publication of two articles by the leader of the Mataro glass workers, who took every opportunity, according to him, 'to produce republican propaganda'. On 6 September 1932, he resigned. The departure of Alaiz, and his move away from the CNT, did stop the elimination of 'treintistas' from the paper. The last victim was the administrator, Pedro Massoni, another signatory of the manifesto, who was forced to resign at the Regional General Meeting of the *Sindicatos Unicos* (industry-wide unions) of Catalonia. Massoni, who was seriously ill at the time, was subjected to all sorts of insults. Distressed at what he saw as unfair attacks on a life dedicated to the organisation, he collapsed. Three months later he died.[5]

The verbal duels between the media allied to the unions and the steering committees of the Catalan Regional Committee and the anarchist publications dependent on the Urales family added a new dimension to the dispute. Federico Urales was director of a small newspaper 'empire', which he had begun to build with *La Revista Blanca* in 1898. His relations with the leaders of the Catalan CNT, be it the moderate syndicalists, anarcho-syndicalists or members of the FAI, were turbulent during the 1930s, although this was not a situation without numerous precedents. He had the support of other members of his family (amongst whom were his wife Soledad Gustavo, his daughter Federica Montseny and her life-long partner Germinal Esgleas) and the unfailing loyalty of anarcho-individualists such as Felipe Alaiz and José Alberola. The source of Urales's influence lay in his proven ability to disseminate his anarchist radicalism, whilst remaining on the margins of union activism, and, above all, in his campaigns denouncing torture and his support for the cause of imprisoned anarchists. The means through which he normally obtained his abundant economic resources were less than transparent. His criticism appeared in *La Revista Blanca* or *El Luchador*, a weekly which he set up just before the declaration of the Republic, and handed out criticism with the cavalier abandon afforded him by his financial independence. It made no difference if they threw him out of meetings or, unexpectedly, offered him a space on the agenda at the general meetings and congresses – Old Urales (he was born in 1864) would continue with his accusations and his systematic and often scandalous criticism.[6]

A proliferation of names existed within the CNT, denominating a variety of political currents. These ranged from a generic anarchism through to the less revolutionary syndicalism. The number increases if we take into consideration the various libertarian publishing houses and the range of journals on sociology, science and art. The publishing houses included *Estudios* in Valencia, *El Libertario* and *Vida y Trab*ajo in Madrid, *Tierra y Libertad* in Barcelona, and they also produced encyclopaedias, pamphlets and books by the fathers of anarchism. The journals included *Orto* or *Etica* and even the *Revista Blanca*, which became a weekly in November 1933. These combined ideological propaganda with union information and aesthetic with social concerns. There continues to be a shortage of data on which to judge the impact of these freethinking publicists. However, there was always a clear distinction between the theoretical discourse of these publications and that of organised labour, which was dominant in those CNT papers dependent on the economic resources generated through the subscriptions of the membership. Furthermore, it was always a problem just to keep the latter afloat. It is worth giving some consideration, therefore, to the two papers with a national circulation on which the organisation could count during the Republic: *Solidaridad Obrera* and *CNT*.

In spite of the apparent power which control of *Solidaridad Obrera* represented, the truth is that the paper was in difficulty. As can be imagined, money was the principal problem. There were two forms in which the CNT received income from its membership. The first was from weekly union subscriptions which were usually 0.25 pesetas (or 0.15 for women and apprentices) during the first years of the Republic. The second was the confederation stamp, of about one peseta a month, which was, theoretically, the only income available to the National and Regional Committees. In Catalonia, two centimes per month of each Confederation stamp should have gone to *Solidaridad Obrera*, which depended on this income, but it was precisely there that the calculations began to go astray. In March 1933, and for reasons which will be examined below, the number of members in Catalonia decreased to 149,000, of whom only 74,955 paid subscriptions. Given that the number of those who did not pay – 'defaulters' and the unemployed – was always around 50 per cent of the membership (and higher still in other areas) and that the Regional Committee did not pass on the correct percentage of the Confederation stamp to the paper, its income was obviously very small. The number of government closures and seizures of copies was very high from January 1932 onwards and added to the losses, which in these years, for example, were greater than the paper's supplementary income. Finally, the serious problems of distribution, combined with the difficulty in collecting the income from sales, jeopardised the stability of an enterprise of that calibre. The logical consequence of a decrease in the number of members and subscriptions was a reduction in circulation. As those responsible for the paper never tired of repeating, under these circumstances 'the life of the paper was frail'.[7]

Things also went worse than expected for the newspaper *CNT*. It had been agreed at the Special Congress in July 1931 that a Confederation paper would be published in Madrid, 'the centre of journalistic activity', which would give detailed information on union, political and ideological issues 'to all of the regions of Spain'. Following a number of failed attempts, there was serious discussion of the project at the National General Meeting of Regional Delegates held in Madrid at the end of August 1932. Avelino González Mallada was appointed as editor with the votes of all delegates, except those of Galicia who abstained and those of Andalucia and Aragon who wanted Valeriano Orobón Fernández. The paper finally made its appearance on 14 November of that year, and from that moment on it did not cease to incur debts – almost 2,000 pesetas a week, or the difference between the 12,000 pesetas it cost to print and the 10,080 pesetas' income from an initial circulation of 31,000 copies (of which 4,000 were always unsold). The numerous police seizures, which cost an average of 1,639 pesetas a week, and the long periods of closure aggravated the difficult economic situation even more. It was closed from 9 December 1933, following the application of the Law of Public Order, and reopened on 21 August 1934. It was closed again on 4 October of this same year and did not reappear until July 1936, after the military uprising.

The attempts to correct the 'untenable' situation were all in vain. Costly projects were undertaken, which only served to accelerate the disaster, such as the purchase of the machinery of *El Imparcial* (a paper which was in crisis at the time) without consulting the National Committee. Avelino González Mallada was replaced as editor following the accusations that he 'had not been sufficiently energetic in his support of the insurrection of 1933'. Liberto Callejas, who had left *Solidaridad Obrera*, became caretaker editor from the summer of 1933 and then officially in June 1934. Some regional delegates blamed the editorial board for the situation and argued that 'they did not know how to capture the spirit of the working classes in their columns'. All of those who took turns in the attempt to resolve the crisis came from the most intransigent sector, people such as Abad de Santillán, Alaiz and García Oliver. However, during the months the paper was in circulation, it generated a powerful wave of revolutionary rhetoric and fuelled the storm that was raging throughout the anarcho-syndicalist organisation, torn apart as it was by internal division and insurrectionary fits.[8]

The gravity of the economic situation in which the anarchist press found itself was an accurate reflection of the state of affairs within the organisation. We have already seen the first link in the causal chain. A substantial part of the membership did not pay subscriptions (even though union regulations stipulated that a member was considered to have 'resigned' after three months) and, according to the information available, the confederation stamp was not paid by more than 100,000 members. In the second place, as Agustín Souchy, the secretary of the AIT, pointed out in the International General Meeting of April 1932, the weekly subscriptions of the CNT were very low in comparison to those of the AIT. In other countries, the rate paid was the equivalent of an hour's labour, while the 25 or 30 centimes paid weekly in Spain were the equivalent of 'a quarter of an hour of the average wage'. Finally, there were the prisoners, whose number grew, along with that of the unemployed, as the Republican period progressed. As will be seen, they ended up becoming a serious burden for the organisation and a permanent source of conflict. In the final analysis, this union movement, without a party and on the margins of institutional life, was also a movement without funds, with problems over subscriptions, and in which there frequently arose 'special' needs, such as those of the prisoners. In spite of not having a paid bureaucracy, it also showed a considerable inability to manage the limited funds it distributed to publicists, managers and editors appointed to the papers. The level of indiscipline was matched by the frequency of calls to order. These were, however, always phrased in such a way as to highlight the animadversion professed towards that concept. 'We reject individual authoritarianism, but accept the collective authority of the majority which has to be obeyed. Without this recognition there is no organisation.'[9]

The ability to organise and mobilise did exist. However, the National Committee was merely 'a post office' which was incapable of co-ordinating 'Confederation activities throughout the country'. This was true to such an extent that, if we are to believe their own reports, the National Committee found out about conflicts, strikes and protest movements when 'the papers reported them'. This was partly due to the federal structure of the CNT. From its basic unit, the union, to the summit of the organisation, the National Committee, organisation passed through a network of local, county and regional committees, which were very difficult to control. The deep conviction that the CNT emerged from the 'heart of the people' obliged it to give unconditional support to the demands of the grass roots, and this did the rest. The local unions called strikes 'without considering in the least the general interests of the organisation', and regional Confederations could cite the concepts of federalism and autonomy in order to decide for themselves, without 'orders from above', the moment in which to mount 'the chimera of revolution'. These organisational defects would often be pointed out, during the 1930s, by AIT observers and delegates, and their comments were always the same. There was no shortage of 'impetus, enthusiasm or revolutionary activism' amongst the CNT or the Spanish people. However, 'this self-sacrifice for the cause of the revolution' was not enough 'to achieve the definitive triumph'. If they continued in this way, without preparing 'the large scale movement', they would run the risk that the 'Republican reaction' would grew ever stronger and the proletariat would find it 'harder every day to defend itself'. If they did not take this risk seriously the proletariat would desert the CNT and this 'potential' would be lost to the 'Communism of Moscow'.[10]

These warnings were of little use at that point in time because the organisational structure was bogged down with overlapping committees. Following the declaration of the Republic, defence committees had been set up which, within the existing federal structure, were supposed to incorporate members of the CNT and the FAI with equal representation. Their principal function was to direct 'readiness' groups or committees, which would 'be activated only at the decisive moment, that is, when a revolutionary insurgency broke out'. They could not, therefore, 'intervene in simple strike actions', nor would they 'have the authority to initiate any sort of mobilisation'. They would be answerable to the CNT, which would be in control. However, what happened in reality was that, once the FAI had managed to take control of the CNT, the management committees of the union organisation and the committees of defence were staffed by the same people. These same people almost always belonged to the FAI. This confusion or, to be more precise, fusion reached its peak, as will be seen, in the attempted insurrection of January 1933. The secretary of the National Committee of the CNT, Manuel Rivas, was at the same time the secretary of the National Defence Committee and a leader of the FAI. When the call to 'launch the movement' arrived, the unions, groups and committees of this confused network could never respond coherently, because they never knew if the call had come from the FAI or the CNT or the defence committees. Afterwards, when the confrontations with the security forces ended in defeat, there would then be a search for those responsible for the disaster.[11]

Reports of the persecution which the anarcho-syndicalists suffered and the campaign in defence of the prisoners formed the basis on which the minuscule group FAI attempted to correct the moderate course which, according to them, the CNT had taken under the guidance of the union leadership. The so-called 'Pro-prisoner Committees' were an ideal instrument in the campaign to convene the 'assembly' in which this group placed so much hope. This assembly would reveal the true level of solidarity amongst the moderate leaders 'for the cause of those persecuted and tortured at the hands of the 'bourgeois Republic'. As there were soon a great many of these, the activities of these prisoner-solidarity committees increasingly gained ground in the organisation. Protest days in support of prisoners multiplied along with 'defensive' mobilisation against government repression. This continual resort to agitation hindered the strategy of the revolutionary trade unionists, whose goal from the beginning of the Republic had been the consolidation of a strong organisation. Accordingly, a willingness to continue the struggle through other means was interpreted as cowardice and betrayal, and the greatest type of betrayal possible: the refusal to support comrades harassed by government brutality. The threats, rhetorical violence and acts of coercion against the moderates grew worse. People who were so weak, lacking in 'virility' and incapable of leading the organisation into general strikes against repression did not deserve to be in charge of the CNT. It was accusations of this type which led to the resignation of Ángel Pestaña from his post as secretary general of the CNT in March 1932 and of Emilio Mira from his post as secretary of the Regional Committee of Catalonia the following month. Replaced by the FAI members Manuel Rivas and Alejandro G. Gilabert, respectively, this change marked the beginning of a new phase for the Confederation. It did not yet mean the expulsion of the '*treintistas*' and the more moderate trade unionists, who continued to put on a brave face in the various union sections, but it was the end of the influence of this stream within the leadership committees.

The issue of prisoners reached such dimensions in Barcelona that unforeseen factors emerged to complicate matters for those attempting to control them. The campaigns generated some money but less than was needed, and the problem of the lack of economic resources came to the fore once more. 'Critical situation', 'exorbitant costs', 'debts' of thousands of pesetas, these were the words which were repeated in the main Pro-prisoner Committee of the Catalan capital and in the General Meetings of the Union Committees. Once more the blame for this situation was placed, not with those who managed these funds, but with the Law of the Defence of the Republic and its repressive mechanisms. Nevertheless, the prisoners remained in prison and began to protest 'energetically' about the 'inefficient work of the Committee'. They demanded the Committee's resignation on various occasions and began a hunger strike in November 1931. They did not understand why they were still in prison after so many months and threatened to reject the support of the organisation and its lawyers. In July 1932, those who had been in prison longest, seven or eight months, complained that they felt 'completely abandoned'.[12]

Those on the outside were not of the same opinion. 'When ideals are defended with heroism and perseverance they will always win', declared the new National Committee. Heroism, pride, courage, virility, responsibility, nobility and 'no trace of weakness and cowardice', these were the traits which always characterised the struggle of the Spanish people represented by the CNT. 'The truly healthy part of the people is entrenched in our organisation and it will not be easy to destroy a history of struggle and wonderful sacrifice like that of this people and our organisation.' The activists of the CNT were brave because they had right on their side. 'They, on the other hand, are afraid, because they see the great Social Revolution growing in the hearts of the people and fear that their irresponsible attitude may precipitate it.' 'They' were the socialists and the bourgeois democrats.

In this way, two sides were formed, 'the proletariat, struggling constantly for its rights and the bourgeois State, with the help of the so-called socialists'. Capitalism, the state and the socialists had united 'in complete collusion' against the 'rebellious spirit of the Spanish people'. And each of the parties brought the worst of itself to this collusion. Capitalism brought exploitation, the cause of the 'miseries and vicissitudes which the revolutionary proletariat has suffered from time immemorial'. The state brought 'machine-gun bullets'. And the socialists, 'the accomplices of the robbery', brought their 'thousands of hangers-on with their fantastically well-paid sinecures' who were always swarming around the corridors of power, 'from the mayors and the civil governors to the county councils and the *jurados mixtos*'. Power was unequally distributed between the sides but it was clearly demarcated in terms of the moral conception of struggle, tyranny and goodness. 'They have emergency laws, means of corruption and weapons. We have an ideal that has taken root in the consciousness of the exploited. And we will overcome!'[13]

Given that this was a 'life or death' struggle, the CNT had to think in terms of 'supremely heroic deeds of such great scope that the guilty would feel the accusatory force of the insurrectionary people'. Heroic and epic deeds were extremely important issues. Anything which a worker did could count as an heroic deed if it was worthy of passing into history as an example of 'courageous struggle for rights'. A heroic deed might be, for example, a meeting, a stoppage, a demonstration or a general strike, and if these deeds were not enough more would be forthcoming in which the 'productive' people would sweep away their oppressors 'with the broom of revolution'. These rebellious deeds required the CNT to be on constant alert, awaiting the signal. This signal for the start of these 'supreme deeds', rather than an ordinary strike, would normally arrive from an external source. It might arrive as a threat of dictatorship, in response to which the CNT would 'declare a general revolutionary strike', or a military coup, the victory of the right in elections or a continued period of repression. In January 1932, following the events of Jeresa, Épila and Arnedo, the anarcho-syndicalist leaders repeated their willingness to participate in an epic deed of this sort. 'Decide comrades. And if you do decide, you know that we await your signal in order to avenge those who fell because of treachery. We are waiting!'

As they waited for the 'Social Revolution', with the leaders in charge and the proletariat as the main protagonist, the route was marked out with days of protest and struggles great and small. These 'trials', regardless of their outcome, always ended in a 'moral triumph'. The adjective 'moral' qualifying the 'triumph' became another trademark of these demonstrations. When they ended with deaths, a frequent occurrence as has been seen, the verbal violence was charged with sacred and religious references. The 'stoic sacrifice of the liber-tarian activists', who offered their lives 'for the redemption of the working people', was contrasted with the heartlessness of the executioners. While they (the socialists and republicans) commemorated the declaration of the Republic with festivals and luxury, the 'workers were bursting with hunger and courage.' The use of religious language gave greater force to the message of recrimination. At least this was what the anarchist propagandists must have believed, given the frequency with which they used it against their enemies. A good example is provided by the commentary directed against the socialists by the paper *CNT*, after a 'banquet in honour' of the prime minister Manuel Azaña. 'After the events of Casas Viejas [a village in the province of Cadiz where an insurrection by anarchist peasants had been bloodily crushed], last night's banquet in honour of the tragic Azaña was an outright provocation of the people. They might just as well have had the gall to say, through the mouth of Prieto, in a parody of Christ's words at the last supper, 'Take this flesh, drink this blood, for this is the blood and this is the flesh of the Spanish people!'[14]

Faced with such evil, the only answer was the 'purifying torch, which is not afraid to leave the bourgeoisie without homes or the clergy without temples'. Furthermore, the blaze would serve to warm the bodies of the workers 'frozen with fear' and avenge their 'humiliation'. This purifying fire played an important role in the insurrections of December 1933 and was widely and powerfully unleashed in the days of revolution during the Civil War. It was justified as a response to the violence with which 'the great religions and political systems' had established themselves. The final 'heroic deed' of the martyred people would be to reduce religions and political structures to ashes.

However, this analysis of the verbal violence and its charge of religious references should not be taken too far. This· was the expression of the radical discourse of a minority, who believed they had been chosen, and it impregnated the pages of papers such as *CNT* or *Tierra y Libertad*. Nevertheless, it should be remembered that for thousands of the CNT's members, the purpose of anarcho-syndicalism was the 'moral and material betterment of its members ... the strengthening of links of solidarity and the unification of all workers in one organisation'. Affiliating to a union in order to achieve these objectives and to end the 'unequal and precarious situation' of all classes of workers through gradual and constant struggle was denounced by the ideologues of the FAI as reformist and not at all revolutionary. It was their realisation that trade unionism to improve daily conditions was precisely what the CNT of the 'treintistas' was about that led these ideologues to the constant reaffirmation of their anti-reformist purity, on the one hand, and to attempt to imbue the union with anarchist spirit, on the other. Their task was facilitated by the intolerance of the state at a time of mass mobilisation.[15]

Naturally, the consequences of these different perceptions of the usefulness of the CNT affected the debate on the revolution. For the most optimistic, the revolution was a matter of 'clear and simple formulas'. 'Are the factories closing? Then we will take control of them. Are the fields of the estate owners left deserted and uncultivated? Then we will do the same as with the factories. Are there opponents who are trying to make life difficult for us? Then let us destroy them without further ado.' The security forces that might prevent the occupation of factories were not a cause for concern. The soldiers were 'sons, brothers and friends ... and for the fifteen million workers in Spain there were only eighty five thousand Civil Guards and police'. Once these obstacles (which the attempted insurrections of 1932 and 1933 and the events of July 1936 would show to be rather more substantial) had been eliminated, the 'anarchist idea' would flourish unfettered in the newly created paradise. As A.G. Gilabert (who would lead the Regional Committee of Catalonia a few months later) wrote at the dawn of the Republic: 'As the means of life are guaranteed under an anarchist regime, who needs money? As no one need take anything from anyone, what need do we have of armies of soldiers and policemen? Once everything belongs to everyone and social classes have disappeared forever, what need do we have of Church and State?'[16]

Anarcho-sydicalists such as Joan Peiró always tried to distance themselves from this naive vision of the revolution and these 'theoretical formulas conceived in the century past'. 'It is ingenuous, something which makes one laugh and cry at the same time, to believe that a plan of insurrection consists in taking control of the land, the factories, the workshops and other centres of production and communication ... How many of these rabid revolutionaries have ever spoken, even in principle, of how the whole of Spanish social life will have to organised after the outbreak of revolution and, above all, after the destruction of the capitalist system.' For Peiró, there was a clear distinction between preparing the revolution and declaring it. Preparation, realisation of the violent act of demolition of the capitalist system and the state and the construction of the society of the future were three distinct stages through which this process would have to pass. This was a gradual process in which the anarchist and Confederation elites must have the support of the popular masses. 'The anarchists and the syndicalists are not ready to accept the responsibility, on their own, for the organisation of production and the economy on the basis of the libertarian conception.' To believe anything else was to feed 'the myth of the social revolution once a week'.

The one thing that everyone was agreed about was that the revolution was inevitable and that it would 'come when it had to come' as the result of a 'series of dramatic events and a 'process of spiritual evolution'. This was an almost biological belief, which recalled ancestral myths and converted the revolution into a 'delicate surgical operation', and when the scalpel was required, the time for theory was over. 'Spain needed and needs a surgical operation and the people must be the surgeon.' The Spanish people, as we have seen repeatedly, had its 'watchful eye' on the CNT and could not be disappointed. Nevertheless, the people, with the CNT at its head, had been let down by the intellectuals, who collectively do not seem to have been particularly attracted by the anarchist populism with its constant references to the workers and the wretched of the earth. 'Attention all writers and artists! Instead of producing for the noble ladies of the salons and the stupid, decadent bourgeoisie, come to the people and interpret their elevated aspirations. Participate in the profound transformation now taking place: the prelude to the approaching revolution.'[17]

There were two conceptualisations of the revolution, because there were two different way of understanding anarcho-syndicalism and the role of the anarchists in the unions. These were closely related to the occupational background of the activists. People like Joan Peiró, Ángel Pestaña, Francisco Arín (of the Transport Union) or Joaquín Cortés (of the Textile Union) defended the vision of a disciplined labour organisation in which the union was always the point of reference for both revolutionary action and the construction of the society of the future. They came from the world of industrial workers with skills and union experience acquired in the most developed sectors of Catalan industry. Activists such as Manuel Rivas, Francisco Ascaso, Juan García Oliver or Buenaventura Durruti (to whom could be added all the libertarian propagandists and teachers who dictated doctrine from the most radical press) came from the construction unions, of semi-skilled and unskilled workers. They began to attend union meetings without having any previous experience of work in industry, and for them the street was the theatre of 'revolutionary gymnastics' against the state. It would not be entirely fair to call the former 'trade unionists' in order to contrast them with the latter on the basis of an apparent lack of anarchist spirit. With the exception of Pestaña, and those who followed him in his more moderate project of creating a political party, these 'trade unionists' were always of the opinion that 'revolutionary syndicalism was not enough on its own' for the conquest of a 'society without a state'. As Peiró stated in 1929, using arguments which he would repeat in 1932, 'without the push or the spiritual impetus of the anarchists, trade-unionism will never achieve any revolutionary deed, and much less social revolution'. Anarcho-syndicalism is the concept which most accurately describes his ideology and practice.

However, it is clear that certain trades tended to be innately more radical than others. Undoubtedly, those who had professional skills and experience combined with job stability had a different perception of the role of the organisation from that of the casual labourers who, having no fixed employment, were the first to end up jobless in times of crisis. The construction unions represented at the Special Congress of the CNT in June 1931 carried considerable weight. And this was the case without taking into consideration the numerous other unions, denominated simply as 'workers' or 'various occupations', which also included agricultural day labourers and unskilled labourers, 77,778 of whom were represented at the Congress. With 74,292 members, the Fabric and Textile Union was the second largest in numerical terms, and the vast majority of these were in Catalonia. The importance of these figures is all the greater when consideration is given to the increasing effect on the construction sector of rising unemployment in the early years of the Republic. The FAI leaders of the CNT construction workers, Manuel Rivas in Barcelona, Joaquín Ascaso in Zaragoza, Cipriano Mera and Miguel González in Madrid, Progreso Fernández in Valencia and José González in Seville, ended up running what were, in reality, unions of the unemployed.[18]

These two versions of the revolution and two different understandings of anarcho-syndicalism and workers' struggle also had clear consequences in the form of a rejection of politics and direct action, 'the backbone of anarchist tactics and the original and distinctive characteristic, in comparison with the rest of the revolutionary groups'. In theory, direct action should have been the basis of the struggle for the life and liberty of the people, at all levels. As is well known, it implied the immediate confrontation between workers and employers, the authorities and the oppressed, the action of the people without recourse to intermediaries, the rejection of participation in the parliamentary struggle of bourgeois society. In sum, it implied the questioning of the fundamental principles of the social, political and economic system, and the affirmation of the will to destroy it. In practice, and when the experience of the Republic eventually brought the CNT and the socialists into confrontation, what was repudiated by the partisans of direct action came down merely to 'wasting time in electoral struggles' and 'participation on the arbitration committees of the *jurados mixtos*'. As the latter has been dealt with in some detail, it will be useful to turn now to consideration of these electoral struggles.[19]

Let us begin at the end. Recent research has led to a revision of the accepted vision of the anarchist refusal to participate in the parliamentary struggle. According to this vision (which was applied as much to the final years of the Restoration period as to the Republic and failed to differentiate between leader and members, men and women, literate and illiterate) hundreds of thousands of workers followed the anarchist slogan of 'Don't Vote'. They did so in November 1933 and the right won. They did not follow the slogan in February 1936 (because the anarchists wanted to get their prisoners out of jail and so they did not pursue it vigorously either), and the coalition of the Popular Front won. The strange thing about this argument, which is repeated in textbooks, histories of the labour movement and ideological tracts produced by both the winners and the losers in the Civil War, is that it has been accepted (and continues to be accepted) without any resort to empirical analysis or detailed study of electoral behaviour. A few citations from anarchist propaganda and the supposed rejection of the political game of bourgeois democracy have been sufficient basis for this thesis. The adoption of this model also explained several factors that did not, apparently, require demonstration. In the first place, the immense anarchist power base was seen as a monolithic whole.

Anarchism and CNT were assumed to be one and the same thing. What difference did half a million members make (membership, which was conjured up from all parts of Spain, was 'calculated' as anything between 500,000, 1,000,000 and 1,500,000) when the important thing was that there were lots of them? Furthermore, the fact that there were so many was fairly reassuring for certain parties of the left. This allowed them to explain the low communist vote and the non-existence of a strong workers' party in Catalonia. Finally, it provided an excuse for the apologists of the *coup d'état* of July 1936: the parliamentary system was a farce not least because it was opposed by this multitude of brutal anarchist gunmen and professional revolutionaries.[20]

New research on Catalonia, where revolutionary syndicalism was most deeply rooted, has brought about a re-evaluation of the interpretation of this electoral behaviour. Ideological abstention (in other words, abstention which was a result of anarchist propaganda) was restricted to a minority of the working class as was also the case with 'committed voters'. The electoral behaviour of the majority of workers fluctuated. They abstained more in 1933 and less in 1936. Their stance depended, fundamentally, on socio-economic factors and on the level of expectations (in the possibility of improved conditions for the working class) that the political situation might provoke. According to this analysis, 'persistent abstainers', 'committed voters' and 'fluctuating voters' were the variable components of electoral behaviour. The first category, which is of most interest here, would always include the most radical anarchists, but not necessarily all of the leaders or principal activists of the CNT. Some of the latter voted in 1931 and 1936, but did not vote in 1933. Numerically, the most important sector of these 'persistent abstainers' was associated with social marginalisation. Levels of literacy and education were, therefore, the determining factors. As Cristina Boix and Mercedes Vilanova have argued:

> Literate men were always those most likely to vote. At a considerable distance, which varied according to the elections in question, came literate

women, who always voted less than literate men, but more than illiterate men and much more than illiterate women.

One quarter of all women in Barcelona in 1930 were illiterate (10 per cent of men were illiterate) and they were always the group that abstained most – 'almost half of illiterate women never voted during the thirties'. By occupation, 'female domestic servants, with a steady abstention rate of 76%, were the city's biggest group of abstentionists'. Day labourers always voted less than white-collar workers, who were the group which made most use of the right to vote. Analysed according to age, the younger sector of the population (25–30 years of age) and those over 60–65 years of age were the groups that abstained most.[21]

It is, therefore, impossible to sustain the thesis that the outcome of the elections during the republican period were decided by the membership of the CNT, and their circle of influence, through their systematic abstention in obedience to anarchist propaganda. Even in those cities in which they had greatest support, there were other generic factors which conditioned electoral behaviour. These included occupation, levels of literacy, the specific political context, the degree to which the policy of the leadership had been successful in achieving the fulfilment of the expectations which their propaganda had generated and the more or less moderate or radical influence of the anarcho-syndicalist leaders. Furthermore, the willingness to participate in the February 1936 elections (which was also the declared position of those leaders who had abstained in 1933) was closely related· to the position which certain groups had begun to adopt after 1934. This position resulted from a combination of the failure of various labour disputes and attempted insurrections, and the appearance of the debate on fascism and the 'workers' alliances'. Finally, two things appear obvious in this first approximation. The arguments used by the most radical section of the leadership in favour of abstention in 1933 were the same as those used against it in 1936. In both cases, it was argued that a good anarchist could not support a government which lived at the expense of the people whilst imposing social order with fire and the sword. However, in 1933 they threatened revolution if the right won, while previous experience meant that there was no revolution to announce in 1936. There was also a reappearance of the distinction, analysed above, between the leadership of the CNT and the majority of the membership, whose main interest was finding employment and bettering their living conditions. This latter group voted for republican parties or, in the case of Catalonia, for the nationalist and 'petit bourgeois' candidates. As a result, the popular understanding of abstentionism as the working-class alternative to electoral mechanisms must be corrected, at least for those years.[22]

How must the commonplace view on the growth of the CNT during these years be corrected? Following a considerable increase from the beginning of April 1931 up until the end of that year (which the sources consulted place at 300,000 members) the organisation entered a period of crisis, from which it began to recover only in the spring of 1936. The differences between the number of representatives at the Madrid Congress in June 1931 and May 1936 in Zaragoza are minimal, 535,565 and 559,294 respectively. However, between these two congresses (and taking into consideration only the figures available for the first two years of the Republic) there are important changes. The Regional Confederation of Catalonia (the most influential and on which most data is available) had 300,533 members in June 1931, which went down to 222,281 in April 1932 and 149,000 in March 1933, with a low point around 100,000 after December 1933. The Regional Confederation of the Levante (which also included the regions of Valencia, and the provinces of Albacete and Murcia) increased from 60,009 members in June 1931 to 99,741 at the end of that year, then decreased to 72,604 in October 1932. Membership decreased even more following the insurrection of January 1933 and the formation of the '*treintista*' opposition unions in March 1934, which took away around 25,000 members. Andalucia, which had 108,975 affiliates representing it at the 1931 Congress, went up to over 300,000 at the end of that year and then began to decrease sharply until it was left with 100,000 in the spring of 1934. In other words (and without needing to continue with figures from other regions with smaller memberships), if June 1931 is taken as the point of reference, by February 1934, following the end of the cycle of insurrections and the consummation of the split within the union, the CNT had lost some 300,000 members, 200,000 of these in Catalonia. If the comparison is made with the point at which levels of affiliation were highest, around 800,000 at the end of 1931, then the loss is of half a million. More importantly, in the most critical moments, only a small proportion of these 200,000 members were actually paying their subscriptions.[23]

This was not merely a question of decreasing membership. From the spring of 1931, it became apparent that there existed a group of anarchists who wanted to set the CNT on what they considered to be the right revolutionary path. In the beginning they were few in number, but they soon found conditions that favoured their expansion. These included the expectations of social change which the advent of the Republic had raised amongst wide sectors of both agricultural and factory workers, the blatant favouritism of the Ministry of Labour towards the UGT, the increasingly hard line taken by the employers, the violence of the security forces acting under the protection of special laws and so on. The economic crisis and unemployment blocked some of the available channels of negotiation. The struggle to better the working conditions and consolidate a strong union organisation gave way to open conflict with the republican regime. This was marked by general strikes, demonstrations and attempted insurrections. The militant sector took control of the organisation, ejecting the group which had led it at the beginning of the Republic, amidst insults, slander and threats. The negative performance of this leadership resulted in the 'alienation of many workers from the ranks of the CNT'. Following the failure of numerous labour conflicts, many workers, especially in Catalonia,

> abandoned the Single Unions of the CNT, because they had no faith in its effectiveness. The image of union efficiency achieved by several leaders, including Salvador Seguí, el 'noi de sucre' ('sugar boy'), a leader of the

sugar workers union who opposed indiscriminate violence and was himself murdered, achieved through the resolution of conflicts (such as the 'Canadiense' strike) had diminished.

The voices of alarm, which even appeared in papers such as the *CNT*, came late. After December 1933, when all factors had finally converged, the CNT found itself submerged in profound crisis, split internally, and without the resources necessary to provide a coherent response to the advances of the right and the employers. Its respectability, which it had possessed for a substantial period of time, had evaporated. The opposition unions failed to adapt to the reformism of the republicans and the radicalism of the anarcho-syndicalists and the FAI failed to channel thé discontent of the workers.[24]

Finally, the CNT failed to address the problems of the agrarian world adequately and misjudged policy on the limited occasions that it did attempt to. This prevented it from expanding solidly in the rural world in comparison, for example, to the socialist Federación Nacional de Trabajadores de la Tierra (FNTT). There can be absolutely no doubt that anarcho-syndicalism neither had any social base in the agrarian world during these years, nor had possessed such a social base previously. In Catalonia, anarcho-syndicalism was an overwhelmingly urban phenomenon. With the exception of Andalucia, the CNT had its roots in the small and medium cities of the Valencian region and its capital, in Zaragoza and in the Asturian mining and ironworking centres. However, one must not forget the weight of the construction unions, and those other unions of 'labourers' or 'diverse occupations', which fell between the agrarian and industrial world and were spread over the rest of Spain. There was no lack of persistent declarations about the need to organise in the countryside, as Spain was a 'fundamentally agrarian' country. And it was not infrequent for the rural delegates to blame this lack of organisation on the urban syndicalists, as a result of their refusal to allow them sufficient autonomy. However, the anarcho-syndicalist leaders never considered agrarian reform (whether the republican law from above or that demanded from below by thousands of agrarian workers and activists of the FNTT) to be an effective solution to the problems of the countryside. The emergence of a mythologised vision of the rural world became apparent as the urban syndicalists were displaced. This vision was conceived in the city and exalted the innate harmony of the rural world and its revolutionary potential. Having no stable organisational structures, it was never capable of providing an alternative which went beyond riots and destabilisation. However, the emergence of this myth will be examined in detail in relation to insurrectionalism.[25]

The CNT was thus a union movement without political allies, in confrontation with the republican regime and alienated from the republican project of reform. Its structures of control operated through channels of ideological formation that led to substantial differences between leaders, activists and the general membership (a large portion of which did not pay its union dues). It did not practise direct democracy, in spite of the myths forged around the concept. It was lacking in economic resources and a large part of its membership were either in jail or unemployed. It tended to ignore the agrarian question and betrayed a lack of understanding of it. Finally, it had entered a phase of deep crisis following an initial boom. These are some of the basic attributes which characterised the entire world of the CNT. They are often left out of those interpretations which focus excessively on ideology, revolutionary rhetoric and the social, political and economic framework which supposedly generates them. The process of fragmentation which the organisation underwent during the first years of the Republic is the last major theme which remains in this approximation to the complexity of anarcho-syndicalism, as a social movement and a movement of protest.

A divided union movement

On 30 August 1931, thirty leaders of the CNT signed a text in which they set out their 'interpretation' of the revolutionary moment, which had begun with the declaration of the Republic, and offered an alternative to the 'classic, simplistic and somewhat superficial concept of the revolution' which had established itself amongst 'certain groups of activists'. The revolution could not be left in the hands of 'more or less audacious minorities'. It would emerge as 'an irresistible movement, of the people as a whole, of the working class marching towards its definitive liberation and of the Confederation'. The riots and revolts, which were 'the rudimentary preparation', had to give way to preparation, discipline and organisation. This organisation 'has the right to control itself, oversee its own movements, act on its own initiative and take decisions on the basis of its own will'. These ideas were clearly recognisable in the programme which had been set out by the principal leaders of revolutionary anarcho-syndicalism since 1918. This involved the consolidation of a strong and permanent workers' organisation which would be independent of political parties and would maintain a distance from the uncontrolled activities of the groups of action. Its ever-present aim would be the abolition of capitalism and the state by means of a revolution 'born from the deep rooted spirit of the people'.

There is no doubt that when the signatories of this manifesto publicly reaffirmed their intention of reinforcing this project they took a step forward. They brought their experience, which had been accumulated during years of union organisation and the dissemination of libertarian ideas. They had under their control the leadership committees and they did not, as is sometimes argued, abandon the revolutionary path. They led the way and warned 'against the chaotic and incoherent concept of the revolution', which had shown itself in some of the strikes and labour conflicts of that summer of 1931. The proposal had originated with Francisco Arín, a member of the National Committee and president of the Barcelona transport workers' union. Using a draft prepared by Ángel Pestaña, the preparation of the final text was undertaken by Progreso Alfarache, a member of the National Committee and president of the Barcelona arts and graphics union, Agustí Gibanel and Ricardo Fornells, both journalists on *Solidaridad Obrera*. It was signed, amongst others, by Joan Peiró, Sebastià Clara and Pedro Massoni, director, editor and administrator of *Solidaridad Obrera*, Joaquín Cortés, the textile workers' union delegate to the National Committee, Juan López, committee member of the construction workers' union and several union leaders from other industrial cities in the region (such as Espartaco Puig from Terrasa, Mariano Prat from Manresa and Pedro Canet from Badalona). As would become clear with time, they were not a uniform group. Roldán Cortada, for example, would end up in the Catalan Communist Party, the PSUC, some years later. He was an activist in that party when he was assassinated in April 1937. Ángel Pestaña, general secretary of the CNT, would found his own party in 1934. However, from that moment on they, and the thousands of activists whom they represented, were known as the '*treintistas*', a stigma of sorts, which they bore throughout the Republic.[26]

The assertion that the FAI undertook the conquest of power in the CNT is fairly widespread. According to this commonplace, the FAI consisted of groups of young intransigent anarchists, the 'shock troop activists and the first on the streets when shots were fired'. With their violent language and deeds they infiltrated the unions and ousted both the traitors and the reformists. Violent, audacious and youthful, they took control of the CNT and set off in search of the longed-for revolution, with often tragic consequences. There was a generational clash within the union, between old militants and youthful enthusiasts. There was also an ideological clash, between simple trade unionists and purist anarchists. And finally, there was a struggle for power between the established leaders (those satisfied, in the words of García Oliver, 'with the mediocre and bourgeois content of the new Republic') and the militant radicals. This latter group were men of action who kept alive the sacred flame of proletarian redemption.[27]

The adjectives 'young' and 'old' do not describe this struggle particularly well. None of those who have gone down in history as the main protagonists were less than thirty years old, with the exceptions of Federica Montseny and Jacinto Toryho, who was of little importance up until the Civil War. It is true that Pestaña (born in 1886) and Peiró (1887) were older than Durruti (1896), García Oliver (1901), Ascaso (1901) and Juan Manuel Molina, known as 'Juanel' (1901). However, there could be found, amongst the '*treintistas*', people like Gibanel (1895), Espartaco Puig (1901) and Juan López (1900), and, among the leaders of the FAI were people like Gregorio Jover 1891) or Felipe Alaiz and Liberto Callejas, who were all over forty. Eleuterio Quintanilla, the trade unionist from Gijón, who had made such a spirited defence of those ideas which now appeared in the manifesto, would be forty-five that year and Valeriano Orobón Fernández, the prestigious defender of an alternative middle way, would be thirty. If a judgement is being made of ideological authenticity (an endeavour of little value to the historian), then there is little tangible evidence on which to judge García Oliver more anarchist, just because he always claimed he was, than Joan Peiró, who also never ceased to do so. Finally, the struggle for power is so caught up in the web of friendships and personal relations that it is almost impossible to follow it through the institutional sources. As with other political parties and social movements, one can find out what changes took place, who lost ground and who gained it, but it is very difficult to trace the route they followed in order to achieve their aims.

The '*treintista*' leaders maintained the support of thousands of followers after they were displaced from power. They fostered, not without difficulty, a parallel organisation with its own competent channels of expression, and always fought for the reunification of the anarcho-syndicalist movement. In constant difficulty, and showered with threats and insults, the majority of them rejected the option of participation in the electoral struggle which Pestaña, a fellow traveller for so many years, offered them. Those who, it is supposed, ejected them from power gained nothing. The CNT, which they claimed to represent, lost members and strikes at the same rate with which they gained martyrs and prisoners. The glorious days of the summer of 1936 served to extol the lives of these men of action for posterity and so concealed the paucity of their contribution to revolutionary syndicalism during the years of the Republic. Even fate held different destinies for them. Massoni and Gibanel died prematurely from illness in 1933 and Orobón at the end of June 1936. Francisco Ascaso and Durruti died as heroes. The former in July 1936 in Barelona, in combat against the uprising, and the latter a few months later on the Madrid front. They became martyrs. The others have never occupied a place of honour in the history of anarchism.[28]

The argument which now follows uses the available information to investigate some unexplored territory. The first step, and this is the area in which most historiographical progress has been made, is to confirm the existence of fundamental ideological differences between the '*treintistas*' and the FAI. It is without doubt that these differences make it possible to speak of 'various anarchisms'. They were apparent throughout the history of Spanish anarchism. However, compared with the previous periods of restrictions on union activity, they became more pronounced in the context of expectations and freedom, created by the declaration of the Second Republic. This context allowed the then leaders of the CNT to feel sufficiently confident to make public their strategy of consolidation and gradual expansion of revolutionary syndicalism. As has already been seen, the frustration of the enormous expectations which had been generated was manifested, above all, in the unsatisfactory and often tragic outcome of numerous labour disputes. This made progress with the strategy of the mass movement impossible. This, in turn, facilitated the rise of groups and individuals who were able to take advantage of the turbulent atmosphere of confrontation with the repressive apparatus of the republican regime.

Various dissenting factions began to appear within the syndicalist movement, which had never been, in any case, a harmonious organisation. The most serious split emerged as a result of the struggle between the '*treintistas*' and the FAI. This struggle ended with the 'imposition', in the words of Schapiro, of those who 'wanted social revolution and did not worry in the least that the conditions might or might not be favourable and who, above all, did not take into consideration … the interests of the National Confederation of Workers'. There were others who, standing apart from the polemic, understood the importance of what the Republic had put on offer. They attempted, in vain, to propose that the union should function within constitutional normality and accept the legislative intervention of the state. The confrontation between the republican regime and the UGT revitalised projects of co-operation with the other labour organisation, a project which had always found resonance within the CNT union movement in Asturias. This was especially the case after the socialists left the government in the late summer of 1933. The position adopted by Ángel Pestaña, with the creation of the Syndicalist Party, was more problematic, because of what it meant in terms of anarchist ideology. Only a few followed him and he angered and scandalised many of his comrades. Nevertheless, he did create a new option. If it had not been interrupted by the Civil War, and given conditions of electoral stability, it might have forced a change in the unsatisfactory relationship between syndicalism and politics. In sum, we have here four examples of the cracks that opened up and that would never be sealed. Therein lie, as we shall see, some of the keys to understanding the weakening of the CNT during these years.[29]

If the FAI succeeded in gaining authority over the CNT it was clearly not as a result of its numerical strength and even less because of its notoriety as an organisation. During the first two years of the Republic, the FAI never even succeeded in becoming an organisation, and afterwards things would only get worse. The FAI consisted of groups, with very little in common, which swarmed around the Peninsular Committee led by Juan Manuel Molina. Their strong point was the nucleus of noteworthy 'journalists' and enthusiastic writers who placed their skills in the service of the revolution. Constantly submerged in economic difficulties, the weekly *Tierra y Libertad* brought them together in an enterprise which, initially, only produced propagandistic enthusiasm. Felipe Alaiz, A.G. Gilabert, José España, Dionisio Eroles, José Alberola, Miguel Jiménez, Severino Campos, José Bonet, Liberto Callejas and Isaac Puente were amongst the names which appeared most, and to which were very quickly added those of Jacinto Toryho and Jaime Balius. These latter two journalists would make a career in *Solidaridad Obrera* during the Civil War. The majority of these names would appear in *El Libertario*, the weekly which they managed to bring out in Madrid from the beginning of the Republic until June 1933. And they would usually have access to the pages of *El Luchador*, the last creation of the Urales family. They had outstanding leaders in Manuel Rivas, on the National Committee of the CNT, and Arturo Parera, on the Regional Committee of Catalonia. And they also had a well-distributed group of activists amongst the most numerous construction unions of the CNT. These included men such as Cipriano Mera and Miguel González Inestal in Madrid, José González in Seville, Progreso Fernández in Valencia, and Joaquín Aznar and Joaquín Ascaso in Zaragoza.

The objective of the FAI as an organisation was to co-ordinate the various groups of like-minded activists. These affinity groups would not usually consist of more than ten people and shortly before the beginning of the Republic they were in a 'disastrous' state of organisation. The FAI was, according to one of the groups in Madrid, absolutely lacking in identity. We must not delude ourselves by pretending to be something we are not or boast of things we do not possess. Our organisation does nothing and influences no one. The regional committees are silent, the groups are silent and the individuals are silent.

Nor had the situation improved much internally by the time of the Regional General Meeting at the end of October 1933, and rival groups continued to co-exist. This meeting brought together 546 groups with 3,986 members, plus 40 groups from the Portuguese Region with 1,000 members, and 27 groups with 250 members from the Anarchist Federation of Spanish Speakers from France. Analysed according to regions, Catalonia, Andalucia and Aragon produced the majority of these members whilst the organisation was very weak in Asturias and Valencia.[30]

The fortunes of these affinity groups improved from the summer of 1933 and, with the deportation of CNT activists which took place after the first attempted insurrection in 1932, things definitely began moving in their favour. It all started gently, with a familiar theme. The CNT was run by opportunists who supported 'the project of the democratic institutions' and were not real anarchists. It was pointed out from time to time that 'syndicalism is only a tool of the working class, used in self defence and in the struggle against capitalism and the state'. However, there was little sympathy for the idea that syndicalism might occupy itself exclusively with the achievement of tangible improvements in working conditions. And there was no message more perfectly suited to the avowal of anarchist purity than the denunciation of the deviation from the revolutionary path to which the CNT was being subjected by its leadership. If this was not enough, the accusation would soon emerge that the '*treintista* spies' were the root cause of government persecution. On 3 February 1933, it was argued in *Tierra y Libertad* that 'the *treintistas* had collaborated enthusiastically in the repression of the CNT'.[31]

The FAI 'lent its banner' to the struggle against 'reformism' in the CNT, against the 'bourgeois Republic' and against those who were drowning Spain in 'proletarian blood'. It was the 'symbol' of the 'spiritual' organisation and the 'moral power' of all those who fought for the triumph of libertarian communism. 'The anarchist idea is not discussed in the heart of the FAI', wrote Alexander Schapiro in his report of the schism. 'It is the alpha and omega of their belief. And it is a belief. One has to have faith. Reason has nothing to do with it.' The touchstones of those who wanted to demonstrate their commitment to the just cause became the reporting of 'crimes' against workers and agricultural labourers, the analysis of the 'inevitable bankruptcy of the bourgeois world', which was the prelude to revolution, and the 'eulogy of the pistol', 'an unquestionable element of equality between men because it perforates the skull of a useless minister in the same way that it tears apart the heart of an imbecile without a wallet'.

With the backdrop of fatalities resulting from the confrontations with the security forces highlighting this message, it was not difficult to win over the 'men of action'. Groups such as 'Los Solidarios' (known as 'Nosotros' from 1933) entered the FAI during this year. They comprised men such as Francisco Ascaso, Durruti, García Oliver and Ricardo Sanz, amongst others. The pre-eminence of direct action placed them in the forefront, as protagonists of 'heroic and rebellious deeds'. And they were assumed, mistakenly, by public opinion, the police and the authorities, to be the leaders of the organisation. In his memoirs, García Oliver attempted to hand down to posterity the idea that what counted was action. Until they arrived, he tells us, the FAI was dominated by a group of 'counter-revolutionaries' such as Fidel Miró, Diego Abad de Santillán, José Peirats and Federica Montseny, 'fugitives from the working class who, as journalists, rationalist teachers and writers' lived off the organisation and made themselves comfortable 'in paid positions'. His testimony may well be doubted, but there are many more who attest to the disputes between the different affinity groups. As a result, the image of the FAI as a united and disciplined organisation with clear and established hierarchies has to be revised.[32]

The gradual displacement of the more moderate anarcho-syndicalists (with influence in the leadership committees, the Council of the Barcelona Unions and the paper *Solidaridad Obrera*) began in the context of the conflict with the state, the increasing disillusionment of a wide sector of the workers with the Republic, and the eulogies to those who had made the 'heroic offering of their lives'. This process lasted almost two years, during which the *'treintistas'* were constantly attacked and expelled from the unions. This culminated in the formation of the 'opposition unions' and the creation of their national organisation, which took the name of the Federation of Libertarian Unions (FSL). Outstanding CNT leaders fell one after the other. This always took place after harsh denunciations, in which the Barcelona Industrial Union of Fabric and Textile Workers, with Durruti and García Oliver in the forefront, led the way. Sometimes a rival could be disposed of by simply reproducing an article they had published making 'serious accusations against activists of the CNT'. This was the case with Juan López and an article published in *Cultura Libertaria*. At other times, the motive was that of having opposed the calls for strikes or demonstrations, or having failed to support them. And this was a very common accusation. There was also no lack of reprehensible accusation such as that of having 'abused a child', for which Joaquín Cortés was 'banned from office'.[33]

On 24 September 1932, the nine unions which constituted the Local Federation of Sabadell were expelled. The hunt for militants who supported the supposed *'treintistas'* intensified in all of the unions of the Local Federation of Barcelona during the last three months of 1932 and the split was hastened after the attempted insurrection in January of the following year. A manifesto which the Manresa Metal Workers' Union sent to all of the unions of the Regional Confederation of Workers in Catalonia contained a denunciation of the 'discrediting' of the CNT which the FAI had caused, 'the alienation of the working classes from their natural organisation' and demanded the convocation of a special Regional General Meeting and the resignation of the National Committee and the editor of *Solidaridad Obrera*. Forty-seven unions from the cities in the Barcelona region signed up to this open declaration of war against the FAI. The General Meeting was held on 5 and 17 March 1933 in Barcelona. It signified the victory of the arguments defended by the Regional Committee and its secretary Gilabert in the conflict, which had begun with the Sabadell unions. A few months later the split was complete. The offensive reaction against the FAI manifested itself in the formation of the opposition unions. These had support in areas such as Sabadell, Manresa, Mataró, Badalona, and also some parts of Andalucia, and had strong support throughout the Valencian region. With the exception of those under the control of the Bloc Obrer i Camperol (the Workers' and Peasants' Block, a small quasi-Trotskyist organisation), they constantly declared their position to be 'libertarian and revolutionary'. By the time these opposition initiatives had succeeded in co-ordinating themselves into the Federation of Libertarian Unions and celebrating their first congress, in July 1934, the CNT was a shadow of that movement which had welcomed the Republic with such expectation. It had been weakened by numerous conflicts and the absolute failure of three attempted insurrections. It had been fragmented by a profound internal schism and its capacity for propaganda and mobilisation had been diminished by the persecution unleashed by the new government of the Radical Party. At that point in time, an abyss lay between those who had supported the two opposing tendencies with such energy. Some, with Ángel Pestaña first amongst them, had packed their bags and left to start a new enterprise in the world of politics. For reasons unconnected to the project itself, Pestaña's endeavour would be short lived.[34]

Before this took place, however, others had begun to reflect in private on the need for a change of attitude within anarchism. Ramón J. Sender was an anarchist novelist belonging to the 'Espartaco' group at the beginning of the Republic and correspondent of *Solidaridad Obrera* in Madrid until the summer of that year. On 16 October 1932, he wrote to his 'comrade and friend' Eusebio Carbó, a veteran anarchist about to celebrate his fiftieth birthday, CNT delegate to the AIT (International Association of Workers) and also an activist in the sector of the FAI which García Oliver has characterised as 'counter-revolutionary'. Given the situation of 'Spanish society' under the Republic, he argued, it was not a propitious moment for dreams of libertarian communism. 'To speak of libertarian communism at this point in time … is a utopia as remote as paradise and the gardens of Mohammed'. Given a state which incorporates 'new processes into its old machine, through laws which no one would have believed in a few years ago, the potential for social integration … and arbitration committees which systematically find in favour of the workers', it was time to think about 'a minimum programme … so widely diffused that there is not one sole worker in the union organisation who is not aware of what the project entails and how it is to be achieved. What is our position on Catalan and regional autonomy? What is our position on the agrarian question … and on the religious question?' There was no need 'to spend so much time speaking about anarchism and libertarian communism' and 'we could do with a little less of this pseudo-revolutionary faith which abounds in the pages of *Solidaridad*'. The solution was to be found elsewhere. 'Let us be conscientious revolutionaries today and undertake an efficient and co-ordinated programme which will be an example of enthusiasm, intelligence and empowerment.'

These ideas alienated Sender from the CNT and from the '*treintistas*', with whom, at the end of the day, he was in agreement (in spite of the verbal aggression he demonstrated in his journalistic and literary activity) and brought him closer to communism. During these years, Sender was a writer activist, 'the most assiduous and outstanding of the new "social" writers' with connections to the daily activities of organised labour. He was poorly positioned for the exercise of any authority in the struggle which is being analysed here. However, the analysis which he sent to Carbó appears to be accurate. He hit the nail on the head with his critique of the CNT, which at this point in time had squandered many of the opportunities which the new republican situation had offered. These were opportunities to find solutions to certain crucial questions about which the new leaders, however, felt no need even to speak.[35]

As has already been seen, the '*treintistas*' spoke out, as did many other anarcho-syndicalist activists who, though sharing the basic postulates, opted not to abandon the confederal organisation. V. Orobón Fernández's 'anarcho-syndicalist synthesis', or the 'third way' proposed by the Asturian syndicalists, widened the range of attitudes and opinions on the crisis of the CNT. Without a climate of understanding, and there was none throughout the first three years of the Republic, all attempts at mediation were in vain. There was no possibility whatsoever of progress along those lines, until the cycle of insurrection had been completed and the atmosphere of polarisation within the organisation had dissipated itself. Orobón Fernández spent the first three months of the year preparing a series of reflections, which others followed, in which he proposed the unification of the proletariat. In other words, he proposed the suspension of hostilities between the two trade-union organisations, the CNT and the UGT. The Asturians were the only group that had previously defended a strategy of alliance, and they now returned once more to this tradition, after two years of bitter struggle. At first they were isolated voices, frustrated time and again by the lack of response in Catalonia, but at least they served to close a cycle of desperate responses to the socialist rivals.[36]

Finally, there is Ángel Pestaña to deal with. He had arrived in Barcelona in 1914, from the town of Santo Tomás de las Ollas in the province of Leon. Within three years, he had become editor of *Solidaridad Obrera* and remained in public prominence until his expulsion in 1932. He took part in all of the debates and dialectical conflicts and had occupied every possible position in the organisation. He was, without doubt, the person who had had most contact with the governmental and political authorities, both under the monarchy and the Republic. Whatever may be thought of him, his personal history and that of the CNT are inextricably linked. Even after he had left the organisation, it was still necessary to talk about him, because his departure was not 'normal'. He made his exit from the organisation having made the most dangerous and scandalous choices possible for an anarchist. He moved into politics and made a decision which would deeply mark the rest of his life. Furthermore, he left almost unaccompanied and as a result he had to explain the reasons for his decision a thousand times over.

First he resigned from the Libertarian Federation of Unions, for 'personal reasons which are of interest to no one by myself'. However, he explained these reasons in a little more depth to Joan Peiró, in a letter signed in Barcelona on 8 January 1934. There is 'no other motive than the need to resolve my economic situation'. Because, 'I am more of a hindrance than a help in my home' and 'one of the means I have of resolving this situation involves activities which might damage the prestige of the organisation'. As well as money, there were other 'small things', such as 'people's apathy' and the desertion of others, who had ended up in the Bloc Obrer i Camperol. 'This has led me to wonder if there is not a need to reconsider our methods of struggle, or even to adopt a more disciplined strategy, embodied in a more concrete project.' In sum, he confessed, 'I am undergoing a personal crisis which has forced me to take the decision of which you are already aware.'

When, in his letter to Peiró, Pestaña dealt with the delicate question of the Syndicalist Party, he suggested that others had made the proposal and that he had merely agreed. In reality, however, he had begun to 'sound out' important anarcho-syndicalists, asking them to be discreet about the affair, in order to see if they would join his project. Regardless of their response, he had continued with the idea until he had achieved his objective. Some, such as Francisco Fenollar, from Valencia, declared, in the words of Francisco Gómez de Lara, from Huelva, their 'unconditional support for everything related to this affair, in all frankness and with complete conviction'. Those he was most interested in, such as his old friends Joan Peiró, José Villanueva and Eleuterio Quintanilla, let him down. The reply sent to him by Quintanilla from Gijón on 18 March 1934 was extremely harsh. 'To what depths of confusion has the unpredictability of events led you?' Just 'when the Spanish Socialist Party is thinking seriously about abandoning bourgeois democracy and, as a result of its experience in government, appears to be willing to dedicate itself to the organisation of the social revolution as the only hope, it occurs to you to create another workers' party, in order to enter municipal and parliamentary politics with a view to the future. Well there is no doubt that you will show your worth in the service you are about to do for the cause of the proletariat!'

Quintanilla recognised that there was a need for much change, 'but not in the body of doctrine or the methods of authentic anarchist and syndicalist action'. These were not responsible

> for the superficiality and lack of merit which anarchism and anarcho-syndicalism have shown in the last few years. There is a need for revision of all this stupid theoretical and tactical dogmatism, which emanates from specific organisations and the leadership of the Confederation, and which is perverting anarchism and the revolutionary action of the proletariat. In sum, there is a need to correct the misdirected libertarian and revolutionary

morale, which is disseminated by certain newspapers and orators and is practised within groups and unions. This is what requires urgent revision, in order to purge anarchism and anarcho-syndicalism of the illegalist and Bolshevising venom which corrodes and sterilises them.

However, 'I do not see that our libertarian and anarcho-syndicalist ideology has failed, either in its theory or its tactics'.

As he had a high opinion of Pestaña, he did not want to see him caught up in this venture of the Syndicalist Party. Rather than that, it would be preferable 'to hold your tongue, keep your lips sealed, and retire into the hearth of your purely private activities. He finished the letter with the advice that, 'I, in your case, would proceed as I have suggested without hesitation. I might lose faith in the ideas I had defended all my life, but I would not contribute to the poisoning of the people's heart when Carthage, with Hannibal, is at the gates of Rome.'

However, Pestaña had already made his decision, from which he would not draw back. A few day later, on 27 March, he presented the statutes of the party, which was officially constituted at the beginning of April. On 16 June of that same year, Pestaña told Juan Torres, from Palma de Mallorca, that 'there is a large sector of opinion with the same understanding of anarcho-syndicalism as ours, but which will never follow us if we do not enter into politics'. Later, in his *Por qué se constituyó el Partido Sindicalista*, he would explain the shift from 'economic and union action' to 'political action' in greater detail. 'The classic conception of the revolution', he argued, had 'suffered a mortal blow with the modern organisation of the State.' It was 'impossible to realise' the revolution in the precise fashion that the anarchists and anarcho-syndicalists had conceived it. The experience of failed insurrections accumulated during the years of the Republic cried out for a party 'which could act in politics in a revolutionary fashion'. This was Pestaña's dream. After October 1934, the dream developed into that of a single 'social and class' party for the entire Spanish proletariat.[37]

As we know, this was a useless dream, and, in any case, Pestaña was not the best placed person to realise it. The way in which he formed the Syndicalist Party left many of his comrades in the FSL 'furious' with him. Eleutorio Quintanilla, who was very offended, reminded him of this in another letter written on 15 June 1934. Those who joined in his project did so more out of loyalty to him in person than attraction to this Copernican turn in the libertarian trajectory. The Syndicalist Party was always a group of friends. Outstanding amongst them were Josep Robusté, who had been editor of *Solidaridad Obrera* during the first three months of 1932, and Marín Civera, a young theoretician and editor of the journal *Orto*. His principal achievement was the underwriting of the manifesto of the Popular Front, which allowed Pestaña to become a parliamentary deputy for Cádiz in February 1936. In a Spain in which arms would soon replace parliament, Pestaña could achieve little in his new profession as a deputy in the Cortes. The Opposition Unions returned to the CNT, which itself entered the government in November 1936. This was something that Pestaña's party, although constituted for this very purpose, never achieved, and the beginning of the Civil War saw Pestaña more isolated than ever. He fell ill with asthma and died on 11 December 1937. Three months previously, he had re-joined the CNT, as a member of the Metal Workers' Union from which he had been expelled in 1932. *Solidaridad Obrera* dedicated a small obituary to his death and a brief note on the burial, which was attended by more 'illustrious politicians' than anarcho-syndicalists.[38]

The CNT had been destroyed by a combination of the 'intrusion of the FAI' and the formation of syndicates of opposition. This took place within an organisation that did not even have the money for propaganda and from which certain leaders left to enter the world of politics. By 1934, what was left of the powerful revolutionary syndicalism which had existed at the beginning of the Republic was in a sorry state. However, the internal struggles were not the only cause of this destruction. The trial of strength with the Republican regime, into which some of the more intransigent of the leadership had led the organisation with a series of attempted insurrections, had far-reaching consequences. Having accumulated spectacular defeats, anarcho-syndicalism was divided and debilitated, but the republican–socialist government was also weakened and discredited, especially after the events of Casas Viejas.[39]

4   On the road to insurrection

On 19 January 1932, the miners of San Cornelio in Figols began a strike. They disarmed the local police and the conflict spread to other areas of the Alt Llobregat and Cardoner. Five days later the army entered the mines of Figols and put an end to the last embers of the uprising. On 8 January 1933, the Regional Defence Committee of Catalonia provoked an armed uprising which spread, without much success, to several towns in Valencia and Aragon. When the uprising had already been put down, the violence and revenge of the security forces were unleashed on Casas Viejas, a small town in the province of Cádiz. Eleven months later, on 8 December, the revolutionary movement reached unprecedented levels of intensity. Spreading through several of the counties of Aragon and La Rioja, it threatened the authorities of Zaragoza for several days. There were three attempted insurrections in two years, initiated by anarchist activists and with a degree of support amongst industrial and agricultural workers. If these are measured in terms of deaths then nothing happened in the first, the second went down in history as the 'tragedy' of Casas Viejas and the third left dozens dead in combat. They began for different reasons, developed differently and had different consequences. Nevertheless, they were identified by some of the leaders of the CNT as landmarks on the same path that lead, through insurrection, to libertarian communism.

There were no preparations for the first uprising. Several days before, anarcho-syndicalist delegates from Barcelona, remembering the atmosphere surrounding the events of Jeresa, Épila and Arnedo, had spoken of 'starting a general revolutionary movement with all of its consequences'. However, the Regional Committee of the CNT in Catalonia found out about the miners' uprising after it had already broken out. Faced with the '*fait accompli*' they agreed to 'make the Figols movement their own and for the areas around Manresa and Berga to extend it with all the intensity which the situation required'.[1]

This particular miners' strike began much more forcefully than the insurrections which followed during 1933 and were announced for a specific date by the leaders of the CNT and the FAI. The advent of the Republic had generated expectations of an improvement of conditions. However, conditions in the mines continued to be atrocious, with long working hours and an absolute lack of safety provision. Furthermore, the fight for union rights continued, as these had still not been recognised under the new regime. These frustrations fuelled an already tense situation, which exploded on the morning of 19 January 1932. It began as a straightforward strike which aimed at the improvement of these conditions, although the most politically conscious did predict the advent of libertarian communism. They were convinced that they would only succeed if they were able to block the armed reaction of the mine owners, and so they disarmed the local police and began to patrol the streets.

The resistance spread to neighbouring towns the next day. In Berga, Sallent, Cardona, Baserany, Navarcles and Súria, the mines and other businesses closed. In Manresa, picketing workers blocked the entry to factories and workshops. The cutting of telephone lines and the replacement of the flag of the Spanish Republic with the black and red banner of the CNT suggested that this was something more than the declaration of a strike over working conditions. That very same day, a delegate of the Regional Committee of the CNT arrived in Figols and, along with the revolutionary committee formed by the striking miners and other anarchists, announced that 'libertarian communism had arrived'.

On 21 January, the prime minister, Manuel Azaña, addressed the Spanish parliament:

> This has nothing to do with labour conflict. No. There was an agreement between employers and workers. I do not know, nor does it interest me at the moment, whether or not this had been honoured or not. A work contract does not give anyone the right, neither employers nor workers, to rise in rebellion against the Republic ... I am not frightened of strikes ... because the strike is a right recognised in law.

However, in the face of 'excesses', the military powers had the obligation to intervene. Effectively, on 22 January, the first military reinforcements arrived from Zaragoza, Lérida, Gerona and Barbastro. By the 23rd they had occupied all of the towns of the area except Figols. They arrived there the following day to discover that the miners had blown up the explosives store and fled to the mountains. By the 25th, order had been restored. Those of the neighbourhood who had opposed the conflict collaborated in the repression. The miners were sacked. Those who had taken least part were later re-employed.

The miners' hopes had been quickly soon dashed and the subversion of order in the mines had come to a swift end. There was no looting nor abolition of private property nor any deaths. Nevertheless, the National Committee of the CNT was spurred on by the desire to 'start the revolutionary strike' which certain union leaders in Barcelona were demanding. They agreed at the meeting on 23 January, when the miners' strike was already drawing to a close, 'to call a strike in all of Spain, accepting all of the consequences'. Only a few isolated towns in the counties of Valencia and Aragon responded. In Sollana, in the Ribera Baixa area of Valencia, a group of anarchists played at revolution for a few hours. In Binefar, in Huesca, the local CNT Sindicato Unico de

Trabajadores called a general strike. Businesses closed and the telephone lines were cut and the railway line to Lleida blocked. There was also a general strike in the area surrounding Belver de Cinca. The order was taken more seriously in the towns around Teruel such as Alcorisa, where activists placed two bombs in the barracks of the Civil Guard, and in Castel de Cabra, a town with no more than five hundred inhabitants in which, according to the governor of the province of Zaragoza, Carlos Montilla, 'the Soviet Republic was declared' for a day. According to the newspapers of the period, on 25 January 'the rebels took over the town hall and destroyed the tax register and all the documents which were to be found in the archive of the municipal secretariat'. They also took control of the explosives stores of the Teruel–Alcañiz railway construction company and barricaded the mayor and his secretary in their houses. Troops from Barcelona and Zaragoza undertook the suppression of the rebellion and by the 27th order had been restored.

The rebellion was followed by several dozen arrests and the closure of all of the CNT's offices in the affected counties. The trial of the sixteen CNT members arrested for allegedly placing the two bombs in the Civil Guard barracks did not take place until November of the following year. At the trial they were defended by Gregorio Vilatela, were absolved and released. Some of them, such as Julio Ayora, had been in prison for twenty months. The Regional Committee of the CNT in Aragón denied any connection with these insurrectionary attempts and had even tried to stop them. However, given the level of repression, the tone of their communiqués became more threatening. 'This makes us think that it might be better to act violently when the occasion presents itself because, as has been clearly seen, responding to evil with goodness is like throwing pearls before swine and places us at risk of always coming out badly.' The paper in which this communiqué appeared, *Cultura y Acción*, disappeared a few days later. On 22 January, *Solidaridad Obrera* had already been suspended from publication, although it did reappear on 4 March. *Cultura y Acción* would not reappear until the spring of 1936.[2]

The persecution gained disproportionate coverage as a result of the infamous and polemical affair of the deportations. On 22 January, a number of anarchist activists had been arrested in Barcelona, amongst them the Ascaso brothers, Francisco and Domingo, Durruti, and the FAI leader Tomás Cano Ruiz. The following day they were transferred, along with other CNT activists, to the merchant ship, the *Buenos Aires*, which was anchored in the port. The news that they were going to be deported (a sentence contemplated in the second article of the Law of the Defence of the Republic) unleashed the wrath of the libertarian media. By the 26th there were already more than 200 prisoners on the ship. A hundred or so began a hunger strike on the 28th and produced a communiqué a few days later, in which they denounced their helpless situation. The ship finally weighed anchor on 10 February from the port of Barcelona with 104 prisoners aboard. In parliament on the same day, the Catalan deputies of the federalist minority requested that the sentences of deportations be commuted. Having collected other prisoners in Cádiz, the *Buenos Aires* passed through the Canaries and Fernando Poo and arrived at Villa Cisneros on 3 April. Some of the prisoners were seriously ill, one of whom had died and some of whom were released on the way. By the time the affair had drawn to a close and the last of the deportees had returned to Spain in September, the leadership group of the CNT and the FAI was in the front-line of conflict with the republican government.[3]

The activists of the CNT were busy on a number of fronts during these months, with reports in the press, public demonstrations all over the Spanish territory, meetings with the government and days of protest and demonstration. After a number of consultations, the National Committee decided to call a twenty-four-hour general strike on 15 February 'as a protest against the deportations'. As had by now become the norm, the day was full of 'virile action' and 'moral triumph'. The 'virile actions' could lead to violent clashes with the security forces, as they did in Zaragoza, where they left four dead in the street and fifteen wounded. The response to the call for a general strike was not, however, as massive as was claimed. Such days of rage and enthusiasm announced for a fixed date were the result of the revolutionary rhetoric which pervaded the propaganda and merely served to increase the sense of victimisation and create new threats. They were always the product of circumstance and had little to do with real labour conflicts.

Perhaps because Pestaña was still secretary at the time, the hatred for the government did not prevent visits to Madrid to visit Casares Quiroga, the Minister of the Interior, or Manuel Azaña. When Azaña received Pestaña and the other three members of the CNT, who had 'come to ask for a pardon for the deportees on the *Buenos Aires*', he blamed them for the length of the repression: 'If there is lasting peace then the term of confinement can be shortened.' Pestaña, according to the President, appeared 'completely broken. He is in a difficult situation amongst the revolutionaries. On the other hand, he will be happy that he has been freed from the domination of the gunmen.'[4]

Broken or not, the fact of the matter is that Pestaña was having a bad time in the organisation which had been his home for many years. On 19 February, in an article entitled 'I accuse', Federica Montseny published an article which was very reminiscent in tone of the denunciations of anarchist persecutions made by her father forty years earlier. She blamed the National Committee of the CNT for having 'sabotaged the agreement on the strike by failing to issue the call in time, by failing to produce the promised manifesto and, in short, by gaining time before making a commitment to the uprising in the Alt Llobregat'. In Montseny's opinion, the reason for the trade-union leader's behaviour was obvious: 'Could Mr Menéndez, Mr Molas and Mr Macià tell us what County Council, Ministry or Civil Governor post they have promised A. Pestaña?' However, the accusations did not stop there as Urales himself began a smear campaign, from the pages of *El Luchador*, against the National Committee which, he argued, was manipulated by Pestaña. Certain anarchists, such as Marcos Alcón and Manuel Rivas, who were also on the committee, reacted against the campaign. Half-way through April, they succeeded in having the General

Meeting of the Regional Committees approve their activities and characterise 'the campaign undertaken by Urales ... as divisive and motivated by personal hatred which will only serve to weaken out movement'.

There is no doubt that this was the case. In March 1932, Pestaña resigned as secretary of the National Committee. Emilio Mira, whom Federica Montseny had also attacked, was sacked from his post as secretary of the Regional Committee of Catalonia a month later. An attempted insurrection and a day of protest, which had been hastily convened and achieved poor levels of mobilisation, had opened the decisive battle in the confrontation which, since the summer of 1931, had festered between moderates and radicals under their respective banners of '*treintismo*' and the FAI. Verbal disputes were abandoned in favour of attacks and expulsions. The new National Committee, led by Manuel Rivas and in which were to be found outstanding activists of the affinity groups such as Alcón, Ricardo Sanz, José Ramos and Miguel Terrén, convoked a 'Day of National Protest' for 29 May, once more against the background of deportations, 'to defend the interests of the working class'. In spite of the fact that the 'mercenary bourgeois press' took it upon itself to argue the opposite, 'the great national protest' had been 'magnificent' and, of course, it represented a 'moral triumph' for the CNT and the workers. It was the definitive end to 'all democratic illusions', because 'the bourgeois Republic' has not resolved 'nor even ameliorated the conditions of the people who have been oppressed since time immemorial'.[5]

Finally, the experience of January 1932 served to strengthen the position of the '*treintistas*'. 'The defensive potential of the bourgeoisie and of the state means that the working class must develop its own potential to the full. Confronted by two powerful and cohesive forces, it would be an error, as costly as that which is currently being paid, to present a dispersed, incoherent and atomised line of battle.' The alternative for the working class was 'a joint action involving the totality of the organisation'. In order for this to happen, it was necessary as 'a matter of life and death, that the CNT should be in control of the various movements'.[6] It did not control them and even less so did it control their leaders. Some of those leaders would be involved a year later in a new insurrection.

On this occasion there were preparations. However, they were carried out so poorly and in such secrecy that hardly anyone heard about them. In the Regional General Meeting of the CNT, held in Madrid on 1 December 1932, the National Committee of the Railway Industry, which represented a minority amongst the railway workers, had asked for economic help (six thousand pesetas) in order to declare a general strike in support of a wage rise. During this month, the usual attempts were made with various regional committees to search for a positive response which would allow the anarcho-syndicalist leaders to throw the organisation into revolutionary action. The railway workers pulled back because more than half of their unions expected the strike to be a 'spectacular fiasco'. Going by the various reports that reached the National Committee, the atmosphere in the CNT was not particularly favourable either. The Regional Defence Committee of Catalonia was extremely irritated by this reticence. Influenced by Juan García

Oliver, they were ready to put into practice his famous 'revolutionary gymnastics', a sort of 'oscillating insurrectional action' which would prevent the consolidation of the 'bourgeois Republic'. They chose 8 January at 8.00 in the evening as the moment. Neither the Regional Committee of Catalonia nor the National Committee paid any attention to their intimidating messages, although Manuel Rivas, who was at the same time secretary of the National Committee of the CNT and of the National Defence Committee, managed to confuse several people with his ambiguous telegrams. His was a curious position in which, as 'representative of the CNT he was opposed to the movement ... but as an activist and anarchist his heart was with those who participated'.

Needless to say it was a fiasco. The army and the security forces occupied strategic positions in the city in which disorder was predicted and the union leaders were arrested. In Barcelona, there were clashes between the neighbourhood defence groups and the security forces. In Zaragoza, on 1 January, the civil governor, Manuel Andrés, had ordered the detention of the leading union leaders. No one did anything. The general strike did affect Valencia and in some areas near the capital, Pedralba, Bugarra, Ribarroja and Bétera, anarchist groups dreamt once more of libertarian communism. The easy inclination towards the use of violence spread to other towns such as Benaguacil, Utiel, Robres and Belver de Cinca. This was a poor result, falling short of the instigators' expectations, but the audacity of a small minority led to prison for many.[7]

The mutual blame and reproaches for what had happened multiplied. In Madrid, distance from events left people uninformed of the preparations. There the newspaper *CNT*, which in just a few months of existence had produced abundant quantities of revolutionary and anti-republican rhetoric, published a surprising editorial on 9 January 1933, 'This is not our revolution'. And it was not 'because our revolution is not simply a conspiracy and will not be brought about by conspiracy. It is an uprising of proletarian consciousness, of an organisation of the producers around syndicalist cores which will move towards the revolution when they have reached the peak of their potential and the organisation of the base – not the committees – decide.' The following day saw a correction on the front page under the headline 'The rebellious gesture of the Spanish proletariat'. The previous editor 'had been misinterpreted'. Finally, on 11 January, a further editorial entitled 'Neither beaten nor humiliated' blames the insurrection on 'the repressive and sectarian policy ... of the Socialists who have usurped power and use it against the interests of the workers'. The revolts were not 'the whim of a minority' but rather, 'they are the result of patent injustice'. It was for this reason that 'once one insurrection has been defeated another begins, once one strike has been resolved another starts and once one uprising has been put down another more powerful breaks out'.

In spite of the correction, the editorial had repercussions. The editor of *CNT* and author of the text, Avelino González Mallada, repeated the idea at the Regional General Meeting at the end of January, with the advantage that experience of failure gave further support to his argument. 'Sudden attacks have to be dropped from our strategy because they do not conform to the anarchist principle', it is the working masses 'who must psychologically determine the revolutionary act'. The more sensible were of a like mind. Nevertheless, the 'unfortunate' timing of the article, the day after the revolutionary uprising, upset a considerable number of the delegates at the General Meeting and it was finally decided that 'the article was the result of nervousness due to the tension of the moment'. The editor offered his resignation which could not be accepted at that moment. A month later, at the Regional General Meeting in June, another rumpus over the same affair led to the resignation of González Mallada and the majority of the editorial board of the paper.

The National Committee of the CNT had been equally unsympathetic to the declaration of the revolution from above either. On 10 January, it declared that 'the events referred to have been of purely anarchist significance and the confederal organisation has not been involved in any way'. They did not condemn it, and neither did *Solidaridad Obrera*, only for reasons of 'conscience and the duty of solidarity'. Nevertheless, this was not their revolution, which would be built 'with guarantees' and 'in the light of day'. Schapiro and Carbó, from the secretariat of the IWO, were of the same opinion, 'the success of a revolution is never dependent on the number of bombs made or the quantity of arms procured. The more that the masses are impregnated with revolutionary consciousness, the smaller the number of bombs required.' The opposition unions, which were still members of the CNT, demanded the 'extirpation from the organisation of these foreign powers' which lead it to the abyss. 'Those who want a revolution every day can do it themselves. Those who want to play at revolutionary chess can go ahead. However, they must take responsibility for it themselves and do it with their own money and not that of others.' The question of money was central in a union movement in which many suspected that part of the subscriptions were used in undertakings and activities which had little to do with the emancipation of the workers. This was the view, for example, of a number of unions, which stopped paying their dues before passing over to the opposition.[8]

While all these mutual reproaches, corrections and accusations were taking place, news began to arrive of the disturbances in the province of Cádiz. There, groups of anarchists and committees of defence had threatened public order in the capital, Jérez de la Frontera, Alcalá de los Gazules, Paterna de la Rivera, San Fernando, Chiclana, Los Barrios and Sanlúcar. That same day, 10 January, Captain Manuel Rojas Feijespán received the order to transfer from Madrid to Jérez with his company of Assault Guards and put an end to the anarchist rebellion. They spent the night on the train. When they arrived in Jérez, the telephone lines had been cut in Casas Viejas, a town 19 kilometres from Medina Sidonia with barely two thousand inhabitants. Following the preparatory instructions issued by the anarchists of the district of Jérez, groups of peasants affiliated to the CNT took up positions in the town early on the morning of 11 January. Armed with pistols and shotguns, they surrounded the barracks of the Civil Guard. There were three guards and a sergeant inside. Following an exchange of fire, the sergeant and one of the guards were seriously wounded. The first died the following day and the second a few days later.[9]

At two o'clock in the afternoon of 11 January, twelve Civil Guards under the orders of Sergeant Anarte arrived at Casas Viejas. They freed their two companions who were left in the barracks and occupied the town. Afraid of reprisals, many of the peasants fled. The others had locked themselves in their homes. A few hours later, four more Civil Guards and more than a dozen Assault Guards sent by Lieutenant Fernández Artal joined those who had taken control of the situation. With the help of the two Civil Guards who knew the locals of the town, the Lieutenant began searching for the rebels. They grabbed two and beat them until they pointed out the family of Francisco Cruz Gurtiérrez, 'Seisdedos' (Six Fingers), a charcoal maker who appeared at the CNT offices from time to time but who had not taken part in the insurrection. However, two of his sons and his son-in-law had and, following the siege of the barracks, they had taken refuge in Seisdedos's house, a tiny shack of mud and stones. The lieutenant ordered the door to be forced. Those inside opened fire and one of the Assault Guards fell dead. Reinforcements arrived at ten o'clock in the evening with grenades, rifles and a machine gun. They began the attack without much success. A few hours later they were joined by Captain Rojas and about forty more assault guards. The General Director of Security, Arturo Menéndez, had ordered them to transfer from Jérez to Casas Viejas to put down the insurrection and they 'opened fire without mercy against anyone who shot at the troops'.

Rojas ordered the shack to be set on fire. By then, some of the occupants had already been killed by rifle and machine-gun fire. Two were riddled with bullets as they ran out fleeing from the fire. María Silva Cruz, 'La Libertaria', the granddaughter of Seisdedos, saved her life because she was carrying a child in her arms. Eight were killed in total, six of them burnt inside the shack. Amongst these were Seisdedos, two of his sons, his son-in-law and his daughter-in-law. The mule was also killed in the corral. It was 12January 1933. The insurrection of Casas Viejas was over.

Rojas sent a telegram to the General Director of Security. 'Two dead. The rest of the revolutionaries trapped in the flames.' He also informed him that he was continuing with the search for the leaders of the movement. He sent three patrols, along with the two Civil Guards from the barracks of Casas Viejas, to search the houses. No sooner had the search started when they killed an old man of seventy-five who was shouting 'Don't shoot! I am not an anarchist!' They arrested another twelve, only one of whom had taken part in the insurrection. They dragged him in handcuffs to Seisdedos's shack. Captain Rojas, who had been drinking brandy, started the shooting and the other guards joined in, murdering twelve. Shortly afterwards they left the town. The massacre was over. Nineteen men, two women and a child had died. The truth about the incident did not emerge for some time, because the first versions had all of the victims killed in the attack on Seisdedos's shack. However, the Republic now had its tragedy.

Dozens of peasants were arrested and tortured. The prisoners blamed Seisdedos and those who had been killed in order to save themselves, although they knew that Seisdedos had nothing to do with the insurrection. The government was attempting to survive attacks from both left and right at the time and refused to take responsibility. 'The government cannot be held responsible in the least', declared Azaña, in his speech to parliament on 3 February of that year.

> As far as we know, nothing out of the order has taken place in Casas Viejas. There was an uprising in Casas Viejas, under the banner of libertarian communism which has turned the heads of the lowest elements of the unemployed and uneducated village working class. Thus a few dozen men raised the flag of this libertarian communism, armed themselves and attacked the Civil Guard, killing several of them. What was the government going to do?

He repeated several times that, faced with 'an armed uprising against society and the State', he had no choice, 'even if there was the risk of some agents committing excesses 'in the pursuit of their duties'. In any case, he declared, again in the Cortes on 2 March, the origins of the rebellion against the state, the Republic and the social order did not lie with the social policy of the government. 'Have we, this government or any government sown the seeds of anarchism? Did we found the CNT? Have we given support, in any way, to those agitators who disseminate the slogans of libertarian communism in the towns?'[10]

In spite of the fact that there was applause for the government's castigation of the revolutionaries in some papers, such as *ABC*, the opposition to the government from both the radicals and the right grew steadily from that point on. Eduardo Guzmán, who visited Casas Viejas along with Ramón J. Sender, questioned the official version in the pages of *La Tierra*. The CNT, which gained nothing from the incident but martyrs for the cause, developed a powerful campaign against 'dictatorial policies and malicious politicians'. It matters not what level of persecution is suffered, they argued in their media because 'in prison and in silence, the voice of the revolution is heard by free spirits'. The demands made with greatest frequency in the demonstrations organised during these months were: freedom for the prisoners, legalisation of the unions, union rights and rights of association, repeal of the 'anti-labour' laws of 8 April 1932, the law of the Defence of the Republic and the arbitration committees. These culminated in the general strike of 9 and 10 May, 'a warning to the government, which rivalled the fascist dictatorship in its despotism'. History was repeating itself. Following an insurrection, there would usually be demonstrations and general strikes, although this time they were fewer than those called against the deportations in 1932. The CNT spent the rest of the year protesting about the growing numbers of prisoners and preparing intensely for the revolution which would once more take the form of failed insurrection. This time, however, with more bloody incidents and also more deaths to report.[11]

The third insurrection had more preparation than the previous one. On 12 September 1933, a new government was formed under Alejandro Lerroux. Lerroux had been attempting to replace Manuel Azaña as Prime Minister for some time but his government lasted only until 3 October. When it was defeated in parliament, the President Niceto Alcalá Zamora called on Diego Martínez Barrio to form a government and call elections. The Constituent Assembly had run its course. General elections were called with the first round taking place on 19 November and the second on 3 December. Given this opportunity (according to A.G. Gilabert, 'we can witness the complete collapse of the authoritarian and capitalist world'), the CNT undertook an unprecedented level of propaganda in favour of abstention. Never had so much been written on the subject in such a short space of time. There were insults of the 'electoral animal. There is not in the whole animal kingdom a being more unhappy and despicable than the man-voter'. There were insults in every direction. 'Vultures, red and yellow [the right], and tricolour vultures [the Republicans]. They are all vultures, all birds of prey, all filthy blackguards that the productive people will sweep away with the broom of revolution.' They had returned to the old arguments but they now employed them against new enemies. The workers are 'tired of being cannon fodder, fodder for the factories and fodder for the mauser', they will not vote. 'They must not vote, because politics means immorality, shameful dealings, greed for advancement, excessive ambition, uncontrolled lust for wealth, the desire to dominate and impose, to hold the privilege of state, the same thing in the name of Democracy as in the name of God, the Fatherland and the King.'[12]

Nevertheless, the CNT was already committed to the insurrection long before the election results provided the excuse. The regional delegates held a plenary meeting in Madrid on 30 October 1933 and, accepting the proposal of the delegates from Aragón, they adopted a sort of revolutionary recipe which made the uprising unavoidable. They intensified their anti-electoral campaign in the knowledge that this would involve 'a direct responsibility towards the Spanish proletariat'. If there was a victory of 'the fascist tendencies, and if, for this or any other reason, the passion of the people was aroused, then the National Confederation of Workers had the duty to inflame this feeling and direct it towards its libertarian communist end'. Furthermore, it was not only the CNT which was bound by the 'rules' of this game. 'It would be enough for one region to begin, that is, as soon as one Regional Committee took the initiative, the others would immediately, and without further orders, go to its support.' Obviously, promising revolution if the right won the elections was an error into which the CNT had never before had the opportunity to fall. The right duly won and they had to fulfil their promise. As they would explain months later, this was because, mistaken or not, 'it would have meant the loss of the moral high ground and as the moral high ground is the most important thing for us, we went to war'.[13]

Even those who did not participate in the fighting contributed to its provocation through their abstention. Benito Pabón, who would be elected as deputy for the Popular Front coalition in Zaragoza in February 1936, recommended 'absolute abstention'. Miguel Abós, a prestigious leader in Aragón, was always under fire from the anarchists in this region because of his moderate position, and because he admitted to having voted in the municipal elections in April 1931. However, he jumped on the bandwagon, arguing that 'the victory of the right would be the warning signal for the implementation of libertarian Communism in Spain'. On 19 November, the day assigned for the 'voter-animal' to act as such, *Solidaridad Obrera* insisted:

> Do not allow yourself to be fooled. Do not vote for the parties of the left, because their victory will hold back your emancipation. Do not be frightened by those who tell you that if you do not vote the right will win. It is preferable that they should win because their victory will favour our project.

The following day, once the prediction had been fulfilled, there was no possibility of turning back. 'Onward People: to the Social Revolution!' This natural force called revolution, a surgical operation capable of purifying the sick body of society, was just around the corner. 'The triumph of the right opens the doors to overt fascism. The proletariat will respond with revolution, in order to prevent its access to power.'[14]

In that same plenary meeting on 30 October, it was decided that the National Committee should transfer to Zaragoza, a city that obtained 230 votes from the delegates against 153 for Madrid and 100 who preferred to remain in Barcelona. The transfer of the National Committee out of Catalonia had been demanded by the opposition unions as a condition for their re-entry into the CNT and it was also supported by the IWO and other veteran activists who were attempting to mediate in the conflict. On 14 November, the Committee installed itself at number 17, Calle Argensola in the capital of Aragón, where it would maintain its headquarters, under the leadership of Miguel Yoldi and Horacio Martínez Prieto, until the summer of 1936. A few days later, on 26 November, a new plenary meeting, held in Zaragoza, charged a revolutionary committee with the organisation of the insurrection. On this committee were to be found Durruti, who had spent several months in the prison of Puerto de Santa María, Cipriano Mera from Madrid, the Andalucians Rafael García Chacón and Rafael Casado Ojeda, the Vizcayan Isaac Puente and the delegates of the Local Federation of Zaragoza, Felipe Orquín, Ramón Andrés and Antonio Ejarque. Puente was a doctor, Andrés a day labourer, Ejarque a metal worker and Durruti had not had a job for some time. The other four were bricklayers, another demonstration of the weight which the construction workers carried in this new CNT, purged now of the representatives from industries in Catalonia. Assisted by two other unemployed bricklayers from Zaragoza, Santiago Baranda and Joaquín Ascaso, the revolutionary committee had a few days in which to hitch together wagons to the train which was about to leave for the revolution. It did not matter to them that messengers were arriving in Zaragoza with the request that the train should delay its departure, because the other regions 'were not prepared'. The decision was already taken. The anarchists of Aragón, who had been telling all and sundry for some time now that this was a place with a sort of special, innate propensity to rebellion, took the crucial step.[15]

On 8 December 1933, following rumours that a revolutionary movement was in preparation, the governor of Zaragoza, Elviro Ordiales, who 'had noticed the presence of outside elements amongst the extremists of Zaragoza', ordered the closure of all of the CNT offices. Forty-five anarchists were arrested. The security forces patrolled the streets and suffered, according to government sources, the first acts of aggression. On the following day, Saturday, the clashes and shootings spread through all of the central neighbourhoods of the city. There was a general strike of shops, taxis, trams and buses. The train lines were blocked and there were attempts to set fire to some convents. A state of emergency was declared and the number of arrests increased. The governor issued a decree prohibiting the printing of pamphlets, union meetings and strikes. The revolutionary committee replied with a manifesto: 'The hour of the revolution has arrived ... We are on our way to the realisation of libertarian communism.' It was obvious that the insurrection would cost dearly. The echoes of gunshots could be heard all over the city. By nightfall, the fighting had left twelve dead and numerous wounded.

The incidents continued until 14 December. The army intervened and, because of the strike, transport had to be manned by the Assault Guards with military escorts. Assault Guards from Burgos, Pamplona and Toledo were brought into Zaragoza to help put down the uprising. The employers' federation helped supply the city with food. The governor imposed order vigorously and suspended the mayor of the city, the radical-socialist Federico Martínez Andrés, 'for his passivity and failure to fulfil the orders given by the authorities'. He had been asked to provide eight municipal drivers and eight urban guards to act as bus conductors. Martínez Andrés had replied that they were needed for the fire services. Furthermore, the employees refused to carry out duties which were not under the strict control of the town hall. Martínez Andrés returned on the 22 December and presented his 'irrevocable resignation'.[16]

On 14 December, there were around four hundred prisoners distributed around military barracks and county prisons. The police searched for the main activists in flats and public places. They discovered a few women who had 'provided munitions to the extremists' and, if their version is to be believed, arrested the revolutionary committee (with the exception of Durruti who was in Barcelona) on 16 December. The arrests are said to have taken place while the committee were having dinner at No. 5 Calle Convertidor, the centre from which they ran their operations. The day before, the National Committee of the CNT had given the order to return to work. The Chamber of Commerce had recommended their affiliates, who had begun sanctions and dismissals, to exercise 'good sense' and 'set an example of calmness and civic spirit'. Photographs of those arrested were published and there were fanciful discoveries of bombs and explosives. The press worked flat out to keep the citizens informed of the extent of the disturbance. The middle and upper classes demanded public tributes for the governor. A plenary session of the Chamber of Commerce praised 'the fortunate outcome he had achieved and the good sense with which he had carried out his duties during the critical moments which the city has undergone'. The leading figures of the city, with the president of the Chamber at their head, visited the governor in order to offer a vote of thanks, and a group of distinguished ladies gave his wife an image of the Virgin of Pilar. Finally, he was given the keys to the city by the town hall, against the votes of the socialists and radical-socialists. In the meantime, while the congratulations were continuing, Lerroux had formed a government.

The battle between the government and the insurgents also broke out in numerous towns of the region. Leaving aside those places in which there were only disturbances of public order, or mere expressions of solidarity to the revolutionary movement, the insurrection was most serious in those places in which an attempt was made to declare libertarian communism. The stages of the process were repeated in most places. Groups led by the anarchists arrived at the barracks of the Civil Guard and took control, or not, depending on the strength of both sides. When they could, the anarchists took over the town and arrested the authorities, other figures of order and the 'powerful', normally without carrying out violent reprisals. They explained their social project to the local population, burnt the property registers and official documents and even began the supply of goods 'according to the norms of libertarian communism'. They did not spread the rebellion to other areas. On the contrary, they waited passively for the arrival of the government reinforcements sent to crush the uprising. They fled, if they could, and in any case suffered a rapid defeat followed by intense repression.

This was repeated, with slight variations, in the towns of Belver and Abalate de Cinca in Aragón and Beceite, Valderrobres and Mas de las Matas in the region of Teruel. One 'extremist' was killed in Valderrobres, another in Calanda and two in Alcorisa. A Civil Guard died in Alcañiz and another in Barbastro. Everything was very well organised with lots of people taking part in the incidents in Albalate de Cinca. Having attacked the barracks, in which there were only two guards, at dawn on the morning of 9 December, 'the extremists imposed libertarian communism, abolishing money and giving out vouchers to the local population so that they could provide themselves with essential goods'. The Civil Guard arrived from Fraga twenty-four hours later to re-establish order. Some two hundred people fled into the countryside. The mayor and the municipal judge, who had been involved in the insurrection, fled there too. Twenty-three men and three women were arrested, amongst them the doctor, a school teacher, the wife and daughter of the mayor, who was known a 'La Libertaria', and the secretary of the town council, Felix Carrasquer, an outstanding young anarchist activist.[17]

If Casas Viejas is taken as the classic model of a rural anarchist rebellion with tragic consequences, Mas de las Matas could be the paradigm of insurrection without violence, in a zone in which small landholders predominated. On 8 December 1933, the CNT members in this locality received a communiqué from the revolutionary committee in Zaragoza. This contained the order to join in the revolution, which would break out 'all over Spain' at one o' clock on the morning of 9 December. Led by Macario Royo (a local who had emigrated to Barcelona and returned as a result of the unemployment crisis of the 1930s), a group of about fifty anarchists, day labourers and small property owners, surrounded the barracks, in which there were six Civil Guards. They took their weapons and arrested three councillors, the priest, his assistant, the secretary of the town council and various landowners. They burnt the municipal archives and the law courts in a bonfire 'that purified all that which had previously justified the existence of capitalist society', and declared 'the municipality free, and establishes libertarian communism'. In the afternoon, a demonstration did the rounds of the entire town 'singing anarchist songs and cheering the Revolution'. A popular assembly appointed an 'administrative revolutionary committee', which 'abolished money' and prepared to organise production. However, they did not have enough time. On 19 December, a major and a captain of the Civil Guard arrived in the town with a hundred guards and re-established order. More than a hundred people were arrested and severely beaten. Royo, with two other activists, fled via Morella and Vinaroz to Barcelona in order to escape to France.

Once order had been re-established, the town council held a special session on 14 December to take stock. The damage to the town hall was minimal although the flag and all of the documents of the municipal archive had been burnt. The mayor and the councillors registered their 'unanimous' protest over the incidents and demanded 'that the courts of law take charge of judging and punishing the leaders'. A few days later, all of the mayors of the zone met in Alcañiz 'to discuss the adequate defence of lower Aragon in the case of a repetition of the revolutionary events'. On 26 January 1934, the municipal authorities of Mas de las Matas agreed to carry out work on the barracks of the Civil Guard, 'in order to enable it to provide the best security and defence possible'. Defence measures aside, the principal task was to re-create the census of rural property, which was in ashes. They negotiated the acquisition of copies of important documents in Teruel and asked the Director General of Properties and Land Tax for authorisation to create a new census. In this particular case, the purifying will of the revolution had more far-reaching consequences than the insurrection itself, which ended without deaths or physical violence.[18]

Groups of revolutionaries in various localities of La Rioja also opted for armed struggle. There was 'much violence' in the capital, with two 'extremists' and an Assault Guard killed in the morning of 9 December, two Civil Guards killed in San Asensio, a local villager was killed in Briones and four in San Vicente de Sonsierra. In Arnedo, where the Civil Guard had left the Plaza de la República awash with blood in January 1932, a group of twenty or thirty men arrived at the town hall 'intent on hoisting the red and black flag on the central balcony ... as a sign that libertarian communism had been declared all over Spain'. When they had achieved their aim, 'they took possession of the assembly hall and remained seated there for about four hours, only withdrawing when the mayor invited them to do so, and without having caused any damage to the town hall or its contents.' A few hours later a detachment of the Civil Guard arrived. They removed the red and black flag, 'hoisted the national flag' and carried out a 'detailed search' of the CNT offices. There they found a notebook entitled *Toque Revolucionario* (The Call to Revolution), a book of minutes with the first page torn out, an ink pad, two copies of *El Orador Popular*, the copy for 7

December of the newpaper *CNT* and a book entitled *Hormiga Roja* (Red Ant). All in all, not very much. They closed the offices and arrested the individuals who had taken part in the incidents. They found twenty-seven, who were to appear before the emergency assizes on 15 January the following year.[19]

Beyond the area of influence of Zaragoza, the echoes of the insurrection reached isolated areas of Extremadura, Andalucia, Catalonia and the mining valley of Leon. Thirteen people died when the Barcelona–Seville express was derailed as the result of a bridge being blown up in the Valencian locality of Puzol. By 15 December, it was all over. The insurrection, which closed the cycle of attempts at libertarian communism, had lasted five days. Of the three uprisings, it was the one which had most serious consequences with 75 dead and 101 wounded amongst the revolutionaries, 11 Civil Guards dead and 45 wounded, three Assault Guards dead and 18 wounded. The prisons were full and there were soon accusations of torture. The emergency assizes, which were a creation of the Law of Public Order approved at the end of July that year, handed down various sentences at the Provincial Assizes of Aragon and La Rioja from the day after the uprising. The CNT was broken, dispersed, and without a press or publicity machinery. Only shreds remained of what had promised to be a devastating force two years before.[20]

As had happened on previous occasions, the leading trade-unionist anarchists, now far from the scene, reacted harshly. 'Between the FAI and the masses of the CNT,' wrote Joan Peiró several days later, 'reigns the most profound divorce.' He accused the FAI of using 'money in vast quantities for an anti-electoral campaign which could be of benefit only to the reactionaries'. Revolutions, he concluded, 'are made by joining forces not dividing them', and this was 'a hard lesson' which 'the congregation of the FAI' would have to learn. Peiró was merely reflecting the official analysis of the 'opposition unions' of the Federación Sindicalista Libertaria. This had been 'a movement of small groups, of guerrillas.' It had nothing to do with a mass movement. Moreover, this view of the divided anarcho-syndicalist organisation was shared by an ever-widening sector. There had to be a point of convergence between these two routes, that of the schism and that of the insurrection. It had to be found, and this is what some did from January 1934. However, before examining this turn of events, some final observations have to be made on the account which has been given here of these failed uprisings.[21]

There can be no disputing the fact that the preparation and launching of these insurrections, especially those of 1933, was the work of groups of anarchists under the influence of catastrophic visions. In order to prove this, one need only read what was repeated, again and again, in their press in the days leading up to the insurrections, when preparations were already under way. 'The revolution is upon us', wrote Gil Bel in *CNT* on 24 December 1932. 'Spain in its entirety is struggling with a terrifying political and economic chaos which is already beginning to give way to the anarchist social revolution and the transformations it will bring', predicted *Tierra y Libertad* on 3 December of the same year. If the diagnosis went beyond mere catastrophe, as Jaime Balius argued in the same FAI weekly on 17 November 1933, 'the logical and correct corollary ... can only be INSURRECTION. We must channel all of our strength towards this end. We must co-ordinate all of the existing rebel forces on Iberian soil, in order to take the battle to the Spanish bourgeoisie at the opportune moment.' What was all this talk of catastrophe about? Simply, claimed A.G. Gilabert on 8 December 1933, that 'the experience of democracy' in Spain had been accompanied by tragedy, cruelty and errors. This being so, 'anarchism had the right to take upon itself the structuring of the new Spain according to its principles and philosophy, the abolition of capitalism, private property and the State, and the implantation of communism in economics, anarchy in politics, and equality of rights and duties for all the inhabitants of the national territory'.

These groups had not suddenly taken up the idea of insurrection simply because they were very revolutionary and very anarchist, always ready to go one further than anyone else. Their rhetoric always made superficial reference to 'social' factors which justified and legitimised, according to them, the 'impassioned state' of the people. Let us summarise these arguments. Under the monarchy there had been many problems in Spain, such as unemployment, the lack of freedom, 'the continual abuse by the employers of the agreements established by the labour unions', 'the constant violation of the norms of justice, in favour of those who had influence and money', *caciquismo* (the disproportionate power of local town bosses), poor land distribution. However, these problems, 'which were acute yesterday ... have not been improved by the Republic, but have, rather, increased considerably. Some of them, such as redundancy and the attacks of the powerful against the organised working class in general, have become incomparably worse.' Furthermore, the causes were patently hunger, misery and injustice. And it was also obvious who was to blame – those who had cheated the people in the name of the Republic. Faced with this situation, 'the people are convinced that they will obtain no justice, nor any respect for their rights, other than those which they are able to impose themselves'. But even if the people were defenceless, the CNT was there to show them the way.[22]

Nevertheless, to believe that the activities of these groups provide sufficient explanation of the insurrections, would be to lapse into the errors of the most traditional and conservative historiography. This has already shown itself to be useless in the explanation of phenomena of the type being examined here. These acts of protest – and that is what these insurrections were regardless of the evaluation made of them – were not merely the product of 'agitators' and 'conspirators,' paid or otherwise, or of anarchists inciting rebellion amongst peasantry immersed in misery.[23]

When specific and well-documented cases are compared, the profile of those who instigated the insurrection and those who supported it are very different. The former tended to be over thirty years of age, activists in the CNT and in the affinity groups and, in general, itinerant, although they might have close connections with the localities in which they operated. The latter were almost always young, or even very young (the majority being no more than twenty), day labourers in the countryside or construction workers and single. In other words, most were willing to risk their own lives, but not those of their families. The insurrection became a form of 'politics by other means' for them, and a way of getting noticed in a system that did not offer them the options of education or the learning of a trade, which would allow them to rise above their situation of low cultural level, illiteracy and marginalisation.

There were aggravating circumstances, such as the poor working conditions and the lack of recognition of basic rights in the mines of the Alto Llobregat, the poor harvests of olives and the strikes of the olive collectors in the winters of 1931–2 and 1933–4 in Bajo Aragón in the province of Teruel, the cruelty and intransigence of men such as José Vela, 'El Tuerto,' who was the main landowner and the 'gentleman' of Casas Viejas (and whom the local peasants pointed to as the principal cause of the insurrection and of the later massacre). There was also the frustration of the expectations of change created on the advent of the Republic, the dream of a better future to be obtained rapidly via the redistribution of wealth. Then there was the behaviour of the republican–socialist governments, which gave special tolerance to the unions of the UGT and demonstrated an energetic desire to eliminate anarcho-syndicalism from the scene. Finally, it is worth pointing out once more that the different manifestations of protest during these years were not only shaped and conditioned by structural factors or the political situation. Repression, the methods of coercion used by the state in favour of the property-owning classes and the day-to-day limitations placed on anyone who parted from these norms all played their part too. In the case of insurrections, and especially in Casas Viejas, the brutality of these mechanisms were laid bare, although, as had already been seen, there were other massacres in which the victims had not opted to channel their protest into armed rebellion.

The comparison of the incidents at Arnedo in January 1932 and December 1933 highlights certain significant factors which support this interpretation. The former originated, as will be remembered, in a strike and a demonstration of women and children drowned in blood in the town square. There were eleven dead and thirty wounded of all ages, old, young, children and middle-aged people. They were there to defend their places of work and those of their families, which were under threat, and show their solidarity with the workers sacked from the shoe-making industry. It was, in any case, a typical type of workers' protest in the rural area. One which had been repeated during these years in other parts of the Spanish territory and which, without leading to an insurrection, ended as it did because the Civil Guard opened fire without motive. Less tragic and altogether more naïve was the attempt to declare libertarian communism in December 1933. Of the twenty-seven arrested and tried, all were males, twenty-four of them single, the majority day labourers, they were very young (the average age was 21.6) and only the man accused of being the instigator and ringleader (who was from the nearby town of Turruncún) was thirty years old.

Moving from Ardedo to Casas Viejas, or the Aragonese localities which supported the uprising, the same characteristics are apparent. There were bricklayers, labourers, day-labourers and small farmers who became wage labourers at harvest times. They were almost all male, young and single. 'Kids of fifteen to twenty years of age steeped in the most misdirected extremism', said the *Heraldo de Aragón* about the revolutionists of the provincial capital, Zaragoza. And in Casas Viejas, with the exception of two of the peasants killed who were over forty and had not taken part, they were all of less than twenty years of age. This is confirmed by the register of the sentences of the 202 tried and sentenced by the emergency assizes in the province of Huesca, which continued to sit until July 1935. The overwhelming majority were single, young wage labourers between eighteen and twenty-five years of age. In most cases, when there had been no arms involved, the sentences were normally less than a year in prison. In the most serious cases, which involved assaults, sometimes homicide or possession of arms or explosives, the sentences ranged from eight to fourteen years. The anarchist campaign in favour of their release did not bear fruit. The most heavily involved were released from prison after the triumph of the Popular Front coalition in the February elections in 1936.[24]

All of the tragic events which accompanied these insurrections were the result of confrontations with the security forces. There were no excesses or acts of anticlerical vengeance. Nor did the authors commit any violence against property or the symbols of economic exploitation, to name a few of the targets against which anarchism acted in the revolution undertaken following the *coup d'état* of July 1936. Nevertheless, the fact that violence was not exercised in this fashion did not soften the character of coercion against the established authorities. There lay behind this a rejection of the institutions of representative government and the belief that force was the only way to liquidate the privilege of class and the abuse inherent in power.[25]

The instigators of insurrection were not particularly interested in first measuring the strength of their opponents, the basis of any rational calculation preceding any move onto the offensive. According to García Oliver, it was a case of 'overcoming the fear complex towards the forces of repression, the army, the Civil Guard and the police through systematic insurrectional activities. When this happened, the reactionaries would have no choice but to attack and this would lead, inevitably, to the downfall of the bourgeois Republic.' This was a simple conception of revolutionary action, but one which appeared very elaborate in comparison with the positions defended by the Urales family or Isaac Puente. The revolution would break out, they tell us, in the rural municipalities, where 'a handful of audacious comrades' would disarm the enemy and arm the revolutionaries. In the city, the workers only had to worry about 'keeping the army in check so that it could not go to suppress the uprising of the peasant brothers'. According to this rhetoric, the conditions necessary for the double objective of installing libertarian communism in the rural villages and starting the revolutionary general strike in the cities were always there but, according to this insurrectionary rhetoric, they were beginning to be particularly favourable from the first months of 1932.[26]

In reality, there were no 'peasant brothers in rebellion', nor could there be many. In comparison with other protest actions undertaken by the CNT, only very small isolated groups took the step forward, when the revolutionary clock struck thrice. Those who had chosen the moment for the movement demonstrated considerably less ability in actually organising it. This was partly because there was not much to organise. It was one thing to organise a strike, a demonstration over bad living conditions or the failure of employers to comply with the agreed working arrangements. An armed uprising was something very different and an action which was absolutely alien to normal union practice. It would obviously not be supported by those trade unionists who had been pushed out of the leadership, precisely for rejecting these tactics of open confrontation with the Republic – tactics which they considered to be not only erroneous, but also suicidal. The new rank-and-file which had joined the union in the first moments of the Republic had often ignored the warnings of the '*treintistas*' and taken part in many of the urban demonstrations. Nevertheless, in the moment of truth, they also ignored the call from the heralds of revolution. Finally, the power of the CNT in the rural world, where local branches were isolated and subordinated to the orders and propaganda of the cities, was limited. They were only successful when they occupied themselves with concrete and achievable projects. The vision of a revolution in the rural world was, therefore, merely a chimera. Even in Andalucia, supposedly the most suitable scenario for this revolutionary dream, the CNT could mobilise the agrarian proletariat only when it organised strikes directly relevant to the concerns of this sector. When it ignored the day-to-day issues (such as wage rises and the reduction of the working day, or the abolition of piecework) and followed the route marked out by the urban leaders and the committees of defence (insurrections and strikes in which these specific demands were marginal) the rural proletariat deserted the ranks. When this happened the socialist organisations of the FNTT took control of the strike movements. Casas Viejas was the outcome of an extreme application of this insurrectionary tactic and we have seen how that ended.

The rivalry for power within the CNT, and its decentralised and inefficient structure, allowed all sorts of uncontrolled actions and the appearance of multiple pro-prisoner and defence committees, which replaced the traditional leadership steeped in day-to-day union practices. This pushed the anarcho-syndicalist movement into a situation of extreme precariousness, in which its primordial objective came to be the mobilisation against repression and the excesses of republican power. The organisation of cohesive mobilisation, in which affiliates acted as a collective, degenerated into actions lead by small groups who could not even agree on which insurrection they were taking part in. As has already been seen, the insurrection of January 1933 was not considered to be authentic by some of the anarchist leaders in Catalonia or by those who were behind the newspaper *CNT* in Madrid. The December uprising of the same year had wider support than ever. However, García Oliver did not participate in the preparation and was not even present because 'revolutionary gymnastics' were meant to install libertarian communism and 'never to overthrow nor set up bourgeois governments be they left or right'. As can be seen, the cycle of insurrection not only exacerbated the differences within the CNT and led to the schism. It also started a phase of mutual reproaches and recriminations between the different sectors vying for control of the considerable power of mobilisation which the CNT possessed in some Spanish cities.[27]

Nevertheless, the ultimate cause of these armed skirmishes is not to be found in this rivalry, nor in the lack of preparation, the 'revolutionary spontaneity', the absence of a social base amongst the peasants. Faced with a state which had kept intact its mechanisms of coercion, an insurrectional strategy based on scattered support can never bring about a general uprising and ends up being easily repressed. The revolution was announced, without clear political objectives, for a set day, which was usually chosen in reaction to the enemy's initiative. It is not surprising, therefore, that the outcome should have been that the prisons were filled to bursting with anarchists and the courts were filled with people on criminal charges. To repeat once more, the Republic stained itself with the 'blood of the people', but, leaving heroic actions aside, the CNT gained little and lost a lot. An internal split, the persecution of its activists and the generalisation of repression were poor propaganda for a movement which hoped to attract the entirety of the proletariat to its ranks. As was shown by the military coup of July 1936, only the collapse of the state's mechanisms of coercion could open the gates to the longed-for revolution.

Many things happened before this became possible. There was a moment of reflection following the insurrections. The constant criticisms which anarcho-syndicalists such as Peiró made of the uselessness of the actions of 'audacious minorities' were seconded by other anarchists, both from the CNT and the IWO, who began to say the same thing. The people had ample reason for revolt. However, although that first necessary step towards the revolution – 'the spirit of rebellion' – had been achieved, the CNT was incapable of the second – the necessary organisation – to unite its forces not divide them, to conserve energy instead of wasting it. A change was necessary to take the CNT away from its recent stormy course.[28]

5   Correcting the route taken

Correcting the route taken meant taking one that was different from that which led to insurrection, and relative to the bloody outcome of the earlier skirmishes, for the CNT, this was a choice that did not bring with it other costs. As is usual with anarcho-syndicalism's own self-analysis, this change in direction was not the result of its own failures nor those of its leaders. Thus, in their reality, they had always been where they should have been, carrying out their duty in the face of adversity and saving revolutionary dignity, which was something similar to the dignity of the proletariat. Rather it was the 'social panorama of Spain' which had changed. Now that bourgeois democracy had failed, the 'possible political solutions' had been reduced to 'the simple antithesis of fascism or social revolution'. The alarm was sounding and the moment had arrived to 'talk seriously about a unified front, an alliance and revolutionary unity'.

Valeriano Orobón was the first anarchist of any authority who dared to make suggestions of 'a class alliance' to overcome the almost irresolvable differences which had separated the two union traditions during the first two years of the Republic. The fact that the suggestion was made in January 1934 and not before was due to the emergence of three new factors. These were 'the crisis of legitimacy of democracy and its political expedients', the 'reactionary radicalisation' of the Spanish bourgeoisie, which had 'shown its true colours' and was marching towards fascism, and 'the theoretical and practical shift within social democracy, which has abandoned its ill-fated collaborationism and returned to its class position'. It was always possible that the desire to make the revolution was not genuine amongst all socialists, but the CNT did not have to worry about this. Given that, if they wanted to defeat reaction, the 'co-ordination' of the Spanish proletariat was an 'unavoidable imperative', the workers of the UGT would end up 'dislodging' the 'Trifones, Besteiros and Saborits', and all of those who plotted against the revolutionary alliance. The alliance was nothing less than 'a tactical necessity imposed by exceptional circumstances'. The anarcho-syndicalists had to leave aside their beloved principles and their excess of rhetoric, and forget the 'foolishness' of the slogan 'we will meet in the streets', which had led to so many disastrous failures.[1]

However, few of the leaders of the committees of the CNT were attracted by Orobón's message. The divisons that had opened up between them and the socialists and the break-away syndicalists had still not been resolved. This is apparent from the discussions which the topic provoked in the Plenary Meeting of Regional Confederations which began in Barcelona on 10 February 1934, the first time the leaders had met since the insurrection of December the previous year. The unions of the central region took the initiative and, under the guidance of Orobón, 'obliged' the National Committee to include a question, which had not been anticipated, in the order of the day. Following the theoretician's arguments, the Local Federation of Trades Unions of Valladolid argued that 'the decision not to collaborate in the so called united revolutionary front would be suicidal'. The regional confederation of Asturias, where Orobón's idea had most support, as well as that of Galicia, under the leadership of José Villaverde, insisted on taking the same step. 'United Front', they declared, (made up) 'purely by workers and without collaborating with the bourgeois sectors'. Workers' front or not, Andalucia rejected it because 'the revolutionary unity of the Spanish proletariat ... has to be undertaken in the streets in the moment of struggle and without political tutelage'. In spite of Orobón, the street was still the scenario. The Catalan delegates went even further. They refused even to discuss this sort of question, as a matter of principle, 'and in the second place because those who support the united front in Catalonia are the greatest enemies of the CNT and its men'. Those who had initiated it, the Workers and Peasants Party, the Left Communists and the Socialist Union of Catalonia were also considered to be enemies and the Federation of Libertarian Unions was seen as the greatest enemy of all. These opposition unions were, effectively, at the forefront of this initiative in Catalonia and throughout the Valencian region, where they had set up the Executive Committee of the Workers' Anti-Fascist Alliance.[2]

The affair ended, as had so many before, with the usual report which served to gloss over disagreement. Between those pushing for unity and those who resisted, there existed a middle ground which seemed to satisfy everyone but which did not, in fact, change anything. The report proclaimed once more how revolutionary the CNT was and what the UGT would have to do to attain similar status. 'The two consecutive years of repression, by the Republicans and Socialists in government, have shown that the arguments of the CNT were correct, in the sense that the Republic, like all conservative and democratic regimes, cannot satisfy the needs and aspirations of the working class.' Given that this same Republic, with reactionaries now in government, was leading 'the country towards the establishment of fascism', the CNT, 'faithful to its revolutionary course and attentive to the declarations of the UGT's representative bodies', was willing, as ever, 'to contribute with all its strength to all revolutionary movements which tends towards the liberation of the working class'. At the end of the day, it was the UGT which had to demonstrate 'clearly and publicly, the nature of its revolutionary aspirations'. Obviously, and this was the final warning, 'when talking of revolution one must not make the mistake of thinking that this simply meant a change of rulers, as had happened on 14 April, but rather the total abolition of capitalism and the State'.

Four months later everything remained the same, or, to be more precise, the same but with greater resistence to this rhetoric. Tired of watching the CNT play at revolution 'every six months, which was the best way to foster the advance of fascism', the anarcho-syndicalists of Asturias signed an alliance agreement with the UGT at the end of March 1934. The best-known promoter of this, José M. Martinez, had to put up with a storm of criticism at the Plenary Meeting of Regional Committees of the CNT held in Madrid from 23 June of that year. Durruti from Catalonia, and above all Eusebio Carbó from the secretariat of the IWO, recalled for the umpteenth time the massacres of the first two years of the Republic. As can be seen, the repression continued to stir passions and keep the torch of sacred principles alight. The strength of this discourse left the Asturians isolated and there was a serious threat of schism. Those who were most outraged with them demanded that a national congress be convened immediately at which the 'revolutionary workers' alliance' would be discussed. They did so confident that the Asturians would have to yield because they had broken with the organisation's resolution on the subject. However, as the congress was taking a long time to organise and the Asturians had no intention of abandoning the CNT, it was the very situation of weakness in which the the organistion found itself that prevented a split. The strange thing about this situation was that these Asturian activists, who had never played at revolution before, would find the occasion to do so a few months later, and all because of this alliance.[3]

The only strike of any length in which both union organisations were united took place in the interval betwen the two plenary meetings. And it took place in Zaragoza, a city which until then had not been particularly propitious for this kind of gatherings. On 26 March 1934, a bomb exploded near a police station, 'an act in which no labour organisation had any involvement'. The bomb was aimed at the police officers who normally changed shift at that time, but it missed its target and killed three civilian passers-by. A number of anarcho-syndicalists were arrested and beaten and the CNT convened a twelve-hour general strike which was prolonged for another twenty-four 'because the strike committee itself was arrested'. A judge and a lawyer were attacked and beaten by more than a hundred prisoners in Torrero prison as they left after taking declarations from prisoners. The Assault Guards had to intervene to re-establish order and the governor and administrator of the prison were forced to resign. Elviro Ordiales, the same provincial governor who had gained notoriety in the repression of the December uprising, imposed severe sanctions and fines on the tram and bus drivers who had supported the strike. Those who were members of the CNT had their driving licences taken away, as a result of which they were dismisssed by their companies. Members of the UGT Union of Tram Drivers were allowed to return to work, but their leaders were obliged to pay a fine of two hundred pesetas each to the management, which amounted to almost a month's wages.

The CNT and the UGT reached agreement to ask the civil governor to revoke these sanctions. Ordiales, who had been so praised by the leading sectors of the city, refused and ordered the hiring of other drivers, who did not even have the appropriate licences. The response of the labour organisations was another forty-eight hour strike from 5 April. The strike concluded when the governor promised to resolve the situation. However, the employers, on the grounds that the strike had been declared illegal by the governor himself, simply informed a large number of employees (two hundred according to the authorities and four hundred according to the unions) that they had been sacked .

The employers in this sector had repeatedly failed to comply with the work contracts approved by mixed panels of arbitration. Many of the small businesses were on the verge of bankruptcy and they took advantage of the situation to streamline their labour force. The CNT had been organising demonstrations for the release of its prisoners since December. These dismissals provided them with an appropriate labour dispute through which to channel their protest. For the UGT, this was also the sector in which they had their most influential union and these lay-offs were the final straw in the 'obstinancy of the bourgeoisie'. In fact, for the UGT, 1934 was the year of 'realities' following the 'harvest of learning' in 1933. The criticism and insults which the UGT had addressed to the CNT, and which had been accompanied by harsh confrontation during the first two years of the Republic, now gave way to calls for reconciliation. Parallel with this truce, each side could still maintain the purity of its principles 'in order to agree on the concrete point which consisted purely and simply in the overthrow of capitalism through revolution'. A joint strike was launched, by some for the sake of their prisoners and by others for the same revolutionary reasons as always. They wanted to show that nothing could be expected from 'bourgeois democracy' especially when government was in the hands of the right. The strike ended up being long and hard because there was more at stake than just the defence of a few hundred sacked workers.[4]

The civil governor, who was not particularly open to negotiation, set the rhythm of the conflict. He gave police protection to the workers who replaced those sacked and refused to re-employ the latter. As the strike progressed, the unions demanded the exclusion of 'blackleg' labour which was essential to the breaking of the 'monopoly' which the CNT and the UGT held in the most important sectors of industry. The resistance of the strikers came to be symbolised by the powerful and emotive image of 'solidarity' when more than five hundred of their children were welcomed by workers in other cities such as Madrid, Barcelona and Vinaroz. 'Zaragoza the invincible', wrote Federica Montseny. The 'Iberian Kronstadt', wrote another. In a somewhat reactionary journey into the past, the anarchist press revived its favourite myths and recalled that the French had never managed to take the city on the Ebro during the 'War of Independence'. The workers won this time round, with an agreement signed on 11 May by the strike committees, the civil governor and the employers' representatives. Those who had been dismissed could return 'under the same conditions as prior to the strike, and undertook to work together with those taken on during the strike'. For its part, the Employers' Federation agreed not to carry out reprisals against any worker'.[5]

The Zaragoza strike did not end the reticence and hostility of the majority of the CNT leaders towards the revolutionary alliance, although it did bring about a change in the hostile relations which the two union movements had hitherto maintained. This change was also noticeable in other cities such as Seville and, even if the CNT refused to recognise it, came as a result of the failed insurrections and the radicalisation of the socialists and their rupture with the Republic from the autumn of 1933. During 1934, the CNT organised several 'defensive' strikes, over the reduction of working hours. It succeeded in keeping these at forty-four hours per week for the iron workers in Barcelona in June and for those in Zaragoza in December. However, the CNT was absent from the two events which dominated labour history for that year, the agricultural workers' general strike in June and the October insurrection in Asturias. As regards the former, the chronic weakness of the CNT in the countryside and their lack of interest in concrete issues such as the application of agrarian reform, working conditions and the restoration of common lands all continued to weigh against the CNT. In Asturias, the anarcho-syndicalists, who were divided over the Revolutionary Workers' Alliance which they had joined, nevertheless took part in the insurrection. The CNT was not to be saved, not even by the myth and heroic legend which was forged around this insurrection, from a bitter debate which betrayed its contradictory nature. On the one hand, there was the feeling that a historic opportunity had been missed. For the others there was confirmation that this was not their struggle, because 'the dilemma is not whether the left or the right governs but bourgeois Republic or libertarian communism'. The socialists had taken what was a new direction for them but which for even the most radical anarchists seemed to have been abandoned because of exhaustion. 'We cannot continue, as we have done till now, with rehearsals. There is a limit and the FAI reached this limit on 8 December 1933', declared *Tierra y Libertad* after it was all over, on 11 October.[6]

The intensity of social struggle dropped sharply after the last insurrections of the republican period. For many, with the employers emboldened by the defeat of the workers, this was the beginning of a truely 'black' period. For the CNT, this 'black' period had begun long before and so this period did not seem darker than the previous one. The reaction of the employers was no harsher towards the CNT's members than it had been in 1932 or 1933, and the attitude of the government towards anarcho-syndicalism was, in any case, conditioned by the degree of resistance that their unions showed towards the Law of Associations of 8 April 1932. That the CNT should go on the offensive in the first two years and then adopt a 'defensive' stance in the second part depended on its strength, internal cohesion and the possibilities of mobilisation at its disposal at any point, and not only on the attitude of the state or their rival unions. In 1935, when unemployment was heavily affecting the CNT's most combatitive sectors, with the prisons full of activists, large numbers of members had left and with others not paying their subscriptions, the organisation was on the verge of collapse. However, this was the extreme symptom of a cumulative crisis which was aggravated from October 1934 onwards by the fact that the government maintained in force the state of preparation, state of alarm and above all martial law, the three states of exception permitted by the Law of Public Order of July 1933. The outcry of the CNT against the Law, which was considerable, was no greater than that of the socialists when they began to feel the effects of its repeated application against them only a few months after its approval.

There were numerous indications of the paralysis of the anarcho-syndicalist organisation in 1935. The National Committee (of which Horacio Martínez Prieto was president from 7 January, taking over from Miguel Yoldi) spent its time sending semi-clandestine circulars full of complaints to the different regional confederations. These rarely received a reply due to the 'functional disequilibrium' which affected the committees and syndicates. The 'consumption' of the confederal stamp, which was central to the financing of this executive body, had been greatly reduced. In the words of its secretary, 'apart from depriving us of elements essential to propaganda, it implies a numerical decline in membership or a drop in the level of militancy'. In February 1935, the National Committee was owed 25,000 pesetas of stamp dues from the organisation (members, unions and regional committees). By the end of the year the amount had gone up to 40,000. The disorganisation and the lack of resources also prevented the holding of the congress which had been announced several times and always been postponed with the excuse of the repression. As a result of this lack of funds, the National Committee was unable to give its share of the confederal stamp income to the National Pro-Prisoners' Committee, whose income was nil just when they were in most need of money. According to this committee, in Asturias there reigned 'chaos ... in the defence of our comrades as a result of the lack of money. They are represented by incompetent lawyers, so bad indeed that they consider the sentences passed down to be not really severe because, given the scale of the movement, they had resigned themselves to harsher punishments.'[7]

The financial ruin also affected the press. The newspaper *CNT* was riddled with debts. The paper owed money to its printing staff whilst it was owed 47,000 pesetas in confederal stamp income, subscriptions and income from distributors. The question had by now become tedious because there was no plenary session or National Committee meeting in which the calamitous state of the paper did not arise. The circulation of the paper was stopped by government order on 5 October 1934. Liberto Callejas had left *Solidaridad Obrera* at the beginning of December 1933 in order to run *CNT* but was only able to do so only from 21 August until 4 October 1934. He was replaced at the Barcelona paper by Manuel Villar. This young man from Burgos (born in 1909) had spent his adolescence in Argentina, under the wing of Abad de Santillán, until he was deported in 1933. He was an activist of the anarchist group 'Nervio', led by Abad de Santillán and which controlled the weekly *Tierra y Libertad* during these years. He remained in his post until June 1936, when a union vote returned Liberto Callejas to the post. During the first year under Villar's editorship, the paper did nothing, due to the repeated closures (during several months following the insurrection of December 1933) and the declaration, by Companies, of the 'Catalan State within the Spanish Federal Republic', on 6 October 1934. In 1935 *Solidaridad Obrera* disappeared 'voluntarily' from 27 April to 1 August. That is to say, it was obliged to close because of lack of funds at a time during which almost all of the unions in Catalonia were closed and only a very few paid their subscriptions.[8]

With the union movement in such a state of weakness and without resources for insurrectional activities, the time had now come to change strategy and start again. It was essential that trade unionism should be legalised again, even if this meant abandoning the energetic rejection of the Law of 8 April 1932. Above all, it was essential to bring about a rapprochement with the opposition unions. Both of these things had been impossible before 1935. There had been a first attempt by the regional committee in Galicia (at the Plenary Meeting of February 1934) to force through the acceptance of the law, with the argument that 'it is easy to get round it'. It was argued that this was the only way for the CNT to emerge from clandestinity. However, the unanimous response of the rest of the delegates had been to 'reject the law even if that means we have to live in clandestinity'. When people like Peiró spoke of the 'conditions' necessary for the return to legality, the paper *CNT* replied, on 21 August 1934, that 'there are no necessary conditions for entering the CNT. When the workers and the '*treintista*' syndicalists want to do so they know that ... there is only one way: that of honour, the door through which all sincere revolutionary proletarians must pass'.

Effectively, the door opened at the Plenary Meeting of Regional Committees, which began in Madrid on 26 January 1936, and without the need to bring questions of honour into play. The Asturian representative opened fire first, as was usually the case with matters of this sort, and requested that 'the opposition unions should be invited to re-join the CNT'. 'Without humiliations', they added, and with the sole condition that they 'adhere to the norms and agreements of the confederal organisation ... leaving aside insults and excesses which might impede co-existence'.

The time was ripe for reconciliation because the insults and slander had abated after the end of the cycle of insurrections. The FAI was on the verge of collapse and the opposition unions had never ceased to affirm their revolutionary and anti-political commitment. For the *treintistas*, the alienation from the CNT had always been the result of 'circumstances'. With the exception of Pestaña's group, which included Josep Robusté and Marín Civera amongst others, almost all of those who had previously been leading figures in the CNT now returned. In total 69,621 members and 85 unions re-joined the organisation at the May 1936 Congress. One third came from the Valencian region and the rest, with the exception of a small group which had remained in Huelva, were from Catalonia.[9]

Whether it was to be succesful or not, the fact that dissidents, FAI activists and anarcho-syndicalists, who had never shared ideological positions, had, nevertheless, joined once more in a single organisation demonstrated two things. Firstly, both of the opposed strategies had failed (be it that which attempted to adapt revolutionary trade unionism to the new political situation which the advent of the Republic had created or that anarchist radicalism which attempted to channel the discontent of the workers into insurrection). Secondly, neither of the two could come up with any alternative solution to the social and political problems of the day beyond their usual abstract formulas for the destruction of the state and the transformation of society. With this being the case, the opposition unions never managed to achieve a support base within other sectors, apart from those which they took with them following the split, and even lost groups of leaders and ordinary members who abandoned anarcho-syndicalism permanently. The defenders of anarchist purity, tied to the colours of the FAI, dragged the CNT to the verge of collapse from which it was only able to pull back as a result of the general elections and the *coup d'état* which, several months later, brought with it unforeseen consequences.

The calling of elections for 16 February 1936 effectively gave the CNT a breathing space. This was a chance to occupy the public sphere once more, mobilise its membership and reorganise, which is the principal aspiration of any social movement. However, once all this was under way, it was necessary to find suitable instruments with which to consolidate this new beginning. This was particularly the case because, as had been demonstrated before October 1934, again during the insurrection of that month and, finally, with the Popular Front agreement signed on 15 January 1936, the possibility of forming a 'revolutionary alliance' exclusively of workers was nil. Furthermore, the formation of the Popular Front left the CNT isolated and, in fact so isolated that now it expressed a willingness to seek alliances. There were to be found the anarcho-syndicalists of Catalonia, with the Barcelona Iron and Construction workers who had previously placed so many obstacles in the way of agreement, now asking the UGT for revolutionary action, 'to destroy completely the existing social regime'. That such a suggestion could be made ten days after the UGT acceptance of an electoral coalition which, if it was victorious at the polls, would control government policy, was indicative of the confusion which reigned within anarcho-syndicalism at this point in time. The leadership in Galicia, Asturias and the regional committee of the North had been occupied for some time, in vain, with the project of an alliance. Coming as it did from those previously hostile quarters, the call came as a pleasant surprise for them. It did not seem like such a good idea to those from Andalucia. The delegate to the Plenary Meeting in which the subject arose reminded his colleagues from Catalonia of the 'contradiction' involved in criticising the socialists mercilessly as authors of the repressive laws which gag us' whilst attempting at the same time 'to form an alliance with the UGT'.[10]

Alone, isolated and without alternatives, ambiguous messages dominated the discussions within the CNT over what to do with the elections. The 'apolitical principles' are untouchable, repeated the Catalan delegates time and again and this meant 'criticising the parliamentary system' and 'combating both right and left', reminding some of the October repression and others of Casas Viejas. 'If the revolution is not to be carried out after the elections then it is impossible to carry out a campaign of abstention', replied the representatives from Aragon, who had learnt the lesson in this respect. The final report contained a little of each sentiment. There was no reason why the CNT should modify 'its traditional attitude towards politics', the 'reasoned' negation of bourgeois, democratic, parliamentary procedures, or the 'objective' criticism of all parties. Nevertheless, the abstentionist campaign of 1933 was not to be repeated. That had been the result of 'contingent circumstances created by the exceptional situation in which the organisation and its activists had been placed. This situation had obliged the activists to reject openly the brutal procedures of which they had been victims.'

In order to maintain a basic level of agreement within this level of ambiguity, it was necessary to centre the discussion as much as possible on those anarcho-syndicalists still in prison. Nevertheless, the difference between 1933 and 1935 did not lie, as has often been said, in the need for the left to win in order for the prisoners to be released. Things were much more straightforward. In 1933, an important sector of anarcho-syndicalism believed that abstention was a fore-runner to revolution and that the latter was an inevitable consequence of the former. In 1936, given the state that the organisation found itself in after that experience, no one was about to announce the revolution for the day after the elections.[11]

There was no need to announce the revolution either. The Popular Front won the elections, and for many this meant the second phase of the task begun in April 1931 and interrupted in the summer of 1933. It was a second opportunity, in fact, for Manuel Azaña, once more in power and with the multitude in the streets. A second chance for the socialists, who once more gained significant political influence in local centres of power. And a second chance for the anarcho-syndicalists who began to regain their capacity for agitation and some of the social support they had lost. However, even if the same protagonists had now returned to centre stage, the atmosphere of this triumph in no way resembled that of the inauguration of the Republic in the spring of 1931. There were riots in some prisons and escapes from others. As soon as the victory of the Popular Front became known, there were crowds in the streets of many of the main cities calling for an amnesty and the re-employment of all dismissed workers. This is what happened in Zaragoza, where the CNT and the UGT declared a general strike and announced a demonstration to demand the liberty of 'social and polit-ical' prisoners. The local military commander General Miguel Cabanellas, who had been in charge of the V Division for only one month, sent groups of soldiers to occupy the official centres and the main streets. The next day, with martial law declared, the city was completely paralysed. The demonstration, which was led by the parliamentary deputies Benito Pabón and Eduardo Castillo, and had attracted several thousand citizens, was crushed by the assault guard. The confrontations and shooting left one dead and many wounded. This was no popular fiesta.

The demonstrations and collective mobilisations resulting from this and other issues raised the political temperature, in spite of the damp and unpleasant weather in the latter days of that winter. All of these demonstrations and activity on the streets tired some and frightened others. 'Neutrality must be re-estab-lished on the streets as soon as possible', argued *El Sol* on 4 March 1936. The streets must be free 'for the traffic to run, as this is a symbol of activity and work, and the material expression of circulating wealth … pedestrians must be free to go about their business, fulfil their obligations and gain their daily bread'. The street 'like the fatherland, belongs to no-one and to everyone'.

'The street belongs to no one yet. We are going to see who conquers it', Ramón J. Sender had written in *Siete domingos rojos* a few years before. Typical of CNT rhetoric, always obsessed with the street, whether it were to occupy it or to oust others from it. For many, filling it was a symbol of power. For others, it was a symptom of the good functioning of order that the streets should be empty and serve 'as a place of honest relaxation for the metropolitan multitudes'. These opposing interpretations were part of what marked out an individual's political identity. This was why there was such interest in returning time and again to this scenario. This was also why a state of emergency was maintained during these months. And finally, this was why the army occupied the streets in July 1936, in order to save a fatherland, which ended up belonging to them and a few others, but not to everyone.[12]

There were a number of deeply important issues with which the new government had to deal and which were the focus of pressure from the streets. These included the concession of an amnesty, the return to their posts of the councillors and mayors elected in April 1931 and suspended by government order from December 1933, and the re-employment of workers who had been dismissed. The expectations were great and once these first steps had been taken, the demonstrators abandoned the streets. Each of the union organisations began, in their own right, to mobilise on the platforms which brought them most members: wage rises, the reduction of the working day and the control of employment and dismissals. On this would depend their strength and their ability to influence the representatives of the employers' organisations in the contracting of their members in construction, the bosses of small workshops or factory owners. The competition over this crucial question divided the two unions once more and there were strikes and confrontations as a result, as in Málaga. This was especially the case when a large sector of UGT activists adopted the procedure which had brought so much success to the CNT. They would simply appear on a site and demand that all of those contracted be union members.[13]

The subversion of the social order, whether it were real or imagined, was felt intensely in the rural world. The programme of the Popular Front contained hardly anything different, in terms of agrarian reform, from that of the first two years of the Republic. However, the electoral victory and the formation of a new government under Azaña placed the struggle for land in the forefront once more. The law of 1932 had been very limited, but even so, during the radical policies in the two years of right-wing government dominated by Gil Robles's CEDA, there had been an attempt to rectify its most threatening social effects. The recovery of lost time and the acceleration of the application of these reforms were, without doubt, two issues which occupied prime positions on the government's agenda. The expectation amongst potential beneficiaries was expressed as a burning desire for the immediate implementation of these reforms.

Logically, the government wanted to control the imminent processes of change. For the agricultural unions representing the farm hands, day labourers, small landowners and agricultural workers in general, this was a question of justice. They saw this as a restoration of their rights to lands which they had cultivated and from which in certain cases, such as that of the ploughmen of Extremadura in 1935, they had been expelled. They now had the support of many of those local authorities who had returned with the elections and they began an offensive which became an open conflict from March 1936. This was the month in which the 1932 decree on the intensification of cultivation was re-established. The Minister for Agriculture authorised the Institute for Agrarian Reform to occupy, for 'social utility', all of those farms 'which could resolve the agrarian problem in any municipality, by putting an end to huge estates, the excessive use of landless workers and non-intensive farming'. Furthermore, the socialists' Spanish Federation of Land Workers organised a massive occupation and ploughing of estates in Badajoz in which 60,000 workers took part and invaded more than two thousand estates. From March until the military uprising, a great deal of land was distributed, seven times more, according to Malefakis, than in the previous five years. There is not complete agreement on the figures, but somewhere around 550,000 hectares were occupied by some 110,000 peasant farmers. This was not much, in the context of the plans elaborated by the technical commission appointed to draw up the agrarian reform of 1932. This had proposed the placing of 150,000 peasant farmers in the first two years of the applicaton of the law of 1932. Nevertheless, it was enough to frighten the employers, the advocates of order and all of those who began to think that the government had lost control of the situation, because it was not preventing these occupations. The occupations of estates were perceived as a threat to all of the existing relations of the social hierarchy.[14]

The data available places in question the usual argument that Spain entered a period of unprecedented levels of strikes in the spring of 1936, 'especially where the CNT had influence', or that this period constituted the moment of the most extreme 'civil disorder in the history of Spain'.[15] If, as these same authors recognise, the statistics available are extremely inadequate, one might assume that the method of counting used by the *Boletín del Ministro de Trabajo* was similarly deficient and conclude that, at most, there were as many strikes in these five months as in all of 1933. However, in order to give a qualitative description of this wave of strikes, other sources of data must be taken into consideration and other factors introduced into the analysis.

In the first place, the CNT was not especially active in this strike movement. It was able to participate in Madrid, Málaga and other urban centres of less importance, but not in Barcelona, Seville or Zaragoza, the cities in which it had greatest support during the first two years of the Republic. The anarcho-syndicalists were not in good shape in Seville or Barcelona and the available figures place them at the lowest level during the whole republican period. When they were forced to abandon the strategy of insurrection, they also had to give up the ideological ties which had distanced them most from the republican regime, and return to the policies they had already practised in the summer of 1931. The evidence is very clear, at least for Barcelona and Zaragoza. There they reached an understanding with the republican authorities instead of continually mobilising their affiliates against them. They were willing to negotiate agreements against unemployment before putting the strategy of direct action into practice. No one spoke about a renuciation of ideals. However, with the prisoners released and without martyrs, the principal concerns during these months of 1936 were unemployment, working conditions and, in particular, the reorganisation of the union. The aggressive language and the martyrised tone of their statements against the socialists and republicans were left aside. The atmosphere within the CNT was very different from that of 1932 and 1933. The workers' centres reopened. The wounds resulting from the *treintista* schism healed. The Confederation press, which suffered censorship but not closures, recovered.[16]

There were good reasons for optimism and even for a return to euphoria. This euphoria which was unleashed, as is logical in these situations, when 649 delegates of the CNT, representing 988 unions and 559,294 members, were able to meet in Zaragoza. This special Congress has always been noted for its famous report on libertarian communism. This was a triumph of the retrograde communal conceptualisations defended with such fervour by Isaac Puente and the Urales family during the republican period. It is in fact astounding, given what lay ahead, that a group of anarchists (amongst whom were to be found Federica Montseny, Juan García Oliver and Joaquín Ascaso) should get involved in exotic discussions about the family and sexual relations in the free communes of the future. However, it should not be forgotten either that this was the first time that the CNT had recognised the error of the insurrectional strategy and left aside speculation on agrarian reform in order to attempt the opposite strategy of concrete demands on wages, working conditions and the recovery of public property. The report on the 'agrarian problem' stated that 'the constructive education of the peasants, in line with our principles, is the most important and difficult mission for anarcho-syndicalism in the countryside'. It was a matter of 'avoiding, in future, those sporadic movements which local regions start of their own accord without the least control, without taking into account the circumstances or the suitability of the moment for revolution, and without the preparation required for the defeat of capitalism'. Organisation, preparation and the building of support amongst the peasantry, these were the principal elements of this strategy. It is difficult to imagine how much this strategy might have achieved because the military uprising forced a new change of strategy.[17]

Recent monographs have also confirmed that this was not a critical moment of social conflict in the rural world. Neither the number nor the types of conflict were any higher or more acute than they had been in the period from 1931 to 1934. The most repeated demands during these months were for the fulfilment of agreements on working conditions and the creation of an obligatory contribution in order to ameliorate the problem of unemployment. There was some bloody repression of these peasant demonstrations, but that was rare by comparison with the abundant bloodshed during the first two years of the Republic.

The massacre of Yeste (Albacete) on 29 May, in which 17 peasants were riddled with bullets by the Civil Guard, did not result in any social mobilisation, no furore against this institution, and did not even revitalise the cult of martyrs which had been so frequent on previous occasions.[18]

However, this story cannot be evaluated merely on the basis of the number of deaths caused. The threat to social order and the subversion of class relations was perceived with greater intensity in 1936 than in the first two years of the Republic. The political stability of the regime was also at greater risk. The language of class, with its rhetoric of social division and the incitement to struggle against opponents had gradually pervaded the Spanish atmosphere from the moment in which the reform projects of the first republican governments came up against insuperable obstacles. Wide sectors of the population remained politically weak and excluded or marginalised, without any form of presence in the political life of the nation. The union organisations were not attempting to defend the interests of the workers within the existing political and economic structures, but rather to change them. Following the failure of the socialist–republican coalition, which had disintegrgated in 1933, which had aimed at the incorporation of large sectors of the middle-class and urban workers into its project, the PSOE abandoned its strategy of peaceful progress towards socialism and raised the flag of revolution. The elections of February 1936 found the socialist movement in a process of fragmentation and internal struggle. This prevented a compromise with the republican government, which was one of the few political solutions that might have given stability to Spanish society at that moment in time.

Given the political fragmentation of the urban middle classes and the inability to attract the small and medium rural proprietors, it is unlikely that this government could have done much to modify the situation, which was not at all favourable to the consolidation of democracy. Once the threat of insurrection, which anarchists and socialists had provoked between January 1932 and October 1934, was over, the greatest threat to the republican regime came from social forces recruited from the medium, poor and 'very poor' rural proprietors, along with the old monarchist oligarchy, under the leadership of the professional urban sectors who had created the CEDA, the first Catholic mass party in the history of Spain. Under the ideological banner of Catholicism, which linked the defence of religion with that of order and property, they took as their objective the extirpation of the socialist and anarchist threat which was so deeply rooted amongst the rural and urban working classes.

This project would not have succeeded if they had not had the support of a large sector of the army. And so it was that the Republic was brought to an end through the force of arms, and not because of popular pressure in the streets, on which the anarchists had placed their faith. It is true that democratic values had not taken root in Spanish society, but it must also be pointed out that they were not given much chance to do so. It is also true that the history of the republican period shows that, for the majority of political forces, and perhaps for all of them, losing an election was the signal for aggression against those who had won. However, the Civil War, which is always seen as the inevitable outcome of this period, was the result of a failed *coup d'état* and not the logical or the expected outcome of the failure of the Republic. The abstract failure of the Republic only became a concrete reality when, five months after the elections of February 1936, a military uprising overthrew the regime. And this is why some historians can speak of this failure today. Conjecture apart, up until this moment anything was possible, including peace.[19]

The military *coup d'état* encountered resistance because Spanish society in 1936 was different from what it had been in 1932. This period had seen the advent of a Republic, and the potential opportunity to deal with unresolved problems. It had encountered considerable factors of instability and had not provided, or rather had not been able to provide, adequate political resources to overcome them. Given the levels of social and political mobilisation, the military coup could not have ended, as it had so many times before in the history of Spain, in a quick and simple *pronunciamiento*. The end of the crisis would require a new and violent solution, one that had already been initiated by Fascism in other European countries. This would cover over and hide the fractures opened up, or increased, by the experience of the Republic.

The coup brought the end of a phase for anarcho-syndicalism. This was a phase in which, as has been seen, it had maintained a difficult relationship with the Republic and had undergone a number of changes in mentality. These varied from the initial expectations of some to the useless insurrections of others, passing through periods in which the majority of the membership was alienated from the organisation. Just as all of these options were being re-evaluated, July 1936 arrived. Suddenly anarcho-syndicalism had before it that which it had searched for in vain for so long. This was the historic opportunity to realise the egalitarian ideal and paradise on earth. That which had been weakness and uncertainty in the spring of 1936 became once more a source of strength and revolutionary imperative. The situation had gone from the 'intoxication of enthusiasm', which arrived with the hurricane of 1931, to the 'revolutionary intoxication' that came with the tempest of July 1936, and, from the power of the streets to that of the force of arms. The second part of this book is dedicated to the analysis of this form of power.

Part II

The people in arms

We are not interested in sashes or medals. We want neither governorships nor ministries. When we have won, we will return to the factories and the workshops from which we have emerged, throwing aside the wealth, for whose abolition we have struggled so much. In the factories, in the fields and in the mines is where the true army of defenders of Spain will be created.

(Buenaventura Durruti, *Solidaridad Obrera*, 12 September 1936)

6   The summer of 1936

On 17 July 1936, sectors of the Civil Guard and of the Regulares Indígenas (native infantry) in Melilla began the uprising against the republican regime. This military coup, which seemed to confirm the catastrophic predictions made on the very next day after the elections, was unable to achieve its desired objectives. Confidence in the rapid triumph of the rebellion evaporated when the rebels were defeated in the majority of large cities. An alliance between the security forces loyal to the Republic and activists of the political and union organisations played a fundamental role in the crushing of the rebellion in Barcelona, Madrid, Málaga, Valencia, Gijón and San Sebastian. Where, on the other hand, this alliance was not created (as in Seville and in Cordoba) or where the Civil and Assault Guards supported the rebels (Zaragoza and Valladolid, for example), the struggle was very one-sided and was quickly settled in favour of the rebel forces.[1]

The republican state maintained its legal existence, but the collapse of its mechanisms of coercion, resulting from the division provoked by the coup within the army and the security forces, destroyed its cohesion and left it teetering on the brink of collapse. In spite of the myths forged around these events, it was not the people unassisted, 'the people in arms', who defeated the rebels in the streets of the most important cities. Nevertheless, having lost its monopoly of arms, the state could not prevent a sudden and violent outburst of revolution in those places where the rebels had been defeated. This was aimed at the destruction of positions of privilege. New armed protagonists, many of whom had made their names in vigorous opposition to this very state, invaded the public sphere. For the labour organisations, it was no longer a question of declaring a new general strike, or of embarking on a new insurrectionary adventure, but rather of opposing an armed movement. What could not be achieved through the constant struggle of a revolutionary minority, with the uneven support of several hundred thousand followers, now came about as a result of the failed *coup d'état*.

The Civil War which followed the failed *coup d'état* imposed a military logic that rendered the trade unionism of protest useless. Two new questions appeared on the horizon, which had not been addressed within the 'romantic' conceptualisation of libertarian communism or in the theoretical elaborations of the anarchists concerning the society of the future. Firstly, a power vacuum had opened up following the defeat of the insurgents. This created the possibility, for the first time, of occupying a considerable amount of territory and so avoiding the isolation which had contributed so much to the defeat of earlier attempts at revolution. Secondly, the 'artificial' division of Spain into two zones marked the beginning of a period in which social conflict would be resolved through armed struggle. This state of affairs, however, did not guarantee the adoption by wide sectors of the population of ideas that had previously been clearly supported by only a militant minority.

In other words, the overthrow of the bourgeois social and economic struc-tures was not as straightforward an affair as had been imagined. Furthermore, it had not been achieved by the labour movement through a mature revolutionary process but rather by military means. This meant that the evolution of that process would be conditioned and limited by the particular circumstances in which the conflict took place. The international situation, centred on the struggle to control or change the capitalist world system, was also of primordial impor-tance from the very beginning of this struggle. This was because both sides were dependent, not only on their own armed factions but also on the military assis-tance of foreign countries. The 'lyrical view of subversion' had imagined the struggle culminating in a great cataclysm which would mark the beginning of an era of bliss, but things had to be modified according to circumstances. In reality, there is nothing strange about this, because all of the 'great' revolutions in history have taken place in adverse circumstances.[2]

These adverse circumstances were barely perceptible during the 'glorious days' of July in Barcelona when, having defeated the military insurgents, the most militant sectors of the CNT and the FAI remained armed. The events in the capital of Catalonia are of such notoriety that today's historian could well be overwhelmed by the abundance of source material. Contemporary accounts of the events and subsequent historiography have left a compendium of distortions, misrepresentations and exaggerations. It will be useful to begin by developing a more nuanced analysis of some of the more conventional visions and common-places. This will allow an understanding of the reality lying beneath that revolutionary storm which began in the summer in Catalonia and spread with unstoppable force through the territory of Aragon.

The first distortion consists in reducing the events of July 1936 in Barcelona to a confrontation between the rebellious army and the working class, which, it is supposed, was entirely organised by the unions of the CNT. Against this vision, there is considerable evidence that only the most committed activists and some of the leadership went on to the streets to fight alongside the loyal sectors of the security forces against the insurgents. The famous people at arms appeared after-wards, when the uprising had been defeated. This was when the streets filled with striking men and women who on 19 and 20 July had stayed in their homes, terrified by the shooting and the gravity of the situation. This was also the moment when the legend began to be cultivated of those who manned the barri-cades, of those who freed Barcelona from the fascist army, and, of those who witnessed Francisco Ascaso fall during the assault on the Ataranzas barracks. He was the first martyr of those days, and would be immortalised in hundreds of posters with his innocent adolescent face.[3]

This victory of the anarchists at the head of the working people left a second vision to posterity. This was the image of a delegation of the CNT–FAI answering the call of President Companys, 'armed to the teeth ... with torn shirts and dirty with smoke and dust'. The President was 'moved' as he received them and told them that, although in the past they had never been treated as they deserved, 'today you are the masters of the city and of Catalonia because you alone have beaten the fascist army. If you do not need me, or if you do not want me as President of Catalonia', Companys is said to have added, 'tell me now and I will become one more soldier in the struggle against fascism'. And the CNT and the FAI, who had beaten fascism in the towns and in the streets, and who had political power at their feet, 'decided in favour of collaboration and democracy, renouncing revolutionary totalitarianism ... and the anarchist dicta-torship of the Confederation'. They were capable of 'obtaining everything' but abandoned this ambition in an act of 'libertarian ethics'.[4]

If we leave to one side the enthusiastic atmosphere of the moment, the account takes on different nuances. In the first place, anarcho-syndicalism had been undergoing a process of reorganisation since the elections in February and was searching for a way out of the crisis in which it found itself submerged. It is obvious that this new direction being undertaken by the anarcho-syndicalist movement was interrupted by the military uprising. That is to say, all these changes came about not as the result of an intensification of the class struggle, but rather because of an outside event with unforeseen consequences. The power vacuum which followed the defeat of the military uprising called for an organised response in the streets and in the factories, on the war front and in the institutions. But there were so many alternatives opening up that few anarcho-syndicalists grasped the gravity of the approaching situation. This chapter will deal specifically with the purifying violence which reigned during the summer of 1936, the social and political transformation which accompanied it and the creation and organisation of the militias which were always held to be the chief manifestation of the new, people's order.

'Proven' fascists have to be assassinated, declared *Solidaridad Obrera* on 1 August 1936. 'Proven' or not, in these first weeks, the purifying torch was applied to conservative politicians, army officers, property owners, the bourgeoisie, busi-nessmen, the clergy, workers who were known in the factories for their moderate views, Catholics, technicians and the heads of personnel in various industries. Before building the new, it was necessary to eliminate the root of social evil and those responsible for it. Blood was spilt by the numerous committees of industry, the neighbourhoods and of committees of the people, and by the 'groups of investigation and vigilance' who were charged with cleaning the atmosphere of 'unhealthy' elements, and all 'in the name of the public good'. Anyone could carry a pistol at that time, in the streets and in the factories.

The anarchist press took it upon itself to remind the people how necessary the spilling of blood was in the consolidation of the revolution against the enemy. Detailed chronicles were published of those victims who were well known. This was the case with generals Goded and Fernández Burriel who were shot at Montjuich castle on 12 August 1936. This was the same spot in which Francisco Ferrer y Guardia had been shot in 1909 and where hundreds of anarchists had been imprisoned and tortured since the beginning of the nineteenth century. A hundred officers and officials from the Barcelona barracks, who had taken part in the uprising, were sentenced to death by the popular tribunals between September 1936 and January 1937 and then shot by firing squad. According to García Oliver (Minister of Justice from November 1936 until May 1937), before the inauguration of these 'revolutionary' tribunals, the 'expedient practice of justice' through which quarrels were resolved, hatred was satisfied. and revenge obtained had been what became known as the 'paseo' (to be taken for a walk). García Oliver's own description of this method leaves little doubt as to its meaning:

> Given that the military uprising had been carried out by the class which historically has imposed public order, it had broken with all social constraints. In the attempt to restore the legal equilibrium, therefore, the spirit of justice returned to its most remote and purest origin, *the people, vox populi, suprema lex*. Whilst the situation of abnormality lasted, the people created and applied its own law and procedure. This was the 'paseo'.[5]

During the first weeks of the war, therefore, the 'hunt for the fascists', the defence of the revolution and the persecution of adversaries were inextricably linked in practice and it was very difficult to find the dividing line. This violence began with those who had participated in the rising against the Republic. It continued as an urgent task in the repression of the counter-revolution and ended up as a question of revolutionary law and order. The moment had finally arrived in which the people would shake off their chains and many participated with enthusiasm in this extremist rhetoric. The anti-fascist committee of Ascó in the province of Tarragona, which assumed judicial duties as did the other revolutionary and militia committees, respected the individual who belonged to the collective within this new situation and 'worked with enthusiasm towards this end'. On the other hand, they applied 'the justice which they deserved' to those who fell under the ambiguous accusation of 'being prominent figures'. Examples of this sort were common across the territory of Catalonia during the autumn of 1936. From that moment on, the reprisals and the 'acts of individual terrorism', as Joan Peiró called them, decreased until they had almost completely disappeared following the events of May 1937. More than half of the 8,360 assassinations that took place in Catalonia were carried out in the period up to 30 October 1936 and the figure had reached 6,400 by the end of the year. A third of the victims were killed in Barcelona. However, if the number of assassinations is placed in relation to the number of inhabitants, then the repression was greater and more intense in the agrarian counties of the interior than in the more industrialised coastal regions.[6]

This purifying fire enveloped the clergy with particular virulence. The public burning of images and sacred objects of religious worship, the use of churches as stables and stores, the melting down of church bells for the production of ordnance, the suppression of religious services, the assassination of both the secular and ordinary clergy, the exhumation of monks and nuns were narrated and publicised at home and abroad, in all its gory detail. In reality, all this anti-clerical practice signified not so much an attack on religion as much as an attack on the specific institution of the Catholic church. The church was supposed to be intimately involved with the rich and powerful. The acts of profanity against religious images were not intended to destroy the power of the sacred symbols (for the iconoclast they had none), but rather to demonstrate their 'uselessness' and the impotence against the attacks they were suffering. However, for many, the incredulous included, it represented a profound disruption to their habits and in their perception of the social order.

An aggressive attitude and ethical reproaches had been common elements in the anti-clericalism of the republicans, socialists and anarchists from the beginning of the century and these were now put into practice. Furthermore, the typical accusations that the clergy were idle, narrow-minded parasites, opposed to the progression of enlightened thought and human liberty, and the criticism of their 'perverse morality' and terrestrial influence were repeated obsessively, as if to justify the slaughter which had already begun. *Solidaridad Obrera* attempted to allay the fears of the petit bourgeois over the possible excesses of the revolution, but made no concessions on the issue of the clergy. 'The religious orders must be dissolved. The bishops and cardinals must be shot. And ecclesiastical wealth must be expropriated.' Obviously, by the time the public of Barcelona had read this front-page headline, on 15 August 1936, the majority of convents had already been ransacked and burnt down, and many of their inmates assassinated, sometimes in collective massacres. More than a thousand regular and secular clergy met their end in this way in Catalonia. Lleida came second, behind Barbastro with the second highest number of assassinations in all of Spain, two regions in which the passing militia left its mark. This issue will be taken up again when we come to examine the part played by the militia in the revolutionary bloodshed that spread over the eastern counties of Aragon.[7]

Leaving anti-clericalism and class repression aside, there were other issues in play during these first weeks. The first was the need to guarantee the continued economic functioning of industry and commerce, which was in turn a guarantee that the workers would continue to be paid. Many workers began to return to their posts from 21 July onwards and, by the end of the month, the initial confusion was at an end, although it would be inaccurate to say that the situation had been normalised. Many owners, managers, technicians and line-managers had been assassinated, had disappeared or were in hiding. The old factory committees, in which the CNT was often the principal organisation, became the 'workers committees of control' and, often without calling a meeting in order to discuss the arrangements for the immediate future, took possession of the factories. Whether or not there was a radical break with the existing economic order was often a case of whether or not there were technicians and managers who had remained behind. The most detailed studies of this process suggest that there were serious conflicts between the sector of manual workers, in which anarcho-syndicalism was predominant, and with those groups from offices and workshops who were affiliated to the UGT and, above all, to the Autonomous Association of Commercial and Industrial Employees (CADCI).

Contrary to what has often been supposed, and been written in the anarchists' own theoretical elaborations on the society of the future, the leadership committees of the CNT were more concerned, in the initial stages, with combating counter-revolution than collectivising the means of production. In other words, 'they concentrated on questions of political and military order and neglected the task of co-ordinating the revolutionary situation as a whole which had emerged on 19 July'. Instead of developing their own alternative or offering concrete suggestions for a new economic organisation of industry and commerce, they joined the new structures of power or the government institutions which already existed. They joined the Central Committee of Anti-fascist Militias on 21 July, the Economic Council of the Generalitat on 11 August and the government on 26 September. The importance of this gradual incorporation of anarcho-syndicalism into government bodies in collaboration with other political forces should not be underestimated and it played an important role in the attempt to overcome the initial chaos. Nevertheless, it is less obvious that, during these first months, there existed dual power, comprising the Generalitat and CNT–FAI, or even a triple power of the Generalitat, the Militias Committee and the Neighbourhoods Committees. The power vacuum which had emerged in the wake of the military uprising gave rise to much more than this. It was a cauldron of armed forces which were difficult to control. In reality, the only people who were truly marginalised in this initial process were the various industry unions. They had received an avalanche of new affiliates following the decree of 10 August on obligatory membership, and had to adapt their old methods to a situation of social change dominated by these powerful armed groups.[8]

Nevertheless, these groups were not the most suitable for the organisation of a programme of collectivisation capable of bettering the living conditions of the workers. It is worth emphasising once more that, since its very foundation, different ideas had circulated within the CNT about how best to organise the activities of the working class in order to combat capitalism and the state and construct the basis of a new egalitarian society. In spite of this heterogeneity of ideology, which had been the cause of more than one split, the CNT had managed to survive and consolidate itself as a movement of social protest against the established order. Once the bourgeois class enemy had evaporated and the arms had been distributed amongst those willing to take them up, the CNT had to take important decisions. These involved something more than the elimination of the adversary or the aesthetic change which the red and black flag brought with it, as it was unfurled over the countryside and on buses and trains. As far as the organisation and management of the collectivised economy was concerned (an issue which will be dealt with in the next chapter), the anarcho-syndicalist organisation was often obliged to participate in the initiatives of technicians and employees of the administration. That is, they had to collaborate with labour sectors they had always regarded as adversaries. Given the lack of experience of their activists and leaders in these affairs, which had never formed any part of their union practice, it would have been very difficult to do otherwise.

Of what, then, did the revolution consist? It consisted of the radical elimination of the symbols of power, be they military, political, economic, cultural or ecclesiastical. It consisted of the overthrow of the existing order and of a state where there was no longer a master to serve. The bourgeoisie had been rounded up and forced to adopt the workers' style clothing if they wanted to save their lives. The revolution consisted in purifying the atmosphere and applying the scalpel to the sick organs of the body politic. In sum, the revolution consisted of fomenting an aggressive rhetoric everywhere, a rhetoric about a society without classes, without parties and without a state. It was not that the CNT did not want to conquer power and 'go for everything'. Power consisted of its activists, in the people. During the initial stages, whilst this euphoria of the armed vigilante committees lasted, with inspection patrols and columns leaving for the front, it seemed as if the CNT was, according to the expression which the anarchists loved so much, 'the undisputed master' of Catalonia. 'The factories, commerce, the banks, the shops, houses, weapons and public order, everything was under its control.'[9]

George Orwell, who had recently arrived in Barcelona in December 1936, found the atmosphere of the city 'exciting and overwhelming ... It was the first time I had ever been in a town where the working class was in the saddle.' The buildings were covered with red and black flags. The churches had been ransacked and the shops and cafés had been collectivised:

> Waiters and shop-walkers looked you in the face and treated you as an equal. Servile and even ceremonial forms of speech had temporarily disappeared. Nobody said 'Señor' or 'Don' or even 'Usted'; everyone called everyone else 'Comrade' and 'Thou', and said 'Salud!' instead of 'Buenos Dias' ... The loud-speakers were bellowing revolutionary songs all day and far into the night ... In outward appearance, it was a town in which the wealthy classes had practically ceased to exist. Except for a small number of women and foreigners there were no 'well dressed' people at all. Practically everyone wore rough working class clothes, or blue overalls or some variant of the militia uniform.

However, these were only appearances: 'I did not realise that great numbers of well-to-do bourgeois were simply lying low and disguising themselves as proletarians for the time being.'[10]

The CNT also experienced this wakening up to the reality of the situation when they realised that they were not alone. There were also the left republicans, the former tutors and defence lawyers of many of their activists who could not be eliminated. They were forced to recognise that they were far from being the undisputed masters of the anti-fascist movement, and even less so the sole holders of power. The break with the past in the factories and in the political institutions was less, however, than appearances suggested. The much-debated political 'collaboration' was a necessary condition for the participation of working-class power in anything more than an armed presence on the streets. In sum, it was necessary to create 'a tactical discipline and a unified rhythm of propaganda', and to begin to 'think politically' in order to 'establish a collective position' on the revolution and the war.

A discourse and practice of this type, which underlined order, discipline and the need to win the war, was at odds with the initial revolutionary rhetoric. As will be seen in the following chapter, it caused controversy and heated debate about the militias, about the army and about power itself, and provoked serious internal conflict, especially over the control of *Solidaridad Obrera* and the committees. This conflict increased in intensity until it culminated in the bloody battle of May 1937. However, while all of this was taking place, and before the winter had begun to freeze revolutionary energies, things seemed much as Orwell described them. This image continued to be repeated subsequently to the point of abuse, by publicists, historians and film directors. According to this schematic vision of the beginning of the Civil War in the republican zone, which is commonly accepted by both critics and apologists, the trade-union organisations rapidly converted their reaction to the military coup into a 'spontaneous revolution' in which the people worked in complete freedom and destroyed all of the symbols of social hierarchy, killing their political and class enemies. Factories and land were collectivised, wages were the same for all workers and the militias were established. The anarchists were behind this chaotic scene, even though no one directed it.[11]

Nevertheless, in order to consolidate this revolution, it was essential to ensure armed control and extend this to other areas. For that reason, some of the first decisions taken were to constitute the Central Committee of Anti-fascist Militias, on 21 July, and to send columns to liberate Zaragoza from the 'fascist beast'. According to the anarchist literature, this was the birth of a model organisation of revolutionary power. In reality, during the first two months of its existence it did little or nothing to 'order' the economic and political activities of Catalonia. Rather, its directives were aimed at the creation of mechanisms of control and revolutionary order, the recruitment and training of the militia (in which García Oliver and Abad de Santillán played an outstanding role) and running of the 'unified command' of operations in the territory of Aragon. To this end, there was created a War Committee for the Aragón front, made up of three CNT members (Buenaventura Durruti, Antonio Ortiz and Cristóbal Aldabaldetrecu), a representative of the UGT (Joaquín del Barrio), one from the POUM (Jordi Arquer) and six military assessors: Franco Quinza, Colonel Villalba, Lieutenant-Colonel Joaquín Blanco, Major Reyes and Captains Medrano and Menéndez. In practice, each column had a 'central committee' and the multiplicity of powers therein totally belied all talk of 'unified command'.[12]

Nothing could be more mistaken than this conventional vision of thousands and thousands of militia ready to take the road to Aragon in order to fight fascism. The photographs and documents of the epoch show us multitudes applauding them as they left. However, it would seem that there were not that many who, inspired by the speeches of their leaders, mounted the trucks with rifles on their shoulders and their clenched fists raised. It is, however, impossible to calculate the total number of militiamen who left Barcelona along with the loyal sectors of the army. The anarchist sources give figures of 20,000 and 30,000 men recruited gradually to cover the entire front in Aragon. According to the Francoist military historian Colonel José Manuel Martínez Bande, there were 15,000 'men' who 'invaded' this region. Astronomical figures have been given for the 'Durruti' column, which was the first to leave in the direction of Zaragoza. Two years later, Abad de Santillán confessed that 'in spite of the enthusiasm, the column was not as big as we had imagined. It had been calculated that a column of 12,000 men would begin the attack on Zaragoza in those days. The column left with 3,000 men'. The 'Ascaso' column, which was so named in honour of the first martyr and led by one of his brothers, Domingo, and Cristóbal Aldabaldetrecu, left in the middle of August with many fewer. The (exaggerated) number, 1,900, were said to have joined the last column to leave at the end of the month, 'Los Aguiluchos' (The Young Eagles), led by García Oliver and the other leaders of the FAI from the 'Nosotros' group: Ricardo Sanz, Aurelio Fernándes, García Vivancos and Severino Campos. The remaining CNT columns, 'Hierro' (Iron), 'Ortiz', 'Carod', the PSUC's 'Karl Marx' led by Trueba and Barrio, and the POUM's 'Lenin' column led by Josep Rovira, all had smaller numbers.[13]

In this initial scenario, of militias leaving for the war front, women, who are normally marginalised in history and by historians, were able to play an important role in what seemed to be a rupture with the dominant cultural norms. The revolution and the anti-fascist war generated a new discourse and a different image of women. This was perfectly obvious in the propaganda and war slogans which transformed the usual representation of women. Those which defined women as the 'perfect wife' and the 'angel of the home' gave way, in the heat of the revolutionary enthusiasm of the first weeks, to those of the militiawoman. They were depicted in numerous posters as attractive young women in a blue uniform and with a rifle on their shoulders, marching decisively towards the front in search of the enemy.

During these first moments, the image of the militiawoman, as an active and belligerent heroine, who was strong and courageous, became the symbol of Spanish mobilisation against fascism. If the rejection of the 'bourgeois suit' was a symbol of political identification for men, 'for women the wearing of trousers or a uniform took on a profound meaning, given that women had never before adopted these masculine styles of dress' which challenged traditional female stereotypes. However, the militiawomen who dressed like the men and demanded equality with them were a small minority. They were members of the CNT, or the sisters and wives of activists and were not representative of the female population. The majority of female workers rejected this style of dress and, needless to say, it did not elicit much sympathy amongst the men. War was a very serious thing which was not to be confused with carnival, it was said, for example in the *Diari oficial del Comité Antifeixista i de Salut Pública de Badalona* (the official newspaper of the Anti-Fascist and Public Safety Committee) on 3 October 1936.

In reality, this aggressive image of women formed part of the spirit of revolutionary adventure, which was present during the summer of 1936. It disappeared very quickly to be replaced by the slogan 'men to the front and women in the rearguard', which was more in keeping with the traditional roles which both sexes were assigned in the war effort. Following the initial revolutionary shake-up, the exaltation of maternity and the right of mothers to defend their children from the brutality of fascism became a much more powerful form of female mobilisation. From September 1936 onwards, with Largo Caballero already Prime Minister, a policy began to be adopted in which women were obliged to abandon the war front. By the end of the year, the posters and propaganda with militiawomen had disappeared and by the beginning of 1937 those heroines with their blue uniforms were already history. As far as is known, none of the female organisations, not even 'Free Women', publicly resisted these decisions, taken by men, which forced women to abandon the armed struggle. All of these organisations, concludes Mary Nash in the best study available on the subject, saw themselves forcibly integrated into female work on the production line of the rearguard as 'an essential component of victory in the war'.[14]

Emphasis on the strength and heroism of the men was unnecessary. In accordance with the cultural norms then in force, courage and virility were something that armies had in abundance, and in this sense the militia was no exception. Similarly courageous and virile were all those who had taken up arms against fascism. It is no coincidence that the main leaders of the militia columns, from Durruti to Ricardo Sanz (who succeeded Durruti as leader of the future 26th division after his death), and including Antonio Ortiz, Cipriano Mera and Gregorio Jover (who later took command of the 28th Division – the Ascaso column), were all 'men of action' and members of the principal anarchist groups of the FAI during the Second Republic. It is also hardly surprising that another 'man of action' such as García Oliver (who did not in fact spend too much time at the front) should use his memoirs to berate 'intellectuals' such as Alaiz, Carbó and Abad de Santillán who spent much time writing, accusing them of contributing little of use with the pen and of being incapable of taking up arms against fascism.[15]

After the defeat of the military insurgents in Barcelona, Tarragona, Castellón and Valencia, those who had taken up arms entered deeply into Aragon with the columns, intent on recovering the three large towns, Huesca, Zaragoza and Teruel, which had been occupied by the forces of the V Division since 19 July. Within the ranks of these columns were to be found the remnants of the army who had remained loyal and of the police who had not rebelled in the cities of Catalonia and the Valencian Region, militant workers affiliated to the CNT unions in these regions and Aragonese peasants recruited in the towns through which the columns passed. They never achieved their main objective as their advance was stopped when they reached the outskirts of each of Huesca, Zaragoza and Teruel. Nevertheless, they dominated a considerable expanse of territory. Within this territory they spread the revolutionary message of expropriation and collectivisation to rural communities whose people, customs and way of life they hardly knew. With the exception of Saturnino Carod, no activist of the CNT in Aragon accepted a position of command in these armed groups. From the very start there was a clear division of labour between the leaders of the CNT from Aragon and those from Catalonia. The former, trade unionists from Zaragoza who had managed to escape the brutal repression begun by the army in that city, took charge of the formation of unions, the organisation of local committees and the initiation of the process of collectivisation. The CNT activists from Catalonia took charge of the columns and of the armed defence of the revolutionary order which these had installed. Aragon was a 'conquered territory' in which the 'liberated people' had to assist 'with their economic sacrifice, the sacrifice of blood made by the fighters'. In exchange, 'the humble, the disinherited and the pariahs' would achieve well-being for the first time in their lives. As will be seen, this supposed union between the 'conquering army' and the 'liberated people' caused mayhem more than once.[16]

When, on 24 July 1936, the first militia column left Barcelona, the military rebels from the Vth Division and the Civil Guard had already imposed their armed control over the principal urban centres of Aragon, with the exception of Barbastro. Within a few days, the advance of the militias modified this situation. With a few exceptions, there was no fighting. Far from Zaragoza and without being able to receive military assistance, the Civil Guard were forced to retreat towards the Aragonese capital. By the middle of August 1936, the front line had already been established in Aragon with its population and its territory divided into two zones. The areas with the greatest density of population and the most important urban centres would be controlled by the military insurgents. The republican zone included the principal mining areas and several large towns, but lacked control of the important industrial centres. This sharp division also affected the union organisations. The areas with the highest density of socialists remained under the control of the rebels, whose authorities undertook the systematic extermination of UGT activists. On the other hand, those areas in which the CNT was best organised, with the important exception of Zaragoza itself, fell within the republican zone. Over and above the influence of the militias in the origin and development of the revolution, this isolation of the UGT should be taken into consideration. This allows an understanding of why the anarcho-syndicalists were initially unopposed as they developed their policies for the transformation of the old social and economic structures.

The effects of the advance of these armed groups was immediate. Under their protection, anti-fascist committees (also known as committees of defence or revolution) were created in all of the towns with the intention of filling the power vacuum, managing the economy and political situation, and maintaining the new order. In those localities in which CNT unions already existed, their leading activists assumed the important tasks of revolutionary committees. The most important examples were to be found in the areas of Valderrobres, Alcorisa, Fraga and Monzón. Some liberal middle-class republicans, conscious of the impossibility of continuing with the preceding regime, participated in the organisation of these committees. However, their principal instigators were peasants who had emigrated to Barcelona in the 1920s (where they had began their union activities), leaders of the CNT from Aragon, a few teachers and veteran anarchists attached to the most radical tendencies within Catalan anarcho-syndicalism. The authority of the militias, on the other hand, was felt more in those towns where the CNT had no unions before the military uprising. In Pina de Ebro, for example, authority was initially held by the war committee of the 'Durruti' column. They appointed a defence committee, 'in agreement with the members of the committee controlling the column', and took control of the town hall, the houses and the 'property of the fascists', destroyed the property register and began the 'return' of land to the peasants. Adolfo Ballano, who maintained close relations with Aragonese anarchists during the 1920s, when he collaborated with the Zaragoza paper *Voluntad*, was the delegate of the column responsible for the organisation of a trade union of various professions and the control of the revolutionary committee. By September 1936 there already existed a union 'with six hundred members' in the town, a popular and cultural *ateneo* and a committee composed of locals from the neighbourhood. Its secretary Juan Arís, however, was a political delegate from one of the groups of the 'Durruti' column.[17]

The combined action of the militias and the committees unleashed a bloody purge. There seemed to be no escape for the large-scale property owners, the *caciques*, the right and those who had supported the uprising. Some were able to flee. Others remained in the towns and, whilst awaiting better times, declared their acceptance of the new revolutionary order. Others were given no option and were assassinated. It was undoubtedly a struggle against both people and symbols. Monographic studies on Cretas, Ibieca (small rural communities) and Caspe (the place with most inhabitants in the republican zone of Aragon) show that there were specific criteria applied in the choice of victims, and this was not as arbitrary as has been assumed. It seems clear today that there was no reason to shoot a priest, someone who had taken arms against the Republic or a property owner who had made his fortune from the labour of his neighbours. However, in the circumstances of the time, many thought that their liquidation was both necessary and just. It was a response to the numerous assassinations carried out by the military in the other zone and was also the consequence of the accumulated hatred against them. What the Republic had failed to achieve with its legal reforms, the war and the revolution would implement by force of arms.[18]

The principal target of this hostility were the shopkeepers, the small industrialists, the comfortable rural proprietors, activists in the most conservative political organisations and affiliates of the Catholic unions. Moreover, political affiliation and class were not the only cause of persecution. Old personal accounts, quarrels and family feuds were settled, in a process which meant for some the beginning of a radical transformation of which they had dreamt and waited for. For others it was a traumatic blow to the 'social peace' which had been guaranteed through neighbourhood links and the relations of subordination and affection with their masters. There are, as can be seen, very different visions of these events. Those who won the war cultivated a coarse, but effective legend around these strange militiamen who spoke Catalan, requisitioned everything and arrested decent people, 'bastards of unknown fathers, men dressed only in underpants and socks ... convicts, Jews and foreigners, all thirsty for Christian blood, hungry for dark Aragonese female flesh, eager for booty and pleasure'. This vision was in no way shared by the leaders of the columns. They were proud of their status as workers, and of having carried out a restraining role in the midst of so much incitement to violence on the part of the very inhabitants of these towns who pointed an accusing finger at their neighbours in order that someone more audacious might finish them off.[19]

We now come back to fire as a symbol of the destruction of the old, of purification and an obligatory stage on the way to the new life.

> The churches were burning. A great pile was then made with all of the documents from the Municipal Archive. It is still burning and will be for days. The property register was also completely burnt. The red and black flag fluttered gloriously over these good things.

So wrote the correspondent of *Solidaridad Obrera* in Hijar (Teruel) on 6 August 1936. And it would appear that this was not merely a rhetorical description. According to testimonies which have been collected, the same story was repeated in many towns and the marks can still be seen. The militiamen, along with the locals, collected the images and objects of religious worship from the houses. They entered the churches with horses, threw the statues of saints to the floor and dragged them into the town square. There they piled them up, 'saints on top of saints', next to the other objects of worship, the municipal and ecclesiastical documents and the property registers, and 'when evening came they set the pile on fire'.

All churches were closed for services and converted into markets, store houses, hostels for militiamen, prisons, dance halls, public canteens or garages. The parish houses were used as living quarters for politicians and army officers, as cultural centres or as offices for the revolutionary committees. There was less violence against the clergy than in Catalonia or the Valencian region, and lower percentages of victims, with the exception of Barbastro where 87 per cent of the priests and almost all of the regular clergy were assassinated. None of the female clergy suffered this fate, although they were obliged to abandon the convents and give up the cloth, after which they were assigned to social work or domestic service.[20]

The beginning of collectivisation in the countryside was also caught up in the heated atmosphere of the summer of 1936. Collective cultivation was organised principally on land which had been abandoned by its owners or on the estates requisitioned directly by the armed groups of the revolutionary committees. Evidently, coercion was greatest in those areas which the columns had chosen as their centre of operations. The need to supply the militias established along a long battle front required production and consumption to be organised on different lines from those habitually adopted and this led to the exhaustion of the already weak economy of many towns. Even those who professed unbreakable faith in the capacity of collectivisation to abolish inequality had to face this reality. This was a war and, as *El Frente*, the paper of Durruti's column, pointed out, 'it is a natural law that armies live off of the land they have conquered'. A proclamation, signed by Durruti himself in Bujaraloz on 11 August 1936, abolished the private property of 'the large landowners'. It claimed as 'property of the people', under the control of the revolutionary committees, 'all the equipment for cultivation, tractors, machines, threshers, etc., of the fascist proprietors', and demanded the 'enthusiastic and unconditional, material and moral' support of the local citizens for 'the armed struggle of the anti-fascist militias which was safeguarding the vital interests of working people'.[21]

It would be inaccurate, in light of this, to describe the process as 'spontaneous'. However, it would also be inaccurate to suggest that the peasants directly rejected collectivisation. There were distinct groups within this sector of society, with very different interests, and for some of them the revolutionary situation which began in July 1936 raised tremendous expectations. If the available sources are accepted, those with the lowest standards of living showed greater willingness to take advantage of collectivisation. The land-less labourers and the very poor owners who did so bettered their standard of living and, above all, gained power and dignity. This same power and dignity was lost by the comfortable owners, patriarchs and owners of the best houses in the towns, who were deprived of that authority, autonomy and the control of production which they had enjoyed as the principal beneficiaries of the pre-war social order.

Many anarcho-syndicalists believed that with the destruction of established legality and this change of property relations, the revolution was already a reality. The events of July 1936 had, in fact, brought about rapid growth of CNT membership. In Catalonia and the eastern half of Aragon, long-standing CNT activists now imagined themselves to be the absolute masters of the situation. They were no longer 'disinherited' prison fodder, or the favourite target of reaction and the government. Now the people, that is to say they themselves, were armed and no one could stop them. Everyone wanted a CNT membership card. With so many people avid for fresh news on the war and the revolution, *Solidaridad Obrera*, which was distributed free during the first days in Barcelona, reached its apogee. Its circulation shot up from 31,000 copies at the beginning of July to more than 70,000 a few days after the military uprising and 150,000 by the end of August.[22]

Nevertheless, no matter how radical and destructive it might appear in the summer of 1936, the revolution had only just begun. The events which followed showed that the skies were not quite so clear. The breach opened by the revolutionaries with the victory in Barcelona could not be extended, even to Zaragoza. For a few weeks, all political organisations appeared to approve of the form of expression which popular power was taking and the overthrow of the old order. It soon became clear, however, that the revolutionary process, or that which others defined as a struggle against fascism within a civil war, was first and foremost a struggle for political and military power. It was a struggle for the control of arms and the changes they brought about, to reconstruct the state which had been weakened by the uprising and popular pressure. The anarcho-syndicalists' inability to use their scattered and diverse revolutionary powers in a coherent way to pursue an overall policy condemned them, from the autumn or 1936 onwards, to become second-rank protagonists. They joined the government only when the most important posts had already been filled. They improvised, with no clear programme, and were subordinated to the events of the war and attacked by multiple enemies, through all of which the revolution ran aground. Badly organised, even more poorly equipped and lacking in discipline, the militias languished until they were finally incorporated into the new army of the Republic. By the summer of 1937, no trace remained of those glorious July days of 1936. In less than a year the anarcho-syndicalist project had demonstrated its fragility. This was its golden age, but it was to be a short golden age, as we will see in the next chapter.

7 War and revolution

> Is the revolution to be carried out before the war, or does the war have to be won before it is possible to carry out the revolution? Both are abstract questions which have nothing to do with reality ... If the war is lost then all is lost, and for half a century or more there will be no discussion of the problem of the revolution.[1]

This thought, so exact in its foresight, was written by Helmut Rudiger, in May 1937, while his Spanish anarcho-syndicalist comrades were still trying to digest the bitter lessons of that month's events. Barely six months earlier, four CNT leaders had, for the first time in history, entered government, after having vainly tried all the possible alternatives. In spite of what was later said, this abandonment of their opposition to conventional politics, the anti-politicism that was one of the anarchist movement's identity marks, was not the cause of chain of disasters which befell it from the moment it took that fateful step. It might be argued that the price that the CNT had to pay for a few seats in the government far outweighed the meagre benefit gained through this collaboration. However, this is not what the majority of its leaders were weighing up in November 1936. Rather, once it became clear that this was a war and not a revolutionary carnival, it was, for them, a case of not leaving the mechanisms of state control in the hands of the other political organisations. It is true that some took longer than others to grasp this. However, there were very few illustrious names who advocated rejecting collaboration. The activists of the FAI and the '*treintistas*' of old were now united in the struggle to obtain the support necessary to put their new political convictions into practice. Those who did not support them and took different routes ended up dead, or defeated on the barricades raised on the streets of Barcelona in May 1937, after having been marginalised from the centres of decision-making.

Power

It all began in September 1936, a month in which the anarchist leaders were obliged to articulate a political solution to the serious problems raised by the military coup. And they were not alone. Until that moment, with the streets, the land and the factories in the hands of the workers' organisations, the republicans (who were responsible, according to some, for not having crushed the military rebellion) did not exercise any power, although, strangely enough, they were the only political groups in José Giral's government. After leaving the government in September 1933, Largo Caballero 'had promised himself that he would never again enter a coalition with the Republican parties'. Nevertheless, now, on 4 September 1936, he agreed to become prime minister of a new government (in which he would also be Minister of War) with a socialist majority, a republican minority, a representative of the Basque Nationalist Party and the participation, for the first time in the history of Spain, of two communist ministers. The CNT were still absent from the government. The leader of the UGT offered them a ministry without portfolio, small beer given the organisation's own estimation of its real power. It was not, therefore, a solution which pleased everyone. However, it seemed to be the only way to combat the collapse of the republicans, win the war and, at the same time, guarantee the revolutionary advances achieved so far. It was, in sum, the first success of those proposals which linked the outcome of the war to the achievement of an overt alliance with other European bourgeois democracies and with the Spanish middle classes who were loyal to the Republic, but extremely frightened of the revolution.[2]

The shift from a republican government, which did not govern anything, to another, led by the well-known leader of the rival union movement and one-time enemy, put the leaders of the CNT on their guard. They had not worried too much whilst the central government was composed of republicans. It was the 'same old bourgeoisie' whom they had scorned for their inability to stop the fascist advance. As long as the people were armed, what need was there to create new structures of power? What mattered was the political and military consolidation of the revolutionary changes which had been brought about in Catalonia, in the eastern half of Aragon, in the Valencian region and in extensive areas of Castilla la Mancha and Andalucia. This would obviously not be done by a phantom government, which was not even able to govern in Madrid. Nevertheless, the arrival of Largo Caballero in government, accompanied by the (not very revolutionary) socialists and the communists, changed matters and also obliged the CNT leadership to modify its rhetoric. From that moment on, the aim of the majority of the CNT leaders was to prevent other organisations using government power for their own benefit.

As might have been expected, the initiative was taken by the anarchists in Catalonia, where the events of July 1936 had given the CNT most influence. Following the defeat of the military insurrection, the organisation found itself in a situation very different from that described in the analyses of the republican years. The '*treintistas*', who had returned to the fold with Peiró at their head, could do nothing to advance their ideas. Their strategy of gradual consolidation had become irrelevant. The best-known anarchist leaders, those who had been expelled at the beginning of the Republic, were occupied at the front, involved with the Central Committee of Anti-Fascist Militias, or busy with other tasks of revolutionary 'cleansing'. The organisation was not, however, leaderless or left in the hands of second-rate activists. The strong man of the moment was the much-respected Mariano Rodríguez Vázquez, 'Marianet'. He was a young activist from the construction industry, born in 1909 and a member of the FAI. He could boast a curriculum of twenty-nine months in prison, the consequence of the six times that he had been detained during the republican years. He had been secretary of the Catalan Region of the CNT since June 1936 and had the support of people as diverse as García Oliver, Abad de Santillán and Federica Montseny. His rhetoric stressed the need for discipline and order which, without renouncing the profound radicalism of the changes already under way, would put an end to unco-ordinated initiatives. Given the structure of the anarchist organisation and the power that the numerous committees had acquired during the summer, this would be a difficult task. And there could be no better way to start than by shifting the orientation of the organisation towards objectives beyond those of the revolution, which it believed was already complete. Through persistent propaganda, the way was to be cleared for anarcho-syndicalist leaders to take up positions of government responsibility. As will be seen, Jacinto Toryho was the man chosen to develop this strategy, first from the CNT Press and Propaganda Office and then from the pages of *Solidaridad Obrera*.

What followed is already well known. On 13 September, *Solidaridad Obrera* began demanding the constitution of 'Regional Councils of National and Revolutionary Defence', which would be the 'genuine representatives of the people in arms'. Two days later, the General Assembly of the Regional Confederations was held in Madrid. At this assembly, there was discussion of the policy that the CNT should adopt, in the immediate future, towards the formation of a government by Largo Caballero. The delegation from Valencia (Domènec Torres, Juan López and Joan Montserrat) supported the idea of entering the government. The Catalan delegation (Francesc Isgleas, Federica Montseny and Mariano R. Vázquez) opposed it and insisted on the proposal already set out in the Barcelona newspaper. Following harsh confrontation, a commission was set up to report on the affair. The final resolution, which was drafted by Montseny, López and Aurelio Alvarez, from the regional confederation of Asturias, supported the Catalan anarcho-syndicalists on the main points. The report called for the 'constitution of a National Council of Defence composed, for the moment, of all the political sectors fighting against fascism'. There would be five representatives of the CNT, five from the UGT, four Republicans and Largo Caballero would be president. The remaining points supported the minimal programme of the CNT 'to assume functions of leadership in the areas of defence and of consolidation in the political and economic areas'.[3]

This resolution was initially presented as firm opposition to participation in government but, in reality, it aimed at the institutionalisation of a new political order via the creation of a stable governing body. However, it did not obtain the desired reception because Largo Caballero's government was already there to fulfil these functions. The differences between these two organisms were also patent. The CNT project excluded the communists. It basically converted the co-operation necessary within a broad-based and heterogeneous anti-fascist movement into a much narrower workers' alliance supported by the republicans. The exclusion of the communists was already impossible by 1936. The relegation of bourgeois forces meant returning to the ideas developed by Orobón Fernández at the beginning of 1934, to the agreement between the CNT and the UGT in Asturias in October of the same year, and to the 'Report on the Revolutionary Alliances' of the Zaragoza Congress. This was what the CNT believed, erroneously, that it had achieved, when it finally agreed to enter the government on 4 November 1936.

This controversy over the choice between the 'National Council of Defence' or government was what Horacio Martínez Prieto found when he arrived on the scene. The anarchists were unanimous in describing him as a 'grey' man, with no flair for meetings or as a public speaker. He had always been in favour of participation in government and this was 'a deeply held conviction'. Martínez Prieto had relinquished the post of secretary of the National Committee of the CNT following the Zaragoza Congress of May 1936, 'because of his complete disagreement with the resolutions adopted there, which he felt were completely out of touch with reality'. The National Committee transferred to Madrid on 18 June and, until a vote could be held on the appointment of a new secretary, the post was temporarily occupied by David Antona. Martínez Prieto was in the Basque Country when the military uprising began. When he was able to get to Madrid he resumed the post of secretary of the National Committee, although it is not known exactly who appointed him. He then undertook 'a systematic campaign to make the CNT take part in government'. At a further nation-wide General Assembly on 30 September, 'he attacked the project of a National Committee of Defence relentlessly' and 'set out once more his arguments in favour of the CNT's participation, pure and simple, in government'. The delegation from Catalonia continued to resist the idea and agreement was delayed. His son, César M. Lorenzo, later claimed that he had succeeded in having his point of view accepted at the General Assembly on 18 October, and that the CNT, therefore, approved of participation at ministerial level. In reality, however, *Solidaridad Obrera* continued to argue, on the 21st of that month, for the need to create a National Council of Defence.[4]

It seems obvious that, leaving aside the fact that the anarchists did not like the word 'government', Mariano R. Vázquez and the Catalan leaders simply wanted to obtain more advantages and benefits than Largo Caballero was willing to concede. The discourse of discipline and order, which Joan Peiró also supported from the pages of *Solidaridad Obrera* at that point, had already led them to enter the government of the Generalitat, the 'Council of the Generalitat', as they called it, on 26 September 1936. This had led to the disbanding of the Committee of the Militias, which was redundant now that a government existed 'in which all the trade union and Republican forces are represented' and which carried out all of the functions previously carried out by the Committee. Two months had passed since Lluís Companys had told those activists, 'armed to the teeth', that all power was in their hands and that if they so desired he would become 'one more soldier in the fight against fascism'. During these two months, the extreme manifestation of this revolutionary power had ended up being welcomed into a Catalan government run by republican nationalists.

The negotiations with Companys were carried out by Mariano R. Vázquez and, apparently, the CNT did not come out badly. It gained control of the Ministries of Economy (Juan P. Fabregas), of Supply (José J. Domènech) and of Health and Social Security (Antonio García Birlán). Garcia Oliver was general secretary of Defence, under Lieutenant-Colonel Felipe Díaz Sandino, whilst Aurelio Fernández and Dionisio Eroles occupied important posts in the management of the police and public order. In reality, the participation of the CNT was essential in order to legitimise the centralisation of power within Catalonia and the subsequent displacing of the multiple committees, which had conquered their place in the sun during the summer of 1936. Two decrees in October of that year, on the constitution of Municipal Councils and Collectivisation, cleared the way for the annulment of what the anarcho-syndicalists had considered to be their greatest revolutionary conquests. The one remaining issue, control of the police and public order, was dealt with in the street fighting of May 1937. By the end of June that year, the CNT had abandoned the government of the Generalitat.[5]

The last phase in the CNT's rise to positions of political responsibility took place on 4 November 1936, two months after the formation of Largo Caballero's government. The last days of October were taken up with 'haggling', between Martínez Prieto and Largo Caballero, over the exact number of ministries that the CNT was going to have. It was finally agreed that there would be four, although Largo Caballero maintained in his 'memoirs' that they had asked him for six. Following the secretary's proposal, the National Committee elected the four who would carry out this exalted mission. The unimportant details of whether, as might have been expected, it was difficult to convince Federica Montseny and García Oliver, whilst, unsurprisingly, Juan Peiró and Juan López accepted immediately, can be left aside. The fact of the matter is that the CNT sent four of its most outstanding leaders into government. It was also clear that these four names represented a balance between the two principal sectors that had struggled for supremacy within anarcho-syndicalism during the republican years, the '*treintistas*' and the FAI. With Pestaña out of the picture, Peiró and López were unquestionably the principal figures of that oppositional trade unionism which, having been expelled, had then returned to the bosom of the mother organisation. There is little to add on García Oliver, who symbolised the 'man of action', 'revolutionary gymnastics and the strategy of insurrection against the Republic. He had risen like froth since the revolutionary days of July in Barcelona. Federica Montseny, on the other hand, came from the CNT's Union of Liberal Professions, that is from a union which was always under suspicion in the worker-oriented rhetoric of the organisation. Her fame came via her family (she was the daughter of anarchists convinced of their own purity) and her pen. She had sharpened her literary skills during the Republic when, from the most intransigent of anarchist positions, she had attacked the '*treintista*' traitors. She would, moreover, become the first female minister in the history of Spain.[6]

The CNT was in government and, according to *Solidaridad Obrera* on 4 November, this was nothing less than a 'transcendental event':

> The government ... has ceased to be a force of oppression for the workers. Similarly, the state is no longer an organism which divides society into classes. And both will be even less oppressive with the participation of elements of the CNT.

The anarchist leaders had never said anything like this about a government and had never before placed their trust in the power of government action. However, war and the revolution had changed matters, or at least, so they believed at the time.

If the CNT's intention in joining the government was not to leave decision-making in the hands of others, then they had left it late. They accepted four ministries – Justice, Health, Commerce and Industry – which had little to do with questions affecting the state, the revolution or the war. The anarchists had to tolerate an agrarian policy with which they did not agree, and they were always excluded from decisions on military matters. Joan Peiró encountered serious obstacles in the application of his industrial policy in the Basque Country and Catalonia, which were precisely the areas in which the principal industries were located. It was here, and not in the decision to join the government itself, that the motives lay for what would later be described as a 'disaster'. They had decided on a course of action that they did not have the resources to carry out. Thanks to the collapse of the republican regime, the anarchists were participating in government through institutions which they themselves had created, the revolutionary committees, local councils of administration, regional and provincial councils of defence. However, when the moment arrived, they showed themselves to be incapable of transforming all of this into an overall programme. This incapacity was something that the other political forces both expected and desired. It was felt to be better to have them in government than outside it. That way they would come up against the harsh realities of power and war and would have to abandon their rhetoric and revolutionary extremism. And without that, the CNT would be nothing.[7]

Some reactions were less enthusiastic. However, there is not much indication of the CNT's entry into government opening up a breach between the leadership committees (who controlled media and propaganda, participated in various regional governments and set out the strategy) and the activists of the trade unions and collectives. If the available sources are examined in detail, there remains no doubt that the principal leadership groups (the National Committee and the regional committees in Catalonia, Valencia and Aragon) and the most influential organs of the press both favoured and accepted this step. The resistance of the 'grass roots' of the union, which is always assumed to have been more revolutionary than its reformist leaders, was minimal. And, as will be seen, what little resistance there was related much more closely to the consequences blamed on the decision than to the actual decision itself. In reality, the rupture of this broad agreement within the CNT, which became so dramatic after the war was over, began with the events of May 1937. It was only after the 'May days' that the collaboration in government began to be considered the greatest 'error' that the CNT had made, and for which the collaborationists were responsible. It was only after these events that the anarchist critique of power acquired particular virulence amongst small sectors of the 'Young Catalan Anarchists' and on the front in Aragon, and amongst groups such as 'The Friends of Durruti', who had already begun to display strong opposition to militarisation. All of those who later wrote memoirs and testimonies, from García Oliver to Federica Montseny and including Ricardo Sanz and Antonio Ortiz, joined this bandwagon. Entry into the government of Largo Caballero had come to be seen as the absolute renunciation of the movement's anti-political and revolutionary principles.[8]

Nevertheless, the opportunity to participate in government had not arrived at the best of moments. The very same day that it took place, Franco's troops arrived on the outskirts of Madrid, where the most decisive battle of the first phase of the war would take place. The government showed itself to be incapable of adequately organising the defence of the capital. On 6 November, at the first cabinet meeting in which the CNT ministers took part, it was decided that the seat of government should be moved from Madrid to Valencia. This hasty departure was carried out in secret and without giving any public explanation. It was seen as abandonment of responsibility and flight by public opinion. Before leaving, Largo Caballero ordered the formation of a Council of Defence which, under the presidency of General Miaja, would exercise authority over a besieged Madrid until 22 April 1937.[9]

On 10 November, *Solidaridad Obrera* expressed its support for the transfer of the government. A few days later, however, at the General Assembly of the Regional Confederations, some delegates expressed their indignation over the way in which this unpopular measure had been supported. Horacio Martínez Prieto was blamed for this abandonment of principles. However, it appears to have been the CNT ministers who were responsible as they had accepted a measure already decided upon by Largo Caballero. Being recently appointed, they felt that they had no authority to voice their opposition. The secretary of the National Committee resigned, or was forced to resign, and there are versions of the story to suit all tastes. Mariano R. Vázquez, the man in charge of the situation in the CNT in Catalonia, took Martínez's place. In his first circular to the various regional committees on 20 November, two days after the General Meeting, Vázquez asked for 'individual and collective discipline' during 'the phase of collaboration to which circumstances oblige us'. This very same day, Buenaventura Durruti died in Madrid. He had died in that undefended Madrid which his old comrades had abandoned. This was the final demonstration of his strength and of the weakness of those who had become entangled in the political game. This was the beginning of the legend of an activist, who had contributed little of importance to anarcho-syndicalism.[10]

Discipline had to start at home and *Solidaridad Obrera* was a fundamental pillar of the CNT home. However, discipline was not exactly one of the virtues of its

editor, Liberto Callejas. His fame as a bohemian who let everyone write whatever they wanted might have been useful during the republican years when he
had been editor of the paper from 1932–3. But at a time when it was necessary
to impose a rhetoric of order and the acceptance of collaboration, these were
hardly appropriate gifts. Taking advantage of his absence at the beginning of
November, while he was ill in a clinic in Seva, he was replaced by Jacinto
Toryho. This young journalist, born in 1911, was twenty-six years younger than
Callejas and had studied journalism at the Catholic newspaper *El Debate* under
the guidance of Angel Herrera, whom he always considered a good friend.
Toryho, under the protection of Mariano R. Vazquez, was the man charged
with the reorganisation of *Solidaridad Obrera* and its adaptation to the needs of the
new policy. He brought in new people, such as the outstanding Salvador
Cánovas Cervantes, the creator and editor of *La Tierra*. He also made use of
already well-known figures such as Montseny and Abad de Santillán, and side-
lined Callejas's group. Amongst the latter was Jaime Balius, an anarchist with a
radical Catalanist background who, as will be seen, channelled his discontent
(along with the groups of militiamen opposed to militarisation) into the formation of 'The Friends of Durruti'.

Toryho's first few months as editor were not peaceful ones. The Union of
Liberal Professionals, which was dominated by Callejas and Balius, accused him
of carrying out a policy opposed to the ideas of anarchism, and of surrounding
himself with 'suspect' journalists in order to expel the true anarchists. The
conflict emerged at the Special Congress of the Catalan Regional
Confederations of Workers, held in Barcelona at the end of February and early
March 1937. There, Mariano R. Vázquez defended Toryho and reminded the
congress of his work in the service of the political line set out by the leadership
of the CNT. Toryho, who had been designated editor without the vote of the
unions, was confirmed in his post by the block vote of 196 unions representing
305,354 affiliates. Almost 120,000 affiliates voted for Callejas and 47,850 for
Felipe Alaiz.

A few days later, on 28 March, the Conference of the Confederal and
Anarchist Press, which had been convened by *Solidaridad Obrera* and the
Propaganda Office, was held in the same city. The principal aim was to control
the press and this appeared as the first point on the agenda, under the heading
'Unitary voice in Propaganda and Doctrinal Positions'. Forty anarchist newspapers from throughout the Republican zone attended. Toryho and the
representatives of the National Committee of the CNT and the Peninsular
Committee of the FAI asked for propaganda to be oriented towards 'the unity of
action' and discipline. Only three papers, *Ideas* from Hospitalet de Llobregat,
Nosotros from Valencia and *Acracia* from Lleida refused, maintaining the line of
resistance on collaboration and criticising the leaders of the CNT and the FAI
for having betrayed their anarchist principles.[11]

Once the press had been brought into line, it was the turn of the militias. The
conflict over militarisation followed similar lines to that over the press. The
setbacks that the militias had suffered, after the first few months of euphoria,

and the entry of the CNT into Largo Caballero's government brought about a change of discourse. 'When it comes to serving the revolution we are the first to take a step forward', declared *Solidaridad Obrera* on 23 December 1936, in an attempt to convince the libertarian movement to accept militarisation as 'a necessity imposed by the war'. For anarchist leadership committees, militarisation was inevitable, if the aim was to continue the armed control of the new social order which, as had been clearly demonstrated, was hardly based on widespread popular acceptance. The only interest of the leaders, both in the rearguard and on the front, was to obtain advantages from militarisation. In other words, to make sure that the CNT lost as little as possible in the battle which had begun for the political control of the republican army. This had been the case from the moment that it became obvious that the militias, that superior force known as the 'people at arms', was useless in a long military campaign, and that the CNT's entry into government implied the conversion of the militias into a conventional army.

Things being so, it is not in the least surprising that this leadership group should suddenly become anxious to go along with the 'necessities imposed by the war'. Furthermore, the situation required the removal of that confusing network of committees, assemblies and general meetings which could impede rapid decisions. Employing the exceptional lucidity with which he grasped those events, Helmut Rudiger declared that:

> Union life is based on agreements and general assemblies and war is based on orders and obedience. There has to be a good system of military authority and political control. However, if we attempt to run the war on the basis of anti-authoritarian principles and general assemblies, then all is lost.[12]

'Federalism' and 'internal democracy' were thrown overboard. Leaders did not ask for opinions and imposed their own ideas 'without consulting those who suffered and fell at the parapet'. This was the final straw for some groups of militiamen. Those from the 'Iron Column' had been registering their protest through the pages of their paper *Linea de Fuego* and they now convened a general assembly of the confederal and anarchist columns. In spite of the fact that they did not, in theory, have the approval of the National Committee of the CNT, it was held in Valencia on 5 February 1937. Three distinct positions had started to emerge in the internal meetings and press since the previous autumn and these could now be heard amidst the intense and impassioned discussion. There was the discourse of discipline and order arguing that the circumstances of war forced beloved principles to be laid aside. In this respect the delegate of the National Committee pointed out that it was 'not an anarchist principle to take a gun and kill another human being either, yet look where we find ourselves'. Without militarisation there would be no arms for the CNT. The anti-militarist prejudices were of no use in circumstances in which a gun was worth a thousand words. What they had to ensure was that the militarisation took place 'on the basis that the command positions, whether of companies, battalions, brigades or divisions, remained under the control of comrades responsible to the organisation'. This position was also shared by the leaders of some of the columns such as Cipriano Mera and Feliciano Benito of the confederal militias of the Centre. However, they complained that this decision had been imposed from the rearguard, without consulting those who were giving their lives in the struggle against fascism. Finally, there was the intractable element who accused the leaders of the CNT of 'worrying too much about the war and too little about the revolution', of renouncing 'the enlightened human future' which the armed victory of the people had announced. 'Are we going to put up with ... the little officers who have been mass-produced in a couple of weeks in some military academy?'[13]

This was the final act in a debate which had already been decided. During the first months of 1937, the majority of the militiamen on the front in Aragon, where the final scenes of the resistance took place, were incorporated into the new army. By the middle of April, the process was completed whereby the armed columns from Catalonia and Valencia, which had reached deep into Aragonese territory, were militarised. Three anarchists, members of the 'Nosotros' group, took command of the three divisions still controlled by the CNT. Antonio Ortiz was commander of the 25th Division, Ricardo Sanz of the 26th, which had been formed from what had been the Durruti column, and Gregorio Jover was now in charge of the 28th Division, which had absorbed 'Los Aguiluchos' and what was left of the other CNT columns. The long front was shared with two other divisions. The 27th was formed from what had been the old 'Karl Marx' column and was now under the command of Antonio Trueba, and the POUM's 29th division was under the command of Josep Rovira. However, the militarisation did not end the struggle for political and military control, which had been under way in that territory since 1936. There were frequent clashes between the 27th Division and those under the control of the anarchists, and these reached a climax in August 1937 with the dissolution of the Council of Aragon and the dismantling of the collectives. As will be seen, the experience of the 29th Division was even more agitated. In the spring of that year it was accused of deserting the front and 'assisting' the plans of the 'fascists'. Rovira was imprisoned and the Division was disbanded.[14]

It was not difficult to escape militarisation in those sectors of the rearguard in which the influence of the CNT was still almost absolute. This was the case for those who took their anti-militarism as an inalienable identity mark, and also for those who opposed it because they felt that it threatened their positions of power. There were desertions from a number of columns such as those of 'Durruti' and 'Carod', and 400 men abandoned the 'Iron Column' when, in March 1937, it was militarised and converted into the 83rd Brigade. The shift from protest over militarisation to desertion was a cause for concern and difficult for the partisans of discipline to accept. All methods of persuasion failed and, short of armed conflict, there was no way to prevent it. Many of these deserters took up arms in the streets of Barcelona in May 1937. There they would finally discover that they had been left on their own.[15]

There was little trace left of the CNT's passage through government. They entered in November 1936 and left in May 1937 and achieved little in those six months. The symbolic significance of four anarchists participating in government has been remembered more than their actual legislative activity. As both the war and the revolution were lost, those ministers would never achieve a dignified place in history. And it could not be otherwise since, with the benefit of hindsight, all misfortunes were blamed on their break with the anti-political tradition. Within the collective memory of anarchism, defeated and in exile, that error and betrayal could only have dire consequences. All of the later anarchist literature which dealt with this question, left aside any analysis in order to unleash the familiar assault of ethical reproach. The revolution was placed on one side of the equation, where it was vigorous and sovereign, and on the other was its destruction, which had been achieved by the offensive carried out from above against the three pillars of revolutionary change: the militias, the revolutionary committees and the collectives. However, this settling of accounts with the past underestimates those aspects of that dramatic change of direction which brought with them both positive and much-needed elements. Both the revolution and war, which had not been provoked by the anarchists, had made necessary the articulation of a policy. This policy obviously had to deviate from the attitudes and doctrines historically identified with anarchism. They were positive because the defence of discipline and responsibility, which made the participation in government into one of their symbols, improved the situation in the rearguard. It helped prevent more useless bloodshed and mitigated the resistance which had been generated by the other maximalist strategy of radical confrontation with the republican institutions.

Obviously, an analysis of this type (in which historians avoid judgements of the doctrinal purity of the protagonists) also takes other forgotten facets into consideration. These might include the fact that it was a 'man of action' such as García Oliver who brought about the consolidation of the popular tribunals or the work camps in place of the 'bullet in the neck' for the 'fascist prisoners'. Or that a lifelong syndicalist such as Joan Peiró should have to take charge of intervention and requisitions in the war industry. Or, finally, that a woman should reach the pinnacle of political power, 'a position which had been absolutely denied to women until then and would be denied again for many decades afterwards'. This was a position from which she was able to undertake a preventive health and medical policy, combat venereal disease (one of the curses of the epoch) and begin a eugenicist reform of abortion which, in spite of advancing little further than a mere initiative, brought forward certain debates which are still current within Spanish society at the start of the twenty-first century.[16]

There remains little to add on the question, so often asked, of whether the anarchists could or should have opted for the imposition of a revolutionary dictatorship, instead of co-operating with the government of socialists, bourgeois republicans and communists. For the anarchists, the revolution represented the overthrow of the existing order and the destruction of all of its symbols. That was why they confused the first act of the revolutionary drama with its definitive consummation. Once they had realised that it would not all end in the streets of Barcelona, or in the fields of Aragon, that they were not alone, that not all industrial workers, and even less so the peasants, were CNT members, and that a revolution within, and subordinate to, a war did not leave any margin for choice, they were obliged to change their rhetoric and its practical application. The conquest of central power was impossible in the existing circumstances. Because it was obvious that the assault on that power, or the installation of a revolutionary dictatorship, would have to be brought about by the same means through which the existing legality had been overthrown, by force of arms. From Barcelona, the CNT had no chance whatsoever of achieving it. In Madrid, where both the combined action of the workers and the destruction of republican legality were impossible, the only option open was that which was taken. They joined the government in which were represented all of the political forces opposed to the military uprising. In reality, the institutionalisation of the revolution and the creation of a new political order, which would be the expression of those revolutionary changes, could be accomplished only in the eastern provinces of Aragon, during the few months in which the Council of Aragon existed.

That organ of regional government was formed on 6 October 1936 (at the General Assembly of the Trade Unions of Aragon held in Bujaraloz) with the express intention of putting an end to the excesses committed by the militias in those territories, of co-ordinating 'the needs of the war and the rearguard' and of controlling 'social, eonomic and political activities'. The first objective was never achieved because the representatives of the columns who attended the Assembly (leaders of the CNT in Catalonia) refused to give the Assembly decision-making power on issues concerning the war . As for the attempt to organise rural society according to anarchist principles, it is clear that more was achieved than their critics have been willing to recognise.[17]

The composition and capacities of the Council were decided at a meeting of the Regional Committe of the CNT in Alcañiz. Seven departments were created, all of which were occupied only by anarchists. Joaquín Ascaso, leader of the Zaragoza construction workers, was appointed as president. He was also the representative of the 'Ortiz' column in the Assembly of Bujaraloz, and on good terms with the members of the most purist sector of the FAI in Catalonia. Ascaso was joined by three teachers, two journalists who wrote regularly for the anarchist press, and two union workers from Zaragoza. There were no peasants, which did not worry these anarchist leaders very much. In a faithful interpretation of revolutionary 'spontaneity', they proclaimed themselves to be the 'spirit of the people, the people itself, which brought together and symbolised the firm will, good wishes and purist feelings of the Aragonese masses'.[18]

Repeated declarations of this type, and the exclusively anarchist composition of the Council, provoked the disapproval of the republicans, socialists and communists. In their opinion, the Council was purely and simply an anarchist dictatorship under the protection of the militias. However, the strongest opposition to the consolidation of this new autonomous government came from the

Generalitat of Catalonia. At the meeting of 3 November, the chief minister, Josep Tarradellas, warned that 'the territory in which it intends to operate is a war zone and cannot, therefore, be under the control of anyone other than the military authorities. And furthermore, the Generalitat is responsable for the civilian population.' The issue was discussed again on 11 November. The communist Joan Comerera argued that if the republican government recognised the Council, 'it would come beween Catalonia and the war front to the detriment of the authority of the leadership', whilst Tarradellas referred to it as the 'psuedo-Council of Aragon'. It was clear that only the participation of the other political forces of the 'anti-fascist front' would bring about the necessary official recognition.[19]

As a first step towards this objective, a delegation headed by Ascaso began a series of conversations with the principal authorities of the Spanish Republic. Following their visit to Barcelona, where Lluís Companys and Manuel Azaña treated them with indifference and disdain, they arrived in Madrid, on 11 November, to see Largo Caballero. They gave him a document which began by stating their 'absolute identification with the Government of the Republic'. It then set out the reasons for the urgent need to set up the Council. These were the need to fill the power vacuum, which the uprising had created in the provinces of Aragon, and to put an end to the 'chaotic situation which threatens to cause economic ruin', and which had, in turn, been caused by the occupation of the region by 'columns which are not fully under control'.

The government was not initially convinced of these good intentions. However, their attitude was changed by the influence of Joan Peiró, who had been the new Minister of Industry since 4 November, the intervention of the National Committee of the CNT and the remaining groups' agreement to participate in the Council. On 25 December 1936 the *Gaceta de la República* published a decree of legalisation and on 14 January Joaquín Ascaso was appointed the 'legitimate' representative of the government of the Republic in Aragon. In the new Council, which transferred its residence from Fraga to Caspe, the CNT kept six departments amongst which were Public Order, Agriculture and Economy, and Supplies. The socialists, republicans and communists shared the remaining six. Joaquín Ascaso continued as president and created the post of secretary general, which was filled by Benito Pabón, a labour lawyer who had also been elected as Popular Front deputy for the city of Zaragoza in February 1936.[20]

The Council attempted to plan and co-ordinate a range of activities through its various departments. The majority of these activities resulted from the radical transformations which had taken place in the republican territories of Aragon during the months between the military uprising and the constitution of the Council. It created its own police force, carried out requisitions, set up rigid mechanisms for the control of the economy, administered justice and, above all, made use of its powerful bureaucratic apparatus to consolidate the power of the CNT. The Council's numerous decrees and proclamations merely show the nature of its policy aims and can, therefore, be left aside. It is the Council's intervention in the economy and the programme of collectivisation which best demonstrates both the success of its strategy and its failures. The area of its activities and their effectiveness were always limited, in every case, by the military occupation of the territory under its jurisdiction, the resolute rejection of the Council by the Generalitat of Catalonia and the energetic opposition of the remaining political groups. Under these circumstances the result was closer to 'war communism' than libertarian communism.[21]

In the final evaluation of the anarchists' passage through the institutions of government, the supposedly negative changes which the organs of power imposed on the revolution has always been an underlying theme. According to this view, this negative contribution is discernible in the distancing from the 'radically democratic inspiration' which the revolution had initially adopted, in the supression of the mass movements and, finally, in the elimination of the most radical, positive and fruitful aspects of the social revolution. It is supposed, following this line of argumentation, that 'the supreme organs of anarchist decision-making favoured the march towards a "strong state"'. In the march towards this tragic outcome, there were three 'fundamental stages'. These were the organisation of the new army to replace the militias, the replacement of the revolutionary committees by municipal councils appointed 'from above', and the freezing of collectivisation via restrictive economic policies and their violent suppression. This perspective also provides a vision of what an unhindered outcome would have been. Without its treacherous leaders, the creative energy of the revolutionary masses, plus the 'refined understanding' of the 'grass roots' of the CNT would have produced an authentic historic revolution. This was the great 'missed opportunity'. In this way, a teleological vision emerges, in which the collective subject, in this case the workers and peasants, are attributed an almost innate revolutionary potential. And they can only be made to deviate from their destiny by the malicious actions of those who abandon, and make the masses abandon, their sacred principles.[22]

In the analysis presented so far here, a very different vision has been elaborated, and this will be defended in what now follows. I have left aside the abundant evidence, with bloodshed and all, of what this revolution entailed, in its supposedly pure state and before it was contaminated, from inside or out. It is also clear that its beginning and end were very different. This is evident in the conversion of the militias into an army, the replacement of the 'spontaneous' revolutionary committees by municipal councils 'formed proportionately from all of the union organisations and anti-fascist parties' and the violent destruction of the collectives. It is, however, quesionable that this was all due to the 'betrayal' of the leaders and the unfortunate decision to collaborate in governmental undertakings. It would seem that the limits to the egalitarian dream are to be found elsewhere. It is a fact that the libertarian attempts to produce a revolutionary alternative following the collapse of the republican state did not correspond to the anarchists' theoretical postulates. However, this was not due to the leadership breaking with these postulates but, rather, to the adverse circumstances in which that theory had to be developed. These circumstances did not entirely dictate what the leadership did, but they did set limits to their actions and define what was feasible. It is in the choices made, which also varied from region to region, that the validity or inconsistency of the anarchist movement's strategies, their contribution to the war effort and the revolution, and the behaviour of their activists have to be situated. The industrial and agrarian collectives provide an excellent context in which to test this perspective, and ask new questions, leaving aside the accepted commonplaces and unfounded assumptions.[23]

The limits of the earthly paradise

The first point to be made is that there does not appear to have been a clear precedent for the peasant collectives. In other words, there was no continuity between the degree and extent of conflict within rural society in the period before the military uprising and the revolutionary period which followed. It is possible, with the data available, to defend this thesis for Aragon and the Valencian region, though with various differences in the areas of Andalucia which remained under republican control and in Castilla-La Mancha. However, it was always the collapse of existing legality which followed the *coup d'état*, and not the pressure or intensity of social conflict, which left the dominant classes unable to exercise their normal functions.[24]

During the initial period, there was only a mixture of expectation and confusion on the horizon. Once the insurgents had been defeated, their arms, and the arms of those who had contributed to their defeat, passed over to the militias and the syndicates. The presence of these armed groups was felt in all of the zones in which the uprising failed, but with particular intensity in the eastern half of Aragon. From the very beginning, in that region, the militias blocked the balance between the trade-union organisations, the armed groups and the civil authorities which was slowly being established in the other republican territories.

It was under the auspices of these new local powers, backed with weapons, that the majority of expropriations took place. It was then on the basis of these expropriations that collective exploitation emerged, although not as quickly as is often maintained. The simple quantitative perspective, adopted universally by the first authors to write on the topic, has merely created controversy, because the incomplete figures eleborated by the Institute of Agrarian Reform never coincide with those produced by the union organisations. Acording to the figures provided by the Institute, based on fifteeen provinces, not including Aragon or Catalonia,` up until August 1938, 5,458,885 hectares had been expropriated (approximately 40 per cent of usable land) and 45 per cent of this had been collectivised legally. In Aragon, which always stands out as the most important focus of agrarian revolution, anarchist sources insist that '75 per cent of the land' was cultivated by collectives. However, we do not have reliable figures on the amount of land confiscated. Furthermore, if we take into account the fact that this new land-holding regime was least applied in the municipalities with the highest levels of population, these estimates do not seem acceptable.[25]

The same problem arises when it comes to calculating the number of collectives. In most cases, one is forced to use these same sources and treat them with caution. If these figures are accepted, then in the provinces of Andalucia there were 147 collectives (42 of the UGT, 36 of the CNT, 38 jointly by the UGT–CNT and 31 run by other organisations). In Castilla-La Mancha, there were 452 (217 of the UGT, 186 of the CNT and 49 mixed CNT–UGT). In Valencia, there were 353 (264 of the CNT, 69 of the UGT and 20 of the CNT–UGT). In Catalonia, there were 95 (43 of the CNT, 3 of the UGT and 18 of the CNT–UGT and 31 from other organisations). In Murcia, there were 122 (59 of the CNT, 53 of the UGT and 10 mixed). Finally, in Aragon there were 306 (275 of the CNT and 31of the UGT).

Once the quantitative approach has been set aside, different types of questions have to be asked with the material available. These allow investigation of the problems which led a considerable number of people, voluntarily or involuntarily, to take the decision to 'live collectively'. Given the initial context of armed groups competing for control of the situation, in which government decisions were applied only with great difficulty outside of Madrid, and with a network of revolutionary committees spread over the republican zone, the search for a new political order became an urgent imperative. It was extremely difficult to maintain respect for legality when this appeared fragmented or barely existent. Within the power vacuum, decision-making lay in the hands of the political and union organisations. It was not a case of forming alliances, but rather of finding emergency solutions which each organisation then attempted to claim as its own success. This explains the impovisation which surrounded military and union activity and the expropriations of the first months of the war.

The collectives emerged on the basis of land which had been abandoned by its owners, or estates which had been requisitioned by the militias and revolutionary committees. The inequality of the sectors involved prevented the acceptance of generalised criteria in the reorganisation of property ownership. The first serious attempt to do so, by the government, ran up against the opposition of the main peasant organisations. The decree of the Minister of Agriculture, Vicente Uribe, had been ratified on 7 October 1936. Whilst this remained in force, the only land subject to expropriation was that of owners who had intervened 'directly or indirectly' in the military uprising, whether or not they employed wage labour. For the CNT and the FNTT, land should only be owned by those who could farm it themselves. At the heart of the matter was the dispute over the definition of the small proprietor. The government claimed it was defending the small proprietor against the 'excesses' of collectivisation, but in reality this was just one more version of the struggle for control by the peasants. For the communists, this decree was 'the instrument of the only true agrarian revolution that has taken place in Spain'. It was the alternative which the Communist Party supported in opposition to the domination of the countryside by the socialists and the CNT. In spite of the meagre presence of this party in the rural sector of republican territory, there was always a communist in the Ministry of Agriculture from the moment that Largo Caballero formed his first government. And this caused problems, at least until the power of the trade unions was reduced.[26]

In Andalucia and Castilla-La Mancha, where the FNTT had its highest level of membership, those working in the collectives refused to give up what they had conquered. In the Valencian region, the UGT and the anarchists argued that the Uribe decree favoured the old absentee estate holders and small landowners to the detriment of the landless workers and the collectives. In the areas of Aragon occupied by the militias, the difficulty in the application of the decree was not due to the late formation of the Qualifying Councils, a problem which seriously affected the republican zone, nor to the excessive bureaucratisation of the Institute of Agrarian Reform. There, the expropriations had started to take place from the very first days of the conflict. The system of cultivation had already been decided upon and the system of collective exploitation was under the armed supervision of the CNT. The ownership of land was still an issue under discussion and there were different positions on this. Some were in favour of the revolutionary committees remaining owners. Others wanted the collectives to be the sole beneficiaries. And finally there were those who wanted the union to be the organ controlling the economy of the collectives. However, the 'nationalisation' of agricultural production, which was one of the fundamental objectives of the Uribe decree, was never considered while the CNT maintained its domination.

Nevertheless, it is fairly obvious that both economic and military considerations also coincided with this political struggle. Given that the principal cereal growing areas of Spain were under the control of the military insurgents, the former helped to create a climate of bitter hostility in the rearguard, and especially in Valencia. The latter, which was present across the entire territory of Spain and throughout the war, left the population of Aragon as a passive, and patient, subject in the constant struggle for power, during which there were frequent changes in administration, purges and armed disturbances.

Some 60 per cent of Valencia's agrarian production went for export. The war disrupted the traditional channels of distribution and commerce. After an initial period of confusion, the union organisations made an effort to reorganise the orange trade, which was the principal source of revenue. In September 1936, the Regional Single Union of Fruit Trade Workers (SURTEF) of the CNT set out a 'Project of Socialisation of Agrarian Exports', which proposed a complete renewal of the sector. A month later, SURTEF and the Union of Workers, Exporters and Associated Sectors of the CNT formed the Unified Council of Agricultural Exporters of the Levant (CLUEA), the organisation which would manage the export of oranges during the harvests of 1936–7. This implied the permanent replacement of the former exporters by a single body run by the workers.

The undertaking was fraught with complications. These included the economic scale of orange production, the complexity of the export industry, the crisis which the sector had been suffering since 1933, the improvisation inherent in a project of this nature and the disorganisation caused by the war. The French and German markets were lost and there was a delay in the start of the harvest in most areas. Added to this was the fact that payments were not reaching the producers. These difficulties, which were to a certain extent normal, created a climate of uncertainty within the economy and ill feeling amongst certain sectors of the workers. Exports began to be carried out clandestinely in order to evade union control and the central government, in Valencia from the beginning of November 1936, never recognised the CLUEA's monopoly of exports. But above all, the CNT and the UGT came up against an energetic competitor when, on 18 October, the communists, with the support of the republican parties, formed the Provincial Federation of Peasants. This organisation was dedicated to the struggle against the 'excesses of collectivisation'. It quickly gained the support of a wide sector of the rural world which had benefited less from the changes introduced by the labour organisations. This was especially the case amongst the share-croppers and small proprietors who had been members of the Catholic unions prior to the uprising.

The conflict became violent and there were clashes and deaths in a number of areas in February and March 1937. During the spring, the CNT complained in Valencia, as they did in Aragon, of virulent attacks against collectivisation. Apart from betraying the tension within Valencian politics, this conflict demonstrated the gradual recovery, by the central government, of the power of intervention in basic sectors of the economy. This task was facilitated even further by the replacement of Largo Caballero by Juan Negrín following the disturbances of May 1937. On 6 September of that same year, the Association of Agrarian Exporters, which was linked to the Treasury, was created in Valencia. In spite of their protests, the CNT and the UGT were not represented on this body. This was the end of worker control of orange exports and the beginning of the end of union control of Valencian agriculture. A few months later the war reached this zone. On 14 July 1938, Franco's army occupied Castellón and the bombardments, forced conscription and food shortages relegated the political struggle to a secondary plane.[27]

These economic factors do not seem to have played such an important role in the violence which began to emerge in the rural sector of Aragon. This zone was split in two. The most densely populated areas and the most important industrial centres had been under the control of the insurgents since July 1936. The militias had taken control of the eastern half, just as the anarchists and socialists were trying (with great difficulty) to reorganise themselves in the aftermath of brutal military repression. Those people who normally exercised authority had been displaced. In the summer of 1936, estates could be found in all of the towns which were either 'without owners' or abandoned, such as the properties of foreigners who in some areas owned almost a third of rural property. Once the confiscations had taken place, this property had to be organised and a new political and economic order established. The CNT was the principal beneficiary. However, it was not clear who would take permanent control, following this initial hegemony – the armed groups who claimed to have 'liberated' the 'miserable rustic' peasants, or the leaders of the CNT in Aragon who were trying to contain the 'uncontrolled' elements. To make things more complicated, the Generalitat of Catalonia was also trying to reaffirm its political and military authority in this same territory.

The formation of the Council of Aragon, in October 1936, cleared the way somewhat, although the militias, who would be converted into an army a few months later, continued to be autonomous powers who took 'whatever they felt like' from the towns. The socialists, communists and republicans attempted energetically to combat the Council, which was not, as is often claimed, the perquisite of a few gunmen who spread terror and stole the peasants' food. Apart from controlling production and consumption, maintaining revolutionary order and regulating wages, the Council collectivised agricultural machinery during the period of harvest, channelled the export of large quantities of oil, almonds, saffron and other agricultural products unavailable in Aragon, through the Port of Tarragona.

It is understandable that the central government would not be happy with a situation of this sort. The President of the Republic, Manuel Azaña, put pressure on Negrín from the begining of June to dissolve 'the anarchists' organ' and put them in jail. The attitude of the communists was even harsher and more threatening. In a meeting of the National Committee of the PSOE held in Valencia on 17 June 1937, the socialist leader Ernesto Marcén (ex-editor of the Zaragoza paper *Vida Nueva*) asked for the intervention of the government in order to 'normalise the situation in Aragon' and put an end to the collectivisation which had been imposed from the 'barrel of a gun'. At the request of the Communist Party, a General Assembly of the Popular Front of Aragon was held in Barbastro at the beginning of August. The principal outcome of the meeting was the decision to make a public appeal for the dissolution of the regional government.[28]

Given so much pressure, it was not difficult to predict the outcome. As part of the preparation of a republican offensive on the Aragonese front, the XI Division, under the command of Lister, was transferred to that territory. On 11 August, the Council of Aragon was dissolved by decree. Its dissolution was accompanied by virulent demonstrations, incited by those who believed that the repercussions of its administration had produced negative effects on the economy and in the war against fascism. Several of its members, including its president, Joaquín Ascaso, and the main leaders of the collectives, were imprisoned. Many of the collectives were destroyed and the expropriated lands returned to their previous owners, or managed by the other political forces. Once the Council had been dissolved, the collectives were destined to disappear. In the months which followed, conditions were not favourable. The battle of Teruel saw new mobilisations and the conscription of landworkers. In March 1938, Franco's army occupied the entire territory on which these revolutionary activities had taken place.

There are no detailed studies available for the remaining provinces of republican Spain, although the characteristics of the anti-collectivisation campaign which started in the summer of 1937 in certain regions of Andalucia are known. Whilst the small proprietors received financial and technical assistance from the Institute of Agrarian Reform, the collectives did not receive credit, seed, fertiliser or machinery for the farming of their land. Whether there were confrontations or not, there exists sufficient evidence that during the last year of the war the government's agrarian policy was imposed through the communist control of the Ministry of Agriculture and the Institute for Agrarian Reform. The call-up of reservists and the growing deterioration of the economic situation heavily conditioned the evolution of many collectives. In these cases there was no need to use force against them as the evolution of the war itself brought them to an end.

The overview sketched above allows an initial conclusion to be drawn. Once the existing order had been destroyed, collectivisation initially proved efficient in maintaining a minimum of co-ordination outside of the market. After a few months, and as a result of the harsh conditions imposed by the war and the absence of planning, the situation deteriorated and the collectives were unable to develop a solution which went beyond the limits of the local economy. As a result of these limitations, which may also have been due to circumstances, the attacks on collectivisation could be justified with convincing arguments. From that point on, there was an intensification of the struggle between 'individualists' and collectivists, between the defenders of the peasant household and the partisans of collectivisation as the most rational form of labour organisation and agrarian production.

Nevertheless, the history of collectivisation is not only a history of political conflict, violence, the struggle for power and controversy over the priority of the war or the revolution. As with all moments of great social change, the armed struggle opened up new possibilities for groups and individuals who had never before been able to participate in political decisions. The war shook up the dominant structure of power, smashed the traditional mechanisms of control and introduced forms of collective mobilisation which, thanks to non-intervention in the First World War, were almost without precedent in Spain. The conjuncture of all of these factors, over which reigned the presence of arms, contributed, more than the revolutionary thrust of trade unionism, to the destruction of the bonds between the subordinate classes and the authorities.

Local and regional studies have attempted to answer the questions of who these collectivists were, what inspired them to work together and what social groups were targeted for this common project.[29] To point out that the membership of the CNT and the UGT were the principal supporters of collectivisation does not tell us much. The trade unionism of the agrarian world cannot be measured solely in quantitative or ideological terms. In reality, in Andalucia and Castilla-La Mancha, where the FNTT had maintained a strong basis before the outbreak of the war, collectives were not formed as quickly as in other rural areas. This was the case, above all, in the eastern half of Aragon, in which the membership of the union organisations was precarious. This observation obviously points to the influence of the militias as the origin of collectivisation. However, it also indicates the absence of a clear socialist strategy towards the peasantry during the first months of the war. Many members of the FNTT who participated in strikes for the improvement of wages and working conditions during the republic were not convinced collectivists. They had other alternatives, such as the co-operatives of 'distribution' which were better able to ensure the loyalty of the small proprietors. And the leaders of the unions did not adopt a clear or homogeneous position on collectivisation either.

Furthermore, an explanation of voluntary adhesion to the collectives in terms of poverty would be dubious, as there was an almost natural tendency towards poverty amongst the lower classes of the social hierarchy. It might be argued intuitively that in the areas of large-scale estates, it was the landless labourers who were most likely to join the collectives, whilst in the areas where small-scale ownership was predominant it would be the agricultural day labourers, share-croppers and 'very poor proprietors' who would benefit most from the practice of collectivisation. But intuition is not enough. In such a complex situation, in which there is an overlapping of aspects as varied as the revolutionary ideology of certain activists, the extreme poverty of many peasants and violence, the question will only be resolved through the analysis of concrete examples.

In Aragon, apart from the harsh conditions imposed by the war, the experi-ence of the collectives was also limited by the peculiar social and economic structure of its agricultural sector. The economy of this sector was based on household units of production with a very high percentage of the population living in small municipalities and with a predominance of small-scale producers. Given these circumstances, it is not surprising that the attempt to implant liber-tarian communism should come up against difficulties, limitations and a diversity of attitudes. There were small proprietors willing to share the cultivation of land and others who gave in to coercion. There were those who became enthusiastic collectivists, because they had never had any land of their own before, and there were terrified peasants. The aim of the CNT was to do away with the land-renting system and, above all, to abolish wage labour. In practice, this required the support of a large part of the peasantry, a minimum of planning and time – three conditions which were unavailable at that point in time. In the absence of these conditions, the collectivist venture was always accompanied by insecurity, uncertainty and fear.

The Aragonese collectivisations were not, therefore, the radical expression of a peasant rebellion against intolerable conditions. The idea of the collectivist was disseminated mainly by union leaders from the cities, who were apologists for the 'natural egalitarianism' of the countryside. They co-ordinated the activi-ties of the collectives and proposed their internal regulations. Everything they proposed had been conceived of in the city, by wage labourers without land, and their project was hardly appropriate for the thousands of small-scale proprietors. Events seem to have developed in a similar fashion in those other regions in which the same conditions predominated (fragmentation of rural society, high levels of illiteracy and poor technical capacity) and made difficult the political expression and organisation of the peasantry.

These conditions also hampered the definition of new social relations between the sexes, a subject which it was never even possible to raise in the rural world. In the words of Pilar Vivancos, the daughter of a small rural proprietor in Beceite (Teruel) and wife of the anarchist leader of the 25th Division, Miguel García Vivancos, 'The subject of women's liberation was not presented as part of the revolutionary process', and in republican Aragon 'the woman's place was in the kitchen or working the land'. According to the available documentation, women did not take part in the leadership committees of the political and union organisations. Nor did they do so in the municipal councils, which were dominated by the CNT until August 1937. As far as equality of opportunity between men and women was concerned, the factor of sex was an important element of differentiation. This is shown by the minimum wage of ten pesetas for men and six for women, set by the anarchist Miguel Chueca at the Department of Labour of the Council of Aragon.

The activists of the anarchist organisation 'Mujeres Libres' (Free Women) were the only group which attempted to eradicate this contradiction between ideas and practice. However, they never succeeded in being recognised as an autonomous sector of the anarchist movement, an objective which the Anarchist Youth movement, for example, achieved in 1932. In spite of their efforts and aspirations, the traditional relationship between men and women, as with many other aspects of daily life, continued without great change within the framework of this revolutionary experience. Or perhaps more precisely, the opportunities which presented themselves during the early stages of revolutionary fervour (and which led, for example, to the exaltation of the female militia member as the heroine and symbol of the mobilisation of the Spanish people against fascism) were blocked as the struggle for power, the re-establishment of order and the war annulled the most radical expressions of popular power.[30]

As the rural world was itself marginalised, women in that context were doubly marginalised. Given this situation, were the peasants the 'victims' of a process over which they never exercised control? Testimonies do, in fact, exist of the ill feeling provoked by the repeated intervention in their cultural and mental world, by the breakdown of their mechanisms of subsistence, by the invasion of alien institutions which took away their autonomy and by the imposition of a war economy. What might have been a protest against the overthrow of certain basic and internalised norms was interpreted by the union organisations as opposition to collectivisation or the class struggle. Whilst for some, collectivisation was the natural expression of the peasant system of values (based, according to this vision, on social equality and local self-government), for others it violated the autonomy of the family-oriented economy and of the 'home', which was the authentic principle of their social identity. For one part of the rural population, the violent suppression of hierarchical social relations (which manifested itself in the assassination of the *caciques*, the rich and the priests) was a liberation. However, for those who were linked to their patrons through their jobs and through personal affection and/or respect, it symbolised the most absolute disruption of traditional peace, which had always reigned in the small Aragonese municipalities.[31]

The collectivisation and domination exercised by the anarchists in many of the municipalities of Aragon did indeed amount to a direct attack on property relations and the established structure of power and authority. Myths and commonplaces aside, there were a series of phenomena which indicate this inversion of social order during the first phase of the revolutionary process. These included the abolition of wage labour, money and private property in the means of production, the organisation of 'popular assemblies' to discuss the new system of production and consumption, the supression of religious acts, and the exercise of power by young people who had, until then, been marginalised from political activity.

This inversion of the social order was also a genuine part of the revolutionary phenomenon in Barelona. Although the characteristics and protagonists were different from those examined in the rural context, recollection of these events provokes the same ambivalence. For some, there was a radical and destructive transformation, while for others it was the demonstration of the creative capacity of the workers in industry without owners, of self-management on the one hand or the imposition of the ideas of a leading minority on the other. Furthermore, this ambivalence is characteristic of those revolutionary phenomena and periods of social change which are, historically, associated with war and international pressure. The concurrence of such diverse and contradictory factors places a question mark over the easy characterisation of that process as the conquest of power by the working class and the end of the class struggle.[32]

After the defeat of the insurgents, the workers did not go immediately to the factories to replace the owners, who had fled or been assassinated, and begin to produce for the construction of a new society. Things did not happen that quickly. The first thing that was done was to create 'workers' management committees' made up in the majority of cases by the union delegates and activists who were already present on the old factory committees. The fact that they were in control from the very first moment does not mean that everything happened spontaneously. Owners, managers and directors had either been eliminated or had abandoned their posts in fear and it was logical, therefore, that there would be disorganisation. The trade-unionist moment had arrived, or rather the moment of those activists who had made a name for themselves during the republican years. The orders were given by the leaders of the various industrial unions of the CNT (especially those sectors in which the CNT was strongest, such as textiles and iron working). These were then transmitted by the factory delegates.

> We assembled the workforce and explained that we had received orders to expropriate the factory. We were relying on them to remain at their posts, as the factory was where everyone earned their daily bread. Everyone decided to support the new organisation. The factory manager and the employees ... Some were more reluctant than others ... From that point on the management committee became the supreme authority.[33]

When work began to be 'normalised' in the first half of August, the state of the majority of factories gave cause for anxiety. Moreover, there was little reason to believe that the change-over to management by the unions could provide a drastic solution to the crisis affecting some of the principal sectors of industry, especially textiles. Catalonia had always been lacking in raw materials for its industry, energy supplies and in a range of food products. As a result of the war, Spanish territory had been divided into two zones. This produced a contraction of demand in certain basic sectors and made imports more difficult, all of which aggravated existing structural problems. Levels of production fell sharply during the first two months of the conflict and the increase in wages was quickly overtaken by the very rapid rise in the cost of living. All of this took place in a region with population densities higher than the Spanish average (91.2 inhabitants per square kilometre as against 48.2) and in which, according to estimates from the Generalitat, there would be more than 300,000 refugees by the end of 1936.[34]

Faced with these difficulties, the improvised solution seemed revolutionary on the surface, but included certain elements of the previous capitalist model. This had not been abandoned, even though everything appeared to be under the control of the unions. The most active groups of the CNT (manual labourers and the most able technicians and office workers) took the leading role in the discussion over workers' control, expropriations and collectivisation, during the summer months of 1936. Various projects and models of internal organisation emerged from the tension and conflict between sectors. These dealt with issues as varied as the running of the collectivised regime to the distribution of profits and the rules governing labour discipline.

The Generalitat was slow to react. One month after the incorporation of the CNT, on 24 October 1936, the Decree on Collectivisations and Workers' Control of the Economic Council was approved. This was the fruit of bitter debate between the political forces represented in the Catalan government. It gave an air of legality to the changes which had taken place in the organisation of industry during August and September of that year. There were two opposed, yet widely held, interpretations of the decree. On the one hand, for some, it represented the legalisation of the 'spontaneous revolution'. On the other, it was said to be the beginning of the counter-revolution under the guise of government control. However, regardless of which interpretation is accepted, there is no doubt that a bureaucratic machine was set up around the decree and this had the support of the anarcho-syndicalist leaders such as the Counsellor (minister) for the Economy, Joan Fábregas.

According to the decree, there was to be collectivisation of businesses whose owners had abandoned them or else been declared to be fascists by the popular tribunals, if they had employed more than a hundred workers before 30 July and if (in a company employing from fifty up to a hundred workers) three-quarters of the workforce were in favour. The branches of foreign companies were given special treatment, a reasonable precaution at that time, and this practice was supported by the CNT from the very first days of the union taking control.[35]

It was not accidental that the technical aspect should be given prime consideration in the decree. This was the instrument through which the republicans, socialists and communists wished to limit the CNT's union power in the factories and centralise from the Generalitat the economic management of industry. The decree divided and weakened the union activists who, as manual workers, were not allowed to occupy key positions on company management boards. It also gave greater importance to the role of skilled workers, technicians and office workers, who were normally affiliated to the CADCI and the UGT. The anarcho-syndicalists' 'economic ideas' amounted simply to the expropriation of property and the means of production and the proclamation of the 'free right to consumption'. Accordingly, the whole bureaucratic framework of 'councils' established by the decree (from the company via the captains of industry to the Generalitat) did not seem to affect them. The anarchists were steeped in received truths on egalitarianism and used 'to operating at an idealistic level detached from economic analysis'. The revolution continued to be, for them, the negation of authority, the change in ownership, the expropriation of the factories and the management of them by the unions. Thanks to their unbreakable faith in the destructive and creative power of the working class, they had no idea how to fulfil their hopes by moving beyond improvisation and taking the crucial step towards proper planning of production and distribution.[36]

It quickly became starkly clear that this idealised belief in the capacity of the working class to manage its own affairs was clashing with harsh reality. As Rudiger pointed out, 'the simple expropriation of a factory and the administration of it does not automatically bring about the miraculous transformation of the entire workforce into responsible men and capable workers'. After the first euphoric moments had passed, most workers began to feel alienated from those who managed, participated or criticised the collectives. It was assumed that they would bring about improvements in social and labour conditions and this may have been the case at the beginning. A few months later, and taking into consideration that collectivisation had taken place in time of war, the opposite happened. The rhythm of work was intensified, wages did not keep up with raging inflation and the shortage of food made the daily struggle to obtain it a basic concern. During that period, Barcelona had to adapt to exceptional circumstances including food shortages, caused by the increase in the price of consumer goods, a fall in the real value of wages, the exhaustion of personal savings and the rapid emergence of a black market. The city also had to create a war industry where it had previously manufactured machines, clothes and chemical products. Finally, Catalan society in its entirety was overwhelmed by an enormous influx of refugees from the territories occupied by the military rebels or in areas where one of the war fronts cut through.

Given this situation, it is logical that various forms of protest should emerge and become caught up with the traditional ideological and political differences between socialists, communists and anarchists. The unions and the administrative and management committees responsible for the organisation of production began to be inundated by demands of all kinds. During October 1936, that is only four months after the initial wave of revolution, the situation was already giving cause for concern. This is clear from the severity of the proclamations which were circulated by the committee of the Local Federation of Sindicatos Unicos (Unions Spread Across Entire Trades) of Barcelona. These were 'times of war to the death against the fascist monster' and the workers 'of both sexes and both manual and intellectual workers' have to consider themselves 'militarily mobilised'. Whilst the war continued, it would be impossible to negotiate new working conditions or even expect, 'above all in the sectors of production which are directly or indirectly related to the anti-fascist struggle', that the agreements on wages and the working day be respected. Week-day holidays were prohibited, 'because they cause a considerable reduction in production and affect the economy', and no one should be paid 'any extra pay for overtime carried out on production used for the anti-fascist war'.

The union committees undertook an active propaganda campaign in favour of this work and productivity drive. The workers were asked to make a greater effort and work harder than they had under 'the capitalist period'. The working day went from 44 to 48 hours in the majority of companies. On 24 April 1937, only a few days before serious disturbances were to break out in Barcelona, *Solidaridad Obrera* pointed out that the First of May should no longer be a day of 'demands, strikes and battles. We no longer have to struggle against capitalism which now is not here but on the other side of our trenches.'

Furthermore, it was not only disputes over wages or the length of the working day that were at issue. Absenteeism, late arrival at work, low productivity, sabotage, indiscipline, theft of tools – all methods used against the old owners – were now demonstrations of protest against the factory committees who were replicating the authoritarian behaviour of the old owners. Popular discontent over the inefficiency of the system of food distribution and supply and protest over the emergence of a black market grew more intense from the end of 1936. Much of this protest was led by women who attacked grocery shops and occupied town halls in order to demand bread and essential provisions for their families. Obviously these protests cannot be separated from the exceptional situation caused by the war and the high number of refugees flooding into Catalonia. Nevertheless, they also provide evidence of the contrast between the luxury and abundance, in which certain elements of the new power structure lived, and the lack of basic necessities from which the majority of the civil population was suffering.[37]

Shortly after it began, then, the revolution came up against problems similar to those which the capitalist owners had encountered in their attempts to increase production and discipline the working class. Differences in attitudes and behaviour were visible amongst the workers and these derived from their beliefs, their level of militancy and commitment to the revolutionary ideal, and the level of responsibility with which they confronted the adverse circumstances. A minority, including the union activists, the office workers and technicians who formed part of the management and administration committees, took an 'active' role in collectivisation and found themselves having to combat the resistence of other workers in the fulfilment of the demands placed upon them. Detailed studies of the reaction to these changes and the levels of participation in collectivisation have served to undermine preconceived schemas of analysis. 'Whilst the activists identified class consciousness with the control and development of the forces of production, the creation of a productionist revolution and a last effort to win the war, the class consciousness of many ordinary workers was expressed in terms of a rejection of the workplace and discipline, much as had been the case before the revolution.' The minority of collectivising activists was composed almost entirely of literate middle-aged men with a sound knowledge of the company and considerable professional capacity. The immense majority of the remaining workers, male and female, were illiterate manual labourers, who had not identified with the social struggles initiated by the anarcho-syndicalists before July 1936. The changes in the organisation of industry and commerce and the labour hierarchy had very little effect on them. They saw these as mere changes of management which still did not free them from their immediate concerns about improving their income and living conditions and working less. Collectivisation brought about under the force of arms was not the best way for them to have these desires addressed. After all, it was far from the social bliss which the revolutionaries had always predicted.[38]

Collectivisation continued to lose ground which was only recovered by its supposed enemies in the spring of 1937. Nevertheless, certain sectors of anarcho-syndicalism which had not initially been critical of collectivisation were now the first to distance themselves from it. It all began with the Decree of Collectivisation. However, it has to be remembered that this coincided with an acceleration of the process which had led the CNT into the government of Largo Caballero, having previously acquiesced in the suppression of the Committee of Anti-Fascist Militias and accepted participation in the Generalitat. The struggle would take place between the new committees of management and administration (which were in favour of the agreement between the different sectors of production and of political collaboration) and the union committees, which had emerged from the previous factory committees and integrated those who had been union delegates during the Republic. This sector saw how the decree reduced the power they had won in the summer of 1936 and made the industrial collectives dependent on the ever-more centralised government. And as far as the war industries were concerned, it made them dependent on the political and military administration of the state. This was a collectivisation which had been watered down with the legality of those same old bourgeois politicians and socialist and communist enemies. 'Socialisation', by which was meant the co-ordination of all of the companies comprising one sector of industry by the relevant single union, became the true revolution's only guarantee, against this, of profound social change. Socialisation was contrasted with government collectivisation and centralisation, and union power was contrasted with political collaboration. This was where the most radical activists of the FAI and the CNT began their struggle to recover lost ground and give back to the anarchist movement the power which, they believed, it should never have lost in the factories, in the economy and on the streets.

Purity meant criticising the betrayal of anarchist principles which had been caused by so much collaboration and bureaucracy. But as well as being radical purists, these activists encountered favourable circumstances of protest on which they were able to capitalise for a few months, essentially the first three months of

1937. The crisis in the Generalitat in the middle of December 1936 represented a rupture of the 'unity', or at least of the pact of collaboration which had reigned during the autumn. The POUM, under attack from the PSUC, which had adopted the Comintern's hardline anti-Trotskyism in order to monopolise the Marxist forces, was forced out of the Generalitat and politically isolated. *Solidaridad Obrera*, which expressed the official anarcho-syndicalist line, interpreted the new composition of the Generalitat (in which the CNT gained one place, the UGT – that is the Communists – gained another, and from which the POUM and Acció Catalana disappeared) as a 'government without parties', dominated by the unions and presided, on an almost honorary basis, by the left republicans. The left republicans were portrayed as the only bourgeois representatives, and petit bourgeois at that, to survive in the face of such apparent union domination.[39]

What actually took place was the opposite of the picture presented by *Solidaridad Obrera*. The powerful ministry of Supply was taken over by the communist Joan Comerera, who replaced the CNT representative José J. Domènech. Comorera suppressed all of the committees of supply, the 'bread committees', which, under the guidance of the CNT, had controlled the supply of food in the main towns of Catalonia until then. The measure coincided with an extreme shortage of bread. According to the communists, this was the result of a lack of planning on the part of the previous minister and of the collectivisation of the production and distribution of bread. In the opinion of the anarchists, it had been provoked by the communists and government control of rationing. The food shortages sparked off a wave of protest. As has been so often the case in history, this was not only a spontaneous reaction of the angry and starving masses. It was, above all, a protest against the immoral attitude of the government which, it was firmly believed, was tolerating the rise in prices, hoarding and speculation. The demands of this popular 'moral economy' are also well known. They wanted the provision of essential commodities at a 'fair' price, a good government and the dismissal of bad ministers.[40]

The bread shortage and the spreading of this conflict coincided with a moment of particular tension both at the front and in the rearguard of the republican zone. The political and union forces were involved in a bitter dispute, during this three-month period of 1937, over the extent of rural and industrial collectivisations, militarisation, control of the war industry and armaments, and public order. This latter issue was of vital importance and led, at the beginning of March, to the dissolution of the security patrols, one of the axes of the CNT's armed power. The cheerful picture of industrial collectivisation gave way to demonstrations, in which women demanded food and fuel, and bloody disturbances which saw a number of deaths among both the demonstrators, including women, and members of the security forces. A notorious case was the assassination of Roldán Cortada on 25 April. An ex-CNT member, Cortada had signed the manifesto of the '*treinta*' in 1931. He was now a member of the PSUC and secretary to Rafael Vidiella, Minister for Labour and Public Works for the Generalitat. A few days later the leader of the local CNT committee in

Puigcerdá, Antonio Martín, known as 'el cojo de Málaga' (the cripple from Málaga), and two anarchists died in a shoot-out with the forces of public order.

Of course, many of these disputes originated in the deep disagreement between the CNT and the PSUC over the conduct of politics in the rearguard. However, in Barcelona it was not merely a case of political differences. There was also a struggle over the control of industrial production. An attempt was made by the Generalitat to abolish the 'socialising' initiative, which the most radical sector of the CNT had put forward as an alternative to the decree on collectivisation. This was done through legislative means and also through the dispatch of armed forces to the factories. For the Generalitat, it would also mean the neutralisation of the dominant influence which the CNT still retained over the manual labourers. The radical activists saw in this conflict the chance to recover the ground lost amongst the grass roots of the confederation, where the great majority had accepted the policy of agreement and collaboration defended by the leadership committees. If their strategy was successful, they would counteract the 'ideological disorientation' which they blamed on the anarcho-syndicalist leadership. These radicals had initially been resigned to the notion of collaboration, but their angry opposition grew as the economic situation deterio-rated, as confrontations between communists and anarcho-syndicalists increased, as protests multiplied against the intensification of the rhythm of production (especially in the metallurgical sector which had now been absorbed into the war industry) and as the limitations of the policies of collaboration with the governments of the Generalitat and Valencia were exposed. It is not coincidental that this anger seemed to bear fruit, just as the CNT lost power in the Generalitat, in the streets, following the dissolution of the patrols and just as the new army was replacing the militias. Nevertheless, not all went as planned. The CNT, under pressure from the other political forces who accused it of provoking economic and political chaos in the rearguard, and from below from the radical activists who were against governmental collaboration, was expelled from both the national and Catalan governments. The maximalist activists gave the republicans, socialists and above all the communists the opportunity they were waiting for, to undertake the final attack on anarcho-syndicalism. As will be seen, the final spectacle which they provided was anything but glorious.[41]

The backdrop of food shortages, political and union conflict and the sense that the revolution had failed was particularly propitious for the radical anarchists to make a show of strength. Following their opposition to militarisation, small but armed groups of militiamen abandoned the front in Aragon and returned to Barcelona, 'doing exactly what the enemies of the CNT wanted, that is, weakening the CNT both numerically and morally'. It was an even more apt moment for those anarchists who had been marginalised after the summer of 1936 for opposing the policy of collaboration. They were now provided with a political and armed vehicle for their personal frustrations over what they were already beginning to call the 'lost opportunity' to make the real revolution.

This was the origin of the group 'Los Amigos de Durruti'. It was composed mainly of anarchists from the Durruti column who had rejected militarisation but who were also united in their struggle against the 'Stalinist counter-revolution'. However, their language of class struggle was also combined, especially in the case of Jaime Balius, with resentment against those responsible for their marginalisation within the anarchist organisation. Jaime Balius had grown up as a Catholic and had passed through Catalan separatism and the anti-Stalinist Bloc Obrer i Camperol before arriving at anarchism. As has been seen, he was dismissed from *Solidaridad Obrera* along with Liberto Callejas. Now, along with Pablo Ruiz and Francisco Carreño, he was the principal organiser of the group. They openly criticised the 'collaborationist' attitudes of the CNT and its lack of a 'revolutionary theory':

> We do not have a proper programme. We do not know where we are going. There is much talk, but at the end of the day we do not know what to do with the enormous masses of workers ... with that mass of people that threw themselves into our organisations.

The street, the much-vaunted street of the most radical anarchists, was once more the point of reference. The CNT had behaved like a 'minority group' when they intervened in politics, 'in spite of the fact that in the streets we are the majority'. However, the only solutions they offered for this lack of 'revolutionary theory' was the formation of a Revolutionary Junta or a National Council of Defence, the 'socialisation' of the economy and the federal organisation of free municipalities. They were obviously not really concerned with the programme, but rather with the need to 'proceed with the greatest energy against those who did not identify with the working class'. This was, in sum, merely the political rhetoric adopted to justify their personal vendettas against their rivals within the anarchist movement. As far as Balius was concerned, there were two names on his hit-list, Mariano R. Vázquez, the secretary of the National Committee of the CNT, and Jacinto Toryho, the editor of *Solidaridad Obrera*.[42]

Radicalism and the desire to win personal conflicts went hand in hand in this crucial moment in the evolution of anarcho-syndicalism in which no one was willing to give way on anything. The leadership bodies were dominated by those same activists and 'men of action' who had sustained a hard battle against the Republic between 1931 and 1933. They now had sufficient force to impose on the dissidents the CNT's position within institutions of government. They had been convinced, since the autumn of 1936, that this was the only possible way to consolidate the revolution and ensure a place on the new political map which the war had drawn up. They acted forcefully against those who, carrying the torch of sacred anarchist principles, attempted to distance them from power. Those who did not accept the official line opted for the strategy of 'action', which, given the circumstances, could only lead to armed confrontation. This is what happened in May 1937, the meeting place of the discontented and the confirmation of the fact that the earthly paradise was far far away.

8 Decline and fall

The first exchange of shots was heard on 3 May. Artemi Aiguader, Minister of Security of the Generalitat, ordered, that very same day, Eusebio Rodríguez, who had been recently appointed general commissioner for Public Order, to occupy the Telefónica building in the Plaza de Catalunya which had been in the hands of the CNT since the 'glorious' days of July 1936. Three lorry-loads of Assault Guards arrived and laid siege to the building. They were met by firing from the CNT activists inside. The rumour quickly spread that there had begun an armed attack against the CNT and against one of the symbols of power that had been conquered months earlier in the struggle against the rebellious military. Armed anarchists arrived to help their besieged comrades and the conflict spread. Many workers left their workplaces and once more barricades were thrown up in the city. Behind them, opposing the security forces, the socialists and the communists, were to be found those militiamen who had refused to join the new army, young libertarians, anarchists from the FAI who were not recognised as such by the organisation itself and activists from the POUM.

The situation was already serious and of great concern on the morning of Tuesday the 4th. Manuel Azaña, defenceless and caught in the crossfire, called for help from the government in Valencia. For him the problem had 'two faces': 'one was that of an anarchist insurrection with all its serious consequences and deplorable effects'. This was already something that, albeit not with such immediacy, he had experienced twice as prime minister in January 1932 and 1933. 'The other was the lack of liberty in which the head of state finds himself not only to move freely but also to carry out his duties.' Largo Caballero urgently called a meeting of the government. It was agreed to send a delegation which would include two ministers from the CNT, García Oliver and Federica Montseny, the secretary of the National Committee of the organisation, Mariano R. Vázquez, and Carlos Hernández Zancajo, a Largo Caballero loyalist on the UGT Executive Commission. Since words would not suffice, they left for Barcelona with around two thousand Assault Guards, a figure soon to be increased to almost five thousand.[1]

On arriving, this delegation met with the representatives of the diverse political organisations of the Generalitat and then immediately broadcast a radio appeal for a cease-fire, and the avoidance of 'provocations', calling further for 'anti-fascist unity, for proletarian unity, for those who had fallen in the struggle'. García Oliver spoke to those on the barricades and told them that those who had died were 'brothers': guards, anarchists, socialists and republicans, all were 'victims' of the anti-fascist struggle. During the night, others also spoke over the radio and said quite different things and called on their 'comrades at the front ... to be ready to come to Barcelona when their help was required'. Between speeches and shooting, considerable amounts of shooting, the night passed.

Agreement was still impossible, and so it remained on 5 and 6 May. It was known that were some illustrious activists to be found amongst the dead: Antonio Sesé, a former member of the CNT who was then general secretary of the UGT in Catalonia; the Italian Camilo Berneri, who had fought in the 'Ascaso' column and who wrote for the anarchist newspaper *Guerra di classe*; and Domingo Ascaso, the brother of Francisco, one of the organisers of the 'Ascaso' column which he had abandoned when it was militarised and converted into the 28th Division. On 5 May, 'a group of some 1,500 to 2,000 men', members of the former 'Red and Black' column, the 127 brigade of the 28th Division, and others from the POUM abandoned the front and were detained a kilometre from Lerida by air-force troops under the command of Lieutenant-Colonel Reyes. In that city, Rovira, leader of the 29th Division of the POUM, García Vivancos, from the 25th Division, and an unidentified delegate from the Regional Committee of the CNT, who were 'seemingly leaders and organisers of the expedition', held an interview with Reyes. They agreed that the air-force troops would be withdrawn in exchange for the deserters returning to the front. The day before, soldiers from the 25th Division commanded by Saturnino Carod abandoned their positions and headed for Catalonia, crossing through the part of lower Aragon in the province of Teruel. Although they did not engage in armed combat, they ran into forces that the General Directorate of Security in Valencia had sent to areas adjoining the provinces of Castellón and Tarragona where, according to anarchist sources, they had smashed machinery and equipment belonging to some of the collectives.[2]

Events were already taking a tragic turn with dozens of dead and wounded in the streets. There were further unsuccessful radio appeals, by Mariano R. Vázquez, Rafael Vidiella and Montseny. The government moved on to the attack and appointed General Sebastián Pozas, as general of the fourth Organic Division (the Catalan Military Region), replacing General José Aranguren. It decreed the take-over of the services of Public Order of the Generalitat which came 'directly to depend on the Government of the Republic' and were to be under the command of Colonel Escobar. On the afternoon of the seventh, normality was, according to Orwell, 'almost absolute'. The Assault Guards that had arrived from Valencia, assisted by activists of the PSUC, occupied the city and finished off the remaining resistance. Official figures stated that there were four hundred dead and a thousand wounded.

On the same day, there were a series of disturbances and bloody events in Aragon. The most serious occurred in Barbastro, where some armed groups, which were returning to the front following the agreement with Lieutenant-

Colonel Reyes, assaulted a military barracks. They seized arms and munitions and also attacked the prison and killed eight prisoners. There was a further assault on the barracks of Monte Julia and some 500 armed men, 'many of whom claimed they had been expelled from the Madrid front', committed 'all kinds of outrages' in the area of Binefar. In all of these violent actions, it appears that Public Order forces of the Council of Aragon took part. One of its ministers, Evaristo Viñuales (Information and Propaganda), 'according to reliable sources though it has not been confirmed ..., led fifty armed men, occupied the frontier post of Benasque and disarmed the border guards who were stationed there'. There was more. In the Huesca village of El Grado, on the same day, three activists from the UGT were found assassinated. According to the documentation concerning the case, the suspected killers who were later brought before a judge belonged to the CNT. Two days earlier in Oliete (Teruel), five others who suffered the same fate as the three UGTistas, amongst them two communists, an activist from the UGT, another from Izquierda Republicana and another being described as a 'rightist'. The members of the CNT who were accused of responsibility for these crimes, included some who, before 19 July 1936, had been 'declared fascists'. Also accused was the president of the municipal council, 'formerly a student for the priesthood'.[3]

Once 'normality' had been re-established, there still remained the question of resolving the virtually inevitable government crisis that had been in the air since the fall of Málaga in February. The loss of the southern port had signified an important loss for the Republic which encouraged the communists openly to criticise the military leadership for which Largo Caballero held the main political responsibility. In reality, 'normality' could not be re-established because things would never be the same again after those events. What had taken place in Barcelona and at the Aragon front went far beyond the limits of conflict between political parties and trade unions, between different unions and between opposing tendencies within the trade-union organisation itself. It was even more than the confirmation of the abyss that separated communists and anarchists (which could no longer be bridged). The cracks were even deeper and weakened the very axes of support on which the Republic depended and they thus endangered the achievement of republican objectives. Here could be found all of the basic problems unresolved and aggravated since the beginning of the war: the constant harvest of military failure, in spite of the subjugation of the militias; governmental incapacity to organise a fair distribution of supplies to the population; and the continued divisions which prevented unity in the social, political and economic spheres.

Barcelona had been the scene of this confrontation because it was hardly a normal city. It was a city at some distance from the front, a symbol of the anarcho-syndicalist revolution, a city that many believed to be essentially proletarian. Its peculiar characteristics facilitated tensions at various levels. In political terms, it was a city divided by an autonomous government significantly dominated by left republicans, a communist party that controlled the UGT and a tiny revolutionary party that was a mortal enemy of the (orthodox) communists. In economic terms, there was the weight of its industrial production for whose control a bitter struggle had taken place. Demographically, the city had high population density, tens of thousands of refugees. All of this contributed towards a city riddled with hostilities. There were also weapons, weapons in abundance, flaunted by the different police forces, the activists of different political organisations and by the ex-militiamen who had brought them from the front. There were also too many revolutionary 'tourists', foreigners who were unable to do anything in their own countries but to whom the Spanish revolution was utterly insufficient. There were also provocateurs of one kind or another to be found all over the place, from the police to the POUM, those whom García Oliver described as 'always playing their own game'. Evidently, they had not themselves created the explosive situation, but they were the first to light the fuse. War-time Barcelona was thus a power-keg, infinitely more dangerous than other cities in republican territory.[4]

Curiously, the outcome of the wider political crisis was the question that most concerned the libertarian leaders. In the cabinet meeting of 13 May, the two communist ministers, Vicente Uribe and Jesús Hernández, demanded that Largo Caballero leave the Ministry of War and also called for the dissolution of the POUM. The prime minister refused to accept the first demand and tried to shelve any decision on the second until reliable information was forthcoming about those supposedly guilty for the disturbances in Barcelona. The communist ministers left the cabinet which meant that the crisis was now out in the open. On 15 May, the CNT and the UGT released similar statements in which they demonstrated their agreement on three basic points: they rejected all responsibility for the crisis; they refused to take part in any government that did not have Largo Caballero as Prime Minister and Minister of War; and they therefore proposed a 'government supported by the workers' organisations'.

On 16 May, Largo Caballero sent a letter to all political forces in which he outlined his own proposals for the composition of the new government. There would be three ministers from the UGT and he would be Prime Minister and Minister for National Defence, which would bring together the former ministries of War and of the Navy and Air Force. The PSOE, PCE, IR and the CNT would each have two ministries and there would be one for Unión Republicana. One representative each from the Partido Nacionalista Vasco and Esquerra Republicana de Catalunya would be ministers 'without portfolio'. The letter received favourable responses from the UGT, Unión Republicana and Izquierda Republicana. The UGT leader's proposals were rejected by the PCE, the PSOE and the CNT, the latter declaring that it was unacceptable that it should be 'put in an inferior position'. The following day, Manuel Azaña, who had expected the demand for a new prime minister to have been made by others, although he was the first to want to be rid of Largo Caballero, whom he had not forgiven for the 'lack of liberty' that he had suffered during his siege in the Palacio de Pedralbes during the May Days, charged Juan Negrín with the formation of a new government. Negrín's cabinet excluded the two trade-union organisations. In its editorial of 18 May, *Solidaridad Obrera* declared: 'a counter-revolutionary government has been formed'.[5]

For a few days, the CNT seemed emboldened, determined not to collaborate with the new government but rather to 'sabotage it', to promote propaganda against it, and 'further pointing out that it was a government of the counter-revolution'. It also called for the intensifying of relations with that part of the UGT that was represented by Largo Caballero: 'We will not accept under any pretext the violence that they might provoke anywhere, since it is obvious that they want to push us into fighting on the streets, something we must avoid.'[6]

Having eliminated the street as the place for the arena of political battle, something that the anarcho-syndicalist leadership had achieved since the autumn of 1936, there was now no alternative other than once more to seek collaboration. By 2 June, the CNT National Committee revealed that it was negotiating with Negrín over its possible participation in the government. And on 17 June, given the 'tragic' situation of the North, which was underlined two days later with the occupation of Bilbao by Italian forces and the Navarrese brigades, Mariano R. Vázquez sent a letter to Manuel Azaña in which he laid out the CNT 'programme'. Demands for changes in republican policy, at least for the CNT leadership, could come only after the return of its organisation to the government.[7]

The events of that spring of 1937 confirmed some of the signs that anarcho-syndicalism was changing, signs of which had been there during the republican years and had been accelerated by the war: the absence of internal discussion, a hierarchical structure and the rupture of the channels of communication between the leadership and the union rank-and-file. The changes could be seen in the conciliatory attitude of the CNT ministers and the National Committee in relation to the recent confrontations between the forces of public order and radical groups of anarchist activists, for whom dissidence was the only option. The same conciliatory and 'serene' position was shown by *Solidaridad Obrera*, which now became the mouthpiece for the policies imposed by the leadership. Already persecuted by censorship, the paper was slow to report the disturbances, trying to play down the news and even praising the behaviour of the forces of public order, something that was unknown in the libertarian movement. It avoided the threatening messages that had been usual in past disturbances in which the CNT participated. It said nothing about the violence of the armed confrontations. The dead from these days were not now, as they would have been in the past, martyrs of the revolutionary cause. Withal, the paper broke with such typical ingredients of the insurrectionary tradition of Spanish anarchism as the glorification of heroes and the call for revenge for the blood that had been spilt.[8]

Yet neither did these days bring a victory for the counter-revolution. The dilemma revolution/counter-revolution, that is if it existed in those terms, had been resolved a good deal before. May 1937 does not constitute, therefore, the dividing line between two very different periods of the Civil War (libertarian social revolution and communist reaction), the culminating moment of confrontation between those who wanted only to make the revolution and those who wanted to win the war. Neither was it the point at which anarchism broke with its revolutionary conceptions. The position that is defended here is that the fundamental elements of this confrontation had already been present at the beginning of the war. There is no doubt, nevertheless, that though the conventional explanation of these events as the triumph of the counter-revolution cannot be accepted, it is certainly the case that, after May 1937, some things changed. The POUM was liquidated, Largo Caballero was isolated and the anarcho-syndicalists saw an acceleration of the loss of their armed and political power. Thus, it was no small matter relative to the special role in the drama played by the anarcho-syndicalist actors.

The radicals were defeated and the leadership committees of anarcho-syndicalism could defend the same arguments that they had made in the autumn of 1936 to open up the way to their participation in political institutions. However, after the 'May Days' of 1937, with the CNT now out of government, strident demands were heard for a settling of accounts over the betrayal of the sacred principles of anti-politicism. The harshest criticisms were heard in the plenary meeting of the International Association of Workers (AIT), held in Paris on 11 July 1937. The secretary of the French delegation, Alexander Schapiro, the very same individual who had been asked to mediate in the internal conflict of the CNT in 1933, and the general secretary of the AIT, Pierre Besnard, theoretical guide of anarcho-syndicalists just as Joan Peiró had been during the early years of the Republic, led strong attacks against the Spanish delegation led by David Antona. Besnard declared: 'If the CNT commits itself to no further collaboration in the government, correcting its current line of conduct ... [the AIT] will formally commit itself to the preparation of a world-wide revolutionary general strike to help the Spanish Revolution.' As Mariano R. Vásquez well perceived, this was 'nonsense ... it may just as well be said to the inhabitants of Mars, but hardly a serious thing to have said in a plenary meeting'. There was further 'nonsense', such as the resolution that attributed the events of May to a 'plan conceived of by the political parties inspired by the Spanish Communist Party, carrying out the orders of the Soviet government ... a plan of an international nature ... serving Anglo-French-American interests'. However, leaving aside the 'nonsense', everything said there was aimed at demonstrating that 'participation in Power' was the cause of 'the suppression of the militias', of giving the government a 'regular army ... a constant danger for the Revolution' and of the 'disappearance of the free municipalities' which had returned to the government 'all of the administration of the country'. It had 'undermined', then, 'the success of the social revolution, subordinating it to a war that could only favour international capitalism'. It is curious to note that all of this was sanctioned by delegates from countries such as Holland, Belgium, Norway and Poland who barely represented between them 1,000 members.[9]

With the star of the once-respected Spanish anarchist heroes already waning, García Oliver and Montseny went to Paris a week later to the Plenary meeting to explain there what they had been expounding for some time: that the CNT could have created a dictatorship and 'led the war and the revolution without forming part of the government'. However, they did not wish to do so as 'international capitalism would have crushed us', and instead they had promoted an 'alliance between all worker and anti-fascist forces'. García Oliver had reached this point in his speech when 'whistling, insults and taunts began. Some shouted "murderer, murderer". What about Camilo Berneri?' The 'violent' incident lasted half an hour and 'blows were exchanged amongst the public present'. The audience was made up of some hundreds of anarchists and Trotskyists.[10]

All of these outbursts of purity enraged the National Committee of the CNT, its secretary and the Spanish delegate to the AIT, David Antona, who called for the replacement of Besnard, 'a man who is exhausted physically and even spiritually'. Collaboration, repeated Mariano R. Vázquez, had been a 'necessity' and 'those who set themselves up as apostles of the anarchist ideal neither understand nor want to understand, even though they could never have even dreamt of the scale of our tragedy or of our struggle'. And these apostles, 'instead of helping us and defending us from the attacks made on us abroad by Marxists and reformists ... all they know is how to criticise us ... [thus] playing into the hands of the enemy, helping its campaign to undermine Spanish anarchism. It seems to forget that our tragedy is that we could not turn to a world anarchist movement capable of providing arms in abundance, capable of pressurising the democratic powers, that could have, to put it in a nutshell, sabotaged fascism.' Vázquez concluded with recognition of the work of Helmut Rudiger, delegate of the AIT in Spain, as the only one that judged the situation with a 'real critical spirit', contrary to those who only 'saw things through the lens of ideas and principles'.

For Rudiger, then, it seemed 'incomprehensible' that international anarchism should attack in this way the only mass movement in the world that libertarians had, 'as though we were in the happy situation of having nothing better to do than to argue about who was the purest ideologically'. The CNT did not need a 'tutor' and did well in defending, as it did in May 1937, the position 'that it had adopted and made its own since the beginning of the war'. Revolution did not consist of 'the brave action of thousands of men' as the anarchists of the nineteenth century thought, or as many Spanish libertarians had assumed before the military revolt of July 1936: 'if the CNT in May had taken its armed movement to its logical conclusion, it would have been an action similar to that of 8 December 1933 ... that is to say a movement of rebellion of a minority faced with the indifference of part of the working class and the active resistance of the other part'. The glory associated with July 1936 was already history.[11]

The star of the anarchists shone even less brightly during those final days of June 1937. On the 26th, a Plenary meeting of Regional Committees meeting in Valencia decided to 'study the means of provoking a cabinet reshuffle to facilitate the entry of the CNT into a new government'. It was one thing to 'study' it but the objective was more distant than ever. Not only would the libertarians not join Negrín's government but, three days later, they would also leave the Generalitat, never to return. They left, as always, with dignity: because, following the events of May, they had shown 'to the world an example of serenity and wisdom'.[12]

As well as dignity, they still had the Council of Aragon, the collectives and the factories. This still signified a great deal although soon it would amount to nothing. The first to disappear was the regional government of Aragon. Following the disturbances in May, Aragon lived through an intense period of conflicts. The tensions between communists and libertarians, with the POUM in between, broke out again with renewed ferocity. The greatest problem was public order. Already on 11 May, representatives of the organisations of the Popular Front of the province of Huesca signed a communiqué protesting about disturbances of law and order in many towns and villages and demanded 'the speedy adoption of measures that will put an end to the murders of honourable anti-fascist peasants'. They also called for the elimination of the Department of Public Order of the Council of Aragon, whose leaders they held responsible for provoking the disorder and inciting violence. On 22 May, in a meeting with the CNT and the president of the Council of Aragon, Joaquín Ascaso, the communists proposed a 're-structuring of the Council' by means of which some departments would be unified and those of Information and Propaganda and Public Order would be eliminated. They also proposed the creation of a forty-man permanent committee 'with an executive powers' to be composed 'equitably' of CNT and the Popular Front representatives. The CNT, however, accepted only the dissolution of the Department of Public Order and rejected the permanent committee because 'as well as being un-economical, it has the deplorable consequence of trying to give life to an Aragonese parliament', something that 'clashes with the racial temperament of our people'. The Council of Aragon, as it was known, was 'the genuine representative of the popular will'.[13]

Equally troublesome was the matter of the POUM, though it was resolved in a much quicker and expeditious way. The Aragonese Communist press helped raise the temperature. The first edition of *Vanguardia*, the newspaper of the Regional Committee of the PCE, demanded on 14 May the immediate dissolution of the POUM, 'Trotyskist provocateurs', 'unconditional ally of the rebel Junta in Burgos'. There was no more damning argument than calling someone 'fascist' at a time when what was being carried out was an 'anti-fascist war'. This was only the beginning. The 29th Division was again accused of having abandoned the front, an accusation that the communists had been making since February 1937. On 16 June, Josep Rovira, the member of the Central Committee of Anti-Fascist Militias who had organised the 'Lenin' column, was detained. Following the protests of the anarchist leaders of the 25th, 26th and 28th Divisions, the Defence Minister, Indalecio Prieto, ordered his release on 10 July. Nevertheless, the 29th Division was dissolved and re-organised and members of the POUM ended up, as is well known, being persecuted and tortured. The worst case was that of Andreu Nin, who was kidnapped, 'disappeared' and was murdered. In spite of the harsh nature of some of the more vehement denunciations made against the POUM, the CNT, itself under attack but angling for its own return to government, limited itself to requesting 'judicial verification' of the accusations and of putting Benito Pabón (general secretary of the Council of Aragon) at the 'disposal of the POUM'. Pabón defended some of the activists in the courts.[14]

With the problems of public order and the POUM despatched, attacks and complaints against the Council of Aragon intensified. Criticism was directed particularly against the organisation of the collectivised economy, to which were added accusations against the CNT for using force to impose its positions. The consequence of all this was that, in the view propagated by the non-anarchist media, whilst the government 'of victory' imposed its authority in the rest of republican territory, in Aragon chaos reigned. According to Manuel Azaña, 'at last', by 12 July, the decree for the dissolution of the Council of Aragon had been prepared: 'all that is now required is to bring them to account for their outrages.' On 6 August he noted: 'The Council of Aragon business is about to be settled.' On the next day, the Aragonese delegation, led by Joaquín Ascaso, went to Valencia to the Plenary session of the CNT. They outlined the Aragonese situation, before which there were only two possibilities: 'to defend ourselves with skill and diplomacy or resort to violence.' The second, proposed by the FAI, was rejected at the request of the National Committee and it was decided 'that the Regional Committee of Aragon opt for the road of skill in keeping the Council in existence. If it is dissolved, then they should aim to position themselves as best they can, by taking part in whatever new body is created to succeed it and thereby neutralise any enemy offensive.'[15]

On 11 August, the decree for the dissolution of the Council was published in the official bulletin, the *Gaceta de la República*. The government delegate in Aragon, Joaquín Ascaso, and the remaining members of the Council were dismissed and the republican José Ignacio Mantecón was appointed as governor-general of Aragon. His first administrative orders criticised the anarchist collectives, commenting that they had been established in 'a heightened moment of revolutionary virulence, during which fear was what drove these new enterprises'. Now 'tyranny' was at an end and 'all individuals or families' that had formed part of the collectives created in Aragon after the military revolt were henceforth 'free to remain within or to leave them, withdrawing, on doing so, any capital invested and any profits that, as a member of the collective, were due to them'.[16]

Hundreds of CNT members were imprisoned. Some, those responsible for the department of Public Order and those accused of crimes related to 'requisitions' and 'robberies', were still in Caspe prison in March 1938, when Franco's major army offensive through Aragon began. The municipal councils controlled by the libertarians were suppressed and replaced by 'committees of administration' designated 'by order of the government'. The CNT was expelled from local power in the majority of the Aragonese villages. The 'committees of administration', with the assistance of the security forces and the army, destroyed the collectives, seized all of their goods and returned land to its owners. Joaquín Ascaso was arrested in Valencia, accused of stealing jewels. Freed on 18 September 1937, he wandered about, preparing one report after another in the hope of preventing his marginalisation. In September 1938, the National Committee expelled him from the CNT.

The delegation of the National Committee sent to Aragon in September 1937 to investigate violence against libertarians was able to do little. They also sent lawyers who ended up clashing with the prisoners. In reality, except for making token protests against the persecution, the leadership committees of the libertarian movement were interested only in ensuring that events did not get out of hand, making sure, in other words, that nothing would hinder negotiations to secure entry into Negrín's government. They could see no use in defending a cause which they had never felt to be theirs. For the National Committee of the CNT, the events in Aragon, within and outside the Council, had brought them only problems and headaches. This was the origin of the criticism of militarisation. This was the justification used by deserters and by the most combative leaders who opposed the policy of order and discipline. Among them could be found, as late as August 1937, many of the young libertarians who continued to demand that the CNT and the FAI withdraw from politics and cease 'begging for charity from the state'. So much criticism and insolence was the last straw for the leadership. For these anarchists from the city, who had defended agrarian reform at other times, collectivisation in the countryside was already a lost cause. In the summer of 1937, energy was being put into other areas, on questions at a much higher level.[17]

The burning question at a higher level was that of a return to government, something that had become a real obsession for the principal committees of the CNT and the FAI. Under vigilance at the battle-fronts, having lost the 'force of the street' and excluded from political institutions, the movement was 'disorientated'. To put an end to this disorientation and 'specify responsibilities', the regional secretaries met in Valencia, which in itself constituted yet another step towards hierarchical and authoritarian decision-making. García Oliver defended 'participation in governing the life of the country' with unimpeachable conviction. Anarcho-syndicalism was left with only three possible choices: 'insurrection, involvement in government or just to wait on events.' 'Realism' advised intervention if the goal was to 'consolidate revolutionary conquests', 'since we are not prepared for insurrection'. All of the leading figures thought more or less the same, ranging from those from the Peninsula Committee of the FAI who called for 'the use of skill to get ourselves into positions of influence with the object of ensuring that we receive the respect we deserve' to the secretary of the CNT from Aragon who, in spite of the persecution that had been unleashed against the CNT in that region, believed that 'what our organisation needs at this time is to be represented in the government'. The final decision was, logically, that 'the National Committee continue working to secure our representation in the government'.[18]

Limiting the major objective simply to 'involvement' was the final proof of the weakness of anarcho-syndicalism, even though there was another parallel road not mentioned by García Oliver, which is actually what ensued: the pact with the UGT, the famous 'workers' solution', the 'revolutionary workers' alliance' which had been aborted so many times. It served for little though that this 'unity of action programme' was finally signed in March 1938, when both union organisations were a shadow of their former selves, the UGT broken and split into socialist and communist factions, the CNT impotent. With their capacity for mobilisation now having evaporated, these unions had little to say and do. Their good intentions brought them, finally, to the government again in April of that same year. This was a government, Negrín's second, that no longer had to fear them. Segundo Blanco, from the CNT in Asturias, where he had defended the workers' alliance in 1934, was appointed Minister of Education and Ramón González Peña, of the UGT, Minister of Justice. Impotence resolved long-standing UGT–CNT hostilities. Whilst both union organisations had the strength, it had never been possible to bridge the gulf that separated them.

The hope that this workers' solution would be better able to respond to the 'needs of the war and economic and social reconstruction' also reached the factories. For the CNT union committees that supported the positions of their leadership, unity with the UGT resuscitated the old myth of workers' power that had nothing to do with politicians and, at the same time, permitted the silencing of those radical sectors which, although they were fatally wounded following the events of May 1937, were still flying the flag of 'socialisation' as the guarantee of an authentic libertarian revolution. However, this move towards trade-union unity was unable to achieve the desired success because it occurred just at the moment when the war began to be felt in Catalonia. The transfer of the government of Negrín to Barcelona at the end of October 1937 relegated the government of the Generalitat to 'a totally secondary role', strengthened central control of the collectives and restricted what little autonomy unions still had in the running of businesses. From a situation of being subjected to government control and restrictions, many factories, particularly in the metallurgical sector, now faced direct requisitioning, which in practice meant the end of collectivisation and trade-union power. The harder the war bit, the more pessimism increased amongst a populace that grew more numerous by the day because of the massive flood of refugees. The people every day drifted further away from the happy state promised by the revolution at the same speed at which their standard of living plummeted.[19]

The revolution was no longer the inevitable point of reference, that devastating force which had swept away the old order. It disappeared from the plans of the CNT, even from its rhetoric. From the spring of 1938, in local and national meetings of the anarcho-syndicalists, the only subjects on the agenda were the war, internal matters, such as the need to give even more power to those who already had it, the supreme efforts which would not be 'sterile, given that when we have achieved victory by crushing the fascist invader, we will consolidate our independence, welfare and liberty, the goals for which we are fighting and indeed the highest ambitions of the people to whom we owe everything'.[20]

The anarchist movement was on its last legs. There was ever less territory to defend. Some of the libertarian newspapers did not survive these difficult months and collapsed before the end of the war. Bankruptcy even hit *Solidaridad Obrera*, which had lived out its golden age, with plentiful resources, during the first months of the revolution. From May 1937, a paper shortage began and the censor was merciless with the newspaper that had once embodied the power of the CNT. Toryho became weary of these continuous attacks and, feeling that he was no longer the star that he had been, engineered his own departure. Toryho had been one of the principal architects of the policies of order, collaboration and discipline imposed by the leadership committees of the CNT from the autumn of 1936 onwards and finally ratified in May 1937. Now, he spent his final days in the editorship of the newspaper absorbed in a 'personal crisis of conscience' which impelled him to criticise all those ideas as useless, as they had achieved so little, and to break the discipline demanded of him by the Regional Committee of Catalonia. He was dismissed on 7 May 1938, together with Abelardo Iglesias, the senior editorialist, who had joined him in those criticisms. The rest of the editorial team showed their solidarity with them and also left the newspaper. Until the conquest of Barcelona by Franco's troops, the paper was run by José Viadiu, a veteran trade unionist linked to Salvador Seguí at the beginning of the 1920s and who was closely involved in the paper during that period. Liberto Callejas, another old and well-known activist, returned. On 24 January 1939, the final edition of the historic mouthpiece of anarcho-syndicalism appeared. Three weeks later, with the city in the hands of the Francoists, on 14 February, *Solidaridad Nacional*, the 'Newspaper of the National Syndicalist Revolution' was published in the *Solidaridad Obrera* premises in the Calle Consell de Cent. From *Solidaridad Obrera* to *Solidaridad Nacional*, from the worker and anarchist revolution to the National–Syndicalist revolution, that is to say, the revolution over which the Falangists expected to preside. It was the beginning, of course, of another very different story.[21]

Epilogue
The uprooting

The Civil War and the revolution left lasting scars on Spanish society. Following the conquest by Franco's army of all territory that had been loyal to the Republic, the old social order was re-established as rapidly as it had been overthrown. The social and cultural structures of clerical power and relations between master and worker were restored after the trauma of the revolutionary experience. Memory of the war and the bloody repression, the spirit of revenge unleashed against the defeated, were maintained by the dictatorship as useful instruments to preserve the unity of the victorious coalition and to intensify the misery of those 'undisciplined wretches' who had dared to denounce the social order. The churches were filled with commemorative plaques for those who had 'Fallen for God and the Fatherland'. The Law of Political Responsibilities, passed in February 1939, gave free reign to the continued physical elimination of the opposition. In official language, for a long time there were only 'victors and vanquished', 'patriots and traitors', 'Nationalists and Reds'.

The 'vanquished' who survived had to adapt to new forms of 'co-existence'. Owners returned to their factories and lands determined to purge them of all those who had participated actively in the collectivisations. Many lost their jobs whilst others, particularly in the rural world, were forced to move to the cities or to other villages. Union activists, those who been prominent in their support of the revolution, suffered most as they were hounded and denounced by informers. On those who had been less involved, many of them illiterate, Francoism imposed silence as the price of survival, forcing them to 'swallow' their own identity.[1]

In exile, activists who had lived through and played a key role in these revolutionary transformations became involved in many bitter polemics over their consequences. Those who condemned the collectivisations, particularly the communists, used the example of republican Aragon to prove that the revolution was imposed on the majority of hostile peasants and that collectivisation failed as a system of production and distribution of food supplies to both troops and the civilian population. Its defenders argued that the revolution was the spontaneous response of the people to decades of repression and that collectivism was the inevitable fruit of mature anarchism, the culmination of the long quest for social justice.

For those who stayed in the towns and villages or returned to them after years of imprisonment and exile, the memory of those events quickly faded because of the effective combination of the bitter taste of defeat, persecution, Francoist propaganda and the fear of denunciation. All that was positive in the experiences in that period when agriculture was reorganised and power redistributed gave way to the weight of negative memories. The first foreign historians who came to Spain at the beginning of the 1970s, ready to interpret for the first time the revolutionary events through the use of oral history, found that almost no one from the defeated side could speak clearly or serenely about their experiences. Some termed them as catastrophic, others emphasised their coercive nature, whilst the most reflective declared that the majority of peasants and workers were not 'ready' to put into practice collective ideals. Women did not want to participate in the interviews and many, under the effects of the anti-communism of Francoist propaganda, confused libertarian collectives with Soviet communism. Evidently, no one-year revolution, however good or bad it was, could survive the assault of four decades of dictatorship.

Prisons, executions and exile drove anarcho-syndicalism into a tunnel from which it would not emerge. Some activists joined the clandestine resistance, taking part in some of the skirmishes and actions of the guerrilla war against the regime as well as other conflicts. Clandestinity, it is true, was nothing new in the history of Spanish anarchism and neither were repression, arrests, torture, executions or prohibition. In reality, clandestinity and repression had gone hand-in-hand following the hysteria surrounding the Cantonal revolt in 1873 and the supposed 'Black Hand' conspiracy in 1882. This was repeated in the 1890s, the early years of the twentieth century and during the dictatorship of Primo de Rivera, all of which were periods of retreat in terms of mobilisation and worker organisation. It was usually at these times that a tendency to violence, 'propaganda of the deed', and terrorism bloomed. Clandestinity gave shelter to violent activists, a shelter where old habits associated with Bakuninism could flourish, but it also permitted reflection and education. During periods of forced inaction within the movement, ideological debates and polemics took place. The movement's newspapers and journals, widely distributed leaflets and books, popular meetings, the creation of 'affinity groups', all these things would keep the flame alive until the next resurgence, until signs of recovery appeared again.

Except in the periods between 1917–21 and 1931–7, when the transition from anarchism to anarcho-syndicalism took place, a period that began with a loose attachment to libertarian ideas and ended with discipline and mass membership, the movement never had a stable membership. It was dominated by chronological and geographical discontinuity, by explosions of protest which always encountered the same punitive response on the part of rulers, landowners and factory-owners. However, although unstable and less persistent than is supposed, anarchism was there, at times disappearing and then returning, with its social project of freedom and of the collectivisation of the means of production, of the abolition of the state, of the organisation of a future society without coercion. All of these objectives would be reached through the authentic trade marks of the movement: apoliticism, the rejection of electoral and parliamentary struggles.

The period of clandestinity which began in 1939, however, bore little resemblance to its predecessors. It was the result of defeat in war, imposed mercilessly by blood and fire. Union life was impossible. Under Franco, there were not even the minimal freedoms that had survived in the harshest of previous periods, freedoms that had permitted doctrinal polemics and cultural initiatives – through leaflets, newspapers and meetings – to make contact with the 'people'. Escaping persecution, evading police vigilance, confronting the armed forces, practising 'revolutionary gymnastics' ceased to be a game, an adventure, as they had been for other 'men of action' such as Ascaso and Durruti, during the years following the coup of Primo de Rivera, and even during the Republic. In the conditions imposed at the end of the war, it was virtually impossible to develop the cult of the people, to discuss the future society, to dream about utopias. All of this was now history, recent but firmly in the past, the great missed opportunity, aborted by the war and by communist rivals, definitively annihilated by Francoist arms. Now there was only silence inside Spain and bitter controversy, confrontations, divisions and splits in exile. The majority had more than enough to do just to survive, just to find somewhere, usually far away, where they could get on with life. Until the end of the Second World War, hope remained. Many anarchists joined the French resistance against Nazism, believing that it was still their war, the war to end all tyrannies of which Franco's was the greatest. They believed that victory in that war would allow them to return to their homes, their work and their land. However, Hitler and Mussolini died, the Axis powers were defeated yet Franco remained in power. Furthermore, Franco endlessly evoked the war and administered bitter punishment to those who had lost it.

Furthermore, it was not only the long dictatorship and its counter-revolutionary terror that swept away anarcho-syndicalism and prevented its return or rebirth after the death of Franco. The extraordinary economic growth between 1961 and 1973 was both accompanied by, and was the result of, profound transformations in Spanish society. The Spanish economy finally took advantage of 'previously lost' opportunities – cheap energy; favourable prices in raw materials and foodstuffs; external financing 'consisting of remittances from emigrants, the profits of tourism and foreign investment'; and the easy acquisition of new technology – which other developed capitalist countries had enjoyed from the beginning of the 1950s. In those years, the value of industrial production exceeded that of agriculture for the first time. The percentage of the population working in agriculture declined from 41.6 per cent in 1960 to 29.1 per cent in 1970. The massive rural exodus ended the historic surplus of labour in the countryside, characteristic of Spanish agriculture until the Civil War. Traditional agriculture went into crisis, as a consequence of the migratory process which profoundly affected the casual day labourers, wage labourers and the small landowners. This redistribution of the population caused a notable increase in agricultural salaries which forced landowners to substitute labour with machinery, something made possible at a time of considerable technological advances.[2]

Industrial growth, the crisis of traditional agriculture and emigration from the countryside had important repercussions for both class structure and the social movements. A new working class emerged which had to initially subsist in miserable conditions and with low wages, under the control of the Falangists and the vertical trade unions, subject to intense repression. However, from the beginning of the 1960s, it was able to use the new legislation on collective agreements to improve employment contracts. The introduction of collective bargaining, 'a means of institutionalising class antagonism', led to significant changes in the theory and practice of unionism, just as it had done in other European countries during the inter-war period. The aims of workers' revolution were shelved in favour of other more immediate aims in terms of wages, the length of contracts and demands for freedom. The union representatives began to develop a 'cushioning' role between workers and bosses.

Obviously, it was no primrose path, because the dictatorship and its police continued to root out any form of rebellion. Given that strikes were prohibited and were harshly repressed, labour conflicts almost always became political ones. They began with demands for higher wages and ended with calls for the overthrow of the dictatorship. Out of this, clandestine unionism, the Workers' Commissions, emerged, created and led by Catholic and communist groups. They infiltrated the Francoist unions, got their representatives voted in, to negotiate with the factory owners. This strategy would be pursued until circumstances changed; meanwhile the new unionists patiently awaited the end to the official structures. There was thus a new union culture, although the UGT had already developed a similar kind of 'indirect action' before the Civil War, in very different circumstances, by using the channels offered by the Primo de Rivera regime. It bore little resemblance to that 'direct' action, which, as it had been adopted and practised by the anarcho-syndicalists, merely brought workers and capitalists, authority and the oppressed, into violent confrontations without union representatives to minimise the conflict. It thereby seemed to reject any possibility that legal mechanisms could be used to the benefit of the working class. Inevitably, amongst the builders of this new union culture, which involved a strategy of negotiation to solve conflicts, were not to be found activists of the CNT, whether those inside Spain or those who, from their exile, still analysed the Spanish situation in terms of the revolutionary experiences of the Civil War.[3]

Nor was the state the same. Its functions increased and diversified, the police and army grew, as vitally important mechanisms of coercion for the maintenance of the order which had been conquered by force of arms in the Civil War but so too was there an increase in the numbers of civil servants and the scale of public services. It was not, of course, a 'welfare' state, like those that existed at that time in the democracies of Western Europe. It left, nevertheless, an impact on the daily life of the population that was more lasting and profound than in previous periods in the history of Spain. It left its traces in a certain liberalisation and rationalisation in the functioning of the capitalist market, in the welfare system and in the services that could be of use for the population. Although police-run, paternalist and technocratic, this state turned out to be stronger and more effective than its predecessors which had allowed anarcho-syndicalism to oppose them in the first decades of the century. It was not that these forms of domination were 'acceptable' and the citizenry did not want to confront them. Rather, it was that the state's organisation, level of development and the absolute control that it exercised over its mechanisms of coercion dramatically diminished any possibilities of insurrection or social mobilisation against it. In the apolitical mind-set which had dominated revolutionary unionism during the Restoration and the Second Republic, the notion of the reform of the state in a democratic direction did not exist and the only possibility was its overthrow. In contrast, included among the objectives of the leadership and the protagonists of the political and union culture that emerged from the 1960s was that of taking advantage of the opportunities for integration that the system offered and for reform of the state. These changes and social mobilisation took legitimacy away from the dictatorship as a form of domination. However, it also rendered irrelevant the anarcho-syndicalists' anti-political discourse, with its rejection of parliamentary politics and electoral struggle as instruments for the representation of the interests of different social groups.[4]

In the final years of Francoism and the early years of the transition, conflicts and mobilisations showed important similarities to the new social movements which proliferated at the time in the industrialised countries of Europe and North America. This was the high point of the student movement, which in Spain confronted not only the education system but also a repressive and reactionary political regime. It was a key moment in the emergence of the peripheral nationalisms, which brought together a good part of the political and cultural elites. Finally, there were also the other forms of collective action linked to pacifism – antimilitarism, feminism, ecology and neighbourhood associations. In the majority of cases, they were movements that abandoned the revolutionary dream of structural change in favour of that of defending a democratic civil society. They adopted less hierarchical and centralised forms of organisations and their members were the young, students and employees of the public sector, meaning people that no longer represented just one particular class, generally the working class, and therefore no longer represented only the interests and demands of that class.

Apparently, these social movements – with their defence of spontaneity and of decentralised organisation, with their denunciation of any method of oppression, their ridiculing of power and their refusal to accept technocratic capitalism – revived elements that were peculiar to the libertarian tradition. This seemed to find expression in some countries with the 'new' left or the conflicts that became identified with the Paris of May 1968. Yet if this was related to anarchism it was with the most individualistic, hedonistic side, which led to elitist positions, and which, more importantly, had little to do with unionism. What had put down roots in Spain from the foundation of the CNT was the notion of solidarity, which always considered equality between men to be an untouchable principle, which placed its trust in the popular 'masses' and which subordinated liberation and personal action to a collective project. In Spain therefore, the supposed rebirth of anarchism within these new social movements clashed with the rigid revolutionary puritanism of the older generation which had fought in the war, and which refused to die even while everything around it had changed.[5]

The period between 1939 and 1975 seems to be insurmountable. Negotiation as the form of institutionalising conflicts had imposed itself. New social movements and new protagonists had substituted class movements and class heroes, those who were from that working class to which had been assigned the historic mission of transforming society. The workers from the countryside who went *en masse* to the cities from the 1950s were doing so to become part of very different industrial sectors. It was not only, as it had been with the emigration of the 1920s, to areas such as construction or in sectors that were intermediate stages between agriculture and industry. The rural proletariat had declined considerably and was no longer at the heart of strikes. Illiteracy had been drastically reduced and was no longer, as was stated in the CNT Congress of 1931 that 'blight ... which has the people sunk in the greatest of infamies'. Environmental and cultural factors in previous periods had permitted the call to ancestral and messianic myths, what Brenan called 'reverse religiosity'. It had been easy to recognise this in anarchism, yet also in other workers' movements of the Marxist type that were also now history. The weak state, which had made possible the hopes and the dreams that revolutions hinged only on the revolutionary intentions of workers and peasants, had transformed itself into one that was stronger, more effective, interventionist and, perhaps, almost a 'benefactor'. Consumerism produced miracles: it allowed capital to spread and for the workers to improve their standard of living. Without the anti-political stance, and with workers who had abandoned radicalism for the prospect of tangible and immediate improvements, who preferred cars and fridges to altruism and sacrifice for the cause, anarchism floundered and ceased to exist.

The panorama offered up by the historic anarchists, those who have been the object of this study, was in the final years of Francoism a discouraging one: some of them by now very old, destroyed by an exile that never achieved the re-unification of different rival groups, scattered throughout France and Latin America, they lived only to recall, with a mix of nostalgia, rage and pride, those heroic years when they had constituted a social force for change. When, with Franco dead, they could again walk on Spanish soil, the fields, the towns and villages, and even the people had all changed. There was no likelihood of reviving anarcho-syndicalism as a mass movement. The old anarchists could stay true to their principles and they did so unto the grave. There was little else for them: their memory and recollections seemed enough. War and cruel dictatorship had uprooted them whilst the changes from the 1950s in the social structure prevented them from putting down new roots. Thus they had no alternative. They were alone and without possible national or international political allies, something enjoyed by, for example, the UGT, the other union destroyed by internal divisions and repression. They did not even have their heritage and buildings returned to them. They, in definitive terms, now belonged to that ruined Spain over which the developmental miracle had been built.

Notes

1 History accelerates

1 Letter in the National History Archive of Salamanca (AHNS), Sección Político-Social, carpeta 886, Barcelona. The term 'wild anarchist' had already been applied to Carbó by the Valencian District Attorney on October 1920 and the text can be found in Serie A de Gobernación, legajo 7, in the National History Archive (AHN) Madrid. The description of the initial trajectory of the Republic as a shift from a 'euphoria of enthusiasm' to the 'awakening of working class consciousness' was used by V. Orobón Fernández in *La CNT y la Revolución* (conference paper, Madrid Academy, 6/4/1932 and published in *El Libertario*, Madrid, 1932, with a prologue by Ramón J. Sender). This is one of the basic arguments in the extensive and important work of Santos' Juliá on the Second Republic. See especially *1931–1934. De la fiesta popular a la lucha de classes* (Madrid, Siglo XXI, 1984) and 'De la revolución popular a la revolución obrera', *Historia Social*, No. 1 (1988), pp. 29–43.

2 These declarations are repeated in the *Memoria del Congreso Extraordinario de la CNT celebrado en Madrid del 11 al 16 de junio de 1931* (Barcelona, Cosmos, 1931), pp. 180–1. The analysis of the culture of mobilisation which 'Lerrouxism' brought to mass politics in Spain provides the underlying thread of José Alvárez Junco's well-known and important book *El emperador del Paralelo. Lerroux y la demagogia populista* (Madrid, Alianza Ed, 1990). See especially pp. 387–97 and pp. 439–41. A further nuance has recently been added to this notion of a 'spontaneous' popular festival by Enric Ucelay da Cal, who defines all of this as a 'plebiscite in the street' orchestrated by the republicans and their working-class allies, 'with the subsequent acquisition of power in councils and other political centres ... following the official cession of power'. See 'Buscando el levantamiento plebiscitario: insurreccionalismo y elecciones' in Santos Juliá (ed.) 'Política en la Segunda República', *Ayer*, 20 (1995), pp. 63–4.

3 Victoriano Gracia's text can be found in legajo 62 of the (AHN) Serie A, Gobernación documents. The phrase 'emerged from the people' is taken from *El Luchador*, 24 April 1931. This was a paper linked to the Urales stream of anarchism, which was not particularly influential in syndicalist publications. The idea of taking advantage of the republican regime in order to strengthen the syndicalist organisation is taken up, for example, in *Solidaridad Obrera* on the 14 April and in the Zaragoza weekly *Cultura y Acción* on the 21 May of the same year. Galo Díez also cites phrases from *El Luchador* in his analysis in the *Memoria del Congreso Extraordinario de la CNT celebrado en Madrid los días 11 al 16 de junio de 1931*, pp. 191–2. There was hardly any vigorous opposition to the Republic expressed initially in anarchist publications. This has been confirmed in recent years by detailed investigations such as Angeles Barrio, *Anarquismo y anarcosindicalismo en Asturias (1890–1936)* (Madrid, Siglo XXI, 1988), pp. 317–18; Enrique Montañés, *Anarcosindicalismo y cambio político. Zaragoza, 1930–1936* (Zaragoza, Institución Fernando el Católico, 1989), pp. 47–9; and Enric Ucelay da

Cal, who uses the term 'honeymoon' to describe the reconciliatory atmosphere which accompanied the advent of the Republic in industrial Barcelona, in *La Catalunya populista. Imatge, cultura i política en l'etapa republicana (1931–1939)* (Barcelona, Edicions de La Magrana, 1982), p. 135.

4 See Santos Juliá, *Manuel Azaña. Una biografía política* (Madrid, Alianza Ed., 1990), pp. 74–5 for this argument and pp. 94–5 for this author's emphasis on Azaña's faith in the state. The reach of this concept for the republicans is summarised in José Alvarez Junco, 'Los amantes de la libertad: la cultura republicana española a principios del sigloXX' in Nigel Townson (ed.) *El republicanismo en España (1830–1977)* (Madrid, Alianza Ed., 1994), pp. 281–83. Townson has dealt with the adaptation of 'Lerrouxism' to the current situation himself in 'Algunas consideraciones sobre el proyecto "republicano" del Partido Radical', in J.L. García Delgado (ed.) *La República española. Bienio rectificador y Frente Popular, 1934–1936* (Madrid, Siglo XXI, 1988), pp. 60–1. The citation referring to anarcho-syndicalism is taken from the *Boletín de la CNT*, No. 5 (February–April 1932) and No. 16 (April–June 1933), and from *CNT*, No. 22, November 1932.

5 Santos Juliá, *Manuel Azaña*, p. 17.

6 A collection of these decrees and laws appears in *La legislación social en la historia de España. De la revolución liberal a 1936* (Madrid, Congreso de los Diputados, 1987) with a detailed introductory article by Antonio Martín Valverde, 'La formación del decreto del Trabajo en España'. See especially pp. LXXVIII–XCIV, which deal with the legislative changes during the Second Republic.

7 Manuel Azaña's note for 21 July 1931 in *Memorias políticas y de guerra, 1* (Barcelona, Crítica, 1981), p. 48. The speech to the Cortes on the 21 January 1932, following the Figols incident, can be found in *Obras Completas* (Mexico, Oasis, 1966–1968), Vol. II, p. 140.

8 Note for 24 July 1931 in *Memorias*, p. 56. For Maura's comments see his *Así cayó Alfonso XIII...*, (Barcelona, Ariel, 1968), pp. 48, 83–4, 266–77 and 289. Azaña wrote this comment about Maura after the incident in the Maria Luisa park in Seville on the 22 July. There were several different versions of the incident. For the Minister of War at the time 'it appeared to be an application of the *ley de fugas*' (the common practice of the Civil Guard whereby prisoners were shot in the back when, allegedly, attempting to escape (p. 55). For Maura 'during an early morning transfer of prisoners from Seville to the port, where they were to be embarked for the penitentiary in Cádiz, several prisoners attempted to escape whilst changing wagon in the middle of María Luisa park. The army unit, under the orders of a young lieutenant, shot and killed four' (p. 285). The following comments on the Civil Guard are taken from Azaña's *Memorias*, p. 362 and Maura's *Así cayó Alfonso XIII*, p. 206.

9 For the exchange of telegrams and a copy of Cabanellas's proclamation, see legajo 16, carpeta 2 in the Serie A Gobernación documents (AHN). On the conflicts in Seville see Manuel Tuñon de Lara, *Luchas obreras y campesinas en la Andalucía del siglo XX. Jaén (1917–1929). Sevilla (1930–1932)* (Madrid, Siglo XXI, 1978), pp. 164–9. For the capital of Andalucia, see José Manuel Macarro Vera *La Utopía revoluvionaria. Sevilla en la Segunda República* (Seville, Monte de Piedad y Caja de Ahorros de Sevilla, 1985). There are also a number of telegrams from some of the provinces of Andalucia, dated July of this year, in which 'advocates of order' ask the Minister of the Interior to 'eradicate the common elements who continue to conspire against social peace' (legajo No. 6, Serie A Gobernación documents). The quote from Manuel Ballbé is from *Orden público y militarismo en la España constitucional (1812–1983)*, Alianza Editorial, Madrid, 1985, where he devotes a chapter to the question, pp. 317–96.

10 Manuel Azaña, note from 8 January 1932 in *Memorias*, Vol. 1, p. 369.

11 This view led them to believe that all of this legislation, which did in fact affect them, and especially the Law of Defence of the Republic of July 1933, was directed against them. For an analysis of the special measures, see Manuel Ballbé, *Orden público y*

militarismo, pp. 323–63, and Francisco Fernández Segado 'La defensa extraordinaria de la República' in *Revista de Derecho Político*, No. 12 (1981–81), pp. 105–35.

12 *Cultura y Acción*, No. 8, October 1931. This threat was repeated on the first anniversary of the Republic when the list of mortal victims of government repression was expressly commemorated.

13 These examples are taken from *Cultura y Acción*, 9 July 1931 and the phrase 'blood of the proletariat' from *Tierra y Libertad*, 16 January 1932. Esteban Bilbao of the communist opposition also considered the 'honourable history of *rebel* activism of the CNT' to be one of the causes of its 'enormous influence amongst the Spanish working classes'. See 'Nuestra revolución y el peligro anarcosindicalista" in *Comunismo*, No. 9, February 1932. José Alvarez Junco has dealt with the power of martyrdom and its function in the mobilisation of these movements in his *El emperador del paralelo*, pp. 255–65.

14 (AHNS) Sección Político-Social, carpeta 886, Barcelona. The contacts with politicians and members of the army in the last years of the dictatorship were discussed, without producing a detailed report, in the Special Congress of July 1931. (*Memoria*, pp. 66–73). For the incorporation of the Catalan CNT unions into the *Sindicatos Libres* (free syndicates or employers unions), see Susana Tavera, 'Els anarcosindicalistes catalans: la Dictadura' in *L'Avenç*, No. 72 (June 1984), pp. 62–7. On the *Sindicatos Libres* in the 1920s, see Colin M. Winston, *La clase trabajadora y la derecha en España, 1900–1936* (Madrid, Cátedra, 1989), pp. 168–218.

15 The timber workers' unions (10,000 members in Barcelona, 4,750 in Valencia and 2,000 in Zaragoza) followed the construction unions in the rejection of this motion. Other important anarchists who rejected the proposal were Vicente Ballester (Cádiz timber union), Germinal Esgleas (Blanes), Progreso Fernández (Valencia construction union), José España (Valencia fabric and textile union), Miguel Chueca (Zaragoza timber union) and Joaquín Aznar (Zaragoza construction union). This is based on the data which appears in *Memoria*, pp. 11–21 and 237–42. There is a good discussion of the issue in 'Actas del Sindicato de Industria de los obreros del Arte Fabril y Textil de Barcelona', June 1931, which was the biggest union in Catalonia. This contains an energetic defence of the creation of federations in industry by Francisco Ascaso. The president of the union at the time was Juan Montserrat, who was delegate to the Congress, and the secretary was Dionisio Eroles. The book of the proceedings and minutes of the republican period can be found in carpeta 501, Barcelona (AHNS).

16 There were also moments of tension when the matter was discussed at the Congress. These began when Eusebio Carbó, who was chairman of the session, attempted to block the criticisms of the project for the creation of national federations in industry. García Oliver countered with the argument that if Peiró had spent 'three months editing the motion which had been read, it was only fair that time should be allowed to oppose it'. This offended the leader form Mataró, who pointed out that he had edited the motion at the behest of the National Committee 'without earning a penny' and closed the matter with the clarification that 'Peiró makes light bulbs and after making those he edits motion', *Memoria*, pp. 136–9. Pere Gabriel provides a useful selection of texts and introduction to this trade unionist's writings in *Ecrits, 1917–1939* (Barcelona, Edicions 62, 1975). See also the articles by M. Rivas and J. Alberola in *Tierra y Libertad*, 18 July, 12 September and 7 November 1931. The National Federation of the Railway Industry was the first to be founded and held its first congress in December 1932 at which point it had 28,326 affiliates. The records and abundant information on this federation can be found in the Internationaal Instituut voor Sociale Geshiedenis, IISG, Amsterdam, sp 190/197. The defeat of the FAI in this discussion has allowed John Brademas to conclude that this 'was the time of the moderates'. See *Anarcosindicalismo y revolución en España (1939–1937)* (Barcelona, Ariel, 1974), p. 69.

17 The term 'extremist minorities' is taken from V. Orobón Fernández's letter to Carbó. Joan García Oliver in *El eco de los pasos* (Barcelona, Ruedo Ibérico, 1978), p. 114 accuses 'Pestaña and his group' of not having allowed 'union democracy' in the preparation of the Congress. According to the author, 'I argued almost alone in the Congress. My voice was an uninterrupted and isolated interrogation until an inflammation of the kidneys forced me to return to Barcelona' (pp. 119–20). This must be the reason why he does not figure amongst those who protested over the 'deviation towards state centric practices' and requested that the discussion on the Constituent Assembly be removed from the agenda and replaced by 'the study of revolutionary options and methods for the immediate establishment of libertarian communism in Spain' (*Memoria*, pp. 176–7). See pp. 188–9 for the personal votes of Mera, Ramos and Benito and p. 212 for the report of the unions supporting the protest. Abundant information on the Congress can be found in *Solidaridad Obrera*, 11–17 June 1931. The reading which 'Juanel' (Juan Manuel Molina), secretary of the Peninsular Committee of the FAI, gave in *Tierra y Libertad*, No. 23, July, of the 'two distinct conceptions of procedure and action' which were discussed at the Congress, was the official line of the anarchist organisation at the time. One line, supported by the FAI, aimed at the preservation of the independence of the CNT from all political parties in order to achieve 'the triumph of our libertarian ends'. The other line 'accepted and supported the plans of the democratic institutions and had for some time been adopting an opportunist procedure of adaptation to the legalistic governmental norms'.

18 There are various sources available for this numerical evolution but, as with all history of Spanish anarchism, one is constrained to accept the figures provided by the organisation itself. The conference reports, the minutes of the various national and regional general meetings and the reports in the anarchist press have been used here. The Regional Congress of Andalucia, 13–17 October 1931, has been taken as the starting point for that region. This was attended by 277 delegates representing 317,672 workers, of whom '50,250 were in involuntary unemployment' (*Boletín de la CNT*, No. 2, November 1931). According to Jacques Maurice, 'the peak was reached in December 1931 with 350,000 affiliates, half of whom were members of the rural proletariat'. See *El anarquismo andaluz, Campesinos y sindicalistas, 1868–1936* (Barcelona, Crítica, 1990), p. 28. For Catalonia, see Susanna Tavera and Eulàlia Vega, 'L'afiliació sindical a la CRT de Catalunya: entre l'eufòria i l'ensulsiada confederal. 1919–1936' in *Revolució i socialisme* (Universitat de Bellaterra, 1989, Vol. II). Some extremely interesting suggestions may be found in the article by Pere Gabriel, '*Sindicalismo y sindicatossocialistas en Cataluña. La UGT, 1888–1938*', *Historia Social*, No. 8 (1990), pp. 47–71. See also Eulàlia Vega, *Anarquistas y sindicalistas durante la Segunda República. La CNT y los Sindicatos de Oposición en el País Valenciano* (Valencia, Edicions Alfons el Magnànim, 1987), pp. 251–8.

19 Some of the regional and provincial monographs already cited confirm that this was also the trajectory in local contexts. See, for example, Angeles Barrio, *Anarquismo y anarcosindicalismo en Asturias*, pp. 317–18, 346–7 and 426–7 or the recent work of Aurora Bosch 'Sindicalismo, conflictividad y política en el campo valenciano durante la Segunda República' in Aurora Bosch, Ana Mª Cervera, Vicent Comes and Albert Girona, *Estudios sobre la Segunda República* (Valencia, Edicions Alfons el Magnànim, 1993), pp. 256–8. José Manuel Macarro supports the opposing thesis of the 'inevitable clash with the state' in his *La Utopia revolucionaria*, p. 469. He has repeated these arguments in 'Sindicalismo y política' in S. Juliá (ed.) 'Política en la Segunda República', *Ayer*, No. 20 (1995), pp.146–7. For the prisoners' support committees, see the 'Actas de la Federación Local de Sindicatos de Barcelona, 1921–1932', which can be found in carpeta 501, Barcelona (AHNS). In the Congress of June 1931, the representative of the Regional Confederations of Aragón, Rioja and Navarra, A. Infante, put forward a demand for 'the immediate repeal of the Corporatist Law' and the 'dismissal of the Minister of the Interior for his excessively reactionary politics

and of the Minister of Labour for his proven lack of impartiality' (*Memoria*, p. 231). The powers given to the UGT by the Ministry of Labour are dealt with in Santos Juliá, 'Objetivos políticos de la legislación laboral' in J.L. García Delgado (ed.) *La II República española. El primer bienio* (Madrid, Siglo XXI, 1987), from which the citation of Largo Caballero is taken (p. 35).

20 All quotations are from V. Orobón Fernandez, *La CNT y la revolución*.

2 The seeds of confrontation

1 The references to Charles Tilly are taken from his introduction to Louise A. Tilly and Charles Tilly (eds) *Class Conflict and Collective Action* (Beverly Hills, CA, Sage, 1981), pp. 13–25. For an application of Tilly's analysis to Spain in the 1930s, see Rafael Cruz, 'Crisis del Estado y acción colectiva en el período de entreguerras. 1917–1939' in *Historia Social*, No. 15 (1993), pp. 119–36. For a good comparative analysis of the development of the workers' movement and its relationship to the economic and political circumstances, see Dick Geary, *European Labour Protest 1848–1939* (London, Methuen, 1984). I have dealt with George Rudé's distinction between the 'pre-industrial' and the 'industrial' in *La Historia social y los historiadores* (Barcelona, Crítica, 1991), pp. 102–9.

2 As is well known, the work of E.P. Thompson constitutes a favourable assessment of the power of collective will and human agency to achieve social change. Class ceases to be an *a priori* category and becomes a process and a historical phenomenon which is a result of the lived experience of the workers and defined in terms of their consciousness. See *The Making of the English Working Class* (London, Victor Gollancz, 1963). I have dealt with this in 'Polèmicas, erudició i història des de baix: el llegat d'E.P. Thompson' in *L'Avenç*, No. 179 (March, 1994), pp. 44–9. A good discussion of this can be found in the work of William H. Sewell Jr., 'Cómo se forman las clases: reflexiones críticas en torno a la teoría de E.P. Thompson sobre la formación de la clase obrera', in *Historia Social*, No. 18 (1994), pp. 77–100. The serious imbalances of the Spanish economy at the beginning of the 1930s is well summarised in Pablo Martín Aceña, 'Economía y política económica durante el primer bienio republicano (1931–1933)' in J.L. García Delgado, *La II República española. El primer bienio*, pp. 125–6. For a good example of the over-simplification, which was previously widespread in the historiography of the Franco regime, of attributing all disorder and political violence up until the end of 1933 to the anarchists, and to the socialists from the beginning of 1934, see Stanley G. Payne, 'Political Violence During the Spanish Second Republic', *Journal of Contemporary History*, No. 25, 2–3 (1990), pp. 276–9.

3 Some of the factors which have determined contemporary protest in Western Europe are dealt with in Charles Tilly's introduction and Louise A. Tilly's conclusion to *Class Conflict and Collective Action*. The relationship between social movements and politics, with a summary of the arguments of Doug Mc Adam, are dealt with in Manuel Pérez Ledesema 'Cuando lleguen los días de la cólera, (Movimientos sociales, teoría e historia)' in VV.AA. [various authors], *Problemas actuales de la historia. Terceras Jornadas de Estudios Históricos* (Salamanca, Ediciones Universidad de Salamanca, 1993). pp. 170–1. According to Manuel Ballbé, the exceptional nature of the Republic should not be evaluated on the basis of 'the greater or lesser application of special laws, but rather, on the existence of these indeterminate and abstract norms which produce a general state of insecurity and intimidation, and by the absence of guarantees of the exercise of basic rights of citizenship' (*Orden público y militarismo*, p. 329).

4 For an explanation of these norms and their consequences, see Paul Preston, *The Coming of the Spanish Civil War. Reform, Reaction and Revolution in the Second Republic*, 2nd edn (London, Routledge, 1994), pp. 80–4.

5 For the petition which was passed on by the Civil Governor of Cáceres to the Speaker of the House, the Minister of the Interior and the Minister of Labour, see

legajo 6 of Serie A of Gobernación (AHN). The same folder contains numerous protests about the 'oppression of the *caciques*' and mayors, of which the socialists of Huelva claim to have been victim. Legajo 43 also contains numerous complaints from Salamanca, Albacete and Alava about the appointment of civil servants 'loyal to the dictatorship' and 'immoral and blind instruments of *caciquismo*'. For an account of some of the clashes which took place in the first months see, Tuñon de Lara, *Tres claves de la Segunda República* (Madrid, Alianza Ed, 1985), pp. 41–60. The author develops a 'typology of conflict' for the period in which he underlines first 'the conflict in the process of elaboration of legal norms ... and in the process of the application of laws, decrees and other decisions' (p. 250). Manuel Pérez Yruela was one of the first to draw a connection, through detailed research, between the structural framework of conflict and the evolution of republican politics. *La conflictividad campesina en la provincia de Córdoba* (Madrid, Servicio de Publicaciones Agrarias, 1979).

6 Confirmation that the demand for the employers to comply with this legislation was repeated in numerous disputes is available from two recent pieces of research on the same province, which are carried out from different interpretative perspectives. Luis Garrido González, *Riqueza y tragedia social: historia de la clase obrera en la provincia de Jaén (1820–1939)* (Jaén, Diputación de Jaén, 1990), pp. 196–7, Vol. II, and Francisco Cobo Romero *Labradores, campesinos y jornaleros. Protesta social y diferenciación interna del campesinado jienense en los orígenes de la Guerra Civil (1931–1936)* (Córdoba, Publicaciones del Ayuntamiento de Córdoba, 1992), p. 481.

7 According to a communication from the sub-secretary of the Ministry of the Interior to the civil governor on 1 May 1932 (legajo 7, Serie A of Gobernación), the contractors of work that was being carried out in Santa Cruz del Grío, Zaragoza 'obliged workers to resign from the Workers' Association as a condition of employment'. Legajos 6 and 7 of Serie A contain numerous requests for money to assist with 'the worsening unemployment situation' and the intense activities of the civil governors throughout the period is also discernible.

8 Ministry of the Interior to the civil governor of Badajoz, forwarding a telegram from Fernando Alvarez del Vayo, a resident of Monesterio, in which he requests 'reinforcement of the civil guard during the harvest of acorns in the "Llano del Corcho" estate' (8 October 1931). For the civil governor to the Ministry on the 19 December concerning the mayor of Calanda, Teruel, see legajo 39, Serie A of Gobernación.

9 'She has failed in her post as Director of Prisons. Altogether too humane and fails to compensate this with the requisite authority' (note for 20 May 1932 in Azaña, *Memorias*, Vol. I. p. 469). He adds that 'We had already decided several days ago to convince her minister, Albornoz, that he should replace her.' Albornoz resisted and blamed the prison guards 'who are unhappy because their wages have not been increased'. However, the campaign against Kent continued 'and she is coming out badly. I suspect that the minister has raised the issue for the party's consideration. These ministers are like that. They have to ask permission in order to sack someone' (p. 470). The comment about fears of escapes and attacks is taken from a telegram which the civil governor of Seville sent to the minister on the same date. Those about altercations caused by the 'social prisoners' and the complaints of 'brutal beating', which was often repeated by the CNT, come from the Central Prison of Puerta de Santa María and the Arcos de la Frontera prison. 'Extremist elements who attempted to disrupt public order' is what the civil governor of Teruel believed to be taking place in Mas de las Matas whilst the local civil guard were occupied in another nearby town, Alcorisa, where an attempted anarchist insurrection had taken place in January 1932. See legajo 43, Serie A of Gobernación.

10 They also committed all sorts of 'outrages', according to the telegram of the civil governor of Teruel to the sub-secretary of the Interior on 5 and 8 March 1932, although the invasion had taken place on 8 February (legajo 7, Serie A); ploughing of land in Concud, Teruel 27 November 1931 (legajo 16); invasion of the estates of

Ossо and Belver de Cinca, Huesca, 6 October 1931 (legajo 6); 'revolutionary' strikes in Torralba de Aragón y Ballovar, Huesca 28 September and 7 October 1931 (legajo 6). For the demonstration against the 'Association of Cultivators' in Bollulos, Huelva on 1 October 1931 see legajo 6. For a brief description of the 'tense atmosphere' see Aurora Bosch, 'Sindicalismo, conflictividad y política en el campo valenciano durante la Segunda República', pp. 248–9. There are numerous complaints by the Associations of Landowners of the towns and regions of Barcelona against share-croppers and *rabassaires* (leasehold grape farmers) 'for not surrendering the landowners' share of the fruit', dated 1932 (legajo 6). The same folder also contains complaints by the landowners of Don Benito y Villanueva de la Serena in Badajoz about 'ploughmen invading estates reserved for cattle farming'.

11 legajo 7, Serie A of Gobernación. For the ploughing question in this province and the dispute over the enclosed land see Emilio Majuelo, *Lucha de clases en Navarra (1931–1936)* (Pamplona, Government of Navarra, 1989), pp.139–58; Luis Germán Zubero, *Aragón en la II República. Estructura económica y comportamiento político* (Zaragoza, Instituto Fernando el Católico, 1984); and José M. Azpíroz, *Poder político y conflictividad social en Huesca durante la II República* (Huesca, Ayuntamiento de Huesca, 1993). The close connection between land ownership, social conflict and the exemplary punishment received by the ringleaders in these disputes over the commons from July 1936 has been dealt with by Julita Cifuentes and Pilar Maluenda, *El asalto a la República Los orígenes del Franquismo en Zaragoza* (Zaragoza, Instituto Fernando el Católico, 1995). The decrees of 26 October 1931 on the communal woodlands and of 1 November of the same year on revision of the leasing of rural estates were found to be inadequate by those concerned, and protests and demonstrations continued with even greater intensity. Only one week after the first decree, activists of the UGT in Erla, a town in the province of Zaragoza in which this was a burning issue, complained to the Minister of the Interior 'against the Decree on communal woodland boundaries … which does not come up to expectations' (legajo 43).

12 Legajo 6, Serie A of Gobernación. On Beceite see legajo 39, carpeta 3. Near Albalate, in Belver de Cinca, the syndicalists called a strike on the 'Monte Julia' estate. The sub-secretary of the Ministry of the Interior asked the civil governor of Huesca to keep a special watch on this estate 'which for some time now has been besieged by working class elements who hinder the realisation of all types of work'. As the matter was not resolved the owner, Julio Sitter Krieg, a resident of Barcelona, asked the minister to 'resolve the dispute caused by the striking workers … who turned up at the estate, threatened the administrator for refusing the working conditions which they demanded and attempted to set fire to the estate' (19 October 1931). The estate was expropriated during the first days of the civil war and the tower situated on it became, for a time, the residence of the Council of Aragón created by the anarchists.

13 All of the citations are taken from Fernando Sánchez Marroyo, whose research and interpretation of this issue is amongst the best. 'Delincuencia y derecho de propiedad. Una nueva perspectiva del problema social durante la Segunda República', *Historia Social*, No. 14 (1992), pp. 26–46. For the empirical bases of his work see 'La delincuencia "sociopolítica" en Cáceres durante la Segunda República', *Norba*, No. 10 (1989–1990), pp. 233–64. Numerous reports of attacks on properties, thefts of wood and acorns, and trespassing on hunting reserves in Badajoz, during 1931 and 1932, can be found in legajo 16 and 39, Serie A of Gobernación. On 7 November, for example, a landowner in Almendralejo reported an incident on his hunting reserve in, which 'a gang of 40 individuals … took whatever game and wood they found'. For a detailed study of these crimes related to property during earlier periods see Francisco Cobo, Salvador Cruz and Manuel González de Molina, 'Privatización del monte y protesta social. Un aspecto desconocido del movimiento campesino andaluz (1836–1920)', *Agricultura y Sociedad*, No. 65 (1992), pp. 253–301. All of this research on

crimes and other forms of protest distinct from other expressions of collective action owes much to the work of James C. Scott, particularly *Weapons of the Weak. Everyday Forms of Peasant Resistance* (New Haven, CT, Yale University Press, 1985).

14 The incident at Peñaranda was reported by the head of the local civil guard to his director general and the Ministry of the Interior. Both reports are in legajo 16, Serie A of Gobernación. A collection of the bibliography on this question in Spanish history, which is already copious, can be found in Carlos Gil Andrés's thought-provoking study *Protesta popular y orden social en La Rioja de fin de siglo, 1890–1905* (Logroño, Instituto de Estudios Riojanos, 1995). See also Thompson's interpretation in his now classic 'La economia moral de la multitud' in *Tradición, revuelta y consciencia de clase. Estudios sobre la crisis de la sociedad preindustrial* (Barcelona, Critica, 1979), pp. 62–134. The persistence of 'pre-industrial' forms of protest in industrial areas has been confirmed by Gareth Stedman Jones in *Outcast London. A study in the Relationship between Classes in Victorian Society* (Harmondsworth, Penguin, 1984) (1st edn, Oxford University Press, 1971). For the role of women developing 'traditional rituals', see Giovanna Procacci, 'Popular protest and labour conflict in Italy, 1915–1918', *Social History*, No. 14, 1 (1989), pp. 31–58.

15 All general works on the period contain an account of the events. Paul Preston provides an accurate version in *The Coming of the Spanish Civil War*, pp. 94–5 and *Doves of War. Four Women of Spain* (London, HarperCollins, 2002), pp. 323–9. The work of Edward Malefakis remains valid as an interpretative synthesis of the debates over land in the 1930s. He also reports these conflicts, although with slight inaccuracies due to his exclusive use of the national press (which reported, for example, the deaths of the first day without taking into account those wounded in the following days, and failed to give exact geographical and demographic details of the towns distant from Madrid, etc.). See *Reforma agraria y revolución campesina en la España del siglo* (Barcelona, Ariel, 1976), pp. 358–60. A more recent chronicle can be found in Jesús Vicente Chamorro, *Año nuevo, año viejo en Castiblanco* (Madrid, Albia, 1985). Ample information on the province without relating the incidents can be found in Francisca Rosique Navarro, *La reforma agraria en Badajoz durante la II República (La respuesta patronal)* (Badajoz, Diputación Provincial de Badajoz, 1988).

16 Aurora Bosch, 'Sindicalismo, conflictividad y política en el campo valenciano durante la Segunda República', pp. 246–7. The events at Épila are summarised accurately in *La Voz de Aragón*, 5 January 1932. The civil governor of Zaragoza, Carlos Montilla, declared that 'absolutely all of the civil guard's actions were taken following my orders, and therefore, I want the responsibility for all of this to rest with me and me alone'. For the CNT's version see *Cultura y Acción* of 7 January. For the socialist version which blames the anarcho-syndicalists see *Vida Nueva*, 9 January: 'Here is how something that started in comic fashion ended in tragedy.'

17 With the exception of the references to the sentence, the information used (from which the citations are taken) comes from the report of the incidents by the then civil governor of Vizcaya, Calviño. Both documents, plus the inquest of the examining magistrate, Infantry Commander Mateo Castillo Fernández, can be found in the Archives of the Military Government of Rioja (unsorted case papers). The information on the meeting of the 5th in the town hall is taken from the letter which the mayor of Arnedo sent on 3 February to the new civil governor (Historical Archives of the Province of La Rioja, Gobierno Civil, Correspondencia Arnedo, caja no. 2). The reference to the UGT is taken from leaflets distributed during the strike call. I am grateful to Carlos Gil for access to all of this information and photocopies of the documents. A version of the events taken from the reports in the newspaper *La Rioja* and the acts of the sessions of the parliament can be found in Roberto Pastor Martínez, 'Una página del movimiento obrero riojano: Sucesos de Arnedo, 5 de enero de 1932', 1st Conference on the History of la Rioja, Logroño, 1, 2 and 3 April 1982 in *Cuadernos de Investigación Histórica*, University College of La Rioja, X, pp.

193–208. For a contemporary report see Clemente Cruzado *La Tragedia de Arnedo* 1932 and the note for 6 January in Azaña, *Memorias*, p. 365.

18 The text signed in Logroño on 28 January 1932 can be found in the Historical Archives of the Province of La Rioja, Gobierno Civil, Correspondencia Arnedo, caja no. 2. There are other examples of fatal incidents which are rarely mentioned, such as that of Luna, in Zaragoza, on 18 March 1933, in which a Civil Guard was killed following the invasion of an estate. The next day, the governor telegraphed the Ministry with a report from the lieutenant-colonel of the Civil Guard in this locality: 'Last night at about three in the morning in the town of Luna, with the suspected killer in the cells of Guard division 29. Believing the bars of the cells which look onto the street were not secure, two guards entered to examine the detainee and decided to tie his feet. One guard left the cell and in that moment the prisoner threw himself on the remaining guard who opened fire seriously wounding the prisoner who was taken to hospital.' He died on the way (Serie A de Gobernación, legajo 39).

19 The concept of the 'very poor land owners' was coined by Juan José Castillo in a text essential to the understanding of the relationship between Catholic unions and rural society, *Propietarios muy pobres. Sobre la subordinación política del pequeño campesino (La Confederación Nacional Católico-Agraria, 1917–1942)* (Madrid, Servicios de Publicaciones Agrarias, 1979). See also José R. Montero, *La C.E.D.A. El catolicismo social y político en la II República* (Madrid, Ediciones de Revista de Trabajo, 1977) and Mercedes Cabrera, *La patronal ante la II República: Organizaciones y estrategia (1931–1936)* (Madrid, Siglo XXI, 1983). The slowness of agrarian reform is summarised by Edward Malefakis: 'Two and a half years after the declaration of the Republic, a mere 45,000 hectares of land had changed hands in benefit of 6,000 to 7,000 rural workers' (*Reforma y revolución campesina*, p. 325. According to Pascual Carrión, the technical commission planned to establish on the land from 60,000 to 75,000 rural workers per year. *La reforma agraria de la segunda república y la situación actual de la agricultura española.* (Barcelona, Ariel, 1973), pp. 128–9.

20 For comparative studies of the different types of urban expansion during these decades see J.L. Garcia Delgado (ed.) *Las ciudades en la modernización de España. Los decenios interseculares* (Madrid, Siglo XXI, 1992). A comparison between various European countries is synthesised in Paul M. Hohenberg and Lynn Hollen Lees, *The Making of Urban Europe* (Cambridge, MA, Harvard University Press, 1985). For the data on the evolution of the different sectors of the economy see 'La economía española en el período de entreguerras (1919–1935)' in Jordi Nadal, Albert Carreras and Carles Sudrià (eds) *La economía española en el siglo XX. Una perspectiva histórica* (Barcelona, Ariel, 1987), pp. 109–110.

21 The comments offered here are only intended as a basic guide towards the interpretation of the conflicts described. The analysis of the characterisation of anarcho-syndicalism and the insurrectional movements which is offered in the following chapters will be essential for a comprehensive interpretation.

22 The telegram can be found in Serie A de Gobernación, legajo 7. A few days before, on 5 September, the governor of Zaragoza had made a report to the minister about the attitude of some policemen 'who instead of limiting themselves to the closure of union offices, destroy documentation and furniture'. More information can be found in Enrique Montañés, *Anarcosindicalismo y cambio político. Zaragoza, 1930–1936*, pp. 53–5. For Seville and the presence of the communists in these conflicts see José Manuel Macarro, *La utopía revolucionaria*, pp. 120 and 124–32. For cities such as Alcoy and Elche, in which the UGT favoured a negotiated outcome to conflict which the anarcho-syndicalists were determined to carry on to the bitter end, see Salvador Forner, *Industrialización y movimiento obrero. Alicante, (1923–1936)* (Valencia, Instituto Alfonso el Magnánimo, 1982), pp. 195–207.

23 *Memorias*, Vol. I, pp. 190, 192 and 465. The complaints of the industrialists and the UGT unions from Barcelona, registered in May 1931, can be found in Serie A de

Gobernación, legajo 7. Albert Balcells referred to this confrontation between the government and the CNT in Catalonia many years ago in his *Crisis económica y agitació social en Cataluña de 1930 a 1936* (Barcelona, Ariel, 1971), p. 138.

24 These complaints were summarised in the text which the secretary of the National Committee of the CNT, Ángel Pestaña, sent to Azaña on 1 December 1931. After pointing out that 'the organisation in whose name we are writing is not in the habit of addressing itself to the constitutional authorities, which it considers to be, in reality, the representative of a determinate social class'. He explained that the reason for this exception was 'the perfunctory and arbitrary attitude which the immense majority of government representatives adopt in their relations with the organised working classes'. The 'offensive' of the employers who 'coerced the workers into joining the UGT' and the demand for the 'freedom of expression' against the 'arbitration committees' were the two most important aspects of the document (*Boletín de la CNT*, No. 3, December 1931). For the opinion of Rivas Cherif, and the citation on Azaña's 'lack of respect', see *Retrato de un desconocido. Vida de Manuel Azaña* (Barcelona, Grijalbo, 1981), p. 252. Azaña wrote the note on 'social peace' on 26 February 1932, after receiving Pestaña and other members of the CNT whom 'I hardly allowed to speak', 'who came to ask for clemency for those deported on the *Buenos Aires*', an affair which, as will be seen later, caused outrage in the anarchist press (*Memorias*, Vol. I, p. 417).

25 *Cultura y Acción*, No. 23, July 1931. For details of these conflicts see John Brademas, *Anarcosindicalismo y revolución en España*, pp. 61–4 and 76–7, and Enrique Montañes *Anarcosindicalismo y cambio político. Zaragoza 1930–1936*, pp. 52–6. On the 'bloody week' of July in Seville see José Manuel Macarro, *La utopía revolucionario*, pp. 147–57. The telephone strike is summarised in Santos Juliá, *Madrid 1931–1934*, pp. 198–207, from which the citation is taken. On the conflict between the Sindicato Unico and the Asturian miners' union see Angeles Barrio, *Anarquismo y anarcosindicalismo en Asturias (1890–1936)*, pp. 320–9; Adrian Schubert, *Hacia la revolución. Orígenes sociales del movimiento obrero en Asturias, 1860–1934* (Barcelona, Crítica, 1984). pp. 188–91; and Samuel Rodríguez, 'Implantación y confrontación en el sindicalismo de clase. 1931–1933', *Estudios de Historia Social*, No. 13 (1984), pp. 108–10. Proof of the tough and rigid attitude of the provincial governors can also be found in Serie A de Gobernación, such as the message sent by Lluís Companys to the Ministry following a meeting of the CNT syndicalists in Barcelona to discuss the inter-union struggle: 'Confederation held meeting last night about the port, attacking Minister of Labour and criticising Governor, but you can remain confident that I am dealing with the matter. Isolated strikes with acts of coercion and sabotage, but I am repressing them and will extirpate them energetically' (29 May 1931, legajo 7).

26 *Boletín de la CNT*, No. 5 (February–April, 1932). The comment about Spain 'kidnapped' and a 'prison' is taken from *Tierra y Libertad*, 16 January 1932 and 15 July 1932. A 'period of calm' comes from an article entitled 'Horas de responsabilidad',' which Avelino González Mellada published in *Solidaridad*, a weekly which he published in Gijón, on 25 July 1931. It is cited by Angeles Barrio in *Anarquismo y anarcosindicalismo en Asturias (1890–1936)*, p. 348. The content of the terms of employment offered by the various sections of the union movement can be followed in the *Boletín de la CNT* and the communications of the civil governors of Zaragoza and Barcelona to the Ministry in the final part of 1931 (Serie A de Gobernación, legajo 7). The protests against the obligatory maternity insurance, a decree law of May 1931 which came into force from the following 1 October, ended in another general strike in Zaragoza where the day of bloodshed left one worker dead and two policemen wounded. The proposal put forward in the decree involved quarterly quotas, 1.90 pesetas to be paid by the employers and 1.80 by the female workers. The Local Federation of CNT Unions considered this insurance to be 'a legalised robbery of the already reduced daily rate they receive', and demanded either its repeal or 'that the employers and the state pay the whole quota'. (Detailed information in the telegram

from the governor to the Ministry, 9 December 1931, Serie A de Gobernación, legajo 6, and information on the general strike and incidents in *Cultura y Acción*, 17 December 1931.)

27 See Serie A de Gobernación, legajo 18, for abundant information on the incidents relating to this law. The comment on the 'repressive' Republic and the disillusioned proletariat is taken from *El Libertario*, 1 May 1932.

28 For the declaration of the National Committee see the *Boletín de la CNT*, No. 9 (August 1932). They returned to the offensive with another manifesto in No. 10 of the following month and there was still more in No. 16 (April–June 1933).

29 The appearance of unemployment as a serious social and political problem, which was the object of political controversy, in the 1920s in Germany and before the First World War in England is dealt with in Richard J. Evans's introduction to the excellent collection of essays and research edited by Evans and Dick Geary, *The German Unemployed. Experiences and Consequences of Mass Unemployment from the Weimar Republic to the Third Reich* (London, Croom Helm, 1987), pp. 1–22. The 'National Fund for Involuntary Unemployment' was created by a decree on 'social provision against involuntary unemployment' of 25 May, although regulation of it was not decreed until 30 September of the same year. For the figures for the unemployed see Manuel Tuñón de Lara, who points out that 'from 1931 onwards, the traditional *emigration* of labour (from 1920 to 1929 there were a total of 277,000 emigrants) became an *immigration* of a similar volume, which in 1931 was already 39,582 and during the first three years of the Republic was over 100,000' in VV.AA., *La crisis del Estado: Dictadura, República, Guerra (1923–1939)* (Barcelona, Labor, 1981), p. 135.

30 The citation is taken from the Zaragozan daily *República*, 30 November 1931 from an article entitled 'El espectro del hambre' [the spectre of famine]. In response to the absence of unemployment insurance, it calls for an economic contribution from the urban landlords, industry and workers in employment. For the relationship between work and social position see John Stevenson, *British Society 1914–1945* (Harmondsworth, Penguin, 1984), p. 182. In order to receive the meagre subsidies which the National Institute of Provision and the town halls were able to provide, the societies had to be recognised and have already established subsidies to the unemployed. The majority of the organisations which could 'take advantage' of these benefits, which were very few in relation to the size of the problem, were in Madrid and belonged to the UGT. For a good analysis of this matter and the different 'perceptions' of the crisis see Santos Juliá, *Madrid, 1931–1934*, pp. 102–44.

31 The criticism of subsidies appear in 'Acta del Pleno de Regionales celebrado en Madrid los días 13, 14, 15, 16 y 17 de diciembre de 1931' in *Boletín de la CNT*, 4 January 1932. The connection between unemployment and the economic crisis is taken up in 'Actas del Pleno de Regionales celebrado en Madrid los días 13, 14, 15, 16 y 17 de diciembre de 1931', *Boletín de la CNT* 6 May 1932. The revolution as the only solution to structural unemployment is also the main theme of *Memoria del Pleno Regional de Sindicatos Unicos de Cataluña, celebrado en Barcelona del 5 al 13 de marzo de 1933* (Barcelona, 1933), pp. 200–1 (I.I.S.G., Sp 910/45). For a good summary of the idea that nothing is preferable to a little in order to get directly to everything, which is the main argument underpinning the rejection of any type of reform, see Abel Paz, 'The unemployed workers did not receive subsidies from the State (they did not want them either, even if the Spanish State had been able to provide such a subsidy, which it was not, because such a subsidy would have weakened the revolutionary capacity and the solidarity of the proletariat)', *Durruti* (Barcelona, Bruguera, 1978), p. 258.

32 This means that it was not only ideological or economic factors which determined the character of this social protest. In other countries with similar or even worse economic problems, unemployment did not lead to radical political action. For England in this respect see John Stevenson, *British Society 1914–1945*, pp. 291–2. The negative impact of the economic depression on union organisation and the ability to

call strikes had been underlined by Dick Geary, *European Labour Protest 1848–1939*, pp. 170–1. The citation is from Manuel Pérez Ledesma. 'El movimiento obrero antes de octubre: de la moderación a la violencia revolucionaria' in VV.AA., *Octubre 1934. Cincuenta años para la reflexión* (Madrid, Siglo XXI, 1985), p. 223.

33 Santos Juliá, 'Gobernar, ¿para quién? Debilidad de partidos y representación de intereses en la II República', *Revista de Derecho Político*, No. 12 (1981–2), p. 148. This author's thesis, which is developed at length in his *Madrid, 1931–1934*, is that through mobilisation of the discontent amongst the unemployed the CNT managed to make headway to the detriment of the UGT. This can be seen to be the case in Madrid. However, in the principal urban centres where the CNT had its greatest presence at the beginning of the Republic, such as Barcelona, Seville, Valencia and in a less unambiguous fashion in Zaragoza, the opposite occurred with a moderate increase in support for the UGT and a noticeable decrease in that of the CNT. In general, the crisis and unemployment did not allow the CNT to grow, something which did happen, as various studies have shown, with the Communist Party (KPD) in Germany during the Weimar Republic. See, for example, W.L. Guttsman, *The German Social Democratic Party, 1875–1933* (London, Allen & Unwin, 1981), pp. 120–1, and Anthony McEligott, 'Mobilising the Unemployed: The KPD and the Unemployed Workers; Movement in Hamburg-Altona during the Weimar Republic' in R.J. Evans and D. Geary, *The German Unemployed*, pp. 228–60. For the employers' opposition to the arbitration panels see Mercedes Cabrera, *La patronal ante la II República*, pp. 202–18.

3 The symbols of identity

1 'Acta de la Asamblea extraordinario celebrada por el Sindicato Unico del Ramo de la Alimentación el día 16 de Noviembre de 1932', *Boletín de la CNT*, 12, 13 and 14 (November/December 1932–January 1933). The occupation of the streets as the 'revolutionary act par excellence' is underlined by Jacques Maurice in *El anarquismo andaluz*, p. 224. That the CNT and the UGT, in spite of their 'profound organisational and strategic differences', shared a 'deep rooted anti-political culture' is one of the principal theses of Santos Juliá, 'Sindicatos y poder político en España', *Sistema*, 97 (1990), pp. 41–62. José Alvarez Junco has drawn attention to the atypical nature of this labour movement which began to appear just at the time when it had vanished in other countries, 'El anarquismo en la España contemporánea' in VV.AA., *El movimiento obrero en la historia de Cádiz* (Cadiz, Diputación provincial, 1988,) p. 43. The international dimension of the direct-action movement is dealt with in Marcel van der Linden and Wyne Thorpe, 'Auge y decadencia del sindicalismo revolucionaria', *Historia Social*, 12 (1992), pp. 3–29.

2 Jerome R. Mintz , *The Anarchists of Casas Viejas* (Chicago, The University of Chicago Press, 1982), p. 164. For a detailed examination of this distinction between the activist and ideological minority and the totality of the membership, see Anna Monjo, 'La CNT durant la República a Barcelona: Líders, militants, afiliats' (Department of Contemporary History, University of Barcelona, 1993), unpublished doctoral thesis. I am grateful to the author for access to this work. See also, by the same author, 'Afiliados y militantes: la calle como complemento del sindicato cenetista en Barcelona de 1930 a 1939', *Historia y Fuente Oral*, No. 7 (1992), pp. 85–98, from which the citations on the relationship between militancy and cultural level are taken. Obviously an analysis of this type in no way presupposes a division between a rebellious minority and a passive majority, an error which George Rudé warned against in *La multitud en la historia. Los disturbios populares en Francia e Inglaterra, 1730–1848* (Madrid, Siglo XXI, 1978), p. 217. Rather, the aim is to recognise the distinct perceptions which various sectors held of the organisation and its struggle, of the mechanisms of

control which the leaders of the unions utilised and the internal dynamics, in terms of weakness, maturity and cohesion, of this labour movement.

3   *Memoria del Congreso Extraordinario celebrado en Madrid los días 11 al 16 de junio de 1931*, p. 182. The liberating power which culture held for the anarchists has been underlined by José Alvarez Junco, providing the most exhaustive analysis which we have of their doctrinal positions. 'To make the worker "aware" is in itself a revolutionary act, because it is a rebellion against the spiritual authority of the bourgeoisie and means taking from the bourgeoisie the most noble aspect of that universal patrimony which it has usurped – culture' (*La ideología política del anarquismo español 1868–1910* (Madrid, Siglo XXI, 1976), p. 73). The relationship between this 'cultural form of suppor', such as groups of fellow travellers, *ateneos*, rationalist schools, and the 'popular success' of anarchism has been dealt with by Pere Solà in 'La base societaria de la cultura y de la acción libertaria en la Cataluña de los años treinta' in Bert Hofman, Pere Joan i Tous and Manfred Tiets (eds) *El anarquismo español y sus tradiciones culturales* (Frankfurt am Main-Madrid, Vervuert-Iberoamericana, 1995), pp. 361–75. For the 'essay on the programme' of libertarian communism' see Issac Puente, *Suplemento de Tierra y Libertad*, No. 10 (May 1993), pp. 147–51. For Frederico Urales version see, *El ideal y la revolución* (Barcelona, Biblioteca de la Revista Blanca, 1932), p. 16.

4   For the letter of resignation see *Solidaridad Obrera*, 22 September 1931. *Cultura Libertaria*, edited by Agustí Gibanel, who died on 1 February 1933, appeared on 6 November 1931 and then changed its name to *Sindicalismo*, the journal of the Federation of Libertarian Syndicalists, edited by Juan López, on 14 February 1933. For further information on the struggle within the paper see Pere Gabriel's introduction to Joan Peiró, *Ecrits, 1917–1939*, pp. 21–4. The difference between the 'workers' journalism' of Joan Peiró and Ángel Pestaña and the 'anarchist publicists' and the 'died in the wool bohemianism' of Felipe Alaiz has been emphasised by Susanna Tavera in 'Revolucionarios, publicistas y bohemios: los periódistas anarquistas (1918–1936)' in the collective work cited above, *El anarquismo español y sus tradiciones culturales*, p. 392. This author has also produced the most complete study of the paper, *Solidaridad Obrera. El fer-se i desfer-se d'un diari anarco-sindicalista (1915–1939)* (Barcelona, Colegio de Periodistas de Cataluña, 1992), in which detailed information is provided on the circulation, suspensions, changes of editors and other aspects which cannot be dealt with here.

5   There is abundant information on the Alaiz 'affair' in the Memoria del pleno Regional de Sindicatos Unicos de Cataluña, celebrado en Barcelona del 5 al 13 de marzo de 1933, pp. 22–3. For Peiró's opinion see Cultura Libertaria, 23 September 1933. For information on the Regional General Meeting of the Sindicatos Unicos of Catalonia, 11, 12 and 13 October, in which Alaiz and the rest of the editors were selected – Cano Ruiz, E. Labrador, Liberto Callejas, Evelio Fontaura, Medina González and Federica Montseny, who did not accept – see Boletín de la CNT, No. 2 (November 1931). The meeting of the Syndicate of Fabric and Textile Workers of Catalonia, which had already made the decision, was held on 9 October 1931 (Libro de Acta, AHNS, carpeta 501 on Barcelona).

6   His poor relationship with *Solidaridad Obrera* continued until the last moments of anarchism. In an undated letter, written to his wife after the outbreak of the Civil War, he complained that the CNT paper would not publish articles of his which appeared in *La Batalla*, the journal of the POUM, and the 'Catalan press': 'It is clear that my temperament, which is essentially anarchist, clashes with the dictatorial spirit which reigns in the CNT and I will end up resigning for good' (AHNS, carpeta 1301 on Madrid). In the same folder, letters dated during the war asking favours – of him and of his daughter who was then a minister – and at other times complaining that they sent money for books published by the family group (above all copies of 'La Novela Ideal') which they never received. The accusations made in *El Luchador* that the

National Committee of the CNT was 'managed by comrade Pestaña', even though he had already been replaced, were discussed in the General Meeting of the Regional Committees held in Madrid on 13, 14, 15 and 16 April, 1932 of which the minutes and proceedings are reproduced in *Boletín de la CNT*, No. 6 (March 1932). His expulsion had already been requested at the Special Congress of June 1931 because of his accusations against the National Committee of which Pestaña was then president (*Memoria*, p. 180). José Alvarez Junco has dealt with the fame he created for himself with his denunciation of the late nineteenth-century anarchists who were tortured in *El emperador del paralelo*, pp. 158–64. For autobiographical data see his extensive work, *Mi vida*, 3 volumes (Barcelona, 1930). For further information see Federica Montseny, *Mis primeros cuarenta años* (Barcelona, Plaza & Janés, 1989).

7 All of this information is taken from the *Memoria del pleno de Sindicatos Unicos de Cataluña, celebrado en Barcelona del 5 al 13 de mayo de 1933*, pp. 164–6. Although the number of representatives according to this *Memoria* reached 208,821–198,764, if we take the figures produced by Susana Tavera and Eulàlia Vega, I have accepted the figures given by the administration of *Solidaridad Obrera* in the Congress, 'results of the count recently carried out', p 165. Data also exists, although it has never been checked, for the circulation of the FAI's main publication, the weekly *Tierra y Libertad*, which sold 22,000 copies (*Suplemento de Tierra y Libertad*, No. 4, November 1932, gives figures of 12,000 copies for this more ideological publication). 'And this given the handful of people that made up the FAI.' No. 8, March 1933 of this *Suplemento* claims that Isaac Puente's *Finalidad de la CNT: El Comunismo Libertario* had sold 15,000 copies in the two months following its publication.

8 The question of the *CNT* is recurrent in all of the National General Meetings. Gil Bel, Miguel González Inestal, Acracio Bartolomé, Angel Gil Roldán and Díez Caneja took part in the first editorial board meeting. Lucía Sánchez, Miguel Cordón, Claro Sendón (Bílbiles), Carlos de Rivero and Liberto Callejas attended the meeting in which he was replaced in the summer of 1933. *Boletín de la CNT*, No. 17 (July–October 1933). The figures on circulation and debts are taken from the 'Pleno de Regionales' held on 12 June and the following days in 1933. *Boletín de la CNT*, No. 17. There is abundant information on the ruinous state of affairs in the 'Actas del pleno de Regionales de la Confederación Nacional del Trabajo, celebrado en Madrid el 23 de junio de 1934 y días sucesivos' (IISG, fondo CNT, Paquete 93 – Film 262 B). The subject was raised again in the 'Pleno Nacional de Regionales de la CNT, celebrado en Madrid el 23 de junio de 1934 y días sucesivos' (AHNS, F-1434 bis). The local and regional press were not unaffected by these problems. Some which had already existed previously, such as the Zaragoza weekly *Cultura y Acción*, reappeared at the beginning of the Republic but were suppressed following the hard line taken by the government after the insurrection of January 1932 and did not see the light of day again until the spring of 1936. The *Boletín de la CNT*, which is a vital source in the analyses of the agreements of an 'intimate nature' and the situation within anarchosyndicalism, was another creation of the republican period. Originally planned as a monthly publication, the first issue appeared in October 1931 and the last which is known of was No. 17, July–October 1933 (the first 15 issues can be found in the IISG and the last two in the AHNS).

9 This phrase appeared in the regulations for members and even on some of the union cards where one could read, 'The confederation stamp is the only income which the National and Regional Committee had. Failure to pay subscriptions is sabotage of the work which you have entrusted to these committees and which they will not be able to carry out for lack of economic resources' (AHNS, carpeta 1119 of Madrid). The complaints of the National Committee that funds did not arrive was repeated in all of the issues of the *Boletín de la CNT*. For Souchy's warning see the 'Dictamen leído por el Secretario de la AIT en el Pleno Internacional', April 1932 (*Boletín de la CNT*, 8 July 1932).

10   The warning is once more Agustín Souchy's from the source already cited. The National Committee as a 'post office' is taken from the 'Informe Schapiro sobre la crisis de la CNT' signed 15 April 1933, following his analysis of the January insurrection of that year. Translated into Spanish by Marta Bizcarrondo in *Estudios de Historia· Social*, Nos 5–6 (April–September, 1978), p. 493. The claim that they found out 'from the press' is taken from the National Committee in the presentation of the *Boletín de la NT*, No. 2 (November 1931). The organisational structure of the CNT is summarised well by John Brademas in *Anarcosindicalismo y revolución en España (1930–1937)*, pp. 22–3, from which the 'chimera of the revolution' is taken.

11   There is a good description of this overlapping of committees in the 'Informe Schapiro sobre la crisis de la CNT', pp. 469–79. The characteristics of these defence groups are described, following the fiasco of 1933, in the 'Pleno de Regionales de la CNT' of 12 June and subsequent issues of that year (*Boletín de la CNT*, No. 9, July–October, 1933).

12   There is abundant information on this question in the 'Actas de los Plenos de la Federación Local de Sindicatos Unicos de Barcelona, 1931–1932' (AHNS, carpeta 501 of Barcelona). The 'critical … situation in which the pro-prisoner Committee' finds itself' was discussed at the General Meeting on 7 November 1931, where it was claimed that the 'debts' amounted to 3,525 pesetas. The hunger strike and the first resignation demand arose in the General Meeting of 29 November. Regarding the Law of the Defence of the Republic, voices were raised, on 24 October of the same year, which suggested 'taking the measures necessary in order to begin a national movement'. In the same session Emilio Mira was elected as secretary of the Regional Committee. After January 1932 he became the target of criticism and had to resign. For more information on the tensions between the prisoners and the Committee, with the texts and reports of the meetings in which the comment 'abandoned' emerged – Alaiz was one of them, and the threat of rejecting support, see carpeta 840 on Barcelona in the AHNS. Gregorio Jover was one of the strong men of the Committee and a member of the anarchist group 'Los Solidarios', which then adopted the name 'Nosotros' in 1933. This group included García Oliver, Durruti, Francisco Ascaso, Aurelio Fernández, Ricardo Sanz and Antonio Ortiz. The changes in the National Committee, where Manuel Rivas of the construction union was accompanied by other known anarchists such as Ricardo Sanz, José Ramos, Miguel Terrén and Marcos Alcón can be followed in the *Boletín de la CNT*, No. 5 (February–April 1932).

13   The last expression in the description of the two sides is taken from *CNT*, No. 7, January 1933, the paper in which the accusations and insults against the socialists appeared most frequently (see, for example, 26 October and 18 November 1932). For the term 'collusion' see the presentation of the National Committee in the *Boletín de la CNT*, No. 8 (July 1932). Following the publication of the Law of 8 April 1932 on 'Professional Associations of workers and employers', the socialists were seen as the sole cause of 'the slide of everything towards repression' (Manifiesto de la CN y los delegados regionales 'a los trabajadoes confederados', *Boletín de la CNT*, No. 10, September 1932). The remaining citations are taken from the manifesto of the National Committee signed in Barcelona in September 1932 entitled 'La Confederación Nacional del Trabajo contra la facciosa Ley de Corporaciones del 8 de Abril' (*Boletín de la CNT*, No. 11, October 1932).

14   15 February 1933. For the 'moral triumph' and the citation on 'heroic deeds' see the *Boletín de la CNT*, No. 8 (July 1932). There are abundant references to 'heroic deeds' in *CNT*, 16 December 1932 and 10 May 1933. 'We are waiting!' is taken from the *Boletín de la CNT*, No. 5 (February–July 1932). The importance of the deed for the CNT was highlighted by Santos Juliá in 'Un sindicalismo de movilización de masas en Madrid de la Segunda Republica' in *Estudios sobre Historia de España. Homenaje a Manuel Tuñon de Lara* (Madrid, Universidad Internacionaal Menéndez Pelayo, 1982), Vol. II, p. 157. See also his more recent 'Poder y revolución en la cultura política del militante obrero

español' in VV.AA., *Peuple, mouvement ouvriers, culture dans l'Espagne contemporaine. Cultures populaires, cultures ouvrièrs en Espagne de 1840 à 1936* (Saint Denis, Presses Universitaires de Vicennes, 1990), pp. 183–5. This mixture of the sacred with rhetorical violence was not much different from that used by Lerroux and republicanism since the French Revolution. See Alvarez Junco, *El emperador del paralelo*, p. 259. Finally, it is odd that the signal for these 'supreme deeds' should have been associated with reactionary coups or the electoral victories of the right. Before the military uprising of August 1932, the National Committee warned that 'reaction' will always be confronted on the streets by the 'forces of the Confederation' (*Boletín de la CNT*, No. 9 August 1932).

15 The social and political problems of confrontation with the state and its labour legislation dominated the demonstrations in spite of the rhetoric. It is also interesting to note that, although there was no shortage of anti-clerical literature and anti-clerical protests as well as an often delirious glorification of the pistol and incitement to individual assassinations, the latter were not very frequent When the CNT occupied the streets the clergy were not, as in the Civil War, the targets of their actions. The behaviour of the insurrectional movements throws considerable light on this issue. Anti-clericalism is the subject of a recent detailed study by Pilar Salomón, 'La critica moral al order social: persistencia del anticlericalismo en la sociedad española (1900–1939)' (unpublished doctoral thesis, University of Zaragoza, 1995). For the 'purifying torch' see *Cultura y Acción*, 3 December 1931. The CNT union constitutions usually specified this aim. The texts used here are the 'Bases de Trabajo de la Industria Fabril y Textil de Cataluña 1931' (NHAS, Serie A de Gobernación, legajo 7) and the constitution of the Sindicato Unico de la Construcción de Vitoria (AHNS, carpeta 1019 of Madrid).

16 'The anarchist ideal' in *El Libertario* Madrid weekly of the FAI, 16 May 1931. For the 'clear and simple formulas' see *CNT*, 14 January 1932.

17 *Suplemento de Tierra y Libertad*, No. 9 (April 1933), p. 105. The 'watchful eye' is taken from the manifesto of the National Committee following the General Meeting of the Regional Committees, held in Madrid half-way through April 1932 (*Boletín de la CNT*, 6 May 1932). For the revolution as a 'surgical operation' see Higinio Noja Ruiz, *El problema agrario en España* (Barcelona, 1932), pp. 65–6. For Joan Peiró's conception see his article, 'La revolución permanente', *Cultura Libertaria*, 18 December 1931. The versions of the revolution included in papers such as *CNT*, *El Libertario* or *Tierra y Libertad* do not do justice to the tradition represented by Peiró, Pestaña and formerly Salvador Seguí, which had such a powerful presence in Catalonia and which expressed itself in so many industrial collectivisations during the Civil War. For this version see Santos Juliá, 'Un sindicalismo de movilización de masas en el Madrid de la Segunda República', pp. 152–3. See also José Manuel Macarro Vera, 'La autovalorización anarquista: un principio de análisis y acción (Sevilla, 1931–1936)' in *Estudios de Historia de España. Homenaje a Manuel Tuñon de Lara*, Vol. II, pp. 145–9. For a detailed statement of these two versions via a reading of the works of the most representative authors see Xavier Paniagua, *La sociedad libertaria. Agrarismo e industrialización en el anarquismo español (1930–1939)* (Barcelona, Critica, 1982).

18 The metal workers' union was in third place with 52,646 members. The Catalan anarchosyndicalists have been focused on because of their dominant position in the organisation during the first part of the Republic. These observations on the relationship between professional occupation, stability of employment and anarchosyndicalist activism could be extended, for example, to José Villaverde in La Coruña, Antonio Ejarque (metal workers' union) and Valeriano San Agustín (distillery and sugar workers' union) in Zaragoza, and Avelino González Mallada (metal workers' union) in Gijón. The figures have been produced on the basis of the union delegates and affiliates represented at this Congress. For Peiró's conception of syndicalism see '¿El Sindicalismo basta a sí mismo?', which appeared in *Despertad*, 28 December 1929 and 'Misión histórica del Sindicalismo, *Cultura Libertad*, 11 August

1932 (both articles are reproduced in Joan Peiró. *Escrits 1917–1939*, pp. 229–36 and 361–4).

19 For the reduced version see the editorial of *CNT,* 'Acción directa', 16 November 1932. For direct action on all levels of the struggle see Joan Peiró, *Solidaridad Obrera*, 14 May 1924 (reproduced in Joan Peiró. *Escrits, 1917–1939*, pp. 71–4). The citation and the definition of direct action is taken from José Alvarez Junco, *La ideología política del anarquismo español*, pp. 587 and 408.

20 This implicit model is explained and then criticised in Mercedes Vilanova, 'Anarchism, political participation, and illiteracy in Barcelona between 1934 and 1936', *American Historical Review*, 97, 1 (February 1992), pp. 96–120, in which the author cites Pierre Vilar and his *Historia de España* as one of the most influential books, as a result of its publication in a number of languages, 'which has contributed to the generalisation of this myth'. The exaggeration of these figures has been dealt with by Susanna Tavera and Eulália Vega in 'L'afiliació sindical a la CRT de Catalunya: entre l'eufòria revolucionària i l'ensulsiada confederal 1919–1936', pp. 245–6. For all of the leaders of the left in the 1930s, from Besteiro and Largo Caballero to Maurín, anarchism was a problem – and its 'apoliticism' was an instrument of the 'interests of the bourgeoisie', which had to be eradicated. According to Besteiro in a lecture given in Zaragoza on 1 May 1930, 'it is nothing more than the final consequence of bourgeois liberty, as opposed to socialism which embodies the scientific doctrine required by the proletariat'. As he was addressing 'one of the cities of Spain in which these tactics were most deeply rooted', he encouraged his listeners to follow the example of the Bolsheviks who had eliminated 'what was left of anarchism'. Today in Russia anarchism has disappeared. It only remains in Spain, a country of exceptions, so think about whether or not it would be useful to make it disappear. (in the volume *UGT. Zaragoza, Curso de Conferencias*, 1930, pp. 127–30). Joaquín Maurín also took pleasure in dismissing this petit bourgeois ideology in *El fracaso del anarcosindicalismo. La crisis de la CNT* (Barcelona, C.I.B., no date, 48 pages).

21 'La participación electoral en Barcelona entre 1934 y 1936', *Historia y Fuente Oral*, No. 7 (1992), pp. 47–83. These authors also relate the level of abstention to the repression suffered after the Civil War. The recorded level of illiteracy in Barcelona was 15 per cent, 18 percentage points lower than the average of 32 per cent for Spain in the decade of the 1930s but seven points higher than Madrid. See also Mercedes Vilanova and Dominique Willems, 'Analfabetismo y participación política en Barcelona durante los años treinta', *Historia y Fuente Oral*, No. 6 (1991), pp. 89–104. The three variants of electoral behaviour are taken from Anna Monjo, Carme Vega and Mercedes Vilanova, 'Trajectoires électorales, leaders et masses sous la IIème République en Catalogne (1934–1939)', *Il politico*, año XLVIII, No. 1 (1983), pp. 91–114. Anna Monjo has also dealt with this question in her doctoral thesis 'La CNT durant la República a Barcelona', p. 13. Rosa Maria Capel has provided useful comments on the connection between women and abstention in *El sufragio femenino en la Segunda República española* (Granada, University of Granada, 1975), pp. 254–5. Since Javier Tusell's pioneering studies at the beginning of the 1970s, the literature on elections in this period has grown enormously and there is now practically no province on which a detailed study does not exist, although, given the scope, they do not usually enter into the type of analysis undertaken here. For a summary of this research see Maria Gloria Múñez Pérez, *Bilbliografia comentada sobre la Segunda República Española. Obras publicadas entre 1940 y 1992* (Madrid, Fundación Univeritaria Española, 1993), pp. 348–87.

22 It will not be possible to abandon it until more studies which take into account the factors used by Mercedes Vilanova's research group for Catalonia are available. José Manuel Macarro had argued, for example, that 'the importance attributed to the abstention of the CNT is a myth'. He arrived at this conclusion after finding that the level of abstention in Seville in 1933 (44 per cent) had only gone up by 2.4 points in

comparison with the elections of June 1931 (42 per cent), while it went down to 31.8 per cent in 1936 and the abstention of the CNT did not provide a convincing explanation of these changes. *La utopía revolucionaria*, pp. 366–7 and 454–6. On the other hand, in other cities with a strong CNT presence, such as Zaragoza, electoral participation was similar in 1931 and 1936 (78.1 per cent and 73.29 per cent) and went down to 55.12 per cent in 1933. Luis Germán discovered that this sharp decrease also took place in other electoral regions of Aragon which had high levels of CNT affiliation and attributed it to the influence and propaganda of the anarcho-syndicalists, which he also saw as the cause of the decline of the 'left republicans'. The socialist leaders of Zaragoza always attributed the strength of the republicans and supporters of Lerroux to the 'romantic surrender of the masses, who were innocently rebellious in union matters, to the politics of the republican parties' (*Vida Nueva* 19 November 1932). After the elections of 1933 they would add that 'it only took the CNT to abstain for the whole republican framework to collapse' (*Vida Nueva*, 2 December 1933).

23 The figures for Catalonia, with the exception of those for March 1930 (for which see Note 7), are taken from Susanna Tavera and Eulàlia Vega, 'L'afiliació sindical a la CRT de Catalunya', pp. 357–8. Those for the Regional Confederation of Workers of Levante are taken from E. Vega, *Anarquistas y sindicalistas durante la Segunda República*, pp. 238–58. Those for Andalucia are from the *Memoria* of the 1931 Congress, the 'Congreso de la Regional Andaluza', 13 and 14 October 1931 (*Boletín de la CN*, 2 November 1931) and the 'Informe de la AIT' to the 'Pleno Nacional de Regionales de la Confederación Nacional del Trabajo', June 1934 (AHNS, carpeta 2437 of Madrid), which state that the membership 'has been reduced to 100,000'. There was also a considerable decrease in Seville, according to the data compiled by José Manuel Macarro in *La utopía revolucionaria*, pp. 46–7. Aragon is the principal exception to this decline in the level of membership. Although there are no reliable figures for 1934 or 1935, the period in which the National Committee was resident in Zaragoza, the 30,000 members, which the organisation had during its highest point in 1931, was maintained in 1936. The greatest increase in membership, between June 1931 (20,899) and May 1936 (29,596), had taken place in the rural sector. I have examined these figures in *Anarquismo y revolución en la sociedad rural aragonesa 1936–1938* (Madrid, Siglo XXI, 1985), pp. 24–9. See also Luis Germán, *Aragón en la II República*, pp. 181–2.

24 The citation in Catalan [referring to the image of efficiency in the original] is taken from Susanna Tavera and Eulàlia Vega 'L'afiliació sindical a la CRT de Catalunya', p. 354. These authors also examine the possible causes of this 'collapse'. For similar explanations see Aurora Bosch, 'Sindicalismo, conflictividad y política en el campo valenciano', pp. 256–8. José Manuel Macarro blames the 'elites who informed the CNT' about these 'disasters', because they demotivated the workers who were 'not willing to follow leaders and a union which wanted to go further than they wanted to go, thus placing at risk the improvements which had been achieved with such effort' ('La disolución de la utopía en el anarcosindicalismo español', *Historia Social*, 15 (1993), p. 155). The 'alienation' of the workers is taken from the evaluation which is made of this crisis in the 'Actas del pleno Regional de Sindicatos de Oposición de Levante, celebrado en Valencia los días 1 y 12 de febrero de 1934,' p. 9 (IISG, Bro 153/11). Symptoms of exhaustion resulting from so much direct action appear in the editorial of *CNT* of 1 August 1933: 'We undertake four or five campaigns at once and abandon them all without having achieved one complete objective. Above all, our enemies show us the red flag and we go at it bravely, but also blindly like the bull.' The Zaragoza publication *Cultura y Acción* already carried a warning in its editorial 'Las huelgas' on 19 November 1931, after demanding respect and good relations from the employers: 'We believe that enthusiasm is enough and throw ourselves into the struggle without taking into consideration the probabilities of success.'

25 For interesting observations on this concept of the rural working class and the weakness of the CNT in the countryside see Xavier Paniagua, *La sociedad libertaria*, pp. 66–96. I had already anticipated the hypothesis that the rejection of agrarian reform in Aragon, especially in the province of Zaragoza where the percentage of land belonging to the nobility was considerable, blocked the expansion of the CNT in the countryside in *Anarquismo y revolución en la sociedad rural aragonesa*, pp. 36–8. This tension between the urban propagandists and the delegates from the rural villages who wanted the autonomy to make propaganda and organise unions arose in the Regional General Meeting at the end of September 1931. (*Cultura y Acción*, 1 October 1931). A few days later, Felipe Alaiz, in an article titled 'The Land Question in Aragón', demanded 'collective expropriation' (*Cultura y Acción*, 15 October 1931).

26 Juan López and John Brademas have recounted the process of eleboration of the manifesto in *Anarcosindicalismo y revolución en España*, pp. 78–80. The text appeared in the Barcelona paper *L'Opinió*. As the various phases of this escalation towards the split and the struggle between the various factions are perhaps the most common themes in the historiography of the CNT and the republican period they will not be focused on here. Introductory analyses can be found in Antonio Elorza, 'La utopía anarquista durante la segunda república española', *Revista de Trabajo*, No. 32 (1971) and Albert Balcells, *Trabajo industrial y organización obrera en la Cataluña contemporánea* (Barcelona, Laia, 1974). The various ideological arguments which came together in the conflict are dealt with in Xavier Paniagua, *La sociedad libertaria*. However, the most detailed study of this process of internal fragmentation has been provided by Eulàlia Vega in *El trentisme a Catalunya. Divèrgencies ideològiques en la CNT (1930–1933)* (Barcelona, Curial, 1933) and her aforementioned *Anarquistas y sindicalistas durante la Segunda República*. The attempt by Manuel Buenacasa, a veteran activist of the CNT and the FAI, to act as a 'friendly chronicler', as he defined himself, has no value other than that of being a text written in the heat of the struggle. See *La CNT, los 'Treinta' y la FAI* (Barcelona, Alfa, 1933). For testimony on the controversy, in which the manifesto is also reproduced, see *El movimiento libertario español pasado, presente y futuro* in *Suplemento de Cuadernos de Ruedo Ibérico* (Paris, 1974), pp. 299–315.

27 The citation and García Oliver's comment are taken from John Brademas, *Anarcosindicalismo y revolución en España* pp. 35 and 80. That 'the activists of the FAI undertook the conquest of the CNT, imposing themselves with violent language and radicalis' is argued by César M. Lorenzo, the son of Horacio Martínez Prieto (secretary of the National Committee of the CNT following the military insurrection of July 1936), in a well-documented work which makes a useful contribution to the question, *Los anarquistas españoles y el poder, 1868–1969* (Paris, Ruedo Ibérico, 1972), p. 52. The commonplaces multiply as the shift is made from specialised texts on anarchism to those dealing with it in tangential fashion. For Edward Malefakis, to cite a widely read author, young men such as Durruti, the Ascaso brothers and García Oliver 'had founded a secret and purely anarchist organisation' which was responsible for the 'spreading to the rest of Spain' of the burning of churches which began in Madrid in May 1931, *Reforma agraria y revolución campesina*, p. 342.

28 For the death of Agustín Gibanel, see the last issue of *Cultura Libertaria*, 9 February 1933. There is an article which commemorates the death of Massoni, 5 June 1933, in *Sindicalismo*, 13 June 1936. For the announcement of the death of Orobón Fernández see *Solidaridad Obrera*, 30 June 1934 and the following day for biographical details.

29 For the 'imposition' of the FAI see the 'Informe Schapiro sobre la crisis de la CNT,' p. 475.

30 *Memoria del pleno peninsular de Regionales de la FAI celebrado en Madrid los días 28, 29 y 39 de octubre, 1933*, 24 pages (IISG,BRO 1034/10). The peninsular Committee, for example, declared that it did not understand 'officially ... why *El Libertario* has ceased publication' and the delegate from *Tierra y Libertad*, in a comment typical of the sort we have already seen repeated regarding other papers, suggested that 'what has

happened is that the editors have not been capable of interpreting the sentiment of their readership' (p. 16). The description of the 'disastrous state' was adopted by the 'Anarchist Cultural Group', *El Luchador*, 6 March 1931. For information on the origin and evolution of this organisation see Juan Gómez Casas, *Historia de la FAI* (Madrid, ZXY, 1977). For a very personal and subjective version of this experience see Juan García Oliver, *El eco de los pasos*.

31 The first accusation was made by Dionisio Eroles from prison and reproduced in *Tierra y Libertad* on 18 March 1932. It was repeated on 15 July 1932 and in a communication of the peninsular Committee of the FAI, of the Regional Committee of Catalonia and the Committee of the Local Federation of Anarchist Groups of Barcelona and reprinted in the same weekly on 4 November of the same year. It was argued that the CNT 'is not anarchist' in *El Luchador* on 19 June 1932. The citation on syndicalism is taken from *Tierra y Libertad*, 9 January 1932.

32 Juan García Oliver, *El eco de los pasos*, pp. 124–5 and 132–3. There are also useful references to these groups in Ricardo Sanz, *La política y el sindicalismo* (Barcelona, Ediciones Petronio, 1978). The image of the FAI united against the 'discredited sector of the union' was widespread amongst the membership at the time and there is a good example in the description which Isaac Puente gives of the division in *Suplemento de Tierra y Libertad*, 7 (February 1933), pp. 35–6. For a challenge to this commonplace image of the FAI during the war, but with observations which are also valid for the republican period, see Susanna Tavera and Enric Ucelay-Da Cal, 'Grupos de afinidad, disciplina bélica y periodismo libertario, 1936–1938', *Historia Contemporánea*, No. 9 (1993), pp. 167–90. For the 'symbol', 'colours' and 'moral power' see Juan Manuel Molina and José Peirats in the declarations reproduced in *El movimiento libertario español. pasado, presente y futuro*, pp. 223 and 237. For Schapiro's comment see the report cited on pp. 480–5. The 'eulogy of the pistol' is the title of an article in *Tierra y Libertad*, 16 September 1932 by Jacinto Toryho, from which the citation which follows is taken. The FAI as a 'spiritual' organisation is taken from an article by Miguel Jiménez in *El Libertario* of 10 and 17 December 1932 entitled 'Problemas orgánicos', in which it is argued that 'one must unite, that is bring into systematic and representative alliance, both the economic and the spiritual organisations for and to the common end of abolishing the state'.

33 'Acta de la Asamblea general del Sindicato de Industria de los obreros del Arte Fabril y Textil de Barcelona', 3 March 1933 (AHNS, carpeta 501 of Barcelona). The 'sacking' of Juan López from the Council of the Single Construction Union of Barcelona on 9 July 1933 was ratified by the union assembly. López was the author of the article 'De cara al porvenir del Movimiento Obrero', *Cultura Libertaria*, 22 June 1932, in which, according to his colleagues in the union, he made 'serious accusations against activists of the CNT' (AHNS, carpeta 886 of Barcelona). He had, in any case, already written, in this same weekly on the 26th of the previous February, that he was not concerned about being left on the margins of the organisation: 'they can have my place so that it can be filled by a more enlightened, more revolutionary and more active comrade willing to give strength and vigour to the unions. I do not want to be an obstacle.' The expulsion of Ángel Pestaña in December 1932 was ratified by the general meeting of the Barcelona Metal Workers (*Boletín de la CNT*, 15 March 1993).

34 For the proceedings of the first Congress of the FSL see *Sindicalismo*, 4 and 11 July 1934. For all of the details of the split in Catalonia see the *Memoria del pleno Regional de Sindicatos Unicos de Cataluña, celebrado en Barcelona del 5 al 13 de marzo de 1933*. For the manifesto of the Manresa unions see *Sindicalismo* 14 February 1933. For precise information on the Valencian areas see Eulàlia Vega, *Anarquistas y sindicalistas*, pp. 148–89.

35 The letter is held in the AHNS, carpeta 886 of Barcelona. Sender put the same words in the mouth of the protagonist of *Siete domingos rojos* (Barcelona, 1932): 'I go out into the street. A bourgeois is not a person, nor an animal. He is less than everything. He is nothing. How would I feel about the death of a bourgeois, I who go out

into the street to kill them?' On Sender's collaboration with the Barcelona anarcho-syndicalist paper see Susanna Tavera, *Solidaridad Obrera*, pp. 61–4. 'Social' writer is taken from José Carlos Mainer's proloque to *Ramon J. Sender. In Memoriam. Antología Crítica* (Zaragoza, Diputación General de Aragón, 1983), p. 10.

36　On the content of the Asturian 'third way' see Angeles Barrio, *Anarquismo y anarcosindicalismo en Asturias (1890–1936)*, pp. 365 and 432. In the General Meeting of Regional Confederations of the CNT held in Madrid at the end of October 1935, the Asturian delegation proposed that the unions which had left should be invited to a future congress in order to resolve the situation. This proposal was rejected by the Catalan representatives who continued to believe that the leaders of these unions should continue to be 'excluded from the CNT … but not the workers who had followed them as a result of their poor orientation' (Actas in IISG, Fondo CNT, Film 262–B). Orobón Fernández's reflections are examined in greater detail in Chapter 5. For his contributions to the debate within anarcho-syndicalism see Xavier Paniagua, *La sociedad libertaria*, pp. 177–82.

37　For all of the letters cited, plus others which provide more of the same, see AHNS, carpeta 272 of Barcelona. *Por qué se constituyó el Partido Sindicalista*, written in October 1935, appeared in Barcelona in March 1936 (76 pages). For a detailed study of his ideas see Antonio Elorza's prologue to *Ángel Pestaña. Trayectoria sindicalista* (Madrid, Ediciones Tebas, 1974), pp. 5–77.

38　For the announcement of his re-joining see *Solidaridad Obrera*, 3 September 1937, 12 December for his death and the 14 of the same month for his burial. Marín Civera replaced him as president of the Syndicalist Party. *Orto* appeared in Valencia in March 1932 as a 'Revista de Documentación Social', was published monthly and the last issue conserved in the AHNS is No. 20. For the intellectual activities of Marín Civera see Xavier Paniagua, *La sociedad Libertaria*, pp.182–90. As might be imagined, the official reaction of the FAI to the formation of the PS was not at all amicable: 'Finally there emerges what was aimed at during all these years of conjuring tricks! How much would have been achieved in the Spanish proletarian revolution if this party had been created ten or fifteen years ago? It would not have stumbled over one of its greatest obstacles, because the worst enemy is the hidden enemy' (*Tierra y Libertad*, 21 April 1934). For the comment of Juan López, whom Pestaña called 'the great López' in a letter to Fenollar on 22 November 1934, see *Sindicalismo*, 18 April 1934.

39　For the damaging influence of the FAI, see the first letter from Quintanilla to Pestaña. There were other leaders who also left the FSL in order to join different organisations. We know (from a letter from Gómez de Lara to Pestaña on 1 April 1934) that Miguel Mendiola, one of the most outstanding leaders of the CNT in Andalucia at the beginning of the Republic and whom they had attempted to win over to the PS, was at that point in time president of the Radical Youth of Seville. Pestaña, who replied to the letter on 6 April, said it was a shame, 'he is a good lad' and if the radical project 'sinks' perhaps he 'might join us'. The radical project sank and Mendiola joined Unión Republicana. The Libertarian Syndicalist Group of Zaragoza was formed at the beginning of January 1934, taking advantage of the repression of the CNT which the insurrection of the previous month had provoked. It was controlled by activists who ended up joining the Communist Party. One of their leaders, José Duque, defended the thesis of 'the democratic conquest of the rural town councils' at the first Congress of the FSL. The proposal was rejected by the secretary of that organisation, Juan López (*Sindicalismo*, 4 July 1934). Duque abandoned the FSL and became regional secretary of the PCE during the Civil War. Pestaña's letter of 22 November to Fenollar provides interesting indications of the difficult situation in which both the PS and the opposition syndicates found themselves following the revolutionary activity of October of that year.

4 On the road to insurrection

1 The statement about 'starting a general revolutionary movement' appears in the 'Minutes of the General Meeting of the Council of Syndicates of Barcelona, 10 January 1932'. According to the representative of the Merchants' Union, 'The moment had arrived for us to throw ourselves into the struggle for the liberty of the People which the present government AHNS has so ignominiously torn from us.' The delegate of the Union of Chemical Workers was of the opinion that 'when a government has taken away the liberty of the people, every moment is ripe for revolution'. That the Regional Committee found out about the strike after it had broken out can be read in the minutes of the meeting of 5 February 1932. More details were given in the meeting of 8 February (Actas in the AHNS, carpeta 501 of Barcelona). The information used here which is not taken from the Actas comes from *Tierra y Libertad*, 6 February 1932, *El Luchador*, 29 January, *Solidaridad Obrera*, 20 and 21 of January and, above all, from the *Boletín de la CNT*, No. 5 (February–April 1932) and No. 6 (May 1932). For the best coverage of these events, with good use of oral sources, see Cristina Borderías and Mercedes Vilanova, 'Cronología de una insurrección: Figols in 1932' in *Estudios de Historia Social*, 24–25 (January–June, 1983), pp. 187–99.

2 For the communiqué see *Cultura y Acción*, 4 February 1932. *Solidaridad Obrera* gave a lot of space to reports of the closure of the unions and the arrests during many days, following its reappearance with Josep Robusté as editor. The case against those prosecuted for the bombing incident in Alcorisa can be followed in the same paper on 12 November 1933. For more information see *La Voz de Aragón*, 17 November of the same year. The defence lawyer Gregorio Vilatela was elected as member of parliament for the Popular Front coalition in the province of Teruel in February 1936 and was shot by the military insurgents in Zaragoza on 10 August of that year. The comment the 'Soviet Republic in Castel de Cabra' was made by Montilla to journalists on the night of 25 January. The minutes of the meetings of the National Committee of the CNT for the days of 22, 23 and 24 January 1932 were reproduced in the *Boletín de la CNT*, No. 6 (May 1932). The miners' uprising caused considerable unease. They felt obliged to respond because 'it was to be expected that all of the Spanish organisation should give it the maximum of enthusiastic support' (23 January), and then the following day, when the strike was seen to be a failure, they annulled the 'call for a general strike, in order to avert a real catastrophe'.

3 For the first-hand testimony of Cano Ruiz, *Nuestra odisea in Villa Cisneros* (Libertad, S.D.) see Gonzalo Santoja, *Las obras que sí escribieron algunos autores que existen (Notas para la historia de la novela revolucionaria de quiosco en España, 1905–1939)* (Madrid, El Museo Universal, 1993), pp. 149–50. The reports of the deportations were given several pages of coverage in the paper *La Tierra* in February, March and April 1932. This paper appeared in Madrid from 16 December 1930 to June 1935 and was founded by Salvador Cánovas Cervantes and had Eduardo de Guzmán as chief-editor. Its relationship with the Barcelona CNT activists was always tense and the latter often accused it of being in the service of the bourgeois press (see for example the 'Minutes of the General Meeting of the Councils of Syndicates of Barcelona', 12 June 1932). In a letter to Eusebio Carbó on 24 March 1933, Cánovas Cervantes apologised for the fact that neither he nor Guzmán had attended the General Meeting of the Regional committees of the CNT in Barcelona and said that he was 'very scared' of dealing with 'the intimate affairs of the CNT ... and much more so in relation to Barcelona where people have become very sensitive about everything related to *La Tierra*' (AHNS, carpeta 886 of Barcelona). During the war, Cánovas Cervantes was commissioned by Jacinto Toryho, editor of *Solidaridad Obrera* from November 1936, to produce a series of articles 'Apuntes Históricos de Solidaridad Obrera' which were collected in a volume published by the CNT of Catalonia in 1937.

4 *Memorias políticas y de Guerra*, Vol. I, Note for 27 February 1932. The deportations not only worried the CNT members. The Chamber of Agriculture and Forestry of Equatorial Guinea wrote to the Secretary of the Interior on 17 February 1932 to express his concern over the government resolution to send the deportees to Bata because these 'undesirables' will have to live amongst 'the indigenous population which we are colonising'. He suggested 'the possibility of deporting them to the coast of the Spanish Sahara where there is hardly any indigenous populations which could create the conflicts caused here (AHN, Serie A de Gobernación, legajo 18, in which can be found the information on numerous incidents related to the Law of the Defence of the Republic). The day of protest against the deportations, its preparation and development can be followed in the 'Minutes of the General Meeting of the Regional committees held in Madrid on 13, 14 and 16 April 1932', *Boletín de la CNT*, No. 6 (May 1932).

5 Montseny's article 'Yo acuso' appeared in *El Luchador* on 19 February 1932. The voices of protest against Urales were unanimous in the General Meeting of the Regional Committees in April and demonstrated, once more, the dreadful relations which he had with the CNT, be it under moderate leadership or that of the activists of the FAI. Urales also signed an article criticising the repression of the anarchist insurrections in *La barbarie gubernamental* (Barcelona, 1933). He copied the title (just as his daughter had done with Zola) from the pamphlet which Ricardo Mella and José Prat had written on the Montjuich trials in 1897. *Cultura Libertaria* replied to F. Montseny's criticism of Mira on 11 March 1932. Mira was not a 'threat' to the CNT but, rather, 'to those who had taken over ... the CNT in order to put the organisation under the control of another extra-union organisation'. For an assessment of the day of protest on 29 May, see the *Boletín de la CNT*, No. 8 (July 1932). It would appear that virility was not the perquisite only of the anarchists. Having been informed of the failure of the strikes which the CNT had called for this day in Huesca, the civil governor wrote the following to the minister on 29 May 1932: 'Public opinion has reacted with virility in every province and the propaganda of the anarchists, whose power amongst the industrial and agricultural workers has decreased visibly, has hardly been noticed' (AHN, Serie A de Gobernación, legajo 16).

6 *Cultura Libertaria*, 5 February 1932.

7 The quote about Rivas is taken from the 'Informe Schapiro sobre la crisis de la CNT', pp. 467–71. Schapiro, who had just arrived in Spain to organise the secretariat of the IWO with Carbó when the insurrection broke out, wrote an acute analysis of the causes and the responsibilities of the organising committee. For all of the information on the railway strike which did not take place and what happened afterwards see the 'Actas del Pleno de Regionales celebrado los días 30 y 31 de enero y 1 y 2 de Febrero 1933', *Boletín de la CNT*, No. 15 (March 1933) The 'revolutionary gymnastics' is taken from Juan García Oliver, *El eco de los pasos*, p. 115, where he claims to have been the main instigator of a plan which was 'meticulously planned', and exaggerates the effects of the movement considerably, 'one of the most important battles between the libertarians and the Spanish state ... which led to the Republican and Socialist parties losing influence over the majority of Spaniards' (p. 131). For the arrest of the anarchists in Zaragoza see *La Voz de Aragón*, 3 January 1933, which gives detailed information on the first fortnight of the events. See also Aurora Bosch, 'Sindicalismo, conflictividad y política en el campo valenciano durante la Segunda República', pp. 265–68.

8 Schapiro and Carbó, who also touched on the delicate topic, thought that 'the subscriptions of the mass of unions should be used exclusively ... in the inevitable daily struggles and above all in the real organisation of the social Revolution'. The communiqué signed by both on 17 January 1933 was reproduced in the 'Informe Schapiro', pp. 475–578. For the manifesto of the National Committee of 10 January see the *Boletín de la CNT* Nos 12, 13 and 14 (November/December 1932–January

1933). The position of *Solidaridad Obrera* emerged on the same day. That of the opposition unions, from which the quotation is taken, is found in *Cultura Libertaria*, 19 January 1933.

9 The account is based on the excellent chronicle of this insurrection by Jerome R, Mintz, *The Anarchists of Casas Viejas*, pp. 189–225. Although all of the general works dealing with this period dedicate a few pages to it, specific bibliography is scarce. Many years ago, Gerard Brey and Jacques Maurice made a brief incursion in *Historia y leyenda de Casas Viejas* (Madrid, ZYX, 1976). Curiously, the recent work of Maurice, *El anarquismo andaluz*, does not analyse the incident and hardly even offers a clue to its interpretation.

10 For these speeches see *Obras completas*, Vol. II, pp. 334–6 and 597. Azaña repeated these and similar arguments on 23 and 24 February and 7 and 16 March. For his reflections and conversations with those directly responsible for the repression, in which the conversation with Rojas is reproduced, in which he denies having murdered the prisoners, see *Memorias políticas*, note for 1–6 March 1933, pp. 546–63. On 6 March, he received the new Director General of Security, Manuel Andrés, following the dismissal of Menéndez. Of the man who had been governor of Zaragoza until that moment, he wrote that 'Everyone says that he is an intelligent, active and energetic man.' The process of investigation, both official and unofficial, is minutely detailed in Jerome R. Mintz, *The Anarchists of Casas Viejas*, pp. 227–66. Manuel Andrés was assassinated in San Sebastián in 1934 (*La Voz de Aragón*, 11 September 1934). Arturo Menéndez was arrested on the night of 19 July 1936 by the military rebels on the Barcelona–Madrid train in the Calatayud station. He was taken to Pamplona and shot by firing squad. Rojas was tried in May 1934 in Cádiz and condemned to twenty years in prison. Released after the military uprising of July 1936, he joined the rebel army with the rank of captain in the artillery and became infamous as a result of his brutal repression in Granada.

11 The development and consequences of this general strike are related with special emphasis on the arrests, by various delegates to the Regional General Meeting held on 12 June and following days. The minutes can be found in *Boletín de la CNT*, No. 17 (July–October 1933). Schapiro himself was surprised 'that the failure of the movement of 8 January can provoke the unanimous call for … a general strike! In other countries, the failure would have been considered a disaster which would result in a long period of depression. Here, for the very reason that the CNT did not sanction the uprising, the CNT itself needs to demonstrate, with its protest, that the working class will respond differently to its orders' (p. 79). The quotations are taken from *CNT*, 28 January and 9 May 1933. For Eduardo de Guzmán's account see *La Tierra*, 23 January 1933. Sender gave his impression in *Viaje a la aldea del crimen (Documental de Casas Viejas)* completed in Madrid, February 1933 and published in 1934 by the Juan Pueyo printing house. In the copy dedicated to his family, which I was able to consult thanks to Inés Ayala Sender, he wrote: 'The first great disappointment for those of you who believed in the Republic.' The National Committee of the CNT also gave its version of the events in *La verdad sobre la tragedia de Casas Viejas*, a pamphlet of 32 pages the profits of which, according to the communiqué of the committee, were destined to 'the prisoners suffering in the slave huts of the Republican "paradise"'.

12 *Solidaridad Obrera*, 21 October 1933. Refusing to give up on the question, they insisted in the editorial on 24 October, on the front page on the 25th and the 29th, from which the term 'voter-animal' is taken, and so on until 19 November. The campaign in *CNT*, from which the term 'vultures' is taken (28 October), was more aggressive and always carried large titles with the slogans 'Workers! Voting is the sad right to choose your rulers and your executioners' (18 November). The quotation of Gilabert, the secretary of the Regional Committees of the CNT in Catalonia and member of the Peninsular Committee of the FAI, is taken from *Tierra y Libertad*, 20 October. All three papers give detailed information on the meetings 'of libertarian and anti-

electoral affirmation', which the CNT and the FAI held across the territory of Spain during these days.

13 Report of the National Revolutionary Committee to the General Meeting of the Regional Committees of the National Confederation of Workers, held in Madrid on 23 June 1934 and following days. (The minutes are conserved in the AHNS, carpeta 2437 of Madrid.) The other quotations are taken from the 'Actas del Pleno de Regionales de la Confederación Nacional del Trabajo, celebrado en Madrid durante los días 30 de Octobre y siguientes de 1933' (*Ibidem* and IISG, Fondo CNT paquete No. 93, Film 262 B). The connection between the triumph of 'reaction' and the social revolution is also discussed in the *Pleno Peninsular de Regionales de la FAI celebrado en Madrid los días 28, 29 y 30 de octubre 1933*.

14 *Solidaridad Obrera*, 23 November 1933. The appeal to the people in *CNT*, 20 November, that abstention would benefit the 'cavemen' was widely repeated in the press sympathetic to Lerroux. *El Radical* in Zaragoza, for example, encouraged the workers, on 23 October, to castigate the socialists with their vote because those who had 'supported' the 'crimes of Arnedo, Parque de Maria Luisa and Casas Viejas' could not call themselves defenders of the workers'. *La Tierra* also declared its support for the 'revolution in progress', although it was not quite clear which. This paper had distinguished itself by rejecting the concession of the vote to women and was at the forefront of those who projected the argument 'that the vote for women has been the principal cause of the triumph of the right in the elections ... These are the results of placing nothing less than the destiny of the whole regime in the hands of women (20 November and 1 December). The position of the anarchists in relation to this issue was not very different. In an article entitled 'The female vote' on 20 October, *CNT* argued that women had been given this right so that they would vote for the right: 'They will vote for the cavemen ... They will support the Pope and the king.' On 15 November, Lucía Sánchez Saornil asked them to abstain, reminding them 'the horizon lay between these two concepts, the kitchen and the brothel'. The future, however, lay with 'the libertarian revolution'.

15 The division between those who said they 'were not prepared' and those who pointed out the duty to 'fulfil the agreement' can be seen quite clearly from the 'Acta del Pleno del Sindicato de Barcelona del día 23 de noviembre de 1993' (AHNS, carpeta 1286 of Barcelona), although they finally decided that 'if the revolution was started by politicians or if a Regional committee took to the streets, the Barcelona Organisation would support that movement energetically'.

16 Martínez Andrés was mayor once more from 21 February 1936. Arrested on 19 July of that year and suspended from his post by the military command, he was the only republican authority of any rank who escaped execution by firing squad following the uprising in Zaragoza. For the conflict with the governor see the 'Acta de la Sesión del Ayuntamiento de Zaragoza, 22 de diciembre de 1933'. The account of the insurrection is based on the Zaragoza newspapers *El Noticiero*, *Heraldo de Aragón* and *La Voz de Aragón* of the month of December and the Madrid paper *La Tierra*. The anarchist press with national circulation was suspended as a result of the uprising. *CNT*, which was still being published on 8 December, did not reappear until 21 August 1934. The weekly *Tierra y Libertad* reappeared on 16 February 1934. For the CNT's analysis of these events see the 'Actas del Pleno Nacional de Regionales, celebrado el día 10 y siguientes de febrero de 1934 en Barcelona' (IISG, fondo CNT, paquete 93–B, film 262) and 'Actas del Pleno Nacional de Regionales de la Confederación Nacional del Trabajo, celebrado en Madrid el 23 de junio de 1934 y días sucesivos'. For a summary, see the 'Memoria que el Comité Nacional de la CNT presenta al Congreso Extraordinario que se celebrará en Mayo de 1936' in *Solidaridad Obrera* from 4 March to 12 April 1936.

17 There were disturbances of public order and shootings in the Aragonese localities of Puipullín, Tormos, Villanueva de Sijena, Barbastro, Lanaja, Sariñena, Alcampel

(where the local tax collector killed a revolutionary and then, finding himself surrounded, shot himself), in the Zaragozan regions of Zuera, Calatayud, Daroca and Puendeluna, and in Alcañiz, Calanda and Alcorisa in the district of Teruel. For details of the province of Alto Aragon, see José María Azpíroz, *Poder político y conflictividad social en Huesca durante la II República*, pp. 162–9. The anarchists offered an account of the events in these Aragonese towns and others in La Rioja, Andalucia, Extremadura and Catalonia in the *Supplemento de Tierra y Libertad*, No. 18 (January, February and March 1934).

18 The information for this account is based on *La Voz de Aragón*, 14 December, the pamphlet by Macario Royo, *Cómo implantamos el comunismo libertario en Mas de las Matas* (Barcelona, 1934), 29 pages (written in Paris a few days after the events and from which the quotations are taken), and an interview with Florentín Cebrián Pastor, a day labourer born in 1914 (interview held on 16 July 1995). All of the towns which tried out libertarian communism in 1933 relived virtually identical events during the Civil War with even greater intensity. This connection can be followed through the pages of my book *Anarquismo y revolución en la sociedad rural aragonesa* and Ronald Fraser, *Blood of Spain. the Experience of Civil War 1936–1939* (London, Allen Lane, 1979), which also dedicates a section to the community of Mas de las Matas, pp. 351–8.

19 This information was obtained from the text which the corporal in charge of the reinforcements sent to the Civil Governor of the province on 10 December 1933, Historical Archive of the Province of La Rioja, Sección Gobierno Civil, Serie Correspondencia, Arnedo (caja 2). For the emergency assizes, as in other cases to which we will refer later, see the same Archive, Sección Judicial, Libro de Sentencias 1934, sentencia No. 23. According to the paper *La Rioja*, of 9, 10 and 12 December, libertarian communism was declared in Ardedo, Fuenmayor, Cenicero, San Asensio, Briones, Abalos and San Vicente de Sonsierra. There were declarations of solidarity with the revolutionary movement in Logroño, Haro, Viguera, Calahorra and Alfaro, and disturbances of public order with some shooting in Rincón de Soto, Quel, Préjano, Ezcaray, San Domingo and Herramélluri.

20 The Zaragozan socialists, who had kept quiet on repression and blamed the CNT in the previous insurrections, now joined in the accusations of 'ill treatment' of workers. The register of Zaragoza prison contains the names of more than 70 prisoners who had to be medically examined on entering prison (*Vida Nueva*, 20 January 1934). The radical-socialist Venancio Sarría, who had been elected deputy for the province of Zaragoza in June 1931, sent a letter to the governor on 22 December 1933 in which he complained about 'the repression and the practice of ill treatment'. On the other side, the landowners and the conservatives sent numerous letters to the Minister of the Interior thanking him for the good work done by the security forces. This, for example, is what the manager of the sugar company in the neighbourhood of Casetas in Zaragoza did, on 31 December, in a telegram in which he asked for the commandant of the civil guard in the area be promoted to sergeant 'as a result of the constant zeal and vigour he demonstrated in his diligent service during the recent events' (AHN, Serie A de Gobernación, legajo 39).

21 Peiró's 'La severa lección de los hechos' appeared in *Sindicalismo*, 29 December 1933. The 'guerrillas' is taken from the same weekly on 15 December. That the right gave money to the CNT in order for it to undertake the campaign in favour of their membership's abstention has been repeated on various occasions but without reliable evidence. This is what Richard A.H. Robinson did some time ago, basing himself on a conversation with Saínz Rodríguez in which the later assured him 'that money was given to the anarchists in the Valle del Ebro, Cádiz and in other parts of Andalucia'. *The Origins of Franco's Spain: The Right, The Republic and Revolution, 1931–1936* (Newton Abbot, David & Charles, 1970), p. 337. If Saínz Rodríguez is to be believed, he had already financed the anti-Azaña campaign of *La Tierra* following Casas Viejas, buying *Cánovas Cervantes. Testimonios y recuerdos* (Barcelona, Planeta, 1978), p. 246.

22 This is the analysis made in the communiqué of the CNT, signed in Barcelona on 4 February 1932, *Boletín de la CNT*, No. 5 (February–April 1932). One could, of course, add that these analyses were recurrent and not only connected with the insurrections. However, it is not without significance that the majority of these elaborations of liber- tarian communism were written by those who defended this direct route to revolution and were published in 1933, the year of the insurrections. For other examples see Isaac Puente's 'Ensayo programático del comunismo libertario', *Suplemento de Tierra y Libertad*, No. 10 (May 1933) and Federico Urales, *El ideal y la revolución* (Barcelona, Biblioteca de la Revista Blanca, 1933). Everything else that was said on the topic, including the famous 'federal conception of libertarian communism' in the Congress of May 1936, had already been invented.

23 These versions were put forward by the right-wing media at the time. For *El Debate*, for example, what was happening in these 'little towns' of La Rioja, themselves pros- perous and peaceful, was due 'to the tenacious and often silent labour and agitation of the revolutionary press, which the government had allowed' and the labour of 'intel- lectual work' which poisoned a 'group in every town' (14 December 1933). *La Voz de Aragón* spoke of 'the propaganda of outside elements, who are to blame', in order to explain the echoes of the insurrection during that month in some towns in the region of Teruel (27 and 29 January).

24 The information on the registers of sentences is conserved in the Provincial Assizes of Huesca and was provided by Pilar Maluenda. For a summary of the professions, marital status and age see José María Azpíroz, *Poder político y conflictividad social en Huesca durante la II República*, pp. 166–8. The emergency assizes from which the infor- mation on Arnedo is taken met on 15 January 1934 and the heaviest sentence for the ring-leader, 'as the author of a crime of non-peaceful demonstration', was a year and a day and a fine of five hundred pesetas. An account of all detentions and sentences drawn up by the Pro-Prisoners' Committee of Aragon, Rioja and Navarra was published in *Tierra y Libertad* on 31 January 1936. For the perception of the peasants of Casas Viejas concerning the responsibility of the local property owners, and espe- cially José Vela, see Jerome R. Mintz, *The Anarchists of Casas Viejas*, pp. 260–4. The participation of 'very young people' in the attempted insurrection of January 1933 in several counties of Valencia is also highlighted in Aurora Bosch, 'Sindicalismo, conflictividad y política en el campo valenciano durante la Segunda República', p. 267. In the absence of more detailed research and thus on the basis only of the register of sentences, the participation of wives was very limited. Only three women, for example, had been tried out of the 202 people tried for insurrection in the province of Huesca in December 1933. A eulogy of the 'heroines' of Aragon, 'the valkyries of this bloody Valhalla', although without concrete data, was produced by Federica Montseny in 'Las mujeres de Aragón', *La Revista Blanca*, 25 January 1934. The same author exalted the figure of Seisdedos's daughter-in-law, who saved her life in the fire and was then assassinated in the first days of the Civil War, in *María Silva, La Libertaria* (Toulouse, 1951).

25 As the history of the Republic demonstrates, from the beginning to the end, the recourse to violence against the parliamentary regime was not the unique perquisite of the anarchists, nor does it appear that the democratic idea was particularly well rooted amongst the political forces or the pressure groups which supposedly acted on the margins. The argument that in the Spain of the 1930s 'there hardly existed polit- ical options which did not see the use of force as the possible alternative to the ballot box' is developed in depth by Enric Ucelay da Cal in 'Buscando el levantamiento plebiscitario: insurrectionalismo y elecciones' in Santos Juliá (ed.) 'Politica en la Segunda República', *Ayer*, No. 20 (1995), pp. 49–80, although it is not as certain that, as in the case of anarchism, these insurrections corresponded to 'strategic calcula- tions' aimed at 'political evolution', as Ucelay maintains himself along with Susanna· Tavera in 'Una revolución dentro de otra: la lógica insurrectional en la política

española, 1924–1934' in Julio Aróstegui (ed.) 'Violencia y política en España', *Ayer*, No. 13 (1994), p. 131.

26 For the quotation of García Oliver see *El eco de los pasos*, p. 115. The quotations on the revolution that would spread from the countryside to the city are taken from Isaac Puente, *Tierra y Libertad*, 22 April 1932. There is a popularising account of the same in Federico Urales, *Los Municipios Libres (Ante las puertas de la Anarquía)* (Barcelona, Biblioteca de la Revista Blanca, 1932). The failure of this tactic did not affect the most firm believers because the editorial of *La Revista Blanca* insisted on the matter in '¿Que es el comunismo libertario?' on 25 January 1934. The weight of this tradition amongst the leadership of the CNT which replaced the 'treintistas' is clear from the communiqué which the National Committee sent to the Regional Committees following the Sanjurjo uprising in August 1932. 'The movement only has the support of the military elements. These ... will be able to dominate only the provincial capitals ... In the provinces in which the respective capitals fall into the hands of the monarchists ... the unions affiliated to the CNT will occupy ... all of the towns and small cities of the provinces threatened by the reactionaries, immediately using all means at hand to crush the monarchism which had triumphed in the capital' (*Boletín de la CNT*, 9 August 1932). The editorial of the Madrid paper *CNT* reached the same conclusion on 23 November 1932: 'Let us disseminate our rebellion amongst the peasants', 'Libertarian communism in Spain will be of an agrarian nature.'

27 For García Oliver's explanation of why he did not participate in this 'republican-socialist' movement and the criticisms of 'egocentric tendencies' by Durruti, who had broken discipline in order to join the revolutionary committee in Zaragoza on his own, see *El eco de los pasos*, pp. 135–6. Nevertheless, Abel Paz places Ascaso at Durruti's side – and so there were two who had broken the unity. He also has the later make the following statement (one of many attributed to him without specifying where precisely he made them). 'This insurrectional movement should be a warning to the Government that the grass root of workers exists and is not willing to bend its knee before a dictator' (*Durruti*, p. 263). John Brademas has already pointed out that, 'instead of providing the pretext for a new analysis of the political and social situation and a rapprochement between the anarchist factions', it had become a reason for further 'reproaches and recriminations' (*Anarcosindicalismo y revolución en España*, p. 89).

28 'The people have ample reason for their dissatisfaction with the Republic and to undertake the revolution', declared Joan Peiró in 'Una tragedia más ...' But 'it is not enough for the people to believe in the social revolution, they must also know the how and for whom of the revolution'. He went on to warn 'these audacious minorities' that 'they live with their backs turned to reality' (*Cultura Libertaria*, 19 January 1933). For the 'rebellious spirit' and 'organisation' see the 'Informe Shapiro', p. 493. That there was a need to not 'waste' energy which 'must be preserved until the moment arrives in which it can be used to best advantage', was the conclusion reached, following the analysis of the insurrection of December 1933, in the report of the AIT to the 'Pleno Nacional de Regionales de la Confederación Nacional del Trabajo, celebrado en Madrid el 23 de junio de 1934 y días sucesivos', p. 6.

5 Correcting the route taken

1 The quotation from Orobón is taken from the article 'Consideraciones sobre la unidad', published in *La Tierra* on 30 and 31 January 1934. With the closure of *Solidaridad Obrera* and *CNT*, this paper became the 'open tribune' of outstanding anarcho-syndicalist publicists. Orobón returned to this topic in 'Para hacer frente al fascismo, que se organiza febrilmente ...' on 1 March of the same year. It is strange that a young firebrand of the FAI such as Jacinto Toryho should defend similar arguments to those of Orobón in the same 'open tribune' and reject the idea, widely spread at the time, that the CNT and the FAI 'could rely on their own forces to carry

out the revolution and install libertarian communism' ('La unidad revolucionaria, imprescindible', 13 February).

2 For the discussions see the 'Acta del Pleno Nacional de Regionales, celebrado el dia 10 y siguientes de febrero de 1934 en Barcelona' (IISG, Fondo CNT, Paquete 93–B, Film 262). For the Valencian Region see 'Acta del Pleno Nacional de Regionales de Sindicatos de Oposición de Levante, celebrado en Valencia los días 11 y 12 de febrero de 1934' (IISG, Bro 153/11). Joan Peiró had already defended the idea of the 'anti-fascist workers' front', without entering into the question of electoral pacts, in *Sindicalismo*, on 15 December 1933. He developed his arguments in greater depth in 'La unidad revolucionaria' on 10 January 1934, and in 'Revolución o fascismo' on 2 May of the same year. For similar arguments by José Villaverde (who was greatly concerned about a distancing from 'the bankruptcy towards which the policy of the FAI has taken us', and to create 'a strong defensive wall against fascism') see the correspondence between this leader from La Coruña and Ángel Pestaña during January 1934 (AHNS, carpeta 272 of Barcelona).

3 'Actas del Pleno Nacional de Regionales de la Confederación Nacional del Trabajo celebrado en Madrid el 23 de Junio de 1934 y día sucesivos' (AHNS, carpeta 2437 of Madrid). José Mª. Martínez was no less severe with those who opposed the alliance: 'If the CNT does not reach a compromise and goes onto the street, as always, to make the revolution, it will be the unknown soldier, as always, who will be exposed to the bullets and will do the suffering so that the leaders of the Socialist Party can win.' And he went on to argue that, 'whilst we reject collusion with the UGT, so as not to "stain our sacred principles", there is no hesitation in inflicting a veritable wound on the dignity of the CNT, prostrating it at the feet of that wily politician, Alejandro Lerroux'. This latter reference was an allusion to the meeting which the National Committee, apparently without consulting the organisation, had held with the then head of government in January 1934. For details of this alliance see Ángeles Barrio Alonso, *Anarquismo y anarcosindicalismo en Asturias*, pp. 394–402.

4 For the 'overthrow of capitalism through revolution' see *Vida Nueva*, 24 February 1934. The same UGT paper welcomed 1934, 'This will be our year!', after arguing that 'in the year which has finished … it became obvious that fascism is on the march in Spain and intends to annihilate the labour movement, which is what is to be expected of bourgeois democracy' (6 January). The account of the conflict is based on the twenty-page report which the strike committees of the CNT and the UGT circulated as *Los treinta y seis días de huelga en Zaragoza* in 1934 (AHNS, F. 2047). It also receives detailed treatment in Enrique Montañés, *Anarcosindicalismo y cambio político. Zaragoza, 1930–1936*, pp. 108–12, and in greater depth in Graham Kelsey, *Anarcosindicalismo y Estado en Aragón: 1930–1938* (Zaragoza, Institución Fernando el Católico-Fundación Salvador Seguí, 1994), pp. 261–76.

5 For the official record of the agreement see *Los treinta y seis días de huelga*, p. 16. 'Invincible Zaragoza' was the title of an article by F. Montseny in *La Revista Blanca* on 11 May 1934 which included the well-known 'eulogies' of the Aragonese: 'These tough, straightforward and rugged men, who would not know how to construct subtle literary works nor poetic speeches, but who give to life the fertility of their actions and that of their blood, are worth of all Spain together.' For the war of independence and other niceties see *Tierra y Libertad*, 19 May 1934. On 3 December 1935, the same paper commented on how quiet the city was as a result of the repression and suggested that this was not the 'rebellious Zaragoza' or the 'Iberian Kronstadt'. The two union organisations, each on its own, struggled thereafter until they achieved the dismissal of the drivers contracted during the strike. Elviro Ordiales was appointed Director-General of prisons at the beginning of July 1934.

6 There is an immense bibliography on Asturias, although that insurrection also had repercussions in many other towns and regions which are only now becoming known as monographic studies emerge. There is a compendium in G. Jackson *et al.*, *Octubre*

1934. Cinquenta años para la reflexión (Madrid, Siglo XXI, 1985), pp. 320–44. The discussion which resulted from this within the CNT, and which is not dealt with here, is summarised in Angeles Barrio, *Anarquismo y anarcosindicalismo en Asturias*, pp. 402–15. For the official position of the CNT see the 'Boletín extraordinario de la CNT sobre los sucesos de octubre de 1934' included in the 'Memoria que el Comité Nacional de la CNT presenta al Congreso Extraordinario que se celebrará en Mayo de 1936' in *Solidaridad Obrera*, 4 March–12 April 1936. For an explanation of the radicalisation of the PSOE, the rupture with the Republic and the split produced in the socialist movement see Marta Bizcarrondo *Araquistain y la crisis socialista en la II República. Leviatán, 1934–1936* (Madrid, Siglo XXI, 1975) and Paul Preston, *La destrucción de la democracia en España*. Juliá has produced an accurate synthesis of this process in 'Republica, revolución y luchas internas' in *El socialismo en España, Desde la fundación del PSOE hasta 1975* (Fundación Pablo Iglesias, 1986), pp. 231–54. For a detailed analysis of the agricultural workers' general strike see Manuel Tuñón de Lara, *Tres claves de la Segunda República*, pp. 130–53.

7 'Informe del C.N.P.P. a los sindicatos para el Pleno Nacional', Zaragoza, 19 March 1935. The basic information which is elaborated here is taken from the 'Informe del Comité Nacional a los sindicatos para el Pleno Nacional', 2 February 1935. (Both are in AHNS, F. 3274.) The General Meeting, in which the agenda was taken up almost completely by the issues of prisoners and the paper *CNT*, was held in Zaragoza on 26 May of the same year.

8 Susanna Tavera, *Solidaridad Obrera*, pp. 74–82. For the history, development and interpretation of these events, see Enric Ucelay da Cal, *La Catalunya populista*, pp. 193–219. Manuel Villar was also the author, under his pseudonym of 'Ignotus', of *El anarquismo en la insurrección de Asturias. La CNT y la FAI en octubre de 1934* (Valencia, Tierra y Libertad, 1935). The weekly *Tierra y Libertad* was suspended after October until 26 April 1935 and had to be published in Valencia from 20 August 1935 to 24 January 1936. Abad de Santillán was also, from July 1935, editor of *Tiempos Nuevos*, the theoretical review of 'Nervio' which served as a springboard for Jacinto Toryho, editorial secretary in the anarchist propaganda press (*Tierra y Libertad*, 11 July 1935).

9 For the figures for the representatives at the Congress see *Solidaridad Obrera*, 7 May 1936. The road for a return, following this formal invitation from the Plenary Meeting in January up to the Congress of May, was no bed of roses either, above all in Catalonia where there continued to be resistance from both sides. The majority of the trade unions of Sabadell and Mataró joined the UGT. Peiró did not go to Zaragoza and did not re-join the CNT definitively until after the military uprising. Juan López, on the other hand, defended unity with fewer conditions and participated actively in the Congress. For the final stages of this incorporation see Eulalia Vega, *Anarquistas y sindicatos durante la Segunda República*, pp. 221–6 and John Brademas, *Anarcosindicalismo y revolución en España*, pp. 152–226. For the Galician initiative, which ended the schism, see 'Actas del Pleno Nacional de Regionales de la Confederación Nacional del Trabajo, celebrado en Madrid los días 26, 27, 28, 29, 30 y 31 de Enero de 1936' (AHNS, F. 1434-bis).

10 *Ibidem*, where the 'report on revolutionary pacts and alliances' which the 'Special Regional Conference of Syndicates of Catalonia' approved is reproduced. In this Plenary Meeting at the end of January, agreement was reached on the proposal of the Catalan unions to include on the agenda of the following Congress, 'and in a preferential position', the usefulness of a 'pact' with the UGT 'from an exclusively revolutionary perspective'. This was done although the only thing that was achieved in May was to ask for new discussions with the delegates of the UGT to seek this alliance. Naturally, the CNT had nothing to do with the fact that the left of the PSOE and the UGT, led by Largo Caballero, decided upon support for the Popular Front pact. It was seen as an opportunity to win the elections, and then they blocked a government coalition with the republicans. Largo Caballero's intention was, in the

words of Santos Juliá, to reinforce, within his own party, 'the left wing in the struggle against the reformist and centrist elements'. *Orígenes del Frente Popular en España (1934–1936)* (Madrid, Siglo XXI, 1979), p. 55.

11 In a Plenary Meeting which followed that of the CNT, the FAI made it clear that there was 'nothing to change in its policy of complete abstention from all collaboration, direct or indirect, with any politician of the State', although it did not enter into 'circumstantial' details about whether or not it was useful to abstain on this occasion. *Memoria del Pleno Peninsular de la Federación Anarquista Ibérica, celebrado en Madrid los días 31 de enero y 1 de febrero de 1936* (AHNS, F.3713). The same ambiguous messages were kept up in the press in the days leading up to the elections, although the necessary relationship between anti-politicism and abstention was played up for the gallery. Commenting on the candidature for Zaragoza, for example, where Benito Pabón was listed as an 'independent trade unionist', *Solidaridad Obrera* argued, on 8 February, that 'Benito Pabón is neither an anarchist nor a trade unionist. He is the worst thing that it is possible to be: a politician.'

12 Maintain the law, re-establish peace and guarantee order, these were the expressions which *El Sol* and other papers repeated insistently from the first day of the elections. The editorial 'La neutralidad de la calle', from which the expression 'place of honest relaxation' is taken, summarises this position well. The novel by Sender was published by Colección Balagué in Barcelona in 1932 and the phrase on the street can be found on p. 77. I have dealt with the conflict in Zaragoza during these months in *Anarquismo y revolución en la sociedad rural aragonesa, 1936–1938*, pp. 60–72. The return of Azaña as the 'national idol' and the new clash with reality from the first day are narrated well in Santos Juliá, *Manuel Azaña*, pp. 459–69. On the permanent state of exception during these months in 1936, in which there was also no attempt of any sort at reform of the political administration, see Manuel Ballbé, *Orden público y militarismo en la España constitucional (1812–1983)*, pp. 387–91.

13 There are examples, signed in May 1936 by the Single Union of the Madrid Construction Industry (AHNS, carpeta 1119 of Madrid), of how this procedure could be converted into a written agreement with the employers 'that all those employees … have to be contracted through the delegates of the UGT and CNT organisations'.

14 The quotation on social utility of the estates is taken from Pasual Carrión, *La reforma agraria de la segunda república*, p. 132. For a summary of the figures of the land occupied and peasant farmers placed on them, by month and province, see Edward Malefakis, *Reforma agraria y revolución campesina en la España del siglo XX* , pp. 432–3. There is detailed information on this period in Manuel Tuñon de Lara, *Tres Claves de la Segunda República*, pp. 166–196. See also Eduardo Sevilla-Guzmán, *La evolución del campesinado en España* (Madrid, Peninsula, 1979), pp. 117–22. For the conflicts between the radical positions of the peasants unions and the attempts at control from above, see Jacques Maurice, 'Problemas de la reforma agraria de la II República (1931–1936)' in Manuel Tuñon de Lara *et al.*, *Movimiento obrero, política y literatura en la España contemporanea* (Madrid, Quadernos para el Diálogo, 1974, pp. 94–7). There is no exhaustive study of the FETT (or of the FNTT before 1934), although there is abundant information on the strength of socialism in the countryside in Paloma Biglino, *El socialismo español y la cuestión agraria, 1890–1936* (Madrid, Ministerio de Trabajo y ·Seguridad Social, 1986).

15 Edward Malefakis wrote that 'Spain experienced the biggest wave of strikes in its history', in *Reforma agraria y revolución campesina*, p. 424, taking the *Boletín del Ministrio de Trábajo* as his source. This has been repeated in the majority of general studies on the period. Santós Juliá (ed.) speaks of 'strike movements on an unprecedented scale', in 'Sistema de partidos y problemas de consolidación de la democracia', *Ayer*, No. 20 (1995), p. 137. The quotation on the CNT is taken from Paul Preston, *La destrucción de la democracia en España*, p. 257. That the spring of 1936 'constitutes the most famous

civil disturbance in Spanish history' is affirmed by Stanley G. Payne in 'Political violence during the Spanish Second Republic', p. 279.

16 I have dealt with the negotiations 'to resolve the unemployment problem', between the authorities, representatives of the banks, and the employers and union leaders during these months in Zaragoza in *Anarquismo y revolución en la sociedad rural aragonesa*, pp. 66–70. On the change in CNT strategy in Catalonia after October 1934, the rapprochement with the republican left [Esquerra Republicana] and the circumstances favourable to the avoidance of confrontation see Enric Ucelay da Cal, *La Catalunya populista*, pp. 223–4 and 269–77. Albert Balcells was one of the first to point out that the abundance of labour conflicts during the spring of 1936, aimed at a restoration of 'the standard of working conditions achieved in 1934', was accompanied by a reduction in the 'violence of the social struggles', in *Crisis económica y agitación social en Cataluña de 1930 a 1936*, pp. 233–4. See also Susanna Tavera and Eulàlia Vega, 'L'afilició sindical a la CRT de Catalunya: entre l'eufòria revolucionària i l'ensulsiada confederal, 1919–1936', pp. 353 and 363. The contrast with Seville between the spring of 1936 with 'a wave of disputes resolved, in the majority of cases, without recourse to strikes', and the elevated number of strikes called in 1931 or the 'serious social radicalisation in 1933', has been examined in detail by José Manuel Macarro, *La utopía revolucionaria*, pp. 72–80.

17 The complete proceedings of the Congress were never published, although there exists a summary in *El Congreso Confederal de Zaragoza. Mayo de 1936* CNT (ed.) (1955). There exists an edition of the report on the *Concepto Confederal del Comunismo Libertario* by the National Committee (Zaragoza, 1936). Typed copies of the report on the 'agrarian problem' and on the 'Análisis de actividad y fijación de normas' are held in the AHNS (carpeta 255 of Madrid). The figures for the Congress are taken from *Solidaridad Obrera* on the 6 and 7 May 1936. Jacques Maurice has dealt with the revision of the strategy on the peasantry which the CNT was obliged to undertake in *El anarquismo andaluz*, pp. 304–6.

18 For a detailed account see Manuel Requena Gallego, *Los sucesos de Yeste (mayo 1936)* (Albacete, Instituto de Estudios Albacetenses, 1983) For a reconstruction, in the form of a novel, see Juan Goyistolo, *Señas de identidad* (Barcelons, Seix Barral, 1976), pp. 122–40. Various monographs are available, providing detailed studies of these conflicts: see Manuel Pérez Yruela, *La conflictividad campesina en la provincia de Córdoba, 1931–1936*, pp. 207–14; Pascual Cebellos, *Luchas agrarias en Sevilla durante la Segunda República* (Seville, Diputación Provincial de Sevilla, 1983); and Francisco Cobo Romero, *Labradores, campesinos y jornaleros*, pp. 445–82. I have undertaken an examination of the characteristics of these conflicts in Aragon, which also illustrated what happened in other areas of the north of Spain in which small property ownership was predominant, in *Anarquismo y revolución en la sociedad rural aragonesa*, pp. 51–9.

19 I have discussed the historiographical explanations of the Republic as a cause of the Civil War in 'Guerra civil, ¿lucha de clases?: el difícil ejercicio de reconstruir el pasado', *Historia Social*, No. 20 (1994), pp. 135–50. Santos Juliá produced a critique of this supposed connection some years ago in 'El fracaso de la República', *Revista de Occidente*, No. 7–8 (1981), pp. 196–211. On the breakdown of the traditional representation of class interest as the principal cause of the weakness of the republican political system, see the same author's 'Gobernar, ¿para quien? Debilidad de partidos y representación de intereses en la II República', *Revista de Derecho Político*, No. 12 (1981), pp. 139–43. For the electoral alliance between the urban middle classes, who provided the basis of support for the Radical Party, and the rural and urban propri-etors who supported the anti-republican right, see Nigel Townson, ' "Una República para todos los españoles": el Partido Radical en el poder, 1933–1935', pp. 194–8. On the lack of democratic tradition and the rejection of election results see Enric Ucelay da Cal, 'Buscando el levantamiento plebiscitario: insurreccionalismo y elecciones', pp. 51–3.

6 The summer of 1936

1 For an extremely detailed account of the uprising, see Luis Romero *Tres días de julio (18, 19 y 20 de julio 1936)* (Barcelona, Ariel, 1967) and Gabriel Cardona, 'El cataclismo de julio' in 'La guerra civil', *Historia*, 16 (1986), Vol. 4, pp. 6–55.

2 This is what Franz Borkenau described (in one of the first examples of what would now be termed the comparative history of revolutions) as 'the objective requirements of revolutionary development ... which are more powerful than any doctrine', in 'State and revolution in the Paris Commune, the Russian Revolution, and the Spanish Civil War', *Sociological Review*, XXIX, 1 (1937), p. 67. For a more sophisticated version of arguments similar to Borkenau's, in relation to the state and revolution, see Theda Skocpol, *States and Social Revolutions. A Comparative Analysis of France, Russia and China*, Cambridge, Cambridge University Press, 1981. In 1937 Borkenau also published a first-hand account of the first few months of conflict, *The Spanish Cockpit* (first Spanish translation, Ruedo Ibérico, París, 1971). The term 'romantic', to describe the CNT's conceptualisation of libertarian communism before July 1936, was coined by Helmut Rudiger, who, as secretary of the IWA in Spain, produced some of the deepest insights into the changes which the anarchist movement experienced during the war. See 'Materiales para la discusión sobre la situación española, en el Pleno de la AIT, el ll de junio de 1937' (AHNS, carpeta 39 de Bilbao). He expanded upon these reflections in *El anarcosindicalismo en la Revolución Española*, Comité Nacional de la CNT, Barcelona, 1938, from which the concept of 'lyrics of subversion' is taken.

3 The legendary status of Ascaso as a martyr (he was born in Almudébar, in Huesca, in 1901) derives from various biographical studies, amongst which see Salvador Cánovas Cervantes, *Durruti y Ascaso. La CNT y la revolución de julio*, Ediciones 'Páginas Libres' (Toulouse, undated); Leo Campion, *Ascaso et Durruti*, (L'Emancipateur, Flemelle-Haute (Bélgica), undated); Antonio Orts-Ramos, *Las grandes figuras de la revolución. Francisco Ascaso* (Ed. Maucci, Barcelona, undated); and Ricardo Sanz, *Figuras de la revolución española* (Barcelona, Ediciones Petronio, 1978). For a critique of this conceptualisation of a homogeneous working class fighting against fascism, which includes a detailed study of the behaviour of the workforce of the Rivière company, see Anna Monjo and Carme Vega, *Els treballadores i la guerra civil. Història d'una indústria catalana collectivitzada* (Barcelona, Empúries, 1986), pp.34–8. Enric Ucelay da Cal has already drawn attention to the idealism implicit in the identification of the proletariat with the workers' movement and this in turn with the CNT in *La Catalunya populista*, p. 306.

4 The first version of this famous scene, which is used here, was provided by Joan García Oliver in *De julio a julio. Un año de lucha* (text taken from the writings collected in the special edition of *Fragua Social*, Valencia, 19 July 1937), pp. 194ff., and has often been cited as evidence of the good faith of the anarchists who did not take advantage of the situation in order to take power. Nevertheless, they crushed and displaced the remaining political forces as soon as the opportunity arose. In an account of the events written decades later, none other than García Oliver took greater pleasure in settling accounts with those anarchists, such as Abad de Santillán, Federica Montseny, Felipe Alaiz and Eusebio Carbó, who 'wanted to exercise leadership in the meetings and assemblies' although they 'had not taken part in the recent activism of the proletariat of the confederation' (*El eco de los pasos*, pp. 176–7). The term 'libertarian ethics' is taken from H. Rudiger, *El anarcosindicalismo en la Revolución Española*, pp. 13–14.

5 *El eco de los pasos*, p. 347. For the 'cleansing necessary for public health', see *Solidaridad Obrera*, 6 September 1936. The 85,490 victims of repression in the republican zone, cited in *Causa general. La dominación roja* (1961), are reduced to 71,744 by Ramón Salas, Larrazábal in *Pérdidas de guerra* (Barcelona, Planeta, 1977) and have been reduced even further as a result of local and regional research. Leaving aside fluctuations in figures, a detailed and exhaustive study of the Catalan case has been provided by Josep Mª Solé i Sabaté and Joan Villarroya i Font, *La repressió a la reraguarda de Catalunya (1936–1939)* (Barcelona, Publicacions de l'Abadia de Montserrat, 1989), which puts

the number of assassinations for the entire duration of the war at 8,360. For an i ntroduction to the character and development of this popular justice see Glicerio Sánchez Recio, *Justicia y guerra en España: Los tribunales populares (1936–1939)* (Diputación de Alicante, Instituto de Cultura, 'Juan Gil-Albert', Diputación de Alicante, 1991).

6 See J.M. Solé i Sabaté and J. Villarroya i Font, *La repressió a la reraguarda de Catalunya*, pp. 458–60, and pp. 337–447 for graphs and statistics for the counties which provide relevant information on the professions involved. For Peiró's condemnation of these 'acts of individual terrorism', and a defence of the popular tribunals, see *Solidaridad Obrera*, 7 September 1936. For Ascó, see the document signed by the committee on 27 September 1936 (AHNS, carpeta 839, Barcelona).

7 A considerable period of time has passed since the publication of Antonio Montero Moreno's famous *Historia de la persecución religiosa en España, 1934–1939* (Madrid, BAC, 1961). However, leaving aside the detailed investigations of figures and the character of this violence in various regions, there is still a shortage of historical investigation explaining this issue. The reader will find accurate accounts of the conviction with which republicans, socialists and anarchists took up this issue in José Alvarez Junco, *El emperador del paralelo*, pp. 397–414, and 'El anticlericalismo en el movimiento obrero', in G. Jackson et. al., *Octubre 1934. Cincuenta años para l reflexión*, pp. 283–300. For a general overview of this phenomenon see Joan Connelly Ullman, 'The warp and woof of parliamentary politics in Spain, 1808–1939: Anticlericalism versus "Neo-Catholicism" ', *European Studies Review*, 13, 2 (1983), pp. 145–76. For an anthropological interpretation, see Manuel Delgado, *La ira sagrada. Anticlericalismo, iconoclastia y antiritualismo en la España contemporánea* (Barcelona, Ed. Humanidades, 1992). The argument used in the text on the acts of desecration is taken from Bruce Lincoln, 'Revolutionary exhumations in Spain, July 1936', *Comparative Studies in Society and History*, 27, 2 (1985), pp. 241–60.

8 For an exemplary study of this process, providing a step-by-step account of the devel-opments at the Rivière company (which had more than a thousand employees in July 1936) and making good use of oral sources, see Anna Monjo and Carme Vega in *Els treballadors i la guerra civil*. The paragraph cited in the text (p. 193) is taken from this work. Mercedes Vilanova has also dealt with these changes making use of 26 biogra-phies in *Les majories invisibles. Explotació fabril, revolució i repressio* (Barcelona, Icaria, 1995). A number of small-scale studies which analyse the economy of the collectives in detail have been published in recent years. See, for example, José Eugenio Borao, 'El impacto de la guerra civil en la economía del Vallés Occidental (1936–1939)', unpub-lished DPhil thesis, Universidad Autónoma de Barcelona, 1989) and the collected volume *Col.lectivitzacions al Baix Llobregat (1936–1939)* (Centre d'Estudis Comarcals del Baix Llobregat, 1989). Josep Mª Bricall was the first to deal with the economy of the collectives in his extensive work *Política económica de la Generalitat (1936–1939)* (Barcelona, Edicions 62, 1970), 2 vols. Albert Pérez Baró's *Trenta mesos de collectivisme a Catalunya (1936–1939)* (Barcelona, Ariel) was published in the same year. A consider-able amount of information and striking interpretations are also to be found in Walther L. Bernecker's *Colectividades y revolución social. El anarquismo en la guerra civil española, 1936–1939* (Barcelona, Crítica, 1982), especially pp. 265–381.

9 This was always the official version and is to be found in the 'Informe que la CNT presenta al Congreso extraordinario de la AIT, convocado en París para el 6 de diciembre de 1937'. Santos Juliá has dealt with the interpretation of the revolution, which was shared by the CNT and the UGT, in 'De revolución popular a revolución obrera', *Historia Social*, 1 (1988), pp. 40–1. The logic which the war imposed on the CNT, obliging it to change its historical hypotheses, is one of the underlying themes in the unpublished work of David Martínez Fiol and Susanna Tavera, 'Corporativism and workers' revolution in Catalonia (1936–1939): The limits of proletarian utopias', to which the authors kindly allowed me access.

10 *Homage to Catalonia* appeared in English in 1938 (the London, Secker & Warburg edition of 1967, pp. 2–4, is used here) and the lucid observations contained in it have been reproduced, and plagiarised, by numerous authors ever since. The shadow of Orwell is clearly present, although with less accuracy, in Ken Loach's *Land and Freedom*, and Vicente Aranda's *Libertarias*, the two most recent films to have success-fully exploited the most emblematic images of those revolutionary times. For dress code as a symbol of the 'proletarianisation' of Catalan society and of the political domination of the working-class images and rhetoric in which women also partici-·pated, see Mary Nash's excellent study *Defying Male Civilization: Women in the Spanish Civil War* (Denver, Colorado, Arden Press, 1995), pp. 50–3.

11 For the quotation on discipline see Helmut Rudiger, *El anarcosindicalismo en la Revolución Española*, p. 13. For a critique of the idealised image of the Barcelona of July 1936 see Enric Ucelay da Cal, *La Catalunya populista*, pp. 286–8. Ucelay and Susanna Tavera have provided an examination of the internal tensions and confrontations in 'Grupos de afinidad, disciplina bélica y periodismo libertario, 1936–1938', *Historia Contemporánea*, 9 (1993), pp. 167–90. For collaboration as an 'a priori condition of workers' power', see Ronald Fraser, *Recuérdalo tú y recuérdalo a otros*, p. 247, Vol. I. For the image of the 'spontaneous revolution' see Raymond Carr, *The Spanish Tragedy. The Civil War in Perspective* (London, Weidenfeld and Nicolson, 1977), pp. 90–1. I have examined the myth and reality of these images in various studies and these chapters merely revise and bring up to date the most substantial part of my arguments and research. See, for example, *Anarquismo y revolución en la sociedad rural aragonesa, 1936–1938* (Madrid, Siglo XXI, 1985); 'Las colectivizaciones', in 'La Guerra Civil', *Historia*, 16, pp. 42–62; 'Anarquismo y guerra civil: del poder popular a la burocracia revolucionaria' in Santos Juliá (co-ordinador), *Socialismo y guerra civil* (Madrid, Ed. Pablo Iglesias, 1987); 'Guerra y revolución: la edad de oro del anarquismo español', *Historia Social*, 1 (1988), pp. 63–76; and Julián Casanova (ed.) *El sueño igualitario: campesinado y colectivizaciones en la España republicana, 1936–1939* (Zaragoza, Institución Fernando el Católico, 1988), pp. 7–15 and 49–60.

12 *El Frente*, Pina de Ebro, 27 August 1936 (Boletín de Guerra de la Columna Durruti), later to become the Boletín de Guerra de la División Durruti y Portavoz de la 26 División. On the Militias' committee see César M. Lorenzo, *Los anarquistas españoles y el poder*, pp. 80–8; Juan García Oliver, *El eco de los pasos*, pp. 179–82; and Diego Abad de Santillán, *Por qué perdimos la guerra. Una contribución a la historia de la tragedia española* (Esplugues de Llobregat, Plaza y Janés, 1977), pp. 69–70. Some authors, such as Walther L. Bernecker argue that the creation of this Committee represented anar-chism's 'break with the tradition of radical anti-politics' and with 'its principles of direct democracy', which implies, in contrast to the argument made in Chapter 3, that 'direct democracy' was one of the symbols of identity of the anarchist movement before July 1936. See *Colectividades y revolución social*, pp. 395–6.

13 Rudolf Rocker, *The Truth about Spain* (New York, Frei Abeiter Stimme, undated), p. 3; Juan García Oliver, *El eco de los pasos*, pp. 198–9; Diego Abad de Santillán, 'Buenaventura Durruti (1896–1936)', *Timón*, November 1938, p. 16. For an even lower figure for the 'Durruti' Column – some 2,000 militiamen – see Abel Paz, *Durruti*, p. 397. According to Francoist historiography, the militias had considerable superiority in men and armaments – 15,000 against 1,500 soldiers in the 5th Division which rose up in Zaragoza. See José Martínez Bande, *La invasión de Aragón y el desembarco en Mallorca* (Madrid, San Martín, 1970), p. 75; Ramón Salas Larrazábal, *Historia del Ejército popular de la República* (Madrid, Editora Nacional), Vol. 1, pp. 330–2. According to General Miguel Ponte y Manso de Zúñiga, who took command of this Division on 21 August 1936, 'the enemy was far superior in numbers, artillery and aviation, they were strongly fortified and had a large number of automatic rifles'. See 'Cuando Aragón era yunque', *Revista del Ejército*, 2 (March 1940). For information on the

'Ascaso' column and 'Los Aguiluchos' see *Solidaridad Obrera*, 14 and 29 of August 1936.

14 I am here led by the research of this author carried out in *Defying Male Civilization: Women in the Spanish Civil War*, pp. 52 and 101–21. She had already dealt with the issue accurately in 'Milicianas and homefront heroines: Images of women in war and revolution 1936–1939', *History of European Ideas*, 11 (1989). Nash's extremely extensive work on women and the civil war (and this is a theme we will return to in the next chapter) began with *'Mujeres Libres'. España, 1936–1939* (Barcelona, Tusquets, 1975). According to *Solidaridad Obrera*, 19 September 1936, the CNT and the FAI organised a female 'century' which was destined for the Aragonese front under the command of Rosario Alvarez. For more information see Montserrat Carreras and Nuria Valls, 'La mujer catalana en las milicias' in 'La Guerra Civil', *Historia* 16, pp. 112–17.

15 Literally, 'They considered themselves to be the intellectual staff, which, it would appear, absolved them from the duty of fighting on the streets. It would later be shown that they were of no great use as intellectuals either' (*El eco de los pasos*, p. 176).

16 The clearest examples of this messianic form of expression are to be found in *El Frente*, 27 and 29 August 1936, although 'sacrifice' is taken from *Solidaridad Obrera*, 14 August of the same year. Saturnino Carod, secretary for agitation and propaganda of the Regional Committee of Aragon, fled from Zaragoza the day after the uprising and began organising, in Tortosa (Tarragona), the column which with the help of Lieutenant Ferrrer and some eighty civil guards under his command, occupied lower Aragon in the region of Teruel from Calaceite to Alcorisa. For his testimony see Ronald Fraser, *Recuérdalo tú y recuérdalo a otros*, pp. 162–3 and 178–84. The information which is developed for this question is also taken from an interview with Antonio Ortiz, carried out in Zaragoza on 6 November 1987 at the home of the CNT activist Luis Muñoz Ortiz, who was affiliated to the wood workers' union in Barcelona. He was born in that city in 1907, appointed as leader of the column by Colonel Díaz Sandino and, in spite of never having had any close ties with Aragon until then, he became one of the most influential CNT leaders in the policies behind the lines in this region.

17 *Solidaridad Obrera*, 13 August 1936; *El Frente*, 2 and 19 September of the same year. Ballano was, furthermore, the chief authority of the 'investigation and vigilance groups' and also for public order under the Council of Aragon. Examples of influential activists during these early stages, which illustrate the argument made in the text, would be Macario Royo, who would lead the insurrection of December 1933 in Mas de Matas and who acted during the war as CNT delegate to Aragon on the National Committee, or Adolfo Arnal, a young member of the FAI (23 years old) and secretary of the Local Federation of Trade Unions of Zaragoza, who would then take charge of the Department of the Economy and Supplies of Aragon. The organisational capacity of some of these teachers was considerable. José Alberola, rationalist teacher and veteran anarchist activist who had participated along with another Aragonese anarchist, Manuel Buenacasa, in the editing and administration of the weekly *El Productor* in 1925 and 1926, was the principal instigator and propagandist of the revolution in the district of Cinca. José Mavilla spread the revolution in the Barbastro area and was secretary of the Regional Federation of Collectives from its foundation until February 1937. Another teacher, Francisco Ponzán, assisted Mavilla with propaganda work. These three were members of the Council of Aragon from its formation in October 1936.

18 Encarna y Renato Simoni, Cretas. *La colectivización de un pueblo aragonés durante la guerra civil española, 1936–1937* (Centro de Estudios Bajoaragoneses, Alcañiz, 1984); Susan Friend Harding, *Remaking Ibieca. Rural Life in Aragon under Franco* (Chapel Hill, University of North Carolina Press, 1984); and Julián Casanova, *Caspe 1936–1938. Conflictos políticos y transformaciones sociales durante la guerra civil* (Zaragoza, Grupo Cultural Caspolino-Institución Fernando el Católico, 1984).

19 The quotation is taken from Sebastían Cirac, *Los héroes y mártires de Caspe*, (Imprenta Octavio y Félez, Zaragoza, 1939) pp. 34–5. The incitement to violence is taken from the interview with Antonio Ortiz, who claims this role for himself for having calmed the thirst for revenge in Caspe. According to his own testimony, Carod gave his column a ticking off, because someone had set fire to the church in Calaceite; see Ronald Fraser, *Recuérdalo tú y recuérdalo a otros*, Vol 1, p. 178. The number of murders claimed by Ramón Salas Larrazábal in the Republican zone of Aragon is 2,922 (*Pérdidas de guerra*, pp. 286–7). In spite of all that has been written about this period of terror, this figure is quite a lot lower than the 8,628 republican victims of the military repression, 941 of which took place in the post-war period following the Nationalist victory. See J. Casanova *et al.*, *El pasado oculto*, p. 231.

20 Pilar Salomón 'La crítica moral al orden social: la persistencia del anticlericalismo en la sociedad española (1900–1939)', Vol. I, pp. 422–37. 'Watch out priest, if we see you in the street you'll end up skinned', the militiamen wrote on the house of a priest in a town on the Teruel front (*Solidaridad Obrera*, 23 August 1936). The account of the burning in the town square of saints and other religious objects is taken from Susan F. Harding, *Remaking Ibieca*, p. 63. An anecdotal account of the same phenomenon in the town of Alcalá del Obispo, in the region of Huesca, is given by Mary Low and Juan Brea, who had enlisted in the POUM: 'We used the painted wooden statues to start the fire we cooked on. They had thrown them into the square when the church was burnt. There was hardly any wood so we smashed up Saint Eduvigis, the virgin martyr, and the next day it was Thomas of Padua' (*Red Spanish Notebook. The First Six Months of the Revolution and the Civil War* (London, Martin Secker and Warburg, 1937), pp. 75–7).

21 *Solidaridad Obrera*, 14 August. The quotation from *El Frente* is from the 29th of the same month.

22 Susanna Tavera, *Solidaridad Obrera. El fer-se i desfer-se d'un diari anarco-sindicalista*, pp. 90–1.

7 War and revolution

1 Helmut Rudiger, 'Materiales para la discusión sobre la situación española, en el Pleno de la AIT del día 11 de junio de 1937', p. 6.

2 For a detailed study of the formation of this government see Santos Juliá, 'España entre dos gobiernos (septiembre–noviembre, 1936)' in 'La Guerra Civil', *Historia*, 16, vol. 7, pp. 8–20, from which the quotation on Largo Caballero is taken. Juliá has conceptualised this government as 'neither trade unionist nor revolutionary', nor of the Popular Front, but rather one 'of national unity, of victory and of anti-fascist union' in 'De la división orgánica al gobierno de unidad nacional', in *Socialismo y guerra civil*, pp. 238–44. For the most detailed study of the different debates and negotiations up until the entry of the CNT into government, with special attention given to his father's participation, see Horacio Martínez Prieto, in César M. Lorenzo, *Los anarquistas españoles y el poder*, pp. 179–90. For the degree of importance to this government that it recover sufficient authority to calm the bourgeoisie both domestically and internationally, see Ronald Fraser, 'The Spanish Civil War' in Raphael Samuel (ed.) *People's History and Socialist Theory* (London, Routledge and Kegan Paul, 1981), pp. 198–9.

3 For the discussion and the report see AHNS, (carpeta 39 of Bilbao). For information on the plenary session see *Solidaridad Obrera*, 19 September 1936. The data on Mariano R. Vázquez is taken from Helmut Rudiger, *El anarcosindicalismo en la Revolución Española*, p. 7.

4 Neither post-war nor contemporary anarchist literature has recognised the key role of this individual in the negotiations which took the CNT into government. César M. Lorenzo, from whom the quotation is taken, argues that his father had been

confirmed in his post 'by the activists of the CNT' (*Los anarquistas españoles y el poder*, p. 179). This was not apparent to García Oliver, who, it might be assumed, gave a vision of Horacio M. Prieto which was diametrically opposed to that of Lorenzo: 'Everyone thought he was overly excitable', he left 'a grey patina on everything he touched', he was always 'dressed up for Sunday', 'one never quite knew what his revolutionary development had been during the military uprising' and 'he was not the sort of activist that the national Committee needed at that point in time' (*El eco de los pasos*, pp. 289–91). That political collaboration was 'part of his character' are the words of Antonio Ortíz and Luis Muñoz in the interview cited (6–XI–1987). For the minutes of the Plenary meeting of 30 September see AHNS (carpeta 2437 of Madrid).

5 It is curious that, contrary to what happened with the Militias Committee, and later with the central government, to which the CNT sent some of its most prestigious leaders, Fábregas, an economist who had never been part of the organisation, was chosen for the Generalitat, along with García Birlán, a FAI publicist with no real links to trade unionism and who wrote under the pseudonym of 'Dionysios'. Also chosen was Juan José Doménech, a 'second rate' activist according to García Oliver. In this case García Oliver (*El eco de los pasos*, p. 278) and César M. Lorenzo (*Los anarquistas españoles y el poder*, pp. 101–2) agree that these appointments were surprising. Federica Montseny also referred to them as 'activists who were little known within the unions' in *Mis primeros cuarenta años* (Barcelona, Plaza & Janés, 1987), p. 97. In her opinion this participation in the Generalitat 'took place in the face of enormous and determined resistance, even by those who brought it about, and which had grave consequences'. The importance that everything related to the 'revolutionary order' held for those union leaders became apparent once more with the appointment of Aurelio Fernández and Dionisio Eroles for those posts. The former, of the group 'Nosotros', had been the real creator of the 'groups of investigation', whilst Eroles, who had spent half of his life in prison, carried out functions similar to the control patrols. For the comment on the dissolution of the Militias Committee see *Solidaridad Obrera*, 2 October 1936. Joan Peiró had been calling for order and discipline at the front and behind the lines, as can be seen from *Solidaridad Obrera* of the 1st and 6th of that month. He returned forcefully to the question, a few days before being appointed as minister, in 'La revolución y la guerra', 28 October 1936.

6 According to García Oliver, Federica Montseny made it a condition of her acceptance of the post that he should also be obliged to do so (*El eco de los pasos*, p. 292). Montseny gives the opposite version and argues that it was García Oliver who said 'I will accept if Federica accepts' (*Mis primeros cuarenta años*, p. 103). Both finally accepted, we are told, out of duty and in both cases Mariano R. Vázquez intervened. For all of the details on the decisive intervention of Horacio Martínez Prieto in the affair see César M. Lorenzo, *Los anarquistas españoles y el poder*, pp. 186–90. The term 'haggling' is taken from Francisco Largo Caballero, *Mis recuerdos* (México, Ediciones Unidas, 1976), pp. 175–6, who also adds that Azaña 'refused to sign the decrees because he found it repugnant to have four anarchists in the government ... He did not realise the consequences that the transformation of Spanish anarchism would have in the future as it moved from terrorism and direct action to collaboration.' Azaña signed them, 'although with reservations', because Largo threatened to resign if he did not. In fact, Azaña would write some months later, when the events of May 1937 removed the CNT from the government, 'that not only against my opinion, but also in spite of my strongest protest, the ministerial modification of November was carried out with the entry of the CNT and the anarchists' ('Cuaderno de La Pobleta', anotación del 20 de mayo de 1937, in *Memorias políticas y de guerra*, II, p. 43).

7 Mary Low and Juan Brea blamed this inability on their 'ideological confusion,' an accusation which was fairly common amongst the activists of the POU (*Red Spanish Notebook. The First Six Months of the Revolution and the Civil War*, p. 247). According to Helmut Rudiger, this could well have been the result of their own history, based on

clearly defensive union practice and 'destructive struggle and pure criticism and protest' (*El anarcosindicalismo en la Revolución Española*, p. 6). Some of the justifications, contemporary reactions and *a posteriori* explanations which have been given of the affair are reproduced in *Anarquismo y revolución en la sociedad rural aragonesa*, pp. 143–50. Burnett Bolloten had already provided a good collection in *El gran engaño*, Luis de Caralt, Barcelona, 1975, pp. 171–4. Horacio Martínez complained about the 'considerable damage' caused by the failure to enter government earlier in *El anarquismo español en la lucha política*, París, 1946, p. 12. García Oliver is also of the opinion that 'we were bad politicians … we allowed the powerful ministries, of War, Navy, Aviation and the Interior to be run by others' (*El eco de los pasos*, p. 414). When García Oliver informed Antonio Ortiz of the decision, he snapped 'What? Join the government for that?' (interview with Ortiz, 6 November 1987).

8 This is a very different opinion from that held by Joan Peiró only a few months before the end of the war, for whom the attainment of anarchism, 'more than on its principles', depended 'on the historical moment and the tactics which are used to achieve it'. The 'nature of war' prevented 'any sort of movement against the state unless we were willing to accept the most serious consequences in terms of responsibilities to ourselves and the world at large … When the historical moment did not coincide with anarchism it would have to be anarchism which put itself at the service of the historical moment' (*Timón*, October 1938, pp. 72–3). The connection between the resistance to this decision and the evolution of the war and the politics of the republican zone constitutes one of the issues which are later termed 'the limits of the earthly paradise'. There are historians, however, who believe that the entry into government opened an irreversible breach between the leadership and the activists of the CNT (Raymond Carr, *The Spanish Tragedy*, p. 113), or that 'many sectors of the anarchist movement', for example 'the immense majority of the press, 'refused to accept it (Julio Aróstegui, 'Los dos Estados', in 'La Guerra Civil', *Historia*, 16, vol. 11, p. 14).

9 For this question see Julio Aróstegui and Jesús A. Martínez Martín, *La Junta de Defensa de Madrid, noviembre de 1936/abril de 1937* (Madrid, Comunidad de Madrid, 1984), which deals with the confrontations between communists and anarchists over public order, a fundamental issue in all of the autonomous and revolutionary sources of power which emerged throughout republican territory.

10 There is much hagiography around Durruti and nothing that resembles a biography. The most documented of these is that cited above by Abel Paz, *Durruti*, who, in order to avoid missing out any detail which might feed this legend, claims that Horacio Martínez Prieto travelled to Bujaraloz in order to convince Durruti to leave the front and join the government, something which, obviously, made the hero 'furious' (p. 474). For different versions of the resignation of Martínez Prieto see Juan García Oliver, *El eco de los pasos*, pp. 323 and 329, and César M. Lorenzo, *Los anarquistas españoles y el poder*, p. 206. Mariano R. Vázquez's circular as new secretary was signed in Valencia which was the seat of the National Committee (AHNS, carpeta 39 of Bilbao).

11 One month after the replacement of Callejas in *Solidaridad Obrera* and with the same aim of supporting the policy of collaboration, Felipe Aliaz, the director of the CNT journal *Tierra y Libertad* suffered the same fate and was replaced by J. Maguid. Alaiz went to Lleida where, along with José Peirats, he published, in *Acracia*, some of the most critical texts dealing with the policy of participation in the political institutions. On 29 December 1936, *Ideas*, the journal of the 'Anarchist Movement of the Region of Baix Llobregat', published articles by Callejas, Balius and other leaders of the FAI such as Severino Campos and José Xena. *Nosotros*, the journal of the FAI in the 'East', joined in with these criticisms of the 'counter-revolutionary' work of the government in which the anarchists were participating. This affair caused a certain degree of confrontation with *Fragua Social*, the journal of the CNT in the 'East', which had

become the 'mouth-piece' of the National Committee during the difficult times which the CNT was experiencing, as usual, in Madrid, according to the 'Pleno Nacional de Regionales celebrado en Valencia el 12 de diciembre de 1936' (AHNS, carpeta 39 of Bilbao). For all of these conflicts between journalists see Susanna Tavera, *Solidaridad Obrera*, pp. 90–102, and in collaboration with Enric Ucelay da Cal, 'Grupos de afinidad, disciplina bélica y periodismo libertario, 1936–1938', pp. 170–90.

12 *El anarcosindicalismo en la Revolución Española*, p. 49.

13 *Acta del Pleno de Columnas Confederales y Anarquistas celebrado en Valencia el día 5 de febrero de 1937*, 63 pages published by 'Los Amigos de Durruti', CNT-FAI. The 'Hierro' column had left Valencia and had established itself in Puebla de Valverde, 22 kilometres from Teruel. In *Línea de Fuego*, which was published in this area, there are numerous examples of these anti-military sentiments which were not, however, shared by all of the members, as can be seen from the expulsions and internal confrontations (there exists an almost complete collection up until 13 December in the IISG of Amsterdam). There is useful information on this column and the other three which established themselves on the Teruel front, which was not under the command of the council of Defence of the Generalitat, in the Servicio Histórico Militar (SHM), Madrid, Sección Ministerio de Defensa, legajo 482, carpeta 8.

14 The order setting out the final organisation, which involved the integration of all these columns into five divisions and two autonomous brigades, was signed on 15 April 1937 by commandant Guarner, acting delegate of the Council of Defence of the Generalitat on the Aragon front (SHM, armario 19, legajo 3, carpeta 6).

15 According to the Regional Committee of the CNT, a 'considerable' number of affiliates, 'under the pretext of not accepting militarisation', had taken up residence in Barcelona and the towns of Catalonia, and even accepted important posts in that region. The same communiqué asked the unions in Catalonia not to endorse them as activists 'let alone give them jobs' (*Solidaridad Obrera*, 2 March 1937). For the testimonies of Saturnino Carod, Ricardo Sanz and Macario Royo on the tensions which militarisation created amongst the CNT activists and their abandonment of the front with their weapons, see Ronald Fraser, *Recuérdalo tú y recuérdalo a otros*, Vol. I, p. 179 and Vol. II, pp. 45–51,

16 Those wishing to evaluate the legislative activities of these anarchist ministers might consult the testimonies (partial and made in the heat of the moment) which these same ministers made on leaving their posts. Juan García Oliver, *Mi gestión al frente del Ministerio de Justicia* (talk given in the Apolo theatre in Valencia on 30 May 1937); Juan López, *Seis meses en el Ministerio de Comercio* (talk given on 27 May at the Gran theatre of Valencia); Federica Montseny, *Mi experiencia en el Ministerio de Sanidad y Asistencia Social* (talk given on 6 June 1937 in Valencia); and Joan Peiró, *De la fábrica de vidrio de Mataró al Ministerio de Industria* (talk given on 3 June 1937 at the Gran theatre in Valencia). For a recent evaluation of Montseny see Mary Nash 'Federica Montseny: dirigente anarquista, feminista y ministra', *Arenal*, 1, 2 (July–December 1994), pp. 259–71, from which the phrase cited in the text is taken.

17 The plenary meeting had been called by the Regional Committee of Aragon in order to comply with the agreement of the National Plenary, taken in mid-September, to constitute regional defence councils (minutes in AHNS, carpeta 39 of Bilbao). *Cultura y Acción*, the journal of the CNT in Aragon, which had reappeared a few days before in Alcañiz, interpreted the two positions which were discussed there as follows: 'Ortiz, Jover and Aldabaldetrecu undoubtedly believed that the constitution of the Council may obstruct the armed struggle against fascism. The towns, on the other hand, believed that the Council was necessary in order to win new ground and consolidate that which had already been won' (10 October 1936). The opinion of the leaders of the columns won the day. No war department was formed and the control of military

operations remained in the hands of the Generalitat, an issue which generated tensions and confrontation between the two institutions.

18 Communiqué to the 'people of Aragon', which appeared in the *Boletín del Consejo Regional de Defensa de Aragón* on 30 October 1936. The appointment of Joaquín Ascaso, a self-educated worker who was poorly qualified and had been in confrontation with some of his colleagues in the Local Federation of Zaragoza in the spring of 1936, was due to the protection and pressure which the leaders of the columns, especially Antonio Ortiz, exerted (the latter's testimony, November 1987). Another teacher, Evaristo Viñuales, was adviser on Information and Propaganda from December 1936. Concerning Ponzán and Viñuales, two teachers from Huesca who, having taken part in the Council and fought in the republican army, died tragically (the former burnt by the Gestapo in Toulouse in August 1944 and the latter shooting himself in Alicante in March so as not to be taken prisoner by the Francoists). See Pilar Ponzán, *Lucha y muerte por la libertad. Memorias de 9 años de guerra: 1936–1945* (Barcelona, Tot Editorial, 1996).

19 The minutes of the Executive Council of the Generalitat were consulted at the 'Servicio Histórico Militar' armario 56, legajo 556, carpeta 3. The intervention of the Generalitat in Aragonese territory also quickly provoked an energetic reaction in the journal *Cultura y Acción*: 'The behaviour of the governmental delegates of the Generalitat is similar to that of the old viceroys in America. Is it logical, anarchist or even autonomous, to interfere in the affairs of others when our own are in such chaos? If not, why does the Generalitat insist on creating Commissions, collecting statistics and running councils in Aragon?' (24 October 1936).

20 For the interview with Largo Caballero and the contents of the document see the *Boletín* of the council for 15 November 1936. Joan Peiró explained his own intervention (against Angel Galarza, Minister of the Interior), demanding the recognition of the Council, in the National Plenary session of Regional committees held in Valencia on 12 December 1936 (minutes in the AHNS, carpeta 39 of Bilbao).

21 I have examined the policy of the Council and the resistance it provoked, in detail, in *Anarquismo y revolución en la sociedad rural aragonesa*, pp. 151–263, although it is worth highlighting once more the confrontations between Adolfo Ballano, councillor for Justice and Public Order, and the Generalitat, which also was responsible for policing posts in Aragonese territory, with clashes over affairs related to his department (correspondence between the two governments in AHNS, carpeta 839 of Barcelona).

22 All of the quotations are taken from Walther L. Bernecker, who summarises this argument perfectly in *Colectividades y revolución social*, pp. 432–6. Bernecker has been used here because his analysis is one of the most rigorous on this subject, but he is himself one of the best-known and widely read examples of this anarchist literature which begins with Peirats and Abel Paz and continues with García Oliver and Camilo Berneri (see, for example, the latter's *Guerra de clases en España, 1936–1937*, Barcelona, Tusquets, 1977). A critique of the teleology 'implicit in the attribution of specific ends or missions to these subjects [classes], in accordance with a predetermined schema of historical development', has been carried out in relation to the populism of Lerroux by José Alvarez Junco in *El emperador del paralelo*, p. 462.

23 In *Anarquismo y revolución en la sociedad rural aragonesa*, I provided abundant evidence of what these changes meant in relation to collectivisation and local power-historical development or 'betrayal', according to one's point of view, of the revolution. The Generalitat of Catalonia was the first to issue a decree, on 9 October 1936, for the replacement of the revolutionary committees by municipal councils in which there was 'proportional representation' of the political forces present in the autonomous government. Largo Caballero's government did the same with a decree from the Ministry of the Interior on 4 January 1937 (*Gaceta de la República*, 7 January). The Council of Aragon followed this measure with a decree signed by Joaquín Ascaso on

19 January. The available information on the composition of 375 municipal councils – that is to say, almost all of the 400 municipalities which were more or less under the control of the administration of the Council –indicate that the CNT continued to be the principal political force in 175 municipalities and the UGT in 19, they shared power in 23 and, in the rest, power was shared between the republicans or other organisations which came under the denomination of the 'Popular Front', although in none did the Communist Party hold the majority. The political power of the CNT in Aragon began a noticeable decline when these councils were replaced, following the dissolution of the Council, by 'administrative commissions' designated by the government.

24 Unless otherwise stated, the references to the various regions which are used here are taken from Aurora Bosch, *Ugetistas y libertarios. Guerra civil y revolución en el País Valenciano, 1936–1939* (Valencia, Institución Alfonso el Magnánimo, 1983); Julián Casanova, *Anarquismo y revolución en la sociedad rural aragonesa*; Luis Garrido, *Colectividades agrarias en Andalucía: Jaén (1931–1939)* (Madrid, Siglo XXI, 1979); and Natividad Rodrigo, *Las colectividades agrarias en Castilla-La Mancha* (Toledo, Servicio de Publicaciones de la Junta de Comunidades de Castilla-La Mancha, 1985). For a summary of the principal theses of these four researchers see Julián Casanova (ed.) *El sueño igualitario: campesinado y colectivizaciones en la España republicana, 1936–1939*. For a detailed quantitative evaluation see Luis Garrido, Fernando Quilis, Natividad Rodrigo and José Miguel Santacreu, 'Las colectivizaciones en la guerra civil: análisis y estado de la cuestión historiográfica' in Julio Aróstegui (ed.) *Historia y memoria de la guerra civil* (Valladolid, Junta de Castilla y León, 1988), Vol. II, pp. 63–134.

25 Félix Carrasquer reduced the figure to 60–65 per cent, even though he raises the number employed on the collectives to 300,000, double the figure given by the Regional Federation of Collectives at that time: *Las colectividades de Aragón* (Barcelona, Laia, 1986). Edward Malefakis concludes, without revealing how he arrives at this conclusion, that 70 per cent of land was expropriated and that the collectives 'probably controlled an even greater portion of the land, given that there were private properties which incorporated themselves voluntarily' ('La revolución social' in 'La guerra de España, 1936–1939', *El País* (1986), 14, p. 217). There is important data available, in this regard, on Caspe and Alcañiz, the two most populated municipalities. In the former, the seat of the Council of Aragon, the collectivists were never more than 10 per cent of the population. In the latter, seat of the Regional Committee of the CNT during the war, 600 collectivists had control of a mere 250 hectares of irrigated land and 1,000 of dry land. See *La reforma agraria en España. Sus motivos, su esencia, su acción*, Instituto de Reforma Agraria, Valencia, p. 67 and Pascual Carrión, *La reforma agraria de la Segunda República y la situación actual de la agricultura española*, pp. 135–6.

26 The quotation is taken from the Spanish Communist Party's official version of these events, *Guerra y revolución en España, 1936–1939* (Moscow, Progreso, 1967–1977), pp. 63–6. The idyllic image of the beginning of collectivisation diffused in the accounts of the activists always contain the same basic elements: the 'politically conscious comrades' took possession of the land, expelled the land owners 'and their surrounding lackies', convoked an assembly of the peasants and all together they agreed, 'democratically', on the collective exploitation of the land and the basis on which this would operate. There is a good example (22 pages) in Rafael Sardá, *Las colectividades agrícolas* (Barcelona, Editorial Marxista, 1937), which describes the process in the communal co-operative of Raimat (Lleida). The pamphlet, which can be found in the AHNS (F. 2883), is fairly unique, being one of the very few testimonies which the POUM left on its position on the agrarian collectives.

27 As well as Aurora Bosch's work, cited above, see Vicente Abad, 'Ideología y práxis de un fenómeno revolucionario: el control sindical de la economía naranjera (1936–1937)' in J. Casanova (ed.) *El sueño igualitario*, pp. 77–93 and Fernando Quilis,

Revolución y guerra civil. Las colectividades obreras en la provincia de Alicante, 1936–1939 (Alicante, Instituto de Cultura 'Juan Gil-Albert', 1992), pp. 83–9.

28 'Informe del Comité Regional del Frente Popular de Aragón al Pleno del mismo, Caspe 2 de agosto de 1937' (SHM, armario 47, legajo 72, carpeta 1). See the minutes of the Regional Committee of the Communist Party of Aragon and the 'Radio Committees' in which the arguments around the Council and the collectivisations can be followed in detail (AHNS, carpetas 373 and 616 of Barcelona). For Azaña's opinion on the dissolution of the Council, a theme which we will return to in the following chapter, see *Memorias políticas y de guerra*, II, pp. 70, 147 and 187. See Marcén's petition in 'Reunión del Comité Nacional del PSOE, 17 de julio de 1937, Valencia' (186-page shorthand text, Fundación Pablo Iglesias, AH, 24–2).

29 See, especially, Aurora Bosch, *Ugetistas y libertarios*, pp. 349–68 and Julián Casanova, *Anarquismo y revolución en la sociedad rural aragonesa*, pp. 193–207, and *Caspe, 1936–1938. Conflictos políticos y transformaciones sociales durante la guerra civil*, pp. 55–6. This theme is dealt with in two other monographs: Encarna and Renato Simoni, *Cretas. La colectivización de un pueblo aragonés durante la guerra civil, 1936–1937*, and Susan Harding, *Remaking Ibieca*. The work of Ronald Fraser, *Recuérdalo tú y recuérdalo a otros*, also provides numerous insights, especially pp. 63–85 of Vol. II.

30 See Pilar Vivancos's testimony in Ronald Fraser, *Recuérdalo tú y recuérdalo a otros*, p. 402, Vol. I. Only one woman, Carmen Gómez, vice-secretary of the Anarchist Youth, ever occupied this leadership post in the anarchist movement during the twenty months of the war in Aragon. For the aims of 'Free Women', amongst which were those of 'emancipating women from the triple slavery which they have generally been and continue to be subjected to: the slavery of ignorance, the slavery of womanhood and the slavery of production', see Federación Nacional de 'Mujeres Libres', *Como organizar una Agrupación 'Mujeres Libres'*, p. 3 (AHNS, F-529). At its height, the organisation achieved a membership of some 20,000. The persistence, in spite of the revolution, of traditional relations between the sexes, was highlighted some years ago by Temma E. Kaplan, 'Spanish anarchism and women's liberation', *Journal of Contemporary History*, 6, 2 (1971), pp. 101–2. It is also one of the conclusions of the recent work of Mary Nash, *Defying Male Civilization: Women in the Spanish Civil War*, p. 139.

31 For a good example of these different perceptions see Susan Harding, *Remaking Ibieca*, pp. 74–5. Using the testimonies of the inhabitants of this town, Harding also confirms that the reorganisation of consumption, which some referred to as 'integral collectivisation' (involving the receipt of vouchers following the delivery of what had been produced in the collectives to the 'common heap'), caused even more problems and upset more peasants than had the collectivisation of the land (pp. 65–73).

32 This, as we have seen, was Orwell's impression on arriving in Barcelona. It was emphatically maintained by anarchists and authors of well-known studies have repeated it ever since. 'The conquest of power by the working class implied the end of the class struggle', wrote Josep Mª Bricall in *Política econòmica de la Generalitat (1936–1939)*, p. 342, I. 'Given that the bourgeoisie no longer existed as such, the element of class struggle disappeared', argued Walther L. Bernecker in *Colectividades y revolución social*, p. 376. The most recent studies, cited in Note 8 of the previous chapter, add further to these assertions either from the perspective of oral history or through their applying detailed analysis of the events in certain industries.

33 For the testimony of a member of the workers' control committee at the Rivière company, see Anna Monjo y Carme Vega, *Els treballadors i la guerra civil*, p. 46. The assembly in which the decision to expropriate was taken was held on 12 September. The company changed its name to 'Trefilería Barcelonesa. Industria Obrera Colectivizada'. This is not, of course, the version given in anarchist literature in which the spontaneity of the decisions is emphasised. For a good example see Agustín Souchy and Paul Folgare, *Colectivizaciones. La obra constructiva de la revolución española*

(Barcelona, Fontamara, 1977), pp. 18–19 (1st edn in *Tierra y Libertad*, 1937). The Regional Plenary Meeting of Anarchist Groups of Catalonia, held in Barcelona on 21 August 1936, which was the first documentary testimony on this issue, discussed and approved 'the expropriation and collectivisation of the establishments abandoned by their owners ... the workers' control of the banking business until the nationalisation of the Bank was carried out ... and the union control of all those industries which continued to be run on the basis of private industry' (AHNS, carpeta 39 of Barcelona). A month later, the Regional Plenary Meeting of the Syndicates of Catalonia agreed 'to move gradually and progressively towards the collectivisation of the land and of all industries (whilst) the bank will be run by Committees of workers' control' (*Solidaridad Obrera*, 26 September, 1936).

34 Josep Mª Bricall, *Política econòmica de la Generalitat*, pp. 33–5, I.
35 On 28 June 1936, in *Solidaridad Obrera*, the Regional Committee of the CNT published a list of 'foreign companies' which were to be 'respected'. See the *Decret de Collectivitzacions i Control Obrer*, Conselleria d'Economia, Generalitat de Catalunya, October 1936, and the analysis made of it by Josep Mª Bricall in *Política econòmica de la Generalitat*, pp. 194–214. Walther L. Bernecker emphasises the fact that, during his period in office (26 September–17 December 1936), Fábregas announced '25 decrees on economic regulation and 86 public orders' in *Colectividades y revolución social*, p. 315. In Valencia, the Economic Council also developed a number of 'Regulations for the expropriation, collectivisation and control of private industries', which were approved by the Popular Executive Committee on 1 December 1936, and which provided for the collectivisation of abandoned companies belonging to owners 'declared to be fascists', and of all those with more than fifty employees. In practice, according to Aurora Bosch, each union took over 'independently, the organisation of the expropriated companies regardless of the number of employees or the political affiliation of the owner', in *Ugetistas y libertarios*, p. 385.
36 The CNT's lack of an economic programme and the predominantly idealistic approach adopted by their activists on the few occasions on which they took part in the discussion of economic policy constitutes one of the central arguments of Helmut Rudiger in *El anarcosindicalismo en la Revolución Española*, pp. 37–41. This argument has also been supported by Xavier Paniagua, *La sociedad libertaria*, pp. 265–78 and Enric Ucelay da Cal in *La Catalunya populista*, pp. 160–1, who highlights the fact that the tendency to 'operate in idealist terms' was shared by republicans, Marxists and anarchists. The argument that the decree limited the power of the CNT in the unions and reconfirmed the technicians and office workers in their posts is dealt with well by Anna Monjo and Carme Vega, *Els treballadors i la guerra civil*, pp. 100–2.
37 Michael Seidman provides the best study of this discourse and the 'Taylorist' practices promoted by the unions of the CNT and the UGT, and the forms of resistance adopted by the workers which, far from being a new phenomenon, had a long history within the industrial societies of the West and in Catalonia. See 'Work and revolution: Workers' control in Barcelona in the Spanish Civil War', *Journal of Contemporary History*, 17, 3 (1982), and 'Hacia una historia de la resistencia proletaria al trabajo: París y Barcelona durante el Frente Popular y la revolución española, 1936–1938', *Historia Social*, 3 (1989), pp. 33–46. Enric Ucelay da Cal has also examined these forms of protest which the workers and political organisations attempted to portray as the 'orchestrations' of their rivals or as provocations of the 'hidden' fascists in *La Catalunya populista*, pp. 309–322. The participation of women in these conflicts has been highlighted by Mary Nash, *Defying Male Civilization: Women in the Spanish Civil War*, pp. 145–6. For the slogans of the Local Federation of Trade Unions of Barcelona see *Solidaridad Obrera*, 14 October 1936, which supported and justified them in its editorial the following day.
38 The quotation is taken from Michael Seidman, 'Hacia una historia de la resistencia proletaria al trabajo', p. 46. Anna Monjo and Carme Vega have given percentages for

the forms of participation in the collectivisation of the Rivière company: 9.5 per cent took part in the committees of control and administration; 23.2 per cent of the company took an 'active' participation in the collectivisation and it was the office workers that stood out amongst this group; 76.7 per cent had a 'passive participation' (*Els treballadors i la guerra civil*, pp. 109–118). Professional qualifications, seniority of more than five years and falling within the middle-age range were the characteristics shared by those participating in these changes.

39 For the CNT's perspective on the crisis of the Generalitat, see César M. Lorenzo, *Los anarquistas españoles y el poder*, pp. 211–14. See also the interpretation of *Solidaridad Obrera*, 17 December 1936. The political struggle between the PSUC and the POUM is dealt with well in Enric Ucelay da Cal, *La Catalunya populista*, pp. 254–64, and in Francesc Bonamusa, *Andreu Nin y el movimiento comunista en España (1930–1937)* (Barcelona, Anagrama, 1977), pp. 349–65.

40 For Comorera's accusations and the anarchist version of these incidents see José Peirats, *La CNT en la revolución española*, Vol. II, pp. 121–4, where, in the pages that follow, Peirats recounts some of the bloody disturbances which beginning in 'La Fatarella', in January 1937, led to the events of May of that year. There is a detailed description of the problem of supplies from the economic perspective, which does not, however, deal with the protests, in Josep Mª Bricall, *Política econòmica de la Generalitat*, pp. 135–55, I. For the POUM's version of this confrontation see Mary Low and Juan Brea, *Red Spanish Notebook*, pp. 211 and 230, who conclude that: 'There was little left to save in Barcelona after January 1937. Militarisation had finished with the militias. The Generalitat, as far as we were concerned, had been lost. There was, of course, the war, but it was the revolution in which we were interested.'

41 The official propaganda of the CNT, which never hesitated in engaging in all sorts of arguments and exchanges of accusations with the communists, remained faithful to the discourse of order and discipline which had been adopted along with policy of collaboration. It never tolerated the disturbances and bloody assassinations which some of its activists, those 'out of control', engaged in behind the lines. A good example of this policy, which would be reflected, above all, in the events of May, was *Solidaridad Obrera*'s condemnation, on 27 April, of the assassination of Roldán Cortada, a figure with whom, in previous times, they would have had no sympathy whatsoever: 'We must put an end to these violent acts against the real workers.' This perspective, which accounts for the tension which led to the events of May in terms of the struggle between various groups within the factories, is well defended by Anna Monjo, Carme Vega and Mercedes Vilanova in 'Socialización y hechos de mayo: una nueva aportación a partir del proceso de Mauricio Stevens (2/6/1937)', *Historia y Fuente Oral*, 3 (1990), pp. 93–103. See also the interesting work by David Martínez Fiol and Sussana Tavera, 'Corporativism and workers' revolution in Catalonia (1936–1937)', pp. 12–13.

42 The first communiqués appeared in *La Noche*, on 2 March 1937, *Solidaridad Obrera*, on 7 March and in *El Frente*, war bulletin of the Durruti column on 8 March. On 11 May of the same year, the first issue of its journal *El Amigo del Pueblo* appeared. Eleven issues are available from the IISG in Amsterdam, the last issue being that of 20 November 1937, the date of the first anniversary of the death of Durruti. From the list of subscribers, it is apparent that they had various groups of supporters both at the front and in the rearguard of Aragon, from where Jaime Balius had promoted collectivisation during the summer of 1936. One of the people who gave economic support was Miguel Chueca, a civil servant in the Department of Labour of the Council of Aragon. His critiques and proposals which are cited in the text are taken from 'Hacia una nueva revolución' (28 pages, undated, of which there is a copy in the Institut Municipal d'Història de Barcelona). That they did just 'what the enemies of the CNT wanted', when they abandoned the front, is taken from Helmut Rudiger, *El anarcosindicalismo en la Revolución Española*, p. 28. There is a defence of this group in

Frank Mintz and Miguel Peña, *Los Amigos de Durruti, los trotsquistas y los sucesos de mayo*, (Madrid, Campo Abierto Ediciones, 1978). Balius's personal conflict with Vázquez and Toryho is dealt with in Susanna Tavera and Enric Ucelay da Cal, 'Grupos de afinidad, disciplina bélica y periodismo libertario, 1936–1938', pp. 177–84. 'All power to the unions' is what they demanded, according to a letter from Jaime Balius to Ronald Fraser, *Recuérdalo tú y recuérdalo a otros*, Vol II, p. 112. At that point in time, the criticism of 'colaborationism' was shared by numerous sectors of the Anarchist Youth of Catalonia, led by Ramón Liarte and José Peirats, with close links to the groups of veteran militiamen on the Huesca front.

8 Decline and fall

1 The version of Azaña in 'Cintas telegráficas entre Presidente de la República en Barcelona y Gobierno central en Valencia, sobre situación interior de aquella capital', 4–6 May 1937 (SHM, armario 53, legajo 461, carpeta 1). The anarchist position in José Peirats, *La CNT en la revolución española*, pp. 137–214; Agustín Souchy, *La verdad sobre los sucesos en la retaguardia leal. Los acontecimientos de Cataluña* (Buenos Aires, Ediciones FACA, 1937); see also the provocative reconstruction of Juan García Oliver in *El eco de los pasos*, pp. 419–34, who attacks 'the so-called Communists of the PSUC', Aiguader and the former member of the CNT Rodríguez Salas, 'El Manco', 'the ideal couple to trigger the events of May'; 'The Friends of Durruti', who could only count on Balius, Ruiz and Carreño, 'none of whom belonged to the FAI'; and J. Merino, Patricio Navarro and Maeztu, 'a dangerous trio' of anarchists who acted 'always on their own'. There is also of course the account of George Orwell in *Homage to Catalonia*; and the monograph by Manuel Cruells, *Mayo sangriento. Barcelona, 1937* (Barcelona, Ed. Juventud, 1977). A Francoist version can be found in Jose Mª Martínez Bande, 'Los sucesos de mayo de 1937 en Barcelona', *Guión* (Madrid), 299 (April 1963), pp. 3–14.

2 Information on desertions and other disturbances from 'Informe que emite la Asesoría Jurídica del frente de Aragón en virtud de la orden telegráfica del general jefe del Ejército del Este' (SHM, armario 62, legajo 788, carpeta 1), a document signed in Sariñena (Huesca), 15 May, supported with 'información adicional' on the 17th of the same month, which contains varying errors in the identification of these forces – for example, it states that the division of the POUM was the 28th instead of the 29th. This is surprising given that it was drawn up by army advisers, and that it tried to show, after the event, that the anarchists and the soldiers of the POUM caused the disturbances. Different versions in *Nuevo Aragón*, 15 May 1937, and *Cultura y Acción*, 7 August 1937. The request for a cease-fire and the speech of García Oliver in *El eco de los pasos*, pp. 425–7. The broadcast request for help from 'comrades at the front' by those who had risen up, in the already cited 'Cintas telegráficas'.

3 'Informe sobre el asesinato de Gregorio Herrero. Datos que se han podido obtener recientemente de los cinco asesinatos ejecutados la noche del 4 al 5 de mayo último en el pueblo de Oliete' (unsigned document, in AHNS, carpeta 397 from Barcelona); and 'Atestado correspondiente a la actuación sobre los sucesos acaecidos en la villa de El Grado el día 7 de mayo' (SHM, armario 47, legajo 71, carpeta 1). The rest of the information is taken from the 'Informe' of the Asesoría Jurídica of the Aragon front. The Council sent a delegation to verify the complaints and rejected the participation of its members. According to this version, included in the 'Informe justificativo de la reciente visita a la Presidencia y de las notas entregadas a la Secretaría de la misma', the dead from Barbastro 'were Rightists who had been judged and condemned by the Popular Tribunal' (SHM, armario 47, legajo 72, carpeta 1).

4 Both libertarians as well as the communists wasted much ink and words in games of that kind whenever there was a confrontation of such a nature, of seeking out the

agent provocateur, of discovering who started it first: Aiguader and Rodríguez Salas, the POUM, the 'so-called Communists of the PSUC', 'The Friends of Durruti', all depended on the point of those looking at it. If on the republican side, no one wanted to take responsibility for the deaths, in the Francoist zone they seemed to want to give out medals. The German ambassador Faupel told his superiors that Franco had told him that 'thirteen' of his agents began the disturbances in Barcelona (David T. Cattell, *Communism and the Spanish Civil War* (Berkeley and Los Angeles, University of California Press, 1955), pp. 146–7).

5 All of the information concerning the proceedings in the crisis and the letter from the CNT to Largo Caballero in AHNS, carpeta 39 from Bilbao. An analysis of the crisis from the perspective of the confrontation between parties and unions in Santos Juliá, 'Partido contra sindicato: una interpretación de la crisis de mayo de 1937', in *Socialismo y guerra civil*, pp. 342–6. The triumph of the parties over the unions following the events of May was dealt with earlier by Raymond Carr in *The Spanish Tragedy. The Civil War in Perspective*, p. 199.

6 'Acuerdos del Pleno Nacional de Regionales, celebrado los días 23 y sucesivos de mayo de 1937', Valencia, 27 May (AHNS, carpeta 39 from Bilbao). In this plenary meeting it was decided 'unanimously to remove from the organisation the advisors to the group the "Friends of Durruti" and that it be prevented, by all means, from forming a movement that would split as a result of it' (the proceedings of the Plenary in AHNS, carpeta 2437 from Madrid). A Catalan Regional Plenary meeting had already decided on 22 May together with a communiqué from the Regional Committee of the CNT, from that of the FAI and from the Barcelona Union Federation demanding from both organisations 'confederal and anarchist ... the expulsion of all of those who belong to "The Friends of Durruti" who do not publicly declare that they are opposed to the position held by the said organisation' (*Solidaridad Obrera*, 28 May).

7 'Acta del Pleno Nacional de Regionales, celebrado los días 2 y sucesivos de junio de 1937'; and 'Documentos remitidos al jefe del Gobierno y al Presidente de la República: fijando la posición de la organización con anterioridad al desastre de Bilbao' (AHNS, carpeta 39 from Bilbao).

8 Domingo Ascaso constitutes a good example. No explanation was given regarding his death. *Solidaridad Obrera* apologised the day after his funeral for not having announced its taking place because of an error in the editorial department ('the note was mislaid'), and that it 'greatly regrets it because it concerned a former activist loved by all' (12 May 1937).

9 The resolutions of the Plenary meeting and the differing reactions of international anarchism towards the positions of the CNT were sent by Mariano R. Vázquez to all the regional organisations on 26 June of that year. They were preceded by a letter from which the word 'nonsense' is taken and which contains, as can also be confirmed, a reaffirmation of the arguments of the National Committee. The organisation with the greatest membership, 3,000, was the General Confederation of Revolutionary Union Labour (CGTSR) from France. Helmut Rudiger presented to this plenary meeting the already cited 'Materiales para la discusión de la situación española'. All of these documents are preserved in AHNS, carpeta 39 from Bilbao. Concerning the influence of Pierre Besnard on Spanish anarcho-syndicalism during the Second Republic and particularly his book *Los sindicatos obreros y la revolución social*, published in Spanish in 1931 with a prologue by Joan Peiró, see Xavier Paniagua, *La sociedad libertaria*, pp. 117–40.

10 This information comes from the documents sent by Mariano R. Vázquez on 26 June. *Solidaridad Obrera* summarised the meeting that took place on 18 June in the 'Velódromo de Invierno', in which David Antona and Benito Pabón also spoke, although it omitted the incidents (23 June).

11 Helmut Rudiger, *El anarcosindicalismo en la Revolución Española*, pp. 25 and 45.

12 *Solidaridad Obrera*, 30 June. Through this newspaper, it is possible to follow the different stages of the crisis that emerged from the 26th. The crisis had seemed already resolved with the incorporation of the three anarchists (Roberto Alfonso Vidal, Juan García Oliver and Germinal Esgleas), yet ended with their outcome that was made public on the 29th. According to the official version of the CNT in Catalonia, its representatives refused, in spite of Mariano R. Vázquez 'pressuring them … not to continue with their refusal' that the historian Pedro Bosch Gimpera be included in the new government, which was what Companys finally did do (César M. Lorenzo, *Los anarquistas españoles y el poder*, pp. 224–5; Proceedings of the Plenary meeting of 26 June in SHM, armario 46, legajo 66, carpeta 3). The day following the Plenary meeting, Galo Díez and Mariano R. Vázquez insisted in a meeting in the Apolo theatre in Valencia on the 'constitution of a Government with representation that is proportionate of all the anti-fascist forces' (*Solidaridad Obrera*, 29 June).

13 'Contestación al proyecto de reforma del Consejo de Aragón', signed by Francisco Muñoz, secretario regional de la CNT, in Alcañiz, 5 June 1937 (SHM, armario 46, legajo 66, carpeta 5). The communist proposal is in 'Acta de las reuniones celebradas por el Comité Regional de Aragón de la CNT, Comité Regional de Aragón del Frente Popular y el presidente del Consejo de Aragón' (SHM, armario 46, legajo 68, carpeta 3). The communiqué of the organisations of the Popular Front of Huesca is in AHNS, carpeta 397 of Barcelona.

14 'Informe sobre la represión llevada a cabo contra el Partido Obrero de Unificación Marxista (POUM)', July 1937, which contains various documents prepared by the CNT and various reports from the lawyers (SHM, armario 47, legajo 71, carpeta 10). Already on 16 February 1937, in an 'Informe de José del Barrio, capitán de la División Carlos Marx, sobre la situación del frente', it stated that 'in Alcubierre we have relieved the forces of the POUM, who have left the front in appalling conditions … in all the time that they have been there, they have not done any work of fortification and they have abandoned seven kilometres of the front which they should have garrisoned' (SHM, armario 56, legajo 556, carpeta 6 bis). The repression against the POUM in Francesc Bonamusa, *Andreu Nin y el movimiento comunista en España (1930–1937)*, pp. 375–94.

15 'Acta del Pleno Nacional de Regionales, celebrado en Valencia el día 7 de agosto de 1937' (SHM, armario 48, legajo 68, carpeta 3). Azaña's notes in *Memorias políticas y de guerra*, II, pp. 147 and 187.

16 *Boletín Oficial de Aragón*, which replaced the *Boletín* of the Council, 22 August 1937.

17 The CNT was unable to achieve the creation of a National Peasant Federation until July 1937, which had been an objective, though an unsuccessful one during the Republic. This timing was at a most unfortunate moment to tackle the problems of the countryside and when the collectives had already entered their period of decline. It never worked although it did bring together the complaints that the delegation from Aragón made over the 'destruction of the work undertaken by the collectives and the detention of their members' ('Pleno Nacional de Federaciones Regionales de Campesinos, celebrado en Valencia los días 20 al 23 de octubre de 1937', SHM, armario 47, legajo 71, carpeta 4). The groups of the Libertarian Youth of Catalonia who were at the Aragonese front re-doubled, following the events of May, their criticism of intervention in politics, to which they attributed the 'failure' of anarchism, in trying to 'leading the destiny of the country from the arm chairs of the State'. Their positions can be found in *Frente y Retaguardia*, where 'begging from the State' appears (17 July) and that concerning the 'armchairs' (the 31st of the same month).

18 The letter calling for the meeting of the regional secretaries in SHM, armario 46, legajo 67, carpeta 3. Information concerning the meeting in the same archive, armario 47, legajo 71, carpeta 4. The proposal from García Oliver constitutes a clear example of memoirs written years later – see his defence of anarchist 'purity' in *El eco de los pasos* – which does not always reflect the same ideas that were proposed at that

time. The breaking of the channels of communication between the leadership and union base accelerated following the summer of 1937. The libertarian movement adopted until the end of the war ways of working that were very similar to those of parties. It is rather difficult though to think that it could have been any other way because events imposed their own harsh reality: the movement supplanted the workers, those it said it was representing, then the leadership supplanted the movement and, finally, it was the main leadership – that had not even been elected – who took all the decisions. The abundant documentation preserved in the Servicio Histórico Militar confirms this process. It is not worth following here the details of those changes in the organisation taken by the CNT and the FAI, amongst other reasons because they turn out to be irrelevant: they do not explain the decline of the movement but rather they are a consequence of it. They can, though, be followed in César M. Lorenzo, *Los anarquistas españoles y el poder*, pp. 227–44.

19 Enric Ucelay da Cal has drawn attention to this loss of enthusiasm caused by the presence of ever more difficult living conditions, *La Catalunya populista*, pp. 347ff. It is here that the 'secondary role' of the Generalitat appears. It is the same secondary role that, according to García Oliver, the Regional Committee of Catalonia attempted to reduce when, following Negrín, 'the national committee of the CNT, with the empty headedness of Marianet, the apathetic and indecisive Horacio Prieto, and with their committees filled with Asturians, showed up in Barcelona' (*El eco de los pasos*, p. 500). This process of worker discontent, from the increase of working discipline to the reduction of union power that took place during the last year of the war in Barcelona, is well described by Anna Monjo and Carme Vega, *Els treballadors i la guerra civil*, pp. 167–77. There are more examples documented in Michael Seidman, 'Work and revolution: Workers' control in Barcelona in the Spanish Civil War, 1936–1938', although this author considers that the CNT, 'often with the participation of the UGT', and in spite of having lost political power following the events of May, retained 'economic control' in many industries until the end of the war. The expression on the hope for the workers' outcome comes from the editorial that *Solidaridad Obrera* devoted to the announcement of the 'programme of unity of action' between the CNT and the UGT on 13 May 1938. A defence of this alliance as the only road for anti-fascist victory is also found in Helmut Rudiger, *El anarcosindicalismo en la Revolución Española*, pp. 21–2.

20 Summary of the National Plenary Meeting of the Regional Committees of the CNT held in Valencia from 2 to 10 August 1938 (AHNS, carpeta 2437 from Madrid). This change in discourse abandoning revolutionary rhetoric to ask for things such as 'independence and welfare' can be easily followed in the *Boletín del Comité Nacional de la CNT*, which was published in Valencia in the autumn of 1937 and in Barcelona from the beginning of 1938.

21 Susanna Tavera, *Solidaridad Obrera. El fer-se i desfer-se d' un diari anarco-sindicalista (1915–1939)*, pp. 108–11. According to García Oliver, Toryho was not dismissed but rather the recently created executive committee of the libertarian movement 'finally accepted his resignation. Toryho was forever presenting his resignation. He liked to do so because when it was not accepted his vanity was flattered' (*El eco de los pasos*, 502). Whilst all this was taking place in *Solidaridad Obrera*, the newspaper *CNT* from Madrid was bogged down in its eternal crisis and its no less eternal deficit, which nobody knew how to resolve: at the beginning of 1938 it had risen to 150,000 pesetas, a figure that the National Committee proposed be met jointly by all the regional organisations (letter from 28 January 1938 to the regional committees, SHM, armario 46, legajo 67, carpeta 3).

Epilogue: the uprooting

1 In the words of Mercedes Vilanova, 'the reaction of the illiterate population to the repression was varied, subtle and skilled. The illiterate had the capacity to remain silent, to go around un-noticed, to become invisible. To a certain extent, their distance from power and from written culture freed them from the repression suffered by literate activists' ('Anarchism, political participation, and illiteracy in Barcelona between 1934 and 1936', pp. 105–6). Vilanova has examined this question in great detail in *Les majories invisibles. Explotació fabril, revolució i repressió. 26 entrevistes.* The consequences of defeat in a collectivised factory can be seen in Anna Mojo and Carme Vega, *Els treballadors i la guerra civil*, pp. 178–92.

2 The crisis of traditional agriculture in Carlos Barciela, 'Crecimiento y cambio en la agricultura española desde la guerra civil', in Jordi Nadal, Albert Carreras and Carles Sudrià (eds) *La economía española en el siglo XX. Una perspectiva histórica* (Barcelona, Ariel, 1987), pp. 270–5. The comments concerning missed opportunities and the factors that allowed for their recovery come from the work of José Luis García Delgado, included in the same volume, 'La industrialización y el desarrollo económico de España durante el franquismo', pp. 177–8.

3 The introduction to collective bargaining in Europe between 1900 and 1940 and its 'cushioning' function and its 'institutionalisation' of conflicts is well summarised by Marcel van der Linden and Wayne Thorpe in 'Auge y decadencia del sindicalismo revolucionario', p. 19. They also account for the decline of revolutionary trade unionism through the changes in capitalist society itself and in the state (pp. 26–7). For a wide-ranging interpretation of these changes in Spanish society and of the process that led to the democratic transition, with particular emphasis on the transformation of the tate, see José Casanova, 'Modernización y democratización: reflexiones sobre la transición española a la democracia', in Teresa Carnero (ed.) *Modernización, desarrollo político y cambio social* (Madrid, Alianza, 1992), pp. 235–76. The emergence of this new working class and a new union culture in Sebastian Balfour, *Dictatorship, Workers and the City. Labour in Greater Barcelona since 1939* (Oxford, Clarendon Press, 1989).

4 The growth of the state and the increasing efficiency of the political apparatus is one of the arguments used by José Alvarez Junco to explain the changes in the repertoire of collective action in the final years of Francoism: 'Movimientos sociales en España: del modelo tradicional a la modernidad postfranquista' in Enrique Laraña and Joseph Gusfield (eds), *Los nuevos movimientos sociales. De la ideología a la identidad* (Madrid, CIS, 1994), pp. 421–2. The theories of Charles Tilly concerning the linkage between the evolution of social mobilisation and the repressive apparatus of the state and those of Sidney Tarrow on the dependence of the social movements with respect to political opportunities, which are backed up by Alvarez Junco, are summarised in Manuel Pérez Ledesma, 'Cuando lleguen los días de la cólera' (*Movimientos sociales, teoría e historia)*', pp. 141–87. The theories of Tilly applied to the case of Spain in Rafael Cruz, 'Crisis del Estado y acción colectiva en el período de entreguerras, 1917–1939', *Historia Social*, 15 (1993), pp. 122 and 131–2.

5 The best synthesis of these two ways of understanding freedom, from which were derived very different doctrinal and tactical conclusions, can be found in José Alvarez Junco, 'Los dos anarquismos', *Cuadernos de Ruedo Ibérico*, 55–7 (1977), pp. 139–56. The bibliography on the new social movements and the theoretical models that explain them is vast. Particularly useful, as well as the already cited book compiled by Laraña and Gusfield, are Claus Offe, *Partidos políticos y nuevos movimientos sociales* (Madrid, Sistema, 1988); Russell J. Dalton and Manfred Kuechler (eds) *Los nuevos movimientos sociales* (Valencia, Edicions Alfons el Magnànim, 1992); Rafael Núñez Florencio, *Sociedad y política en el siglo XX. Viejos y nuevos movimientos sociales* (Madrid, Síntesis, 1993); Paul D'Anieri, Claire Ernst and Elizabeth Kier, 'New social movements in historical perspective', *Comparative Politics*, 22, 4 (1990), pp. 445–58; and the monograph edition

of *Social Research*, 52, 4 (1985), under the title of 'Social Movements', co-ordinated by Jean L. Cohen, with articles by Cohen herself, Charles Tilly, Alaine Touraine, Alberto Melucci, Claus Offe and Klaus Eder.

Appendix

Anarchism in Spanish contemporary history[1]

There are three previous well-written, stimulating works that the reader will find useful and readable. *El proletariado militante*, by Anselmo Lorenzo, which appeared in two parts, in 1901 and 1916 (complete edition in 1974), is an autobiographical source and is indispensable for the study of the First International in Spain and the libertarian movement between 1868 and 1883. *Historia de las agitaciones campesinas andaluzas* (1928, new edition in 1967), by Juan Díaz del Moral, which was the first interpretation to take into account the millenarian characteristics of the anarchist movement and linked it to a national idiosyncrasy which was derived from the persistence of a mode of communal life. Finally, *The Spanish Labrynth*, by Gerald Brenan (1943), which revived these ideas, though simplifying the theses of Díaz del Moral, and explained anarchism as an ethical-religious reaction against the corruption of the church and its collusion with the rich and the powerful.

Except in the brief but provocative approach of Eric Hobsbawm (1959), the linking of anarchism with millenarianism and religious legends was shelved for some time as it was considered to be lacking in 'scientific' objectivity. New detailed scholarly studies began to appear, almost always produced in universities. They tried to explain anarchism as an understandable response to determined historical periods and social groupings. They were the beginnings of a 'social' history, with the workers' movement at its centre, which rescued from oblivion the accounts of committed and learned workers' activists of the 1920s and 1930s. In spite of the subsequent criticisms made (José Álvarez Junco and Manuel Pérez Ledesma, 1982), they were the starting point for dealing with problems that had been ignored or eradicated by Francoist historiography. Following the pioneering and, at the time, isolated study of Father Casimir Martí (1959), the subsequent silence was broken by Catalan historians such as Albert Balcells (1965, 1971) and Josep Termes (1972), influenced by the teaching of Jaume Vicens Vives, and they opened up new approaches to research. Foreign historians of Spain, such as Clara Lida (1972, 1973) and Temma Kaplan (1977), and Spanish authors, such as Manuel Tuñón de Lara (1972), who had studied in foreign universities, continued this work. Although the study by Tuñón, the teacher of many in the subject, was a much wider general history of the workers' movement, the common thread amongst all of these authors was the quest for the origins of anarchism. This took the form of an attempt to answer the perennial question of the reasons why Bakuninism attained such strength amongst Andalucian peasants and the manufacturing proletariat and urban artisans of Catalonia. The study by Termes continues to be an essential account of the penetration of the First International into Spain and its organisation in the form of the Spanish Regional Federation (FRE), and the split between Marxists and Bakuninists, which would have far-reaching consequences.

From the AIT to the Civil War, there were almost seventy years in which it seemed that, compared to what happened to other countries in Western Europe, the weight and persistence of the libertarian phenomenon in the workers' movement was a Spanish peculiarity. And the investigation of such a peculiarity required the dusting off of 'official' sources, from the press to the proceedings of meetings, as well as hundreds of leaflets left by libertarians. Thus, there emerged documentary accounts, which were both positivist and descriptive and narrated the 'institutional' history of organised anarchism. They followed in the footsteps, albeit with greater material resources, of the analyses of the anarchist writers in exile (José Peirats, 1971; Diego Abad de Santillán, 1962–71; César M. Lorenzo, 1972). The sources dictated the nature of this kind of history: periods of expansion were identified when the sources were abundant and of depression when they were lacking. Since it was taken for granted that Spanish anarchism was a stable and persistent phenomenon in contemporary Spain, the moments when the movement appeared weaker were attributed to repression. Anarchism appeared, disappeared, re-emerged. Thus, with all manner of detail, the transition from anarchism to anarcho-syndicalism, symbolised by the birth and consolidation of the CNT (Xavier Cuadrat, 1976; Antonio Bar, 1981), has been amply explained. Yet we have little by way of analysis of the periods of clandestinity (Clara Lida, 1995), the complicated question of terrorism in the 1890s (Rafael Núñez Florencio, 1983) or the experience under the dictatorship of Primo de Rivera (Antonio Elorza, 1972–4). Studies on the Civil War, seen as the golden age of Spanish anarchism, have proliferated, whilst the work of John Brademas – who concluded his period of research in Oxford at the beginning of the 1950s and whose book was not published, and then only in Spanish, until 1974 – continues to be almost the only point of reference for all of those interested in the institutional role of the CNT in trade unionism during the Second Republic.

There were, even so, other contributions that provided new methodological approaches, which opened up paths to previously unknown areas and allowed for different readings. First, there was the analysis of anarchism as political ideology. This was first looked at by Antonio Elorza (1973, 1972–4), and then exhaustively explored by José Álvarez Junco (1976), giving us the best overall approach to the subject. This approach has been completed by Xavier Paniagua (1982) with an analysis of the varying doctrinal positions that supposedly guided the revolutionary practice of the anarchists of the 1930s. The second group directed its attention towards social conflicts, and the movements and classes that were their central protagonists. Given that they occurred in very concrete and extraordinary periods in the history of Spain, these conflicts allowed for the extraction of wide-ranging conclusions and were not limited only to anarchism or organised labour. There is much of this to be found in the work of Joaquín Romero Maura (1974), Enric Ucelay da Cal (1982), Santos Juliá (1984) and, more recently, in the work of Joan Culla (1986) and José Álvarez Junco (1990); or in two studies (Carlos Forcadell, 1978; Gerald Meaker, 1978) that have produced the best examinations of the years of organisation, maturity and splits in the labour movement that coincided with the First World War and the latter part of the political system of the Restoration. The third approach, inspired by new developments in regional and social history, produced important results when, instead of merely confirming the already established general theses, it undertook the task of analysing the attitudes and behaviour of anarchists and trade unionists in the areas of greatest influence. Finally, numerous works arrived that centred their focus on partial aspects of the libertarian movement, from its cultural traditions through to education. They also looked at the relations between anarchism and feminism and, through asking new questions of the sources, provided a wide repertoire of hypotheses, questions and empirical proofs that had been omitted from institutional histories. To these local histories and those focused on specific questions, which have been enriched by oral and social history, we owe some of the most rigorous monographs offered by the historiography of anarchism in Spain.[2]

Such a remarkable production of literature on anarchism, enormous in comparison with other subjects, has imposed subtle differences and clarifications in respect of interpretations previously held to be axiomatic. Anarchism was not, then, an 'exceptional' and 'extraordinary' phenomenon in the history of Spain, if by 'normal' and 'ordinary' is understood what took place in the other countries of Western Europe, until well into the twentieth century, when there occurred the transition from anarchism to anarcho-syndicalism, from forms of organisation based on ideological affinity to the more formal and disciplined union organisation based on the particular trade or branch of production in which the membership worked. It was only with the constitution and consolidation of the CNT as a mass movement in the years 1917–21 and 1931–7 that there began the so-called 'atypical' nature of Spain, because during those periods, except in Argentina and Sweden, revolutionary trade unionism, apolitical and based on direct action, had disappeared from the rest of the world (Marcel van der Linden and Wayne Thorpe, 1992; José Álvarez Junco, 1986b). Until this conversion into anarcho-syndicalism, Spain had experienced trends in labour associationism that were very similar to France and Italy, the adoption of Bakuninist positions, the decline of the First International, the appearance of terrorism in the 1890s and the expansion of the doctrine of revolutionary syndicalism during the first fifteen years of the twentieth century. Not even the CNT was a persistent and stable phenomenon: it maintained an important presence only in very specific periods and except in Catalonia and some cities such as Seville or Zaragoza it shared this presence with the UGT, a form of unionism which also cultivated, until the Second Republic, the anti-political and anti-statist tradition inherited from the First International (Santos Juliá, 1990).

In the light of all this, it is appropriate to pose once more the familiar question concerning the popular basis of anarchism in Spain. The various arguments that have been put forward, and which José Álvarez Junco (1976) earlier classified into social-economic, religious and political-institutional interpretations, are not so much explanations for these popular roots as general observations concerning the culture of social protest in Spain. That was a culture shaped by the weak and ineffective character of the state, and was the heir to beliefs, behaviour and religious and millenarian impulses that must be recognised but which were shared to a great extent by anarchists, republicans and those in the UGT until the Second Republic, which were propagated in areas as different as· industrial Barcelona or rural Andalucia. It was a culture uprooted by the sword and the cross of the victors in the Civil War.

The broad lines of the interpretation of anarchism as political ideology and as a social movement of protest are already marked out. Yet it is likely that, in terms of local history and of studies giving particular emphasis to concrete data, the subject will never be exhausted. It would be of great interest, if it is a question of widening and enriching the study of anarchism, to continue by using the techniques of cultural history and of the research into the modes of expression of the popular classes that has been begun by French Hispanists in recent years (Paul Aubet et al., 1986; Jean-Louis Guereña, 1991). We should also stress the importance of studying the internal functioning of anarcho-syndicalism in the workplace and in its methods of mobilisation outside the unions, just as Anna Monjo has done (1992, and in her unpublished doctoral thesis, 1993). It would also be useful to opt for a biographical approach and for the use of the autobiographies written by activists themselves (Adrian Shubert, 1990). It is time definitively to abandon the excessive piety that continues to be applied to leaders such as Durruti. Rather we should be looking at unravelling the characteristics of the leaders, how they reached positions of power and how this power was exercised. We have some good introductory studies to the thought and opinions of some leaders (Antonio Elorza, 1974, and Diego Abad de Santillán, 1976, on Ángel Pestaña; Pere Gabriel, 1975, and Federica Montseny, 1979, on Joan Peiró; Isidre Molas on Salvador Seguí, 1975). Yet we know virtually nothing about their lives, their work, their families, their interests or their education. There are some autobiographies of leading activists (Federico Urales, 1930; Anselmo Lorenzo, 1974; Angel Pestaña, 1974; Adolfo Bueso, 1976–8; Juan García Oliver, 1978; Antonio Rosado, 1979; and Federica Montseny, 1987). These though are only used as political testimony and not as a source of social history that illuminate their experiences as workers and flesh and blood individuals. Cultural history, research on the internal union and extra-union worlds, biography and the use of autobiographical sources are all, in my opinion, areas that still need to be explored to expand our knowledge of the historical development of anarchism, of the various anarchisms, in contemporary Spain.

Works cited in the appendix

Abad de Santillan, Diego (1962–1971), *Contribución a la Historia del Movimiento Obrero Español*, Cajica, Puebla (México).

——(1976), *El anarquismo y la revolución en España. Escritos 1930/38* (selección y estudio preliminar de Antonio Elorza), Ayuso, Madrid.

Álvarez Junco, José (1976), *La ideología política del anarquismo español (1868–1910)*, Siglo XXI, Madrid (new edn 1991).

——(1986a), 'La subcultura anarquista en España: racionalismo y populismo', in *Culturas populares. Diferencias, divergencias, conflictos*, Casa de Velázquez, Universidad Complutense, Madrid, pp. 197–208.

——(1986b), 'El anarquismo en la España contemporánea', *Anales de Historia Contemporánea*, Murcia, 5, pp. 189–200.

——(1990), *El emperador del Paralelo. Lerroux y la demagogia populista*, Alianza, Madrid.

—— and Pérez Ledesma, Manuel (1982), 'Historia del movimiento obrero ¿Una segunda ruptura?', *Revista de Occidente*, 12, pp. 19–41.

Aubert, Paul, Brey, Gérard, Guereña, Jean-Louis, Maurice, Jacques and Salaün, Serge (1986), *Anarquismo y poesía en Cádiz bajo la Restauración*, Ediciones de la Posada, Córdoba.

Balcells, Albert (1965), *El sindicalismo en Barcelona (1916–1923)*, Nova Terra, Barcelona.

——(1971), *Crisis económica y agitación social en Cataluña de 1930 a 1936*, Ariel, Barcelona.

Bar, Antonio (1981), *La CNT en los años rojos. Del sindicalismo revolucionario al anarcosindicalismo (1910–1926)*, Akal, Madrid.

Barrio Alonso, Angeles (1988), *Anarquismo y anarcosindicalismo en Asturias (1890–1936)*, Siglo XXI, Madrid.

Bernecker, Walther L. (1982), *Colectividades y revolución social. El anarquismo en la guerra civil española, 1936–1939*, Crítica, Barcelona.

Borderias, Cristina and Vilanova, Mercedes (1983), 'Cronología de una insurrección: Figols en 1932', *Estudios de Historia Social*, 24–5, pp. 187–99.

Bosch, Aurora (1983), *Ugetistas y libertarios. Guerra civil y revolución en el País Valenciano, 1936–1939*, Institución Alfonso el Magnánimo, Valencia.

Brademas, John (1974), *Anarcosindicalismo y revolución en España (1930–1937)*, Ariel, Barcelona.

Brenan, Gerald (1950; 1st edn 1943), *The Spanish Labyrinth*, Cambridge University Press, Cambridge.

Bueso, Adolfo (1976–8), *Recuerdos de un cenetista*, Ariel, Barcelona, 2 vols.

Calero, Antonio María (1973), *Historia del movimiento obrero en Granada (1909–1923)*, Tecnos, Madrid.

——(1974), 'Los "por qué" del anarquismo andaluz. Aportaciones del caso de Granada', in Manuel Tuñón de Lara and Jean-François Botrel, *Movimiento obrero, política y literatura en la España contemporánea*, Cuadernos para el Diálogo, Madrid.

——(1976), *Movimientos sociales en Andalucía (1820–1936)*, Siglo XXI, Madrid.

Casanova, Julián (1985), *Anarquismo y revolución en la sociedad rural aragonesa, 1936–1938*, Siglo XXI, Madrid.

——(1988a), 'Guerra y revolución: la edad de oro del anarquismo español', *Historia Social*, 1, pp. 63–76.

——comp.(1988b), *El sueño igualitario. Campesinado y colectivizaciones en la España republicana, 1936–1939*, Institución Fernando el Católico, Zaragoza.

Cuadarat, Xavier (1976), *Socialismo y anarquismo en Cataluña (1899–1911)*, Revista de Trabajo, Madrid.

Culla I Clara, Joan B. (1986), *El republicanisme lerrouxista a Catalunya (1901–1923)*, Curial, Barcelona.

Diaz del Moral, Juan (1967), *Historia de las agitaciones campesinas andaluzas–Córdoba*, Alianza, Madrid.

Elorza, Antonio (1972–4), 'El anarcosindicalismo español bajo la Dictadura', *Revista de Trabajo*, 39, 40, 44, 45 and 46.

——(1973), *La utopía anarquista bajo la Segunda República*, Ayuso, Madrid, pp. 351–468 (editado antes en *Revista de Trabajo*, 32, 1971).

Forcadell, Carlos (1978), *Parlamentarismo y bolchevización. El movimiento obrero español, 1914–1918*, Crítica, Barcelona.

Forner, Salvador (1982), *Industrialización y movimiento obrero. Alicante, 1923–1936*, Institución Alfonso el Magnánimo, Valencia.

Gabriel, Pere (1988), 'Historiografía reciente sobre el anarquismo y el sindicalismo en España, 1870–1923', *Historia Social*, 1, pp. 45–54.

Garcia Oliver, Juan (1978), *El eco de los pasos*, Ruedo Ibérico, Madrid.

Guereña, Jean-Louis (1991), 'Hacia una historia socio-cultural de las clases populares en España (1840–1920)', *Historia Social*, 11, pp. 147–64.

Hobsbawm, Eric J. (1959), *Primitive Rebels. Studies in Archaic Forms of Social Movements in the 19th and 20th Centuries*, Manchester University Press, Manchester.

Hofmann, Bert, Joan i Tous, Pere and Tietz, Manfred (eds) (1995), *El anarquismo español y sus tradiciones culturales*, Vervuert-Iberoamericana, Frankfurt am Main-Madrid.

Juliá, Santos (1984), *Madrid, 1931–1934. De la fiesta popular a la lucha de clases*, Siglo XXI, Madrid.

——(1990), 'Sindicatos y poder político en España', *Sistema*, 97, pp. 41–62.

Kaplan, Temma (1977), *Anarchists of Andalucia 1868–1903*, Princeton University Press, Princeton, NJ.

Kelsey, Graham (1991), *Anarchosyndicalism, Libertarian Communism and the State: the CNT in Zaragoza and Aragon, 1930–1937*, International Institute of Social History, Amsterdam.

Lida, Clara E. (1971), 'Educación anarquista en la España del ochocientos', *Revista de Occidente*, 97, pp. 33–47.

——(1972), *Anarquismo y revolución en la España del siglo XIX*, Siglo XXI, Madrid.

——(1973), *Antecedentes y desarrollo del movimiento obrero español (1835–1888)*, Siglo XXI, Madrid.

——(1995), 'El discurso de la clandestinidad anarquista', in B. Hofmann, P. Joan i Tous and M. Tietz (eds), *El anarquismo español y sus tradiciones culturales*, Vervuert-Iberoamericana, Frankfurt am Main-Madrid, pp. 201–14.

Linden, Marcel van der and Thorpe, Wayne (1992), 'Auge y decadencia del sindicalismo revolucionario', *Historia Social*, 12, pp. 3–29.

Litvak, Lily (1981), *Musa Libertaria. Arte, literatura y vida cultural del anarquismo español (1880–1913)*, Antoni Bosch, Barcelona.

Lorenzo, Anselmo (1974), *El proletariado militante*, Alianza, Madrid (con prólogo, notas y cronología de José Alvarez Junco).

Lorenzo, César M. (1972), *Los anarquistas españoles y el poder, 1868–1969*, Ruedo Ibérico, París.

Macarro Vera, José Manuel (1985), *La Utopía revolucionaria. Sevilla en la Segunda República*, Monte de Piedad y Caja de Ahorros, Seville.

Marti, Casimir (1959), *Orígenes del anarquismo en Barcelona*, Teide, Barcelona.

Maurice, Jacques (1990), *El anarquismo andaluz. Campesinos y sindicalistas, 1868–1936*, Crítica, Barcelona.

Meaker, Gerald H. (1974), *The Revolutionary Left in Spain, 1914–1923*, Stanford University Press, Stanford, CA.

Mintz, Jerome R. (1982), *The Anarchists of Casas Viejas*, University of Chicago Press, Chicago.

Monjo, Anna (1992), 'Afiliados y militantes: la calle como complemento del sindicato cenetista en Barcelona de 1930 a 1939', *Historia y Fuente Oral*, 7, pp. 85–98.

——(1993), 'La CNT durant la II República a Barcelona: líders, militants, afiliats', doctoral thesis, Department of Contemporary History, University of Barcelona.

——and Vega, Carme (1986), *Els treballadors i la guerra civil. Història d'una indústria catalana collectivtzada*, Empúries, Barcelona.

Montañes, Enrique (1989), *Anarcosindicalismo y cambio político. Zaragoza, 1930–1936*, Institución Fernando el Católico, Zaragoza.

Montseny, Federica (1979), *Escrits politics* (selección de textos e introducción a cargo de Pere Gabriel), Edició de la Gaya Ciencia, Barcelona.

——(1987), *Mis primeros cuarenta años*, Plaza & Janés, Barcelona.

Nash, Mary (1995), *Defying Male Civilization: Women in the Spanish Civil War*, Arden Press, Denver, CO.

Nuñez Florencio, Rafael (1983), *El terrorismo anarquista (1888–1909)*, Siglo XXI, Madrid.

Paniagua, Xavier (1982), *La sociedad libertaria. Agrarismo e industrialización en el anarquismo español*, Crítica, Barcelona.

——(1992), 'Una gran pregunta y varias respuestas. El anarquismo español: desde la política a la historiografia', *Historia Social*, 12, pp. 31–57.

Peirats, José (1971), *La CNT en la revolución española*, Ruedo Ibérico, París, 3 vols.

Peiro, Joan (1975), *Escrits, 1917–1939* (selección e introducción de Pere Gabriel), Edicions 62, Barcelona.

Pestaña, Angel (1974), *Trayectoria sindicalista* (edición y prólogo de Antonio Elorza), Tebas, Madrid.

Romero Maura, Joaquín (1974), *'La Rosa de Fuego'. Republicanos y anarquistas: la política de los obreros barceloneses entre el desastre colonial y la Semana Trágica, 1889–1909*, Grijalbo, Barcelona.

Rosado, Antonio (1979), *Tierra y libertad. Memorias de un campesino anarcosindicalista andaluz*, Crítica, Barcelona.

Segui, Salvador (1975), *Escrits* (selección y prólogo de Isidre Molas), Edicions 62, Barcelona.

Shubert, Adrian (1990), 'Autobiografia obrera e historia social', *Historia Social*, 6, pp. 141–59.

Sola i Gussinyer, Pere (1980), *Educació i Moviment Libertari a Catalunya (1901–1939)*, Edicions 62, Barcelona.

Tavera, Susanna (1977), 'La premsa anarco-sindicalista (1868–1931)', *Recerques*, 8, pp. 85–102.

——(1992), *Solidaridad Obrera. El fer-se i desfer-se d'un diari anarcosindicalista (1915–1939)*, Diputació de Barcelona, Barcelona.

—— and Ucelay da Cal, Enric (1993), 'Grupos de afinidad, disciplina bélica y periodismo libertario, 1936–1938', *Historia Contemporánea*, 9, pp. 167–190.

Termes, Josep (1972), *Anarquismo y sindicalismo en España. La Primera Internacional (1864–1881)*, Ariel, Barcelona (new edn Crítica, Barcelona, 1977).

Tiana Ferrer, Alejandro (1987), *Educación libertaria y revolución social (España, 1936–1939)*, U.N.E.D., Madrid.

Tuñon de Lara, Manuel (1972), *El movimiento obrero en la historia de España*, Taurus, Madrid.

Ucelay da Cal, Enric (1982), *La Catalunya populista. Imatge, cultura i política en l'etapa republicana (1931–1939)*, La Magrana, Barcelona.

Urales, Federico (1930), *Mi vida*, Biblioteca de la Revista Blanca, Barcelona.

Vega, Eulàlia (1980), *El trentisme a Catalunya. Divergències ideològiques en la CNT (1930–1933)*, Curial, Barcelona.

——(1987), *Anarquistas y sindicalistas durante la Segunda República. La CNT y los Sindicatos de Oposición en el País Valenciano*, Edicions Alfons el Magnànim, Valencia.

——(1988), 'Anarquismo y sindicalismo durante la Dictadura y la República', *Historia Social*, 1, pp. 55–62.

Vicente, Laura (1993), *Sindicalismo y conflictividad social. Zaragoza, 1916–1923*, Institución Fernando el Católico, Zaragoza.

Vilanova, Mercedes (1992), 'Anarchism, political participation, and illiteracy in Barcelona between 1934 and 1936', *American Historical Review*, 97 (1), pp. 96–120.

——(1995), *Les majories invisibles. Explotació fabril, revolució i repressió. 26 entrevistes*, Icaria, Barcelona.

Notes

1   This appendix does not aim to be a historiographical essay nor an overview of the extensive bibliography available on the subject. Rather it simply offers a selection of the
arguments and questions that have been raised by the best studies aimed at a non-
specialised public. In no case are explanations offered that are not formulated explicitly in
these works. A selection of this type requires brevity and thus runs the risk of not doing
justice to the richness of the theses of some authors or of leaving out aspects or research
that others may consider to be relevant. I have preferred, nevertheless, to assume this risk
rather than just providing a list of articles and books. So as not to make the text unneces-
sarily long, I have omitted the complete references of the works that are mentioned though
they can be easily found, in alphabetical order, in the bibiography at the end. Bibliograph-
ical essays and interpretations can be found in Pere Gabriel (1988), Eulàlia Vega (1988) and
Julián Casanova (1988a), and can be completed with Javier Paniagua (1992).

2   The list is long and again it is necessary to be selective. Bibiliographic production about
Catalonia is, obviously, the most abundant. The work by Mercedes Vilanova (1992, 1995)
and her research group (Cristina Borderías and Mercedes Vilanova, 1983; Anna Monjo,
1992; Anna Monjo and Carme Vega, 1986) stand out, particularly through their use of
oral testimony in the account of libertarian experiences; those of Eulalia Vega on the
internal divisions of the CNT during the Republic (1980, 1987); and those of Susanna
Tavera on the press and journalism (1977, 1992; and with Enric Ucelay da Cal, 1993).
Reconstructions of the history of anarcho-syndicalism from a regional or local focus are
found in Antonio María Calero (1973, 1976), Salvador Forner (1982), José Manuel
Macarro Vera (1985), Ángeles Barrio (1988), Enrique Montañés (1989), Laura Vicente
(1993) and Graham Kelsey (1991). On Andalucian anarchism, whose deep-rooted tradition Calero examined some time ago (1974), see the recent synthesis of Jacques Maurice
(1990), which brings together a good part of the previous research by other authors; there
is a good model of oral history in Jerome R. Mintz (1982). There are regional monographs
on collectivisations in Aurora Bosch (1983) and Julián Casanova (1985, 1988b); a general
analysis in Walther L. Bernecker (1982). Concerning the cultural influences in anarchist
ideology to attract the popular classes see José Álvarez Junco (1986a). A collection, though
of varying quality, showing the new concerns of many authors on the subject can be found
in Bert Hofmann, Pere Joan i Tous and Manfred Tietz (1995). A predecessor of the studies
on the relationship between art, anarchism and literature was Lily Litvak (1981).
Concerning education, see Clara Lida (1971), Pere Solà i Gussinyer (1980) and Alejandro
Tiana Ferrer (1987). The presence of women in the revolutionary experiences during the
Civil War has been extensively dealt with by Mary Nash (1995).

Index